Performance Measurement Systems

MÜNSTERANER SCHRIFTEN ZUR INTERNATIONALEN UNTERNEHMENSRECHNUNG

Herausgegeben von Peter Kajüter

Band 19

Zu Qualitätssicherung und Peer Review der vorliegenden Publikation

Die Qualität der in dieser Reihe erscheinenden Arbeiten wird vor der Publikation durch den Herausgeber der Reihe geprüft.

Notes on the quality assurance and peer review of this publication

Prior to publication, the quality of the work published in this series is reviewed by the editor of the series.

Henrik Schirmacher

Performance Measurement Systems

Design and Adoption in German Multinational Companies

PETER LANG

Bibliographic Information published by the Deutsche Nationalbibliothek
The Deutsche Nationalbibliothek lists this publication in the Deutsche
Nationalbibliografie; detailed bibliographic data is available in the internet
at http://dnb.d-nb.de.

Zugl.: Münster (Westfalen), Univ., Diss., 2020

Printed by CPI books GmbH, Leck

D 6
ISSN 1868-7687
ISBN 978-3-631-82193-0 (Print)
E-ISBN 978-3-631-82855-7 (E-PDF)
E-ISBN 978-3-631-82856-4 (EPUB)
E-ISBN 978-3-631-82857-1 (MOBI)
DOI 10.3726/b17231

© Peter Lang GmbH
Internationaler Verlag der Wissenschaften
Berlin 2020
This publication has been peer reviewed.

www.peterlang.com

Preface

Performance measurement systems (PMSs) play a crucial role for multinational companies (MNCs). In fact, MNCs' head offices implement PMSs at their subsidiaries not only to receive performance information that allows well-informed decision-making, but also to influence the subsidiaries' decisions.

Despite the importance of PMSs in practice, the management accounting literature has not adequately addressed these systems. In particular, the existing literature lacks a detailed description how MNCs' head offices design PMSs. Furthermore, and even more important, there are several calls to analyze in depth how PMSs are adopted by MNCs' subsidiaries.

Consequently, Henrik Schirmacher investigates both the design of PMSs at head office level and the adoption of these systems at subsidiary level. The empirical analysis is based on interviews with management accountants of five German MNCs. Besides interviewing experts at the MNCs' head offices, Henrik Schirmacher held interviews with ten subsidiaries stemming from three continents and nine countries.

For describing the design of PMSs, the study builds on four elements, namely performance measures, targets, link to rewards, and IT infrastructure. The results indicate, for example, that head offices use performance measures from multiple perspectives for which they set targets based on budgeting processes and past performance. To analyze the adoption at subsidiary level, Henrik Schirmacher scrutinizes how the case companies' subsidiaries use the PMS and whether and how they develop their own, unofficial PMS. The results indicate that subsidiaries do not necessarily follow the instructions of their head offices in adopting the PMS. For example, subsidiaries use the head office-designed PMS in a ceremonial way, which means that they only pretend to use it. Furthermore, subsidiaries might develop an own, unofficial PMS that serves as an alternative to the head office-designed PMS and that contains different performance measures and targets. Finally, the study explores factors that influence the adoption of PMSs at subsidiary level. The results suggest that both characteristics of the PMS implemented by the head office – such as the relevance of selected performance measures – and peculiarities of host countries and subsidiaries – such as economic and cultural differences – affect the subsidiaries' adoption.

By analyzing the design and adoption of PMSs, Henrik Schirmacher's study provides insights into current management accounting practice. Furthermore, it contributes considerably to the management accounting literature since it does not only describe the design of PMSs, but also sheds light on how subsidiaries adopt these systems – a topic that has been ignored in the literature for a long time. The results have several implications for academics and practitioners. They might be a basis for further research using larger samples. Management accountants in MNC's head offices, for example, can use the findings of this study to design PMSs that are by accepted their subsidiaries and hence adopted according to their intentions.

Given the importance of PMSs in practice, the effort in the empirical analysis as well as the contribution of the results, I strongly wish that Henrik Schirmacher's work will receive attention from many academics and practitioners.

Münster, January 2020   Prof. Dr. Peter Kajüter

Acknowledgement

I have written this thesis during my time as a PhD student and research assistant at the Chair of International Accounting of the University of Münster. The Münster School of Business and Economics accepted this thesis as a dissertation in January 2020.

In this acknowledgement, I would like to express my deep gratitude for all the support I have received while writing this thesis. First of all, I sincerely thank my academic teacher and supervisor Prof. Dr. Peter Kajüter for being enthusiastic for the project from the first moment. His guidance, advice, and feedback paved the way for successfully completing this thesis. I also thank him for enabling me to present my work at national and international conferences, which was a great experience from both a professional and personal perspective. Moreover, I would like to thank Prof. Dr. Martin Artz, who reviewed my thesis as second referee as well as Prof. Dr. Bernd Kempa for being the third referee at my disputation.

This empirical study would not have been feasible without the interview experts of the participating companies. I am grateful for the energy and effort all interview partners dedicated to my study. Even though I cannot name the persons involved due to reasons of confidentiality, I would like to give my sincere thanks to everyone.

Furthermore, I am blessed having wonderful colleagues and friends at the Chair of International Accounting. In addition to giving me plenty of comments and ideas that enhanced the quality of my thesis, they brought me a lot of unforgettable memories. I joyfully think back to our sailing cruises in the Netherlands, doctoral seminars in Düsseldorf and Cologne, spontaneous office parties, table tennis matches at late hours, and awesome graduation parties – to name just a few. This team spirit made the time as a PhD student extremely enjoyable and cheered me up in challenging times.

From the very beginning of my PhD, I had the pleasure to meet and make friends with Tobias Langehaneberg, the good soul of our chair, who always put me in a good mood during countless coffee and lunch breaks. I sincerely thank him for being a great companion, his hospitality in Metelen, and his conscientious support in all administrative matters. Likewise, I am thankful for having Martin Vogelpohl on my side, who always has a sympathetic ear for my problems. I am grateful for all the fun and laughter we share and I very much appreciate our burger and sushi dinners as well as our running laps on Münster's promenade. Many of them were accompanied by Dr. Max Meinhövel, my officemate at the start of my PhD. By sharing the same sense of humor, we had a lot of fun together both inside and outside of our office. I am also thankful for his valuable comments on my empirical results and, not to forget, for our experience of running a half-marathon in Bonn. Moreover, I appreciate all brown-bag sessions on qualitative research with Dr. Matthias Nienaber. With his positive mindset, he was an inspiring companion who always supported me when needed.

I was lucky having Manuel Herkenhoff on my side sharing the responsibility for organizing several rounds of the chair's sailing seminar. He was not only a great teammate on the sailing boat, but also did (and still does) an excellent job in organizing and preparing the seminar. I sincerely thank Stephanie Eckerth for always lending me a helping hand

and for taking care of all team members. I very much appreciate our humorous discussions whether Düsseldorf or Cologne has the better soccer club (Cologne!). Furthermore, I joyfully think back to competitive and entertaining table soccer matches with Friedrich Kalden, which helped to clear my mind. For his valuable feedback on the conceptual basis of my study and all fruitful discussions on research design issues, I thank my fellow qualitative research colleague Daniel Gayk. Furthermore, I owe thanks to Kai Schaumann for being an excellent co-author and companion at doctoral colloquiums such as the ACMAR. For his creativity and expertise in creating doctoral hats and for continuously providing our team with various kinds of sweets, I thank Marcel Baki. I also owe my gratitude to Dr. Stefan Hannen and Jonas Pöhler for their constructive comments on my literature review and research design. Similarly, I thank Dr. Alexander Schulz and Dr. Thomas Blades for sharing their knowledge and experience in conducting interviews and Dr. Christian Reisloh for his support in acquiring interview partners. I also dedicate special thanks to Tobias Gerwing, Niklas Kerkhoff, Florian Kooke, Arne Lessenich, Christoph Mauritz, Christian Rave, Moritz Steffien, and Maximilian Wirth for our frequent paper discussions and for introducing me to darts.

Moreover, I like to thank the student assistants of the Chair of International Accounting. All of them contributed to the great atmosphere and team spirit at our chair. In particular, I like to thank Max Wullenweber for his extraordinary commitment to support my research project and for proofreading all chapters of this thesis. I also owe special thanks to Florian Bunn, Carolin Elnser, Katharina Göcking, Katharina Högemann, Tobias Peterssen, Alexandra Quitmann, Max Walde, and Saskia Warm for their excellent and reliable support during the different stages of my thesis.

Above all, I want to express my gratitude to my family. Without the unconditional support of my parents, Edda and Alfred Schirmacher, this thesis would not have been possible. They selflessly put their own needs behind those of their children and make everything possible for us. I am deeply grateful for their love and dedication. Together with my brother Robert and my sister Luisa, I have spent so many cheerful and amusing moments, in which I was able to forget the efforts of writing this thesis. I am looking forward to all the adventures we will experience together in Göttingen, Montpellier, and Münster. I also thank my parents-in-law Rita and Dieter Meyer for their great encouragement over the past years and for welcoming me warmly into their family.

Last but foremost, I want to say thank you to my beloved wife Sarah. I am so grateful for your never-ending patience in listening to my ideas and in discussing the structure of chapters (again and again...). No matter whether in conversations during the day or in nightly talks on our balcony, you have always been on my side and never stopped encouraging me. With your positive way, your selfless care, and your expertise in finishing a dissertation, you gave me the trust and energy to cope with all challenges on the way. Most importantly, however, I would like to thank you for your infinite love and all the happiness we experience together.

Münster, March 2020   Henrik Schirmacher

Contents overview

Contents

List of figures

List of tables

List of abbreviations

BI	Business intelligence
BSC	Balanced Scorecard
CEO	Chief Executive Officer
Cf.	Confer
CFO	Chief Financial Officer
CFROI	Cash flow return on investment
COO	Chief Operating Officer
CVA	Cash Value Added
Dr.	Doctor
EBIT	Earnings before interest and taxes
EBITDA	Earnings before interest, taxes, depreciation, and amortization
Ed.	Editor
E.g.	Exempli gratia (for example)
Eds.	Editors
EMEA	Europe, middle east, and africa
ERP	Enterprise resource planning
Et al.	Et alii
Etc.	Et cetera
e.V.	Eingetragener Verein (registered association)
EVA®	Economic Value Added
Ext.	External
HR	Human resources
http	Hypertext Transfer Protocol
I.e.	Id est (that is)
Int.	Internal
IT	Information technology
IUR	Lehrstuhl für Internationale Unternehmensrechnung (Chair of International Accounting)
Kg	Kilogram
M&A	Mergers & Acquisitions
MNC	Multinational company
n.a.	Not applicable

NIS   New Institutional Sociology

OECD   Organisation for Economic Co-operation and Development

p.   Page
PES   Production Excellence System
PMS   Performance measurement system
pp.   Pages
Prof.   Professor

QDA   Qualitative data analysis

R&D   Research and development
ROI   Return on investment
ROS   Return on sales
RQ   Research question

SAP   SAP SE (formerly "Systemanalyse und Programmentwick-
                            lung" – Systems, Applications & Products in Data Pro-
                            cessing)
SG&A   Selling, general, and administrative expenses

T&A   Travel and advertisement

UK   United Kingdom
UAE   United Arab Emirates
UNCTAD   United Nations Conference on Trade and Development
URL   Uniform Resource Locator
US   United States
USA   United States of America

Vol.   Volume
Vs.   Versus

www   World Wide Web

XBRL   Extensible Business Reporting Language

List of symbols

&	And
€	Euro
$	Dollar
%	Percent
m^2	Square meter
#	Number
✓	Item included in the parent-PMS/local-PMS

1   Introduction

1.1   Motivation and research questions

Multinational companies (MNCs)[1] are of **tremendous importance for the world economy**. They account for more than one-third of global production, around half of worldwide exports, and about a quarter of global employment (*Cadestin et al.* (2018), p. 4; *Cadestin et al.* (2019), p. 8). Of particular importance for MNCs are foreign subsidiaries (*Kim et al.* (2005), p. 44; *Kretschmer* (2008), p. 1; *Dörrenbächer/Gammelgaard* (2016), p. 1250). In fact, foreign subsidiaries import and export more goods and services than MNCs' head offices and domestic subsidiaries (*Kim et al.* (2005), p. 44; *Dörrenbächer/Gammelgaard* (2016), p. 1250; *Cadestin et al.* (2019), p. 10). Furthermore, the sales of foreign subsidiaries have increased by more than 380% in value between 1990 and 2018 according to latest figures of the *World Investment Report* (*UNCTAD* (2019), p. 18).

Due to this high importance of foreign subsidiaries for MNCs, it is undoubted that head offices need effective mechanisms to control their subsidiaries (*Roth/Nigh* (1992), pp. 277-279; *Egelhoff* (2010), pp. 420-428).[2] The management accounting literature suggests that **performance measurement systems (PMSs)**, which head offices implement at their subsidiaries (parent-PMSs), can fulfill this role:

> *"Parent-PMS portray an important control mechanism in MNCs as they reflect the intentions of headquarters and are able to improve relationships between headquarters and subsidiaries. They translate subsidiary activities into measurable outcomes and provide a common basis for decision-making at all levels of the MNC, including foreign subsidiaries."*
>
> (*Mahlendorf et al.* (2012), p. 689)[3]

As pointed out in the literature, head offices pursue **two objectives** with parent-PMSs (*Dossi/Patelli* (2008), pp. 128-131; *Mahlendorf et al.* (2012), p. 689; *Wu* (2015), pp. 9-11).[4] First, head offices employ parent-PMSs to obtain performance information on their world-wide-dispersed subsidiaries to **facilitate decision-making** (*Austin* (1996), pp. 25-28; *Quattrone/Hopper* (2005), p. 742; *Horváth/Seiter* (2009), p. 396). Information on the performance of the subsidiaries allow head offices, for example, to allocate resources within the MNC (*Kaplan/Norton* (2001), p. 158; *Henri* (2006), p. 77; *Dossi/Patelli* (2008), p. 132). Second, head offices implement parent-PMSs to **influence the decisions** of the subsidiaries (*Dossi/Patelli* (2008), p. 131). This is to ensure that the subsidiaries contribute to the overall goals of the MNCs rather than pursuing local goals (*Mahlendorf et al.* (2012), p. 689; *Wu/Schäffer* (2015), p. 109). Given these two important objectives of parent-PMSs, it is not surprising that these systems are **widespread in practice**. For example, *Dossi/Patelli*

---

[1]   Cf. section 2.1 for a definition of MNCs.
[2]   Cf. also *AlHashim* (1980), pp. 37-39; *Cray* (1984), pp. 85-88; *Doz/Prahalad* (1984), pp. 58-61; *Schmid/Kretschmer* (2010), pp. 219-220; *Mahlendorf et al.* (2012), p. 689; *Wu* (2015), pp. 9-10.
[3]   Cf. also *Busco et al.* (2008), pp. 108-109; *Dossi/Patelli* (2008), p. 130; *Schäffer et al.* (2010), p. 309.
[4]   Cf. section 2.2 for a detailed description of the objectives of parent-PMSs.

show that almost all head offices in their sample implement parent-PMSs at their subsidiaries (*Dossi/Patelli* (2008), p. 134).

However, despite the high importance practitioners and scholars attach to parent-PMSs, **two research gaps** on parent-PMSs are prevailing in the management accounting literature. First, research has neglected important developments concerning the **design** of parent-PMSs. Admittedly, research on the design of parent-PMSs has a long-lasting tradition, but older empirical studies (e.g. *McInnes* (1971); *Choi/Czechowicz* (1983)) mainly deal with financial performance measures and targets only (*Schmid/Kretschmer* (2010), p. 225). However, nowadays parent-PMSs are no longer regarded as purely financial systems (*Chenhall/Langfield-Smith* (2007), p. 267). Instead, the literature suggests that the design of parent-PMSs has changed during the last decades in several ways (*Bourne et al.* (2000), pp. 754-755; *Klingebiel* (2001), pp. 17-18; *Gleich* (2011), pp. 10-19). First, parent-PMSs today are expected to contain both financial and non-financial performance measures and targets (*Lynch/Cross* (1995), p. 38; *Klingebiel* (2001), pp. 17-18). Second, conceptual studies suggest that parent-PMSs should be linked to the remuneration of the subsidiaries' management and staff to effectively influence their decisions (*Atkinson* (1998), pp. 553-556; *Otley* (1999), p. 366). Finally, it is common sense that parent-PMSs nowadays need an information technology (IT) infrastructure, which consists of, for example, enterprise resource planning systems and business intelligence systems (*Horváth/Seiter* (2009), p. 402; *Heinicke* (2018), p. 480).

Despite this newer and broader understanding of parent-PMSs, many studies (e.g., *Quattrone/Hopper* (2005); *Kihn* (2008)) still only address single design elements of parent-PMSs, such as performance measures or IT systems. By providing descriptions of single elements, these studies cannot describe how the different design elements of parent-PMSs are connected to each other. Furthermore, many studies (e.g., *Kihn* (2008); *Dossi/Patelli* (2010); *Du et al.* (2013) have an explanatory focus and therefore do not describe the design of parent-PMSs in detail. Thus, the management accounting literature lacks a description of the design of parent-PMSs based on **multiple design elements.**

The second research gap relates to the **adoption** of parent-PMSs at subsidiary level, which has received scant attention in the literature:

> *"For multinational enterprises (MNEs), the adoption of practices by various subsidiaries remains an interesting but insufficiently discussed management issue [...]. This issue requires attention from both researchers and managers because it affects the managerial performance of MNEs."*

> (*Cheng/Yu* (2012), p. 82)

> *"There are not many studies in the accounting literature which explore whether and how locals reshape global management control systems when mobilising them to conduct their day-to-day activities. [...] It seems to be assumed, therefore, that the management control systems used by the parents will simply be reproduced [...]."*

> (*Cruz et al.* (2011), p. 414)

As expressed by the quotes above, the literature has ignored how subsidiaries adopt parent-PMSs for a long time (*Dossi/Patelli* (2008), p. 144; *Cruz et al.* (2011), p. 414). In fact, the literature has mainly looked at the design of these systems or has simply assumed that subsidiaries adopt parent-PMSs as intended by the head offices (*Cruz et al.* (2011), p. 414). However, recent studies (e.g., *Siti-Nabiha/Scapens* (2005); *Dossi/Patelli* (2008); *Mahlendorf et al.* (2012)) provide preliminary evidence that subsidiaries might deviate from head offices' intentions in **two ways** when adopting parent-PMSs.

First, the subsidiaries' **use** of the parent-PMS might deviate from head offices' intentions (*Dossi/Patelli* (2008), p. 138; *Mahlendorf et al.* (2012), p. 689). In fact, the few existing studies indicate that subsidiaries might only pretend to use parent-PMSs without actually incorporating them in the day-to-day business (*Siti-Nabiha/Scapens* (2005), p. 58; *Dossi/Patelli* (2008), p. 138; *Mahlendorf et al.* (2012), p. 689). For example, subsidiaries might report the performance measures of the parent-PMS to their head office but do not discuss them in local meetings (*Ansari/Euske* (1987), pp. 561-564; *Siti-Nabiha/Scapens* (2005), p. 47). Second, the management accounting literature provides evidence that subsidiaries might develop their own PMS when they are dissatisfied with the design of the parent-PMS (e.g., *Siti-Nabiha/Scapens* (2005), p. 65; *Dossi/Patelli* (2008), p. 140). These so-called **local-PMSs** are unofficial PMSs, which are not approved by the MNCs' head offices (*Kilfoyle et al.* (2013), pp. 385-386; *Goretzki et al.* (2018), pp. 1888-1892). A subsidiary might develop a local-PMS to have an alternative to the parent-PMS or to compensate for the perceived weaknesses in the parent-PMS design (*Siti-Nabiha/Scapens* (2005), p. 65; *Cruz et al.* (2011), p. 413; *Cooper/Ezzamel* (2013), pp. 291-293).

When subsidiaries adopt parent-PMSs differently than expected by their head offices, the parent-PMSs might not have the head offices' desired effects (*Siti-Nabiha/Scapens* (2005), p. 58; *Dossi/Patelli* (2008), p. 140; *Rehring* (2012), p. 96). Since this jeopardizes the overall goals of the MNCs (*Mahlendorf et al.* (2012), p. 705; *Wu* (2015), p. 10), the adoption of parent-PMSs should be considered in more detail. In particular, several aspects deserve further attention. First, quantitative studies on the use of parent-PMSs only examine the extent to which subsidiaries use the parent-PMSs but do not describe how subsidiaries use these systems. The existing qualitative studies mainly examine the use of parent-PMSs at domestic subsidiaries or joint ventures. Thus, the literature lacks a detailed description of different **usage types** of parent-PMSs. Second, most prior studies (e.g., *Dossi/Patelli* (2008); *Schäffer et al.* (2010) only document the existence of local-PMSs but not describe the **design** of these unofficial PMSs.[5] This hinders understanding how the local-PMSs differ from the parent-PMSs implemented by the head offices. Moreover, most prior studies (*e.g., Dossi/Patelli* (2008); *Schäffer et al.* (2010)) examine the use of parent-PMSs and the development of local-PMSs separately. Therefore, there is no study providing a **typology** of the adoption of parent-PMSs. Finally, little is known about the **factors** that influence how subsidiaries adopt parent-PMSs. Prior studies only indicate that subsidiaries deviate from head offices' intentions in adopting parent-PMSs because standardized parent-PMSs *"do not fully interpret the local contexts or satisfy local demands"* (*Wu/Schäffer* (2015), p. 109; cf. also *Vance*

---

[5]   Exceptions are *Cruz et al.* (2009); *Cruz et al.* (2011); *Cooper/Ezzamel* (2013).

(2006), p. 42). However, scant evidence exists on the parent-PMS characteristics (e.g., subsidiaries' participation in the parent-PMS design) that affect the adoption of parent-PMSs. Furthermore, little is known about the local contexts (e.g., national culture) that influence how subsidiaries adopt parent-PMSs. Hence, management accounting research should examine **how** parent-PMSs are adopted at subsidiary level and **what influences** this adoption.

Overall, research is needed on the design and adoption of parent-PMSs in MNCs. Consequently, this study addresses both topics by answering the **research questions** depicted in Figure 1–1.

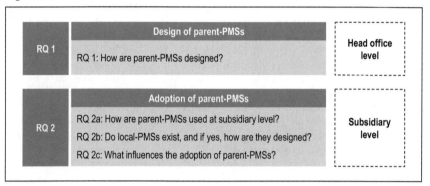

Figure 1–1: Overview of research questions

The first research question (RQ) relates to the **head office level**. It aims to provide a description of the design of the head offices' parent-PMSs. This description also serves as the basis for investigating the second research questions, which shift the focus to the adoption of parent-PMSs at **subsidiary level**. RQ 2a seeks to describe how the subsidiaries use the parent-PMSs. By addressing RQ 2b, this study aims at investigating the existence and design of local-PMSs. Based on the use of parent-PMSs and the existence and design of local-PMSs, this study intends to carve out a typology of the adoption of parent-PMSs. Finally, RQ 2c aims at exploring factors that influence how the subsidiaries adopt parent-PMSs.

These research questions are addressed by conducting **case studies** of five German MNCs. This research approach is particularly suitable due to the explorative stage of prior research, especially on the adoption of parent-PMSs. At each case company, interviews are conducted at both head office and subsidiary level. The interviews at head office level provide information on the design of the parent-PMSs. At subsidiary level, experts from two subsidiaries of each case company are interviewed to examine the adoption of the parent-PMSs. The resulting empirical data is analyzed both within and across the cases.

Addressing these research questions **contributes** to management accounting research and practice in several ways. First, this study describes the design of parent-PMSs based on multiple elements, which allows the designers of parent-PMSs in MNCs' head offices to compare the design of their own parent-PMS with the design of other parent-PMSs. Second, examining how subsidiaries use parent-PMSs enhances researchers' understanding of the differences between a functional and dysfunctional use. This is also relevant for designers of parent-PMSs, as it shows how subsidiaries can deviate from head offices' intentions when using parent-PMSs. Third, this study contributes to management accounting research and practice by carving out characteristics of local-PMSs and by describing the design of these systems. This sharpens the distinction between parent-PMSs and local-PMSs. Furthermore, the typology of the adoption can be used by other researchers when examining, for example, the prevalence of the different adoption types. Finally, identifying factors that influence the adoption supports management accountants in MNCs' head offices in developing parent-PMSs that are adopted by the subsidiaries in accordance with their intentions.

1.2 Scientific positioning

In **scientific projects,** which are projects that systematically search for knowledge (*Fülbier* (2004), p. 266; *Kornmeier* (2007), p. 4), it is important to decide on and justify the scientific positioning. This allows other scholars to evaluate whether the research is conducted in an appropriate way (*Brühl* (2017), pp. 1-2). The scientific positioning includes the objectives of the research, the research strategy, and the underlying research paradigm (*Fülbier* (2004), pp. 267-271). The following paragraphs discuss these three aspects.

Research objectives

Scientific projects can pursue four different **objectives** (*Schweitzer* (1978), pp. 3-9; *Fülbier* (2004), pp. 267-268). First, the descriptive objective aims at depicting and illustrating concepts and phenomena (*Schweitzer* (1978), p. 3). Based on these depictions and illustrations, the objective of explanation seeks to shed light on the causes and consequences of these phenomena (*Schweitzer* (1978), pp. 4-5; *Fülbier* (2004), p. 267). Third, pragmatic research intends to serve as a basis for decision-making and to provide recommendations (*Schweitzer* (1978), pp. 6-7; *Kasanen et al.* (1993), p. 253; *Fülbier* (2004), p. 267). Finally, normative research provides prescriptions for practical problems (*Kasanen et al.* (1993), p. 256; *Fülbier* (2004), pp. 267-268).

The objectives of this study are **twofold.** First, this study aims at describing the design and adoption of parent-PMSs in MNCs (descriptive objective). Based on these descriptions, the second objective is to provide implications for practice. For example, this study strives to inform management accountants in MNCs' head offices on the factors that influence the adoption of parent-PMSs at subsidiary level (pragmatic objective).

Research strategy

Based on the chosen research objectives, researchers have to decide on a **research strategy.** Management accounting researchers usually choose between three strategies, namely a conceptual strategy, an analytical strategy, and an empirical strategy (*Wagenhofer* (2006), p. 10; *Messner et al.* (2008), p. 141).

The **conceptual** strategy provides arguments, reflections, and ideas on a certain topic without empirically testing them (*Kasanen et al.* (1993), p. 256; *Messner et al.* (2008), p. 141). This strategy aims at explaining relationships between variables and presenting recommendations for practitioners (*Grochla* (1978), pp. 72-78).

When using an **analytical** strategy, researchers develop quantitative models that can be used for simulating the effects of decision alternatives. In this vein, this strategy supports researchers and practitioners in finding optimal solutions for a certain problem (*Grochla* (1978), pp. 85-93).

The **empirical** strategy aims at describing and explaining actual practices (*Kaplan* (1986), p. 432). For example, management accounting researchers examine budgeting systems or PMSs at certain companies. When applying an empirical research strategy, researchers refer to theories that are tested or that are used as lenses to understand phenomena (*Chua* (1986), p. 607; *Grochla* (1978), pp. 78-85; *Lukka/Modell* (2017), p. 40).

This study applies an **empirical** research strategy, as this study aims at examining the design and adoption of parent-PMSs in practice. It is not in the scope of this study to provide normative evidence on, for example, the design of parent-PMSs. Furthermore, an empirical research strategy is in line with using a case study approach for addressing the research questions.

Research paradigm

Finally, researchers have to reflect and explain the **paradigm** that underlies their research (*Kuhn* (1970), p. 43; *Hopper/Powell* (1985), p. 429; *Lukka* (2010), p. 11). A Research paradigm consists of the standards and doctrines of doing research and therefore "*builds boundaries between what is acceptable and what is not*" (*Lukka/Mouritsen* (2002), p. 807).[6] In management accounting research, two concurring research paradigms are prevalent: positivist and interpretive research (*Chua* (1986), p. 603).

Positivist research bases on the assumption than an objective reality exists, which is independent of the observer (*Richardson* (2012), p. 84; *Haynes* (2017), p. 284). Consequently, positivist researchers see themselves as neutral observers, who create knowledge by describing and explaining this reality (*Furlong/Marsh* (2010), pp. 193-199). Within the paradigm of positivism, the most commonly applied approach is the critical rationalism according to *Popper* (*Fülbier* (2004), p. 268; *Brühl* (2017), p. 181). The basic idea of this approach is to create knowledge by **falsifying hypotheses** (*Popper* (2005), pp. 16-19; *Brühl* (2017), p. 181). To falsify hypotheses researchers follow two main steps. First, they formulate hypotheses based on prior literature and theories (*Lingnau* (1995), p. 124). Second, they test these hypotheses usually by employing quantitative methods such as surveys, experiments, and archival studies (*Chua* (1986), p. 607; *Tomkins/Groves* (1983), p. 362). Through this process of testing theory-based hypotheses, researchers accumulate knowledge (*Chua* (1986), p. 607). However, the critical rationalism assumes that knowledge is only valid for a limited period of time (*Brühl* (2017), p. 181). In fact, it is only valid until other researchers have falsified prior assertions (*Fülbier* (2004), p. 268).

The **interpretive** paradigm has several strands in management accounting research (*Ahrens et al.* (2008), p. 841; *Lukka/Modell* (2017), p. 38). The most commonly applied strand is the social constructivism based on *Berger/Luckmann* (*Chua* (1986), p. 613, *Ahrens* (2008),

---

[6] Cf. also *Lukka* (2010), p. 111; *Hopper/Powell* (1985), p. 429.

p. 296; *Brühl* (2017), p. 60). In contrast to the positivistic approaches, the social constructivism does not assume that an objective reality exists (*Berger/Luckmann* (1991), pp. 33-42;
Richardson (2012), p. 84). Instead, researchers following the social constructivism state that
reality is socially constructed (*Chua* (1986), p. 613; *Furlong/Marsh* (2010), p. 185). Thus,
humans are not neutral observers of a given reality but construct reality based on their experiences and interpretations (*Hopper/Powell* (1985), p. 446). Since there is no objective
reality for researchers following the social constructivism, they do not strive for describing
or explaining an objective reality (*Chua* (1986), p. 613). They are rather interested in the
subjective perceptions of their research subjects (*Hopper/Powell* (1985), p. 446). They create
knowledge by **interpreting** these perceptions and meanings (*Chua* (1986), p. 613). Consequently, researchers following the social constructivism mainly rely on qualitative research
methods such as case studies (*Dey* (2017), p. 148; *Parker* (2012), p. 59). This shall provide
"thick descriptions" (*Parker/Northcott* (2016), p. 1103) and *"deep understandings"* (*Macin-
tosh/Quattrone* (2010), p. 47) of management accounting phenomena. Therefore, researchers do not formulate and test theory-based hypotheses, but use theories as lenses to understand phenomena (*Lukka/Modell* (2017), p. 40).

This study follows the **interpretive** paradigm for several reasons. First, the interpretive paradigm allows capturing different opinions that employees from MNCs' head offices and
subsidiaries have on parent-PMSs. For example, the designers of parent-PMSs in the head
offices might have a different opinion on the usefulness of these systems than the subsidiaries, who are expected to adopt these systems. Second, by following the interpretive paradigm, this study can provide a deep understanding of the design and adoption of parent-
PMSs. For example, New Institutional Sociology is used as a theoretical lens in this study
to develop a typology of the adoption of parent-PMSs at subsidiary level. Finally, the exploratory stage of research does not yet allow formulating and testing theory-based hypotheses as it is done in positivist research.

1.3   Outline of the study

This study consists of seven chapters (see Figure 1–2). The **first chapter** motivates the topic
and research questions by outlining their relevance for both research and practice. Furthermore, it presents the scientific positioning of this study.

The **second chapter** describes the conceptual basis for this study. The first section of this
chapter sets out a definition of multinational companies, which is a key term of this study.
The subsequent sections present the objectives that head offices pursue with parent-PMSs
and provide a conceptualization for describing the design of parent-PMSs. Afterwards, the
focus is shifted towards the subsidiary level. Therefore, the fourth section of the chapter
introduces the adoption of parent-PMSs at subsidiary level by outlining the use of parent-
PMSs and the existence and design of local-PMSs.

Based on the conceptual basis, the **third chapter** reviews prior empirical literature. Consistent with the research questions of this study, the review includes studies on the design
of parent-PMSs and on the adoption of these systems at subsidiary level. The chapter con-
cludes by summarizing the findings of prior literature and by laying out the research gaps
that this study addresses.

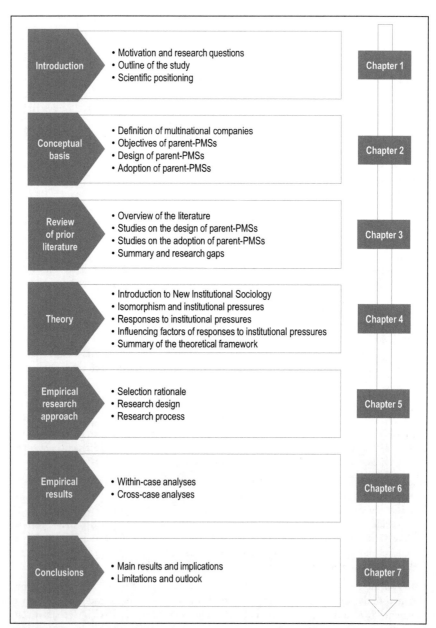

Figure 1–2: Outline of the study

The **fourth chapter** introduces the theoretical framework based on the New Institutional Sociology. In particular, different concepts of this theory are linked to the design and adoption of parent-PMSs. Furthermore, the theoretical framework is used to derive factors that influence how the subsidiaries adopt parent-PMSs.

The **fifth chapter** introduces the empirical research approach that this study follows. The first part of the chapter justifies and explains the choice of a qualitative case study approach. The second part presents the research design of this approach, sets out the sampling process, and describes the selected case companies. Finally, the chapter describes the research process by explaining the access to the case firms, the data collection and analysis, and the criteria that are used to judge the quality of the research process.

After having developed the conceptual and theoretical basis and having explained the research approach, the **sixth chapter** provides the empirical results of this study. The chapter starts by presenting the results of the within-case analyses. In particular, the within-case analyses describe the case firms' profiles, the objectives and design of the parent-PMSs, and outlines how the subsidiaries adopt the parent-PMSs. Subsequently, the chapter presents cross-case analyses of the objectives of parent-PMSs, the design of parent-PMSs, and the adoption of these systems at subsidiary level. The results are discussed by referring to prior literature and to the theoretical framework of this study.

Finally, the **seventh chapter** summarizes the key findings of this study. Subsequently, this chapter reveals the study's limitations. The chapter closes by providing an outlook for future research.

2   Conceptual basis

This chapter presents the conceptual basis of parent-PMSs in MNCs. Section 2.1 provides a definition of multinational companies. Section 2.2 describes the objectives that head offices pursue with parent-PMSs. Subsequently, the design of parent-PMSs is outlined (section 2.3). Finally, section 2.4 deals with the adoption of parent-PMSs at subsidiary level.

2.1   Definition of multinational companies

Defining the term "multinational company" is particularly important since the literature has brought several different definitions of MNCs (*Sundaram/Black* (1992), p. 731; *Aggarwal et al.* (2011), pp. 557-560; *Kutschker/Schmid* (2011), p. 244). A very early definition of this term stems from *Lilienthal* (*Kutschker/Schmid* (2011), p. 244), who defines MNCs as follows:

> *"Such corporations – which have their home in one country but which operate and live under the laws and customs of other countries as well – I would like to define here as multinational corporations."*
>
> (*Lilienthal* (1960), p. 119)

According to this definition, companies are labeled as MNCs if they sell their products and services not only in their home country, but also in foreign countries as well (*Kutschker/Schmid* (2011), p. 224; *Behringer* (2018), p. 215). As this early definition encompasses all companies that are exporting goods and services to foreign countries, it is rather broad (*Kutschker/Schmid* (2011), p. 224).

In later work, researchers have further specified which companies should be referred to as MNCs (*Kutschker/Schmid* (2011), p. 224). They provide **several additional criteria** that MNCs have to fulfill. These criteria require from MNCs, for example, to employ people abroad (e.g., *Rolfe* (1970), p. 17), to have production facilities in foreign countries (*Rolfe* (1970), p. 17), and to carry out research & development (R&D) activities outside the home country (e.g., *Rolfe* (1970), p. 17; *Maisonrouge* (1974), p. 8).[7] Even though each study proposes slightly different criteria, the literature agrees that companies that are purely exporting goods or services should not be labeled as MNCs (*Kutschker/Schmid* (2011), p. 224). Furthermore, the literature requires from MNCs to have resources, knowledge, and capabilities in multiple countries (*Sundaram/Black* (1992), p. 733; *Cruz et al.* (2011), p. 412; *Mahlendorf et al.* (2012), p. 689). In this vein, *Annavarjula/Beldone* argue that MNCs need to have *"value-adding activities"* (*Annavarjula/Beldone* (2000), p. 49) in foreign countries.

Based on these considerations, MNCs are defined in this study as companies having **value chains** that are spread over **multiple countries**. Thus, MNCs have, for example, production plants outside their home countries (*Annavarjula /Beldone* (2000), p. 49).

Because this study examines how MNCs' head offices design parent-PMSs and how their subsidiaries adopt these systems, the terms "head office" and "subsidiary" also have to be

---

[7]   Other examples of such criteria are direct capital investments in foreign countries (*Michel/Shaked* (1986), p. 92) and the control of assets in more than one country (*Dunning* (1974), p. 13).

defined. This study takes an **operational** rather than a legal perspective to define these terms (*Borchers* (2000), pp. 124-125). In contrast to a legal perspective dealing with MNCs' ownership structures, an operational perspective looks at the internal organizational structures that are used for operating and managing the MNC (*Lervik* (2011), pp. 237-239; *Macharzina/Wolf* (2012), p. 480; *Ruggie* (2018), p. 4; *Macharzina/Wolf* (2012), p. 480).[8]

From such an operational perspective, MNCs do not necessarily have only a single head office, but might have head offices on **multiple levels** that are involved in designing parent-PMSs (*Egelhoff* (1988), p. 3; *Cooper/Ezzamel* (2013), p. 293). Depending on their organizational structures, MNCs have, for example, corporate, regional, and/or divisional head offices (*Heenan* (1979), p. 410; *Lasserre* (1996), pp. 30-33).[9]

Subsidiaries are also defined from an **operational** perspective and are therefore not defined as legal entities (*Raupach* (1998), pp. 86-88; *Borchers* (2000), pp. 124-127; *Borchers* (2006), pp. 240-241). As operational entities, subsidiaries are, for example, responsible for the MNC's activities in a certain country or region (*Pla-Barber et al.* (2018), pp. 537-538). They are independent from the legal structure and can include several legal entities or can be just one part of a legal entity (*Borchers* (2000), p. 124).

2.2 Objectives of parent-PMSs

This section outlines the objectives that head offices pursue with parent-PMSs.[10] As Figure 2–1 shows, there are **two objectives** of parent-PMSs (*Austin* (1996), pp. 21-28; *Horváth/Seiter* (2009), p. 396; *Speklé/Verbeeten* (2014), p. 134). These objectives coincide with the roles of management accounting more generally, namely facilitating and influencing decisions (*Sprinkle* (2003), p. 288).

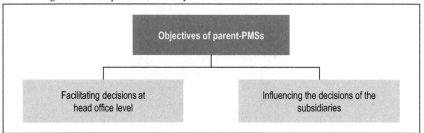

Figure 2–1: Overview of objectives of parent-PMSs

---

[8] Taking an operational perspective in this study is appropriate since parent-PMSs follow MNCs' internal organizational structures (*Malmi/Brown* (2008), p. 295). These internal organizational structures might deviate from the legal structures of the MNC (*Borchers* (2000), pp. 124-127).

[9] Because multiple head offices can be involved in the design of the parent-PMSs (*Cooper/Ezzamel* (2013), p. 293), experts from the different levels of head offices are interviewed for examining the design of the parent-PMSs (see chapter 5).

[10] This is important for two reasons. First, the objectives that a head office pursues with the parent-PMS affect the design of that system. Second, a delineation of head offices' objectives is necessary to assess how subsidiaries adopt parent-PMSs. In fact, only by knowing head offices' objectives, it is possible to judge whether the subsidiaries adopt parent-PMSs as intended by their head offices.

Facilitating decisions at head office level

Head offices implement parent-PMSs at their subsidiaries to obtain performance information that **facilitates decision-making** (*Austin* (1996), pp. 21-28; *Horváth/Seiter* (2009), p. 396; *Speklé/Verbeeten* (2014), p. 134). Receiving information on subsidiary performance is particularly important for head offices for two reasons. First, MNCs often have a large number of subsidiaries that are spread across several countries and continents (*Egelhoff/Wolf* (2017), p. 73). This **internal complexity** requires formal systems such as parent-PMSs, which provide a regular and pre-defined exchange of information between MNCs' head offices and subsidiaries (*Egelhoff/Wolf* (2017), p. 85). For example, the performance reports of parent-PMSs provide head offices with information on the subsidiaries' actual and planned performance (*Henri* (2006), p. 77; *Busco et al.* (2008), p. 108). Second, subsidiaries often **contribute considerably to the MNC's overall revenues and profits** (*Kretschmer* (2008), p. 1; *UNCTAD* (2019), p. 18). Therefore, it is important for head offices to track the performance of their subsidiaries (*Kretschmer* (2008), p. 1).

Depending on the decision that the head office has to make, parent-PMSs can provide information on

- the performance of the subsidiary as an operational entity or on
- the performance of the subsidiaries' management and staff.

(*Welge/Holtbrügge* (1999), p. 571)

The former allows MNCs' head offices to evaluate whether the **subsidiary as an operational entity** achieves its targets (*Austin* (1996), pp. 25-28; *Busco et al.* (2008), pp. 108-109; *Mahlendorf et al.* (2012), p. 689). This information facilitates head offices' decision-making in several ways. First, it allows the head office to get a consolidated picture of the MNC, at least if the parent-PMS is implemented at all subsidiaries (*Dossi/Patelli* (2008), p. 129). Second, the performance information supports a head office in allocating resources within the MNC (*Kaplan/Norton* (2001), p. 158; *Dossi/Patelli* (2008), p. 132). Head offices also use the performance information to decide on whether to continue investing in the subsidiary or to abandon or sell the entity (*Pausenberger* (1996), p. 186). Moreover, information on the subsidiaries' performance allows the head office to evaluate the success of the MNC's strategy (*Chenhall* (2005), p. 397; *Langfield-Smith et al.* (2006), pp. 655). In addition, parent-PMSs reveal cause-and-effect-relationships between performance measures and hence help the head offices to better understand which factors drive performance (*Lebas* (1995), pp. 27-34; *Atkinson et al.* (1997), pp. 30-31). Finally, head offices use the performance information to compare the results of their various subsidiaries among each other (*Schmid/Kretschmer* (2010), p. 225). In particular, they receive feedback which subsidiaries need to be looked at more closely (*Atkinson et al.* (1997), p. 30; *Dossi/Patelli* (2008), p. 131).

Performance information on the **subsidiaries' management and staff** allows evaluating the performance of individual persons (*Pausenberger* (1996), p. 186; *Welge/Holtbrügge* (1999), p. 571). Based on this evaluation, the head offices decide on the future career opportunities of the evaluated employees (*Welge/Holtbrügge* (1999), p. 571; *Ferreira/Otley* (2009), pp. 272-273). Furthermore, this information can be used at the head office level to decide on bonus payments for the subsidiaries' management and staff (*Gleich* (2011), p. 13-14; *Fitzgerald* (2007), pp. 228-229).[11]

Influencing decisions of the subsidiaries

In addition to obtaining performance information, head offices develop parent-PMSs to **influence the decisions of the subsidiaries' management and staff** (*Dossi/Patelli* (2008), p. 131; *Mahlendorf et al.* (2012), p. 691).[12] In this vein, *Vance* argues that parent-PMSs

> "*[…] can serve as an effective human resource control mechanism for implementing MNE [multinational entity; added by the author] strategy and carrying out important objectives despite significant distance and cultural barriers […].*"
>
> (*Vance* (2006), p. 38)

Following this quote, head offices implement parent-PMSs at their subsidiaries to ensure that the subsidiaries do not pursue their own local goals, but the overall goals of the MNC (*Dossi/Patelli* (2008), p. 131; *Mahlendorf et al.* (2012), p. 689). As pointed out by *Vance*, this is important in MNCs for two reasons (*Vance* (2006), p. 38). First, head offices cannot directly observe the behavior of the subsidiaries' management and staff due to the **large geographical distances** between the head offices and the subsidiaries (*Mahlendorf et al.* (2012), p. 694; *Wu* (2015), pp. 9-10). This increases the risk that the subsidiaries pursue their own goals rather than the goals of the MNC (*Vance* (2006), p. 38; *Busco et al.* (2008), p. 109). Second, there are **cultural distances** between the employees in the head offices and the subsidiaries, which can reinforce the risk of divergent interests in MNCs (*Kostova/Roth* (2002), pp. 217-220; *Vance* (2006), p. 38; *Wu* (2015), pp. 9-10).

Two mechanisms shall ensure that parent-PMSs influence the decisions of the subsidiaries. First, by selecting and defining performance measures, the **perception** of the subsidiaries' management and staff shall be influenced (*Hopwood* (1990), p. 9; *Busco/Quattrone* (2015), p. 1237). In fact, parent-PMSs are intended to influence which issues the subsidiaries consider as important and therefore put on the agenda (*Roberts/Scapens* (1985), p. 448; *Busco et al.* (2008), p. 108). For example, the selection of the performance measure "customer satisfaction" shall draw the attention of the subsidiaries' management to this issue and shall ensure that they do their best to improve the satisfaction of their customers (*Busco et al.* (2008), p. 108). This argumentation corresponds to the frequently quoted expression of "*what gets measured gets done*" (e.g., *Otley* (1999), p. 368; *Sandt* (2004), p. 1; *Weber/Schäffer* (2016), p. 88).

Second, setting and evaluating targets shall increase the **motivation** of the subsidiaries (*Busco et al.* (2008), p. 108; *Dossi/Patelli* (2008), p. 131). In fact, head offices employ parent-PMSs to stimulate greater effort by the subsidiaries' management and staff, which shall result in a higher performance of the MNC (*Austin* (1996), p. 21). This can be reinforced by linking the target achievement to the compensation of the subsidiaries' management and staff (*Hopwood* (1972), pp. 156-157; *Banker et al.* (1996), pp. 196-197). In this way, the

---

[11] Cf. the description of the link between parent-PMSs and rewards (section 2.3).

[12] Cf. also *Busco et al.* (2008), pp. 108-109; *Cruz et al.* (2009), p. 97; *Cruz et al.* (2011), p. 414.

head offices try to create goal congruence between the subsidiaries and the head offices (*Mahlendorf et al.* (2012), p. 694; *Wu* (2015), pp. 9-10).

Overall, head offices implement parent-PMSs at their subsidiaries for receiving performance information and influencing the decisions of the subsidiaries (see Figure 2–2).

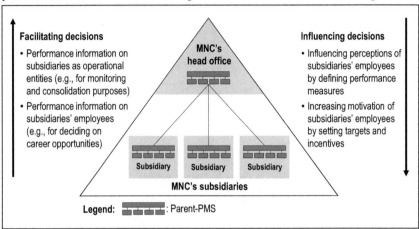

Figure 2–2: Objectives of parent-PMSs

However, the two objectives of parent-PMSs are **often not separable in practice** (*Austin* (1996), pp. 29-31). This is because it is almost impossible to develop a parent-PMS that addresses just one of the two objectives (*Austin* (1996), pp. 29-31; *Speklé/Verbeeten* (2014), p. 134). A parent-PMS intended for informational purposes only may still affect the decisions of the subsidiaries' management and staff. In fact, providing them with performance measures might make them feel that these performance measures are particularly important and hence might change their decisions (*Ridgway* (1956), p. 247; *Austin* (1996), p. 30). A parent-PMS that is intended to influence decisions must nevertheless provide information so that the head offices are able to verify whether the subsidiaries behave as expected (*Austin* (1996), pp. 30-31). In practice, it is therefore often not important for head offices to decide between one of the two objectives, but to decide which objective they consider to be more important (*Austin* (1996), p. 30; *Sprinkle* (2003), p. 288).

After this description of the objectives that head offices pursue with parent-PMSs, the following section provides a conceptualization on the design of parent-PMSs.

2.3 Design of parent-PMSs

2.3.1 Overview

When describing the design of parent-PMSs, it is necessary to specify the **design elements** that are examined. This study builds on prior literature, which suggests that parent-PMSs consist of multiple elements. First, parent-PMSs contain **performance measures** (*Gleich*

(2011), p. 215). While earlier studies focused primarily on financial performance measures (e.g., *McInnes* (1971); *Choi/Czechowicz* (1983)), nowadays the literature proposes that parent-PMSs should complement financial performance measures with non-financial ones (*Fitzgerald* (2007), p. 223; *Klingebiel* (2001), pp. 17-18).[13] Second, the literature agrees that parent-PMSs should contain **targets** for the financial and non-financial performance measures, as this allows head offices to compare the subsidiaries' actual and planned performance (*Austin* (1996), p. 130; *Chung et al.* (2000), p. 653; *Simons* (2000), pp. 208-210).

Third, conceptual studies suggest that parent-PMSs should be linked to the **remuneration** of the subsidiaries' management and staff to effectively influence their decisions (*Atkinson* (1998), pp. 553-556; *Otley* (1999), p. 366). Finally, it is common sense that parent-PMSs nowadays need an **information technology (IT) infrastructure**, which consists of, for example, enterprise resource planning systems and business intelligence systems (*Horváth/Seiter* (2009), p. 402; *Heinicke* (2018), p. 480).

Based on these considerations, this study describes the design of parent-PMSs based on **four design elements**: Performance measures, targets, link to rewards, and IT infrastructure (see Figure 2–3).

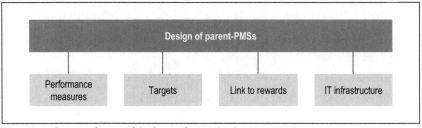

Figure 2–3: Conceptualization of the design of parent-PMSs

By using these four design elements, this study **does not limit itself to specific examples** of parent-PMSs such as the BSC or the Performance Pyramid. Instead, the four design elements can be used to examine the design of any parent-PMS. Furthermore, it should be noted that the four design elements are used solely to **describe** the design of parent-PMS. It is not in the scope of this study to examine or argue whether these elements should necessarily be included in parent-PMS.[14] Thus, this study does not intend to provide normative evidence on the four design elements (*Ferreira/Otley* (2009), pp. 266-267).[15]

When designing parent-PMSs, MNCs' head offices tend to implement parent-PMSs at their subsidiaries that are **highly standardized** (*Cruz et al.* (2009), p. 97). Thus, head offices

---

[13] However, there is no consensus on the non-financial perspectives that should be addressed (*Franco-Santos et al.* (2007), p. 769).

[14] In this vein, this study does not assume or require that parent-PMSs necessarily include all four design elements in practice. It is rather the aim of this study to examine and describe whether and how parent-PMSs address these design elements (*Franco-Santos et al.* (2012), p. 80).

[15] As indicated by contingency theory, the optimal design of PMSs depends on several internal and external context factors (*Hoque* (2004), p. 487; *Ferreira/Otley* (2009), p. 266). For an overview of influencing factors, cf. *Chenhall* (2003).

do not adapt the design elements to the local conditions of the subsidiaries (e.g., the region in which the subsidiary operates), but rather implement the same parent-PMS at all subsidiaries (*Hoffjan/Weide* (2006), p. 391; *Vance* (2006), p. 39).[16] For example, all subsidiaries of a MNC have to report the same performance measures to the head office and have to use the same IT infrastructure. The most important advantages of standardizing parent-PMSs are a better comparability of performance results between the subsidiaries and the fact that all subsidiaries are guided in the same direction (*Hoffjan/Weide* (2006), p. 391; *Vance* (2006), pp. 38-39; *Busco et al.* (2008), p. 106). The main disadvantage is that standardized parent-PMSs do not address local conditions and could therefore be perceived as less useful by the subsidiaries (*Vance* (2006), p. 39).[17]

After this overview of the design of parent-PMSs, the following sections present the four design elements in detail.

2.3.2   Design elements

2.3.2.1   Performance measures

Performance measures as a design element are introduced in two steps. The first step defines the term "performance measure" and outlines criteria on the selection of performance measures. The second step is to distinguish financial from non-financial performance measures.

Definition and selection criteria

The basic idea of parent-PMSs is to make subsidiary performance (e.g., the efficiency of production processes in the subsidiaries or the success of the subsidiaries' sales teams) measurable and hence visible for MNCs' head offices (*Gleich* (2011), p. 215; *Quattrone/Hopper* (2005), p. 737). Parent-PMSs contain performance measures, which condense information on subsidiary performance by **quantifying** this information (*Atkinson et al.* (1997), p. 33; *Horváth/Seiter* (2009), pp. 389-390; *Gladen* (2014), p. 9). In this vein, *Neely et al.* state that performance measures *"are used to quantify both the efficiency and/or the effectiveness of an action"* (*Neely et al.* (1995), p. 80). Therefore, performance measures express subsidiary performance always in numbers (*Gladen* (2014), p. 15). Examples are absolute values (e.g., €, m^2), ratios (e.g., €/hour or €/m^2), and indices (e.g., customer satisfaction index) (*Gladen* (2014), p. 15). Qualitative information such as texts and figures are not in the scope of performance measures (*Choong* (2013), p. 116).[18]

---

[16]   However, standardization and differentiation should not be considered as either-or issue but as a continuum (*Hoffjan/Weide* (2006), p. 391; *Busco et al.* (2008), p. 106).

[17]   There are several further advantages and disadvantages of a high degree of standardization. For a discussion in the context of parent-PMSs and other management accounting instruments, cf. *Hoffjan/Weide* (2006), p. 392; *Horváth/Seiter* (2009), pp. 395-396; *Schulz* (2018), pp. 36-40.

[18]   An example of qualitative information is a written statement on the strengths and weaknesses of a new competitor.

In the literature, sometimes other terms such as **"metrics"** and **"indicators"** are also used to refer to performance measures (*Choong* (2013), p. 116). While most studies (e.g., *Itt-ner/Larcker* (1998); *Günther/Grüning* (2002); *Ferreira/Otley* (2009)) use these terms as synonyms, others (e.g., *Choong* (2013); *Weber/Schäffer* (2016)) argue that there are differences in these terms. Studies following the latter approach distinguish between performance measures and metrics on the one hand and indicators on the other hand (*Gladen* (2014), p. 9; *Weber/Schäffer* (2016), p. 177). They argue that performance measures and metrics address aspects that can be observed and measured directly, such as the number of customer visits and the subsidiaries' sales revenues (*Gladen* (2014), p. 9; *Schmid/Kretschmer* (2010), p. 224). The term indicator is then used for issues that can be observed only indirectly (*Gladen* (2014), p. 9). For example, customer satisfaction is not directly observable and must therefore be measured in an indirect way (e.g., by surveying customers) (*Schmid/Kretschmer* (2010), p. 224). However, as the distinction between directly and indirectly observable issues is not always clear-cut (*Schmid/Kretschmer* (2010), p. 224), this study does not distinguish between performance measures/metrics and indicators. Instead, the three terms are treated as **synonyms** in this study.[19]

For selecting performance measures, the literature proposes **several criteria**. First, performance measures should be **relevant** for both the persons who measure the performance and the persons whose performance is evaluated (*Lebas* (1995), p. 24; *Atkinson et al.* (1997), p. 34; *Gleich* (2011), p. 298). Thus, when selecting performance measures, head offices should make sure that the performance measures are also relevant for the subsidiaries. Otherwise, they might resist the parent-PMS (*Vance* (2006), pp. 42-43). Second, the selected performance measures should be **reliable**, meaning that there are at least as possible errors in quantifying events and actions at subsidiary level and that performance measures should be hard to manipulate (*Atkinson et al.* (1997), p. 34; *Günther/Grüning* (2002), p. 8; *Artz et al.* (2012), p. 447). Third, the literature argues that head offices should consider the **cost effectiveness** of performance measures (*Gleich* (2011), p. 286). Following this criterion, the costs of data collection and measurement should not outweigh the value that the performance measure has for the MNC (*Tangen* (2004), p. 728).[20]

Furthermore, head offices should choose performance measures that are **easy to communicate** and hence **easy to understand** by the subsidiaries (*Atkinson et al.* (1997), p. 34; *Tangen* (2004), p. 728; *Ferreira/Otley* (2009), p. 271). This requires selecting performance measures that are clearly defined and that are not too complicated (*Maskell* (1991), p. 40; *Langfield-Smith et al.* (2006), p. 674). This is also necessary to ensure that employees from both MNCs' head offices and subsidiaries understand the performance measures in the same way (*Atkinson et al.* (1997), p. 34). To support a common understanding, head offices can issue guidelines and handbooks on the performance measures and can carry out workshops and trainings (*Schedler* (2005), p. 66).

---

[19] To avoid confusion, only the term "performance measure" is consistently used throughout this study.

[20] However, it is difficult for head offices to determine the value of performance measures. Nevertheless, head offices should always ask themselves whether each performance measure is really needed and should regularly revise the selection of performance measures (*Tangen* (2004), p. 728; *Schäffer/Heidmann* (2007), p. 69).

Finally, literature agrees that parent-PMSs should **not contain too many** performance measures due to the limited cognitive capabilities of the users of parent-PMSs (*Weber/Schäffer* (2013), p. 46; *Tangen* (2004), p. 728; *Gladen* (2014), p. 13). In fact, too many performance measures bear the risk that subsidiaries cannot give attention to all performance measures of the parent-PMS and therefore focus only on a few of them (*Ferreira/Otley* (2009), p. 127; *Artz* (2010), p. 2-3; *Schäffer/Weber* (2015), pp. 37-39). However, literature does not provide evidence on how many performance measures parent-PMSs should contain at maximum. This is rather company specific (*Ferreira/Otley* (2009), p. 127). Table 2–1 summarizes the selection criteria of performance measures.

Criterion	Description
Relevance	Parent-PMSs should contain performance measures that are relevant at both head office and subsidiary level
Reliability	Performance measures should be subject to as least as possible measurement errors and should be hard to manipulate
Cost effectiveness	The costs of data collection and measurement should not outweigh the value that a performance measure has for the MNC
Communication	Performance measures should be easy to communicate to the subsidiaries
Comprehensibility	Parent-PMSs should consist of performance measures that are clearly defined and easy to understand by the subsidiaries
Number	Head offices should select a reasonable number of performance measures

Table 2–1: Criteria for selecting performance measures for parent-PMSs
Based on *Atkinson et al.* (1997), p. 34; *Tangen* (2004), pp. 727-729.[21]

Financial vs. non-financial performance measures

The literature proposes several reasons for including non-financial performance in parent-PMSs (*Dossi/Patelli* (2010), p. 501-502). First, the literature argues that financial performance measures alone **are not useful for making operational decisions** (*Kaplan/Norton* (1996), pp. 196-198). In this vein, it is also claimed that non-financial performance measures can be used as **predictors for financial performance** (*Dossi/Patelli* (2010), p. 502). For example, it is often argued that customer satisfaction is a good predictor of future revenues (*de Haas/Kleingeld* (1999), p. 251; *Langfield-Smith et al.* (2006), p. 660).[22] In addition, literature recommends including non-financial performance

---

[21] Cf. also *Maskell* (1991), p. 40; *Gleich* (2011), p. 298; *Schäffer/Weber* (2015), pp. 37-39.
[22] Therefore, financial performance measures are often labeled as lagging or result indicators, while non-financial performance measures are often described as leading or process indicators that are able to explain future financial performance (*Kaplan/Norton* (1996), p. 32; *de Haas* (2000), p. 29). However, this distinction bases on the assumption that there are causal relationships between financial and non-financial measures. As pointed out by *Nørreklit*, this (assumed) causality does often not exist in practice (*Nørreklit* (2000), pp. 81-82).

measures in parent-PMSs by arguing that they support the implementation of strategies. In particular, it is argued that non-financial performance measures help to **understand linkages between a MNC's overall strategic objectives and operational actions** that need to be taken (*Maskell* (1991), pp. 19-21; *Dossi/Patelli* (2010), p. 502). Finally, literature argues that including non-financial perspectives **stimulates communication** between head offices and subsidiaries (*Atkinson et al.* (1997), pp. 25-27; *Dossi/Patelli* (2010), p. 502).

Despite these arguments for including non-financial performance measures in parent-PMSs, the management accounting literature does not provide a consistent definition of non-financial performance measures. Instead, **two approaches** exist to demarcate financial from non-financial performance measures. (*Fisher* (1992), p. 32). Following the **first approach**, financial performance measures are those performance measures that are expressed in **monetary units** (*Weber/Schäffer* (2016), pp. 174-176). Thus, according to this approach, financial performance measures are denominated in currencies such as $ or € (e.g., turnover in € million), as ratios of currencies and other measurement units (e.g., €/number of employees), or as changes in monetary units (e.g., percentage growth in turnover).[23]

The **second approach** distinguishes between financial and non-financial performance measures according to the **perspective** that they relate to (*Ittner/Larcker* (2003), p. 717). This approach is inspired by *Kaplan/Norton's* well-known BSC,[24] which distinguishes between a company's financial perspective and non-financial perspectives (*Kaplan/Norton* (1992), pp. 72-79; *Kaplan/Norton* (1996), pp. 43-146). The financial perspective addresses the **shareholders' concerns** (*Kaplan/Norton* (1992), p. 72). It includes traditional and value-based financial performance measures (*Hussain/Hoque* (2002), p. 162; *Ittner/Larcker* (1998), pp. 209-210). Examples of traditional financial performance measures are profit, sales revenues, return on investment (ROI), or cash flow (*Schmid/Kretschmer* (2010), p. 224). The basic idea of value-based financial performance measures is to take the cost of capital into account when determining the firm's value that the management achieves over a certain period of time (*Ittner/Larcker* (1998), pp. 209-210; *Otley* (2002), pp. 13-17). Examples are the economic value added (EVA), cash value added (CVA), and cash flow return on investment (CFROI).[25]

The non-financial perspectives relate to **other stakeholders** such as customers and employees (*Gleich* (2011), p. 24; *Körnert* (2006), p. 159). Examples of performance measures relating to the perspective of customers are market share and customer satisfaction, while accident rate and absenteeism rate are examples of performance measures relating to the employee perspective (*Dossi/Patelli* (2008), p. 551, *Horváth et al.* (2015), p. 286). Which non-perspectives a head office includes in the parent-PMS is company specific. However,

---

[23] Cf. *Merchant/van der Stede* (2012), p. 413, for similar examples.

[24] However, as pointed out by *Tuomela*, the idea of including non-financial perspectives in PMSs is older than the BSC. For example, the French Tableau de Bord, which has been used since the early 1960s (*Bourguignon et al.* (2004), p. 116), already included non-financial perspectives (*Tuomela* (2005), p. 300). For a detailed description and discussion of the *Tableau de Bord*, cf. *Lebas* (1996).

[25] For a detailed discussion of value-based performance measures, cf. *Bouwens/Speklé* (2007), pp. 245-268; *Gladen* (2014), pp. 113-178.

the literature argues that parent-PMSs should address the perspectives of multiple stake-holders (*Henri* (2006), pp. 81-82; *Dossi/Patelli* (2008), p. 132).

In this study, the **second approach** is used to distinguish financial from non-financial performance measures. The rationale behind this decision is that this approach is widely accepted and used in studies on parent-PMSs (e.g., *Dossi/Patelli* (2008), *Dossi/Patelli* (2010); *Mahlendorf et al.* (2012); *Abdallah/Alnamri* (2015)). Adopting the second approach therefore increases the comparability of this study to existing literature. Consistent with prior studies, this study distinguishes between the MNC's **financial perspective** and three non-financial perspectives, namely MNC's **customers, internal processes,** and **employees** (see Table 2–2).

Financial performance measures	Non-financial performance measures
Traditional performance measures	**Customers**
Examples: Sales revenues, costs, cash flows	Examples: Market share, customer satisfaction
Value-based performance measures	**Internal processes**
Examples: EVA, CFROI	Examples: Delivery reliability, lead time
	Employees
	Examples: Accident rate, absenteeism rate

Table 2–2: Comparison of financial and non-financial performance measures
Based on *Dossi/Patelli* (2010), p. 551; *Horváth et al.* (2015), p. 286.

2.3.2.2 Targets

This section deals with the targets included in parent-PMSs. *Austin* compares the role of targets with those of a **thermostat**. With a thermostat, a desired room temperature can be set. A thermometer in the thermostat measures the actual room temperature and compares it with the pre-defined temperature. If the room temperature is too low (high), the thermometer signals the system to heat (cool down) the room (*Austin* (1996), p. 130).

In a similar way, head offices **set a desired level of performance**, that the subsidiaries are expected to meet (*Chung et al.* (2000), p. 653; *Simons* (2000), pp. 208-210). By using performance reports and review meetings, the head offices **evaluate** the subsidiaries' target achievements (*Austin* (1996), p. 130; *Ferreira/Otley* (2009), p. 271). This is comparable to the role of the thermometer in the thermostat. By evaluating performance, the head offices receive feedback on the subsidiaries' performance and can initiate countermeasures (*Gleich* (2011), pp. 25-26; *Austin* (1996), pp. 130-132). Furthermore, by discussing these deviations with the subsidiaries, they gain a better understanding of the cause-and-effect-relationships between the performance measures of the parent-PMS (*Lebas* (1995), pp. 27-34; *Atkinson et al.* (1997), pp. 30-31). The following paragraphs depict in more detail how head offices set and evaluate targets with parent-PMSs.

Target setting

When setting targets, head offices have to decide on the **types** of targets they want to use. As Figure 2–4 shows, the literature proposes **three** target types, which can be used on their own or in combination (*Appleyard et al.* (1991), p. 117; *Schmid/Kretschmer* (2010), p. 225).

Figure 2–4: Types of targets included in parent-PMSs

Based on *Appleyard et al.* (1991), p. 117; *Schmid/Kretschmer* (2010), p. 225.

When using **past performance-based targets**, head offices set desired levels of performance by referring to the performance of previous periods (*Schmid/Kretschmer* (2010), p. 225). For example, a head office compares a subsidiary's actual performance with the performance of the previous year (*Appleyard et al.* (1991), p. 117.) However, head offices might not simply carry forward subsidiaries' past performance, but might also require a certain degree of improvement compared to the past performance (*Hronec* (1996), pp. 163-164; *Langfield-Smith et al.* (2006), p. 675).[26] For example, a head office might increase target levels of subsidiary performance by a fixed percentage rate each year (*Ferreira/Otley* (2009), p. 272).

Head offices can also use **budget-based targets**, which are the outcome of a MNC's budgeting process (*Emmanuel et al.* (1990), p. 175).[27] Budget-based targets allow head offices to compare the subsidiaries' actual performance against the budgeting plan (*Demski/Feltham* (1978), pp. 336-337). MNCs can determine budget-based targets by top-down, bottom-up or counter-flow planning (*Scholz* (1984), pp. 96-98; *Nevries et al.* (2009), p. 238). When using a **top-down approach**, the subsidiaries are not involved in the target setting process. Instead, the target levels are solely defined at the head office level. In contrast, a **bottom-up** approach means that the subsidiaries define target levels by themselves (*Scholz* (1984), p. 96). Finally, a **counter-flow** approach is a compromise between top-down planning and bottom-up target setting. Thus, in counter-flow planning, target levels are negotiated between head offices and subsidiaries (*Nevries et al.* (2009), p. 238; *Horváth et al.* (2015), p. 99-101).

When deciding between the three ways of setting budgets, head offices should be aware of the advantages and disadvantages associated with these approaches. The main advantage of top-down planning is that it prevents excessive discussions between head offices and their subsidiaries and therefore it is **little time-consuming** (*Horváth et al.* (2015), p. 100). At the

---

[26] If head offices have lower expectations, they can also adjust the past performance downwards. However, this is less common in practice (*Ferreira/Otley* (2009), p. 272).

[27] Budgeting processes can be defined as those processes which "*weave together all the disparate threads of an organization into a comprehensive plan […]*" (*Hansen et al.* (2003), p. 96).

other side of the coin, top-down planning does not involve the subsidiaries, which might **negatively affect their motivation and commitment** to the targets (*Chong/Chong* (2002), pp. 79-82; *Merchant/van der Stede* (2012), p. 317; *Matějka* (2018), p. 17). Furthermore, the participation of the subsidiaries in the budgeting process can lead to targets that are **more realistic** (*Chong/Chong* (2002), pp. 79-82). This is especially important in MNCs since subsidiary managers often have superior knowledge compared to head offices about processes, opportunities, and challenges at subsidiary level (*Merchant/van der Stede* (2012), p. 311). However, at the same time, the subsidiaries also gain the **ability to include slack** in the target levels, which is defined as *"the excess of the amount budgeted over what is necessary"* (*van der Stede* (2001), p. 31). In decentralized entities such as MNCs, it is especially difficult for the head offices to detect budgetary slack (*van der Stede* (2001), pp. 31-32). Counter-flow planning **reduces the ability of the subsidiaries to include a high amount of slack** since targets are revised by the head office (*Feichter et al.* (2018), p. 32). However, a main disadvantage of counter-flow planning is that it often **needs several discussion rounds** between head offices and subsidiaries (*Matějka* (2018), p. 13).

Finally, targets can be derived from a **benchmarking** of performance results. Two forms of benchmarking are differentiated (*Appleyard et al.* (1991), p. 117). First, targets can be derived from an **internal** benchmarking. For instance, head offices might compare the achieved performance of one subsidiary with the performance of other subsidiaries of the MNC (*Hyland/Beckett* (2002), p. 303). Since head offices receive performance reports from all their subsidiaries, this form of benchmarking is available at low costs and helps the head offices to identify best practices within the MNC (*Drew* (1997), p. 429; *Langfield-Smith et al.* (2006), p. 670). Second, head offices can compare the performance of their subsidiaries with the performance of **external** partners (*Hyland/Beckett* (2002), p. 293). For example, head offices can compare the performance of their subsidiaries with the performance of similar subsidiaries (e.g., in their size) of other MNCs (*Drew* (1997), p. 429; *Langfield-Smith et al.* (2006), p. 670).

In addition to choosing the types of targets, head offices have to decide on the **level of detail** of the targets (*Gleich* (2011), pp. 300-301; *Casas-Arce et al.* (2017), pp. 1052-1053). Head offices can specify desired levels of performance only on subsidiary level or they can additionally define sub-targets (*Casas-Arce et al.* (2017), pp. 1052-1053). These sub-targets might refer, for example, to products, brands, or teams within the subsidiaries (*Ferreira* (2002), p. 476). If targets are only agreed for the subsidiaries as a whole, the head offices only get an overview of the subsidiaries' performance, but cannot see from which products, brands, etc. target deviations stem (*Gleich* (2011), p. 301). However, too detailed target levels can lead to an information overload at the head office level (*Tangen* (2004), p. 728).

Target evaluation

Concerning the evaluation of targets, the type and frequency can be distinguished. Head offices can use **two different types** of evaluating targets, namely formal and personal target evaluation (*Schmid/Kretschmer* (2010), p. 226-227). **Formal** performance evaluation bases on written performance reports (*Horváth/Seiter* (2009), p. 397). Performance reports that are issued on a regular basis at a given time are called standard reports (*Weber/Schäffer*

(2016), pp. 237-249). In addition to standard reports, deviation reports are created when actual performance falls below a pre-defined threshold (*Horváth* (2008), p. 21). Furthermore, head offices might request ad-hoc reports from their subsidiaries on special events or circumstances (*Küpper et al.* (2013), p. 232; *Gleich* (2011), p. 301). In contrast to evaluating performance based on written reports, head offices can evaluate performance in **personal** interaction with subsidiaries. Examples of personal performance evaluation are review meetings via phone or video conferences and personal visits by head offices (*Jaeger* (1983), p. 95; *Kretschmer* (2008), p. 23). Formal and personal performance evaluation should not be seen as mutually exclusive, but are often used in combination (*Child* (1984), p. 158; *Kretschmer* (2008), p. 23). For example, written performance reports often serve as the basis for discussions in review meetings (*Merchant/van der Stede* (2012), p. 309).

Relating to the **frequency** of performance evaluation, periodic and ad-hoc performance evaluation can be distinguished (*Küpper et al.* (2013), p. 239). When performance is evaluated **periodically**, head offices evaluate performance regularly (e.g., daily, weekly, monthly, or yearly) based on standard reports or regular meetings, for example (*Gleich* (2011), p. 301). **Ad-hoc** performance evaluation is driven by special events or outstanding (positive or negative) performance and typically bases on ad-hoc reports and short-dated phone calls between head offices and subsidiaries (*Malina/Selto* (2001), p. 80; *Küpper et al.* (2013), p. 239).

2.3.2.3 Link to rewards

Head offices can link their parent-PMSs to the reward systems of the MNCs (*Coates et al.* (1995), p. 128; *Dossi/Patelli* (2008), p. 132; *Mahlendorf et al.* (2012), p. 707). The basic idea behind this is to increase the motivation of the subsidiaries' employees to achieve the targets (*Merchant/van der Stede* (2007), pp. 394-395; *Gleich* (2011), p. 298). Furthermore, rewards shall ensure goal congruence between head offices and subsidiaries (*Mahlendorf et al.* (2012), pp. 692-694; *Coates et al.* (1995), p. 128). Reward systems can be defined as

> "*[...] processes, practices and systems that are used to provide levels of pay and benefits to employees.*"
>
> (*Langfield-Smith et al.* (2006), p. 627)

Following this definition, monetary and non-monetary rewards can be distinguished (*Merchant/van der Stede* (2007), p. 394; *Ferreira/Otley* (2009), p. 273). Whereas monetary rewards include incentives such as bonus payments, stock option plans, and salary increases, non-monetary rewards comprise, for instance, dinner invitations or appreciation by superiors (*Langfield-Smith et al.* (2006), p. 627; *Otley* (1999), p. 373). This study focuses on **monetary rewards**, for the following reasons. First, literature argues that monetary rewards are more important than non-monetary rewards (*Roberts* (2010), p. 127; *Bartol/Srivastava* (2002), p. 66; *Aguinis et al.* (2013), pp. 242-243). Second, non-monetary rewards such as appreciation by superiors are only subtly expressed and therefore difficult to capture by empirical research (*Ferreira/Otley* (2009), p. 273). Finally, focusing on monetary rewards is consistent with prior studies dealing with the link of parent-PMSs to rewards (e.g., *Coates* *et al.* (1995); *Dossi/Patelli* (2008); *Mahlendorf et al.* (2012)). The following paragraphs outline the linkage of performance measures and rewards and outline the differences between individual and group rewards.

Linking performance measures to rewards

When linking parent-PMSs to rewards, head offices have to decide on the performance measures that shall be linked to the variable compensation of the subsidiaries' management and staff (*Coates et al.* (1995), p. 128). Literature proposes that head offices should follow the **controllability principle** when linking performance measures to rewards (*Drury/Tayles* (1995), pp. 267-268; *Merchant/van der Stede* (2007), p. 33; *Burkert et al.* (2011), p. 143). The basic idea of controllability is that only those performance measures should be linked to rewards that **can be influenced** by the person who is rewarded (*Hopwood* (1972), p. 158; *Langfield-Smith et al.* (2006), p. 674; *Merchant/van der Stede* (2007), p. 33). For example, a production manager at subsidiary level should only be rewarded based on performance measures within his area of responsibility such as the failure rate of produced goods (*Langfield-Smith et al.* (2006), p. 674).

In a strict sense, the controllability principle also advocates to **eliminate the effects of uncontrollable events** when rewarding the subsidiaries' management and staff (*Merchant* (1987), p. 336). Eliminating uncontrollable effects shall ensure that the subsidiaries perceive the rewarding as **fair** (*Merchant/van der Stede* (2007), p. 533; *Burkert et al.* (2011), p. 143). This is especially relevant in MNCs because there are several events that affect subsidiary performance that are outside the control of the subsidiaries' management and staff. Examples are decisions taken by a MNC's head offices (e.g., decisions on transfer prices) or the host country's government (e.g., regulation) (*Welge/Holtbrügge* (1999), p. 570). However, there are also arguments for head offices not to apply the controllability principle in a strict sense (*Burkert et al.* (2011), p. 143). First, head offices can **share risks** by rewarding subsidiaries' management and staff based on uncontrollable effects (*Drury/Tayles* (1995), p. 276). If uncontrollable effects are not taken into account, the risk of uncontrollable events and corresponding negative performance consequences is solely taken by the head office (*Demski/Feltham* (1978), p. 340; *Merchant* (1987), p. 318). Second, head offices **motivate the subsidiaries** to take precautions for uncontrollable events when including them in determining bonus payments. Examples of precautions are insurances and other hedging strategies (*Merchant/van der Stede* (2007), pp. 533-537).

Individual vs. group rewards

When linking parent-PMSs to rewards, head offices can choose between individual and group rewards or might use them in combination (*Ferreira/Otley* (2009), p. 273). When using **individual rewards**, an employee receives one or more personal targets that he has to achieve to gain his monetary incentive (*Merchant/van der Stede* (2007), p. 406; *Ladley et al.* (2015), pp. 2412-2413). These personal targets might refer to performance measures of the parent-PMS or might include other aspects such as qualitative targets (e.g., the regular participation in training courses) (*Coates et al.* (1995), p. 128).

Group rewards refer to the target achievement of groups of persons (*Ferreira/Otley* (2009), p. 273). As Figure 2–5 shows, group rewards can refer to different levels of MNCs (*Merchant/van der Stede* (2007), p. 405). First, head offices can reward teams within the subsidiaries based on the performance of these teams. For example, head offices reward production workers based on the failure rate of the production line. Second, head offices can reward the subsidiary's management and staff based on the performance of the subsidiary. For instance, the bonus payments of the subsidiary's management depend on the subsidiary's earnings before interest, taxes, depreciation, and amortization (EBITDA). Finally, the bonus payments of the subsidiaries' employees can also depend on the MNC's overall performance. For example, the bonus payments of the subsidiaries' management might depend on the MNC's EBITDA (*Merchant/van der Stede* (2007), p. 405; *Ferreira/Otley* (2009), p. 273).

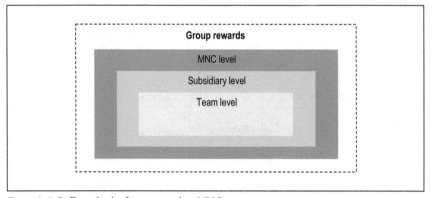

Figure 2–5: Different levels of group rewards in MNCs

Group rewards have advantages and disadvantages compared to individual rewards. On the one hand, a major advantage of group rewards is that they **create a culture of ownership** by remunerating employees for a good overall performance of the MNC (*Hansen* (1997), pp. 37-38; *Ferreira/Otley* (2009), p 273). On the other hand, group rewards enable employees to act as **free riders**, especially in case of a weak relationship between individual and group performance (*Hansen* (1997), pp. 37-38; *Ladley et al.* (2015), p. 2415). Furthermore, the higher the level of the group rewards (e.g., subsidiary level and MNC level), the **weaker is the link** between the performance of the individual employee and his reward (*Merchant/van der Stede* (2007), pp. 405-406).

2.3.2.4 IT infrastructure

Nowadays, one can hardly imagine parent-PMSs without underlying IT systems (*Marr* (2005), p. 647; *Horváth/Seiter* (2009), p. 402; *Vallurupalli/Bose* (2018), p. 73).

IT systems serve several purposes. First, they support firms in **recording and storing performance information** (*Folan/Browne* (2005), p. 537; *Hyvönen et al.* (2008), pp. 52-53).[28] This is especially important in MNCs, since a large amount of information is generated from the MNCs' several locations such as foreign production or sales sites (*Quattrone/Hopper* (2005), p. 736). IT systems help MNC's to centrally store the data and to integrate various data sources. Second, IT systems facilitate the **reporting and sharing of performance information** throughout the MNC (*Dechow et al.* (2007), p. 627; *Horváth/Seiter* (2009), pp. 402-403). Given that head offices and subsidiaries are distant in both time and space, a fast reporting of performance information is inevitable in MNCs (*Schuler et al.* (1991), p. 370; *Quattrone/Hopper* (2005), pp. 739-743). To speed up information flows between the dispersed locations, MNCs can draw on recent developments in IT such as real-time reporting (*Rikhardsson/Yigitbasioglu* (2018), pp. 44-45; *Sageder/Feldbauer-Durstmüller* (2018), p. 19). Third, IT systems help employees in MNCs' head offices and subsidiaries in **conducting statistical analyses** through data mining techniques (*Chen et al.* (2012), p. 1166). Finally, IT systems can be used to **visualize performance information** in dashboards and scorecards (*Folan/Browne* (2005), p. 537; *Rikhardsson/Yigitbasioglu* (2018), pp. 44-45; *Kajüter et al.* (2019), pp. 145-146).

As Figure 2–6 shows, head offices can choose between different **types of IT systems** or use them in combination (*Marr* (2005), p. 647-648; *Richards et al.* (2019), p. 189).

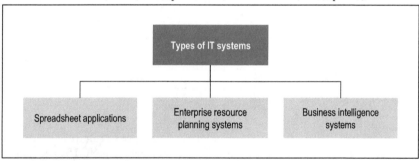

Figure 2–6: Types of IT systems in parent-PMSs
Based on *Marr* (2005), p. 647-648; *Richards et al.* (2019), p. 189.

First, **spreadsheet applications** (e.g., Microsoft Excel) are the **simplest** type of IT systems that can be used for parent-PMSs (*Horváth/Seiter* (2009), p. 402; *Franco-Santos et al.* (2012), p. 80). Despite their few functions compared to more sophisticated IT systems such as enterprise resource planning (ERP) systems, they play an important role in practice (*Marr* (2005), p. 648). On the one hand, advantages of spreadsheet applications are their low implementation costs and their flexibility (*Horváth/Seiter* (2009), p. 402; *Allen et al.* (2017), p. 4). On the other hand, spreadsheet applications are also criticized for being slow, work-intensive, and prone to error (*Bititci et al.* (2002), p. 1280; *Bange et al.* (2004), pp.

---

[28] This study does not distinguish between data and information, as the focus of this study is not on the information processing of individual persons. For a discussion of the two terms, cf. *Steiners* (2005), p. 23.

11-13). Furthermore, spreadsheet applications are less useful for processing large amounts of information, which is the case in MNCs (*Marr* (2005), p. 648; *Quattrone/Hopper* (2005), p. 736).

Second, head offices can base their parent-PMSs on **ERP systems** such as SAP R/3 or Microsoft Dynamics NAV (*Quattrone/Hopper* (2005), pp. 753-736). Following *Dechow et al.* ERP systems can be defined as follows:

"An integrated information system taking care of all information flows of an organization; operates on a centralized database where data is entered once at the point of transaction."

(*Dechow et al.* (2007), p. 637)

By implementing ERP systems, head offices strive to **integrate and consolidate performance information** from different data sources that exist at several locations of the MNC (*Quattrone/Hopper* (2005), pp. 735-736). This shall ensure that head offices and subsidiaries have access to a single, integrated database providing standardized performance information (*Dechow/Mouritsen* (2005), p. 692; *Quattrone/Hopper* (2005), pp. 735-736). However, ERP systems also have two main disadvantages. First, the implementation of these systems takes more time and is more costly than the implementation of spreadsheet applications (*Tarn et al.* (2002), pp. 26-27). The second disadvantage arises from the standardization of the ERP system, which makes it more difficult to adapt these systems to different conditions (*Granlund/Malmi* (2002), pp. 306-307; *Al-Sabri et al.* (2018), p. 943).

Finally, head offices can use **business intelligence (BI) systems** as an IT infrastructure of parent-PMSs (*Vallurupalli/Bose* (2018), p. 73). *Richards et al.* define BI systems as follows:

"BI systems are generally considered to be software applications that deliver information to decision makers to help maintain business performance. Most BI systems include different technological components such as databases, visualization tools, and on-line analytic processing (OLAP) that allow decision makers to view and work with subsets of data."

(*Richards et al.* (2019), p. 189)

As expressed in the definition above, BI systems (e.g., SAP Business Warehouse, IBM Cognos 8 Business Intelligence) provide software for **analyzing, reporting, and visualizing** performance information (*Dechow et al.* (2007), p. 636). To do so, they access information usually from ERP systems (*Ranjan* (2008), p. 463). An advantage of BI systems is that they allow head offices to make sophisticated analyses of the performance information included in ERP systems (*Richards et al.* (2019), p. 189). Furthermore, they allow head offices to visualize the results of these analyses in interactive dashboards and reports (*Janvrin et al.* (2014), p. 31-32; *Kajüter et al.* (2019), pp. 145-146). The main disadvantage of BI systems as IT infrastructure for parent-PMSs is that they cannot function on their own but always need a supporting infrastructure such as ERP systems (*Ranjan* (2008), p. 463; *Richards et al.* (2019), p. 189).

2.3.3 Summary

For describing the design of parent-PMSs, **four design elements** are used, namely performance measures, targets, link to rewards, and IT infrastructure (see Figure 2–7).

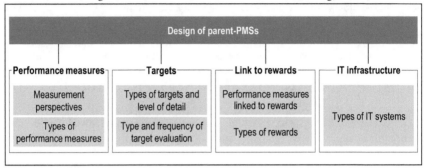

Figure 2–7: Summary of the design of parent-PMSs

2.4 Adoption of parent-PMSs

2.4.1 Overview

Many studies (e.g., *Pausenberger* (1996); *Chung et al.* (2006), *Kihn* (2008)) examine parent-PMSs only at **head office level** (*Cruz et al.* (2011), p. 414; *Cheng/Yu* (2012), p. 82; *Kornacker et al.* (2018), p. 24). Thus, these researchers are only concerned with the objectives and the design of parent-PMSs. They ignore how subsidiaries adopt parent-PMSs or simply assume that the subsidiaries adopt these systems as desired by their head offices (*Cruz et al.* (2011), p. 414).

This study explicitly examines how parent-PMSs are adopted at **subsidiary level**. The adoption of parent-PMSs consists of **two aspects** (see Figure 2–8).

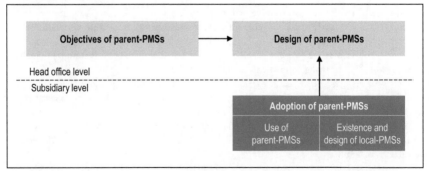

Figure 2–8: Overview of adoption of parent-PMSs

First, this study examines how the subsidiaries **use the parent-PMSs** implemented by their head offices. This is important, since parent-PMSs only influence the behavior of the subsidiaries,[29] if they are *"de facto"* (*Kornacker et al.* (2018), p. 24) used at subsidiary level (*Bruns* (1968), p. 469; *Langfield-Smith* (1997), p. 226; *Dossi/Patelli* (2008), p. 127). However, it is difficult for the designers of (parent-)PMSs to make sure that their systems are actually used as intended, as pointed out by *Austin*:

> *"The designers of a measurement system are usually powerless to guarantee that measurement information will be used in accord with their intentions, if not from the moment of the installation then certainly by the time the system has been in place for a while."*

(*Austin* (1996), pp. 29-30)

Consequently, it is not simply taken for granted in this study that the subsidiaries use parent-PMSs according to the head offices' intentions. Instead, it is explicitly acknowledged that the subsidiaries can **deviate** from the intentions of their head offices when using parent-PMSs (*Siti-Nabiha/Scapens* (2005), pp. 47-49; *Kornacker et al.* (2018), p. 26).

Second, the adoption of parent-PMSs at subsidiary level is addressed by examining the **existence and design of local-PMSs**. This is based on prior findings (e.g., *Siti-Nabiha/Scapens* (2005); *Dossi/Patelli* (2008); *Mahlendorf et al.* (2012)) that subsidiaries tend to develop their own PMS, which differs in its design from the parent-PMS (*Dossi/Patelli* (2008), p. 140, *Cruz et al.* (2011), pp. 419-424; *Cooper/Ezzamel* (2013), p. 298). Therefore, it is not simply assumed in this study that a MNC has a single, integrated parent-PMS. Instead, this study explicitly examines whether and for what reasons the subsidiaries deviate from the intentions of their head offices by developing and designing local-PMSs.

The following sections outline the use of parent-PMSs (section 2.4.2) and the existence and design of local-PMSs (section 2.4.3) in more detail.

2.4.2   Use of parent-PMSs

In the literature, the use of parent-PMSs is examined in **three** different ways (*Menon/Varadarajan* (1992), p. 54; *Schröder* (2014), p. 27). First, the literature investigates the **extent** to which the subsidiaries use parent-PMSs (*Schröder* (2014), p. 27). This is mainly done in quantitative large-scale studies that are interested in how extensively parent-PMSs are used on average at the subsidiary level (e.g., *Dossi/Patelli* (2008), *Mahlendorf et al.* (2012)). Second, the literature examines the **prevalence** of specific types of parent-PMSs such as the BSC or the Performance Pyramid (e.g., *Speckbacher et al.* (2003); *Kraus/Lind* (2010)). Finally, the literature refers to different usage types for examining **how** the subsidiaries use parent-PMSs (e.g., *Siti-Nabiha/Scapens* (2005); *Schäffer et al.* (2010)).

In this study, it is examined **how** the subsidiaries use parent-PMSs. Different from the first two approaches, this allows to examine whether subsidiaries use the parent-PMSs in a func-

---

[29]   As shown in section 2.2, influencing the behavior of the subsidiaries' employees is one of the two objectives that head offices pursue with parent-PMSs.

tional or dysfunctional way (*Ferreira* (2002), p. 43). The **functional** way describes a situation in which subsidiaries use the parent-PMSs as desired by their head offices (*Ferreira* (2002), p. 43). Thus, the functional way fulfills the objectives that the head offices pursue with designing and implementing parent-PMSs (*Horváth/Seiter* (2009), p. 396). In contrast, the **dysfunctional** use means that subsidiaries deviate from the intentions of their head offices when using parent-PMSs (*Ferreira* (2002), p. 43; *Siti-Nabiha/Scapens* (2005), p. 47). In this case, the head offices' objectives of designing and implementing parent-PMSs are not or only partially achieved (*Austin* (1996), pp. 10-12; *Horváth/Seiter* (2009), p. 396). In the following, the functional and dysfunctional use of parent-PMSs are described in more detail.

Functional use

The literature provides **several usage types** for describing the functional use of parent-PMSs (e.g., *Simons* (1995); *Atkinson et al.* (1997); *Henri* (2006); *Schäffer et al.* (2010); *Speklé/Verbeeten* (2014); cf. also *Nitzl et al.* (2018), p. 689). Although these usage types are often named differently by the different researchers, they overlap with regard to many aspects (*Henri* (2006), p. 80; *Schäffer/Steiners* (2004), p. 378; *Speklé/Verbeeten* (2014), p. 134). In fact, **four** functional usage types can be derived from the literature.

First, the literature proposes a **decision-making use** of parent-PMSs (*Henri* (2006), p. 81; *Schäffer et al.* (2010), p. 312).[30] The decision-making use aims to answer the question which *"[...] of the several alternatives [...] is rationally the best?"* (*Henri* (2006), p. 81). Thus, it enables the subsidiaries to **decide between decision alternatives** (*Atkinson et al.* (1997), p. 32; *Schäffer et al.* (2010), p. 312). Furthermore, the decision-making use includes the **development of counteractions** in case of poor performance (*Henri* (2006), p. 81).

Second, subsidiaries can use the parent-PMSs for **monitoring** purposes (*Atkinson et al.* (1997), p. 33; *Henri* (2006), pp. 80-81; *Schäffer et al.* (2010), p. 312).[31] The monitoring use provides the subsidiaries' employees with **feedback** on the performance of the subsidiary (*Henri* (2006), pp. 80-81; *Speklé/Verbeeten* (2014), p. 135). For example, they can use the performance reports of the parent-PMS to obtain information on the subsidiaries' actual and targeted performance (*Simons* (1995), pp. 60-61; *Schäffer et al.* (2010), p. 312). In addition, the subsidiaries can conduct **deviation analyses** based on the performance information of the parent-PMSs to detect the causes of target deviations (*Henri* (2006), pp. 80-81; *Schäffer et al.* (2010), p. 312).

Third, parent-PMSs can be used at subsidiary level for **attention focusing** purposes (*Henri* (2006), p. 81).[32] In this way, the managers of the subsidiaries **make their subordinates aware** of the performance measures and targets of the parent-PMS (*Simons* (1995), pp. 97-98; *Henri* (2006), p. 81). This can be done, for example, by regularly discussing the performance measures and corresponding targets with the subsidiaries' employees (*Schäffer et al.* (2010), p. 312). Furthermore, the discussions with the subordinates shall ensure that

---

[30] *Henri* refers to the decision-making use as *"strategic decision making"* (*Henri* (2006), p. 81).
[31] *Simons* refers to this usage type as the *"diagnostic use"* (*Simons* (1995), p. 7). In the typology of *Speklé/Verbeeten*, the term *"operational use"* (*Speklé/Verbeeten* (2014), p. 135) is applied.
[32] *Atkinson et al.* labels this the *"coordinating role"* (*Atkinson et al.* (1997), p. 31).

each employee of the subsidiary **understands how he contributes** to the performance of the subsidiary (*Atkinson et al.* (1997), p. 31).

Finally, subsidiaries can use parent-PMSs for **learning** purposes (*Simons* (1990), p. 137; *Speklé/Verbeeten* (2014), p. 135). This includes getting a **better understanding** of the subsidiary's business situation (*Schröder* (2014), p. 31). Furthermore, subsidiaries can use the parent-PMSs to **understand the cause-and-effect relationships** between the several performance measures (*Atkinson et al.* (1997), p. 33; *Henri* (2006), pp. 80-81; *Schäffer et al.* (2010), p. 312). Finally, subsidiaries can use the performance information of the parent-PMS to predict future developments (*Burchell et al.* (1980), p. 15; *Schröder* (2014), p. 136). For example, subsidiaries can create forecasts and scenarios based on the performance measures of the parent-PMSs.

Dysfunctional use

Different from the functional use, research on the dysfunctional use of parent-PMSs is **scarce** (*Kornacker et al.* (2018), pp. 24-25). In fact, most studies (e.g., *Schäffer et al.* (2010); *Speklé/Verbeeten* (2014)) are only concerned with the functional use of parent-PMSs and ignore that subsidiaries can also use parent-PMSs in a dysfunctional way (*Cruz et al.* (2011), p. 414).

However, evidence on the dysfunctional use of parent-PMSs stems from *Ansari/Euske*, who study the use of a cost accounting system in a US military organization. The authors find that the members of the military organization use the cost accounting system not for decision-making, but for making the Congress' members believe that the military organization acts in a rational way (*Ansari/Euske* (1987), pp. 561-564; cf. also *Schäffer/Steiners* (2004), p. 381). In fact, the military organization's members follow the official instructions on cost accounting and regularly provide cost reports to the Congress, but **do not consider this information** in their daily operations (*Ansari/Euske* (1987), pp. 561-564). The authors conclude that the members of the military organization *"put on an appropriate façade for the world to see"* (*Ansari/Euske* (1987), p. 552).

Transferred to the context of this study, subsidiaries can **pretend to use** the parent-PMS in a functional way (e.g., for decision-making, monitoring, attention-focusing, and/or learning), which is labeled as **ceremonial** use (*Siti-Nabiha/Scapens* (2005), p. 47). [33] Following *Ansari/Euske*, the subsidiaries can pretend to use the parent-PMS by, for example, reporting the performance measures to the head office and by attending the regular review meetings (*Ansari/Euske* (1987), pp. 561-564; *Siti-Nabiha/Scapens* (2005), p. 47). In this way, the head offices believe that the subsidiaries use the parent-PMS as intended (*Siti-Nabiha/Scapens* (2005), p. 54; *Kornacker et al.* (2018), pp. 35-38).

Through the ceremonial use, **only one of the two objectives** that head offices pursue with a parent-PMS is fulfilled. In fact, since the subsidiaries pretend to use the information from the parent-PMS by reporting the performance measures and attending review meetings, the objective of receiving information is fulfilled (*Siti-Nabiha/Scapens* (2005), p. 47; *Kornacker*

---

[33] This is to avoid confusion with the term institutional theory, which is introduced in chapter 4. For a similar argumentation, cf. *Schröder* (2014), p. 34.

et al. (2018), pp. 44-47). However, the ceremonial use does not fulfill the head offices' objective of influencing the behavior of the subsidiaries, as the information from the parent-PMS is actually ignored at the subsidiary level (*Ansari/Euske* (1987), p. 563; *Siti-Nabiha/Scapens* (2005), pp. 63-64).

Figure 2–9 summarizes the functional and dysfunctional usage types that are addressed in this study.

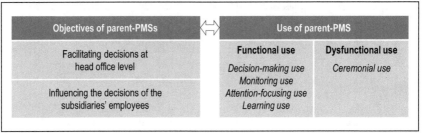

Figure 2–9: Summary of the use of parent-PMSs

2.4.3   Existence and design of local-PMSs

This section deals with the second aspect of the adoption of parent-PMSs, namely the existence and design of local-PMSs. The **existence of local-PMSs** is a topic that has been ignored in the literature for a long time (*Cruz et al.* (2011), p. 414; *Cheng/Yu* (2012), p. 82). In fact, many prior studies on parent-PMSs simply assumed that subsidiaries use the design of the parent-PMS as specified by the head office (*Cruz et al.* (2011), p. 414). However, recent studies (e.g., *Siti-Nabiha/Scapens* (2005); *Dossi/Patelli* (2008); *Cooper et al.* (2013))[34] provide evidence that subsidiaries might prefer a different design than their head office (*Dossi/Patelli* (2008), p. 140; *Schäffer et al.* (2010), p. 312). For example, subsidiaries miss performance measures in the parent-PMS or consider performance measures of the parent-PMS to be irrelevant (*Schäffer et al.* (2010), p. 312). However, a subsidiary cannot simply adapt the design of the parent-PMS, as this would lead to conflicts with the head office (*Siti-Nabiha/Scapens* (2005), p. 65).[35] In fact, a head office expects their subsidiaries to follow the design of the parent-PMS (*Clancy/Collins* (1979), pp. 22-23; *Kilfoyle et al.* (2013), pp. 385-386). Thus, for example, a subsidiary cannot simply delete a performance measure from the parent-PMS's performance report or add a performance measure to this report (*Clancy/Collins* (1979), pp. 22-23; *Kilfoyle et al.* (2013), pp. 385-386). The head office would notice these changes and would demand the subsidiary to provide the report according to the rules of the parent-PMS (*Siti-Nabiha/Scapens* (2005), p. 54).

If the subsidiaries consider the design of the parent-PMS to be inappropriate at subsidiary level, they can **develop a local-PMS** (e.g., *Siti-Nabiha/Scapens* (2005), p. 65; *Dossi/Patelli* (2008), p. 140; *Schäffer et al.* (2010), p. 312). However, even though the literature acknowl-

---

[34]   Further examples are *Schäffer et al.* (2010); *Cruz et al.* (2009); *Cruz et al.* (2011); *Mahlendorf et al.* (2012).

[35]   Subsidiaries tend to avoid these conflicts because they depend on the legitimacy of the head offices (*Meyer/Rowan* (1977), pp. 352-353; *Kostova/Zaheer* (1999), pp. 67-68; also see chapter 4).

edges the existence of local-PMSs, **little is known about their characteristics**, which hinders the understanding of these systems (*Dossi/Patelli* (2008), p. 144; *Rehring* (2012), p. 120). Consequently, this study carves out characteristics of local-PMSs by demarcating these systems from parent-PMSs. In particular, local-PMSs are compared with parent-PMSs according to **three** criteria: Their status within the MNC, their designers, and their objectives.

First, parent-PMSs and local-PMSs differ in their **status** within the MNC. This idea stems from a strand of literature dealing with managers' self-generated information systems (e.g., *Clancy/Collins* (1979); *Hopwood* (2009); *Kilfoyle et al.* (2013); *Goretzki et al.* (2018)).[36] The self-generated information systems[37] of managers can be described as follows:

> *"Managers and staff often keep informal, non-legitimized sets of records [...]. These records are kept on any available media from paper scraps to complex, but secretive computer files. Instead of the records being kept by an outside unit (i.e. the accounting or data processing department), the records are usually kept by the person who directly uses the data."*

> (*Clancy/Collins* (1979), p. 22)

An example of a self-generated information system is a customer list that a sales manager creates because he does not get this information from the firms' official information system (*Kilfoyle et al.* (2013), p. 384). As the example shows, the literature on self-generated information systems distinguishes between, on the one hand, a firm's official information system and, on the other hand, a firm's unofficial information systems (*Clancy/Collins* (1979), p. 22; *Kilfoyle et al.* (2013), p. 384; *Goretzki et al.* (2018), pp. 1888-1892). The **official** system is legitimized by the company's hierarchy. In fact, there is a department in charge of developing the official systems, which is also given the power to implement and enforce this system (*Kilfoyle et al.* (2013), pp. 385-386). In addition to the company's official information systems, managers might create their own, **unofficial** information systems. These unofficial systems are not sanctioned by the department that is responsible for designing the company's official accounting system (*Kilfoyle et al.* (2013), pp. 385-386; *Goretzki et al.* (2018), pp. 1888-1892). Therefore, only the managers who create the unofficial information systems consider them as appropriate (*Clancy/Collins* (1979), pp. 22-23; *Kilfoyle et al.* (2013), pp. 385-386).

Even though the literature on self-generated information systems does not deal with PMSs, the idea of official and unofficial systems can be transferred to this study. In this vein, a parent-PMS is considered here as the MNC's **official** PMS. The status as the official system is legitimized by the head offices' hierarchical power over their subsidiaries, which allows the head offices to implement the parent-PMSs at the subsidiaries (*Cruz et al.* (2009), p. 103). To support the adoption of the parent-PMSs at subsidiary level, the head offices' management accountants define the rules of the parent-PMSs (e.g., specifications on the

---

[36] Cf. also *Simon et al.* (1954); *Hall* (2010).
[37] Different expressions exist for these systems. Examples are *"bootleg reports"* (*Simon et al.* (1954), p. 34), *"alternatives to formal information systems"* (*Hopwood* (2009), p. 801) or *"vernacular accounting systems"* (*Kilfoyle et. al* (2013), pp. 382-383).

design) in official documents such as handbooks, guidelines, and presentations. Furthermore, head offices might offer trainings for the subsidiaries' employees on the correct adoption of these systems (*Schedler* (2005), p. 66-71). In contrast, a local-PMS is a MNCs' **unofficial** system and therefore not approved by a MNC's head office (*Kilfoyle et al.* (2013), pp. 385-386; *Goretzki et al.* (2018), pp. 1888-1892). The local-PMS is only considered as legitimate within the subsidiary in which it is created, but it is not shared with employees from other subsidiaries or the head office (*Clancy/Collins* (1979), p. 22; *Kilfoyle et al.* (2013), pp. 385-386). Therefore, the employees from other subsidiaries or the head office **do not necessarily know** that local-PMSs exist at subsidiary level (*Goretzki et al.* (2018), pp. 1888-1892).

Second, local-PMSs differ from parent-PMSs with respect to their **designers** (*Dossi/Patelli* (2008), p. 127). Parent-PMSs are **centrally designed in MNCs' head offices** and then implemented at the subsidiaries (*Dossi/Patelli* (2008), p. 127; *Mahlendorf et al.* (2012), p. 689). In particular, the head offices' management accountants are responsible for designing these systems (*Cruz et al.* (2011), p. 103). Depending on the size of the MNC, several management accounting departments from different head office levels (e.g., corporate head office and regional head offices) might be involved (*Cooper et al.* (2013), pp. 229-300). In contrast, local-PMSs are developed at **subsidiary level** (*Dossi/Patelli* (2008), pp. 140-144; *Egbe et al.* (2018), p. 706). In fact, the designers of these local systems stem from, for example, local management accounting departments at the subsidiaries (*Dossi/Patelli* (2008), p. 127; *Schäffer et al.* (2010), p. 312).

Finally, parent-PMSs and local-PMSs can be compared according to their **objectives**. Head offices use parent-PMSs to obtain information on the subsidiaries' performance to **facilitate decisions** at head office level and to **influence the decisions of the subsidiaries** (*Austin* (1996), pp. 21-28; *Horváth/Seiter* (2009), p. 396; *Speklé/Verbeeten* (2014), p. 134).[38] Concerning the objectives of local-PMSs, little is known in the literature. The few studies dealing with this topic yield conflicting results. On the one hand, the literature provides evidence that the subsidiaries develop local-PMSs when they reject the parent-PMSs (*Dossi/Patelli* (2008), p. 143; *Siti-Nabiha/Scapens* (2005), p. 65). This is the case, for example, if the subsidiaries' management accountants do not trust the information of the parent-PMSs (*Kilfoyle et al.* (2013), p. 386). The local-PMSs then serve as unofficial **alternatives** to the parent-PMSs (*Siti-Nabiha/Scapens* (2005), p. 65; *Dossi/Patelli* (2008), p. 134). On the other hand, the subsidiaries might develop local-PMSs to **support the functioning of the parent-PMSs** (*Cruz et al.* (2009), p. 113; *Cruz et al.* (2011), p. 413; *Cooper/Ezzamel* (2013), pp. 291-293). This is the case, for example, if the subsidiaries perceive that the parent-PMS ignores relevant information that is necessary at subsidiary level (*Clancy/Collings* (1979), pp. 22-24; *Cruz et al.* (2011), p. 413). In this case, the subsidiaries might develop local-PMSs that contain the missing information (*Dossi/Patelli* (2008), p. 140; *Schäffer et al.* (2010), p. 313). Table 2–3 summarizes the characteristics of parent-PMSs and local-PMSs.

---

[38] Cf. section 2.2.

Characteristics	Parent-PMSs	Local-PMSs
Status	MNC's official PMS, which is legitimized by the head office's authority and power. It can be described in official documents such as guidelines and presentations and can be accompanied by trainings.	Unofficial PMS that is not officially sanctioned by the MNC's head office. The existence of the local-PMSs is not necessarily known by the employees of other subsidiaries or the head office.
Designers	Designed by the head offices' employees (e.g., in the corporate management accounting department) and implemented at the subsidiaries.	Designed by the subsidiaries' employees (e.g., in the local management accounting department).
Objectives	Head offices develop parent-PMSs for facilitating decisions at head office level and influencing the decisions of the subsidiaries.	Local-PMSs can serve as alternatives to parent-PMSs or to support the functioning of the parent-PMSs.

Table 2–3: Characteristics of parent-PMSs and local-PMSs

Design of local-PMSs

As outlined in the previous paragraphs, the subsidiaries are the designers of their local-PMS (*Dossi/Patelli* (2008), pp. 140-144; *Egbe et al.* (2018), p. 706). Thus, they decide on their own on the design of the local-PMS (*Schäffer et al.* (2010), p. 313). In particular, they might take elements from the parent-PMS when they consider them to be appropriate (*Dossi/Patelli* (2008), p. 140). For example, they could include performance measures of the parent-PMS in their local-PMS. Furthermore, subsidiaries might take elements from the parent-PMS and change them (*Cruz et al.* (2011), pp. 422-423; *Cooper/Ezzamel* (2013), pp. 307-312). For instance, subsidiaries could take a performance measure that is included in the parent-PMS but change the definition when including it in the local-PMS (*Cooper/Ezzamel* (2013), p. 304). Finally, subsidiaries can design own elements that are not included in the parent-PMS (*Cruz et al.* (2009), pp. 110-111; *Cruz et al.* (2011), pp. 422-423). For example, subsidiaries select performance measures that are not included in the parent-PMS (*Siti-Nabiha/Scapens* (2005), p. 65).

The resulting local-PMS **differs** from the design of the parent-PMS (see Figure 2–10). However, differences in the design of the parent-PMS and the local-PMSs should not be considered as an either-or issue but as an **extent**. The extent of the design differences might depend on the objective that the subsidiary pursues with the local-PMS (*Cooper/Ezzamel* (2013), pp. 291-293). If the subsidiary develops the local-PMS as an alternative to the parent-PMS, the design differences might be considerably **large**. In this case, the local-PMS includes, for example, other performance measures and targets than the parent-PMS (*Siti-Nabiha/Scapens* (2005), p. 65; *Dossi/Patelli* (2008), p. 140). If the subsidiary develops the local-PMS to support the functioning of the parent-PMS, the differences in the design might be **rather small**. For example, the local-PMS might contain the same performance measures as the parent-PMS plus one or two additional ones (*Cooper et al.* (2013), pp. 303-307).

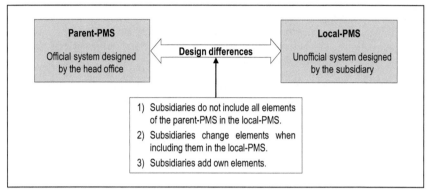

Figure 2–10: Design differences between parent-PMSs and local-PMSs

2.4.4 Summary

Figure 2–11 summarizes the conceptualization of the adoption of parent-PMSs at subsidiary level. The adoption of parent-PMSs is addressed by examining the use of parent-PMSs and the existence and design of local-PMSs.

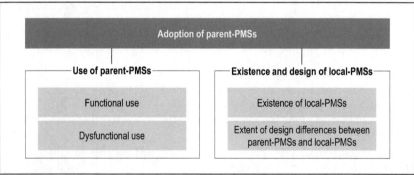

Figure 2–11: Summary of adoption of parent-PMSs at subsidiary level

3 Review of prior research

3.1 Overview of the literature

This chapter reviews **empirical studies** on parent-PMSs in MNCs. Following the two research questions addressed in this study, existing literature is classified into two parts (see Figure 3–1).[39]

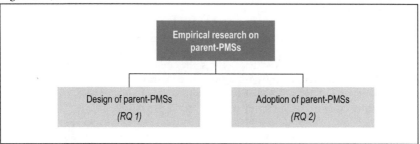

Figure 3–1: Classification of the literature on parent-PMSs

The first part deals with studies describing[40] the **design of parent-PMSs.** Therefore, the first part reviews and outlines evidence on the four design elements of parent-PMSs (performance measures, targets, link to rewards and IT infrastructure).

The second part includes studies describing and/or explaining the **adoption of parent-PMSs by subsidiaries.**[41] Thus, it reviews studies dealing with the use of parent-PMSs at subsidiary level and with the existence and design of local-PMSs. Furthermore, the second part reviews evidence on the factors that influence the adoption of parent-PMSs at subsidiary level.

The following sections present the two parts: Section 3.2 reviews studies on the design of parent-PMSs. In section 3.3, studies on the adoption of parent-PMSs at subsidiary level are presented. Finally, section 3.4 summarizes the findings of both parts and carves out the research gaps that this study addresses.

---

[39] The two parts can be related to *Granlund/Lukka's* distinction between a macro and a micro level of management accounting (*Granlund/Lukka* (1998), p. 154). Macro-level studies deal with the design of management control systems, while micro-level studies examine *"the practical 'doing' of management accounting in the everyday life of organisational actors"* (*Hoffjan et al.* (2012), p. 6). Consequently, the first part relates to the macro perspective, while the second part investigates the role of parent-PMSs in the everyday life of subsidiaries' employees.

[40] Consistent with the research objective of describing the design of parent-PMSs, the first part only deals with descriptive evidence. However, studies with a different focus (e.g., explanatory studies) that additionally provide descriptive evidence are also included in this literature review.

[41] Due to a deficiency of studies examining the adoption of parent-PMSs at subsidiary level, the second part also includes one study (*Kornacker et al.* (2018)) investigating the adoption of budgeting systems at foreign subsidiaries.

3.2   Design of parent-PMSs

The descriptive evidence on the design of parent-PMSs is structured along the four design elements of parent-PMSs: Performance measures, targets, link to rewards, and IT infrastructure.

Performance measures

Evidence on performance measures included in parent-PMSs stems from single-country settings as well as from studies comparing the design of parent-PMSs in MNCs from different countries. In a **single-country setting**, *Demirag* (1988) examines the performance measures that MNCs from the UK employ to evaluate the performance of foreign subsidiaries. By surveying 105 UK-based head offices, the author finds that the head offices perceive cash flow potential, return on investment, and profits as **most important performance measures** for evaluating subsidiary performance (*Demirag* (1988), p. 262). However, the questionnaire contains only a few performance measures from which the head offices can choose. Therefore, it could be that the head offices also consider other performance measures as important that are not surveyed by the author. In this vein, a further limitation of this study is that it solely deals with financial performance measures and thus does not describe the non-financial performance measures that head offices use for evaluating subsidiary performance.

Another study in single-country setting stems from *Appleyard et al.* (1991). The authors conduct interviews with head offices of eleven MNCs from the UK to examine the performance measures that the head offices employ for evaluating subsidiary performance. The authors find that the head offices perceive **profits, return on capital employed, cash flows, and return sales** as most important financial performance measures. For evaluating the subsidiaries' non-financial performance, the head offices mainly rely on **market share, productivity, and growth** (*Appleyard et al.* (1991), p. 116). However, the authors do not examine whether the head offices consider financial and non-financial performance measures to be equally important. Furthermore, the results of this study should be interpreted with caution due to the small sample size.

Pausenberger (1996) examines the kind of performance measures that German MNCs employ to evaluate the performance of foreign subsidiaries. Analyzing the answers of 19 German head offices to his survey, the author finds that **financial performance measures are more important** than non-financial measures in evaluating the performance of foreign subsidiaries. In particular, the survey respondents rank sales, earnings before taxes and cash flow as the most important performance measures (in a descending order). Nevertheless, the author also documents that 13 of 19 MNCs complement financial with non-financial measures (*Pausenberger* (1996), pp. 188-189). However, due to the small sample size the results of the study should be interpreted cautiously. A further drawback of the study is the fact that it does not disclose which non-financial performance measures the surveyed head offices use to evaluate the subsidiaries' performance.

Further evidence in a single-country setting stems from *Kihn's* (2008) survey on Finish MNCs. Even though this study is mainly concerned with the determinants of including financial and non-financial performance measures in parent-PMSs, it also provides some descriptive evidence. Particularly, the author shows that 49 out of 60 surveyed head offices put a high or very high **emphasis on financial performance measures** when evaluating the subsidiaries' performance. Only four companies put a higher emphasis on non-financial performance measures than on financial ones. Thus, financial performance measures are more important than their non-financial counterparts for the surveyed companies in evaluating the subsidiaries' performance. Despite the low weight the surveyed head offices put on non-financial measures, more than half of them at least include non-financial performance measures in the parent-PMS (*Kihn* (2008), p. 162-164). However, similar to *Pausenberger* (1996), *Kihn* (2008) does not reveal which non-financial performance measures are included in the parent-PMS.

Another study from a single-country setting is the study by *Dossi/Patelli* (2010) on the determinants of including non-financial performance measures in parent-PMSs. As opposed to the aforementioned studies, *Dossi/Patelli* (2010) do not survey MNCs' head offices, but their subsidiaries. Particularly, the authors survey management accountants from Italian subsidiaries on the performance measures that they have to report to their head offices. The authors document that 67% of the 141 surveyed subsidiaries have to report **more financial than non-financial performance measures**. In addition, *Dossi/Patelli* (2010) also provide detailed descriptive evidence on the financial and non-financial performance measures included in parent-PMSs. In fact, the authors show that sales revenues, operating income, and contribution margin are the most frequently used financial measures while process productivity rate, market share, and people training expenses are the most commonly used non-financial measures. Furthermore, the authors find that the three examined non-financial perspectives (customers, internal processes, and people) are equally represented in parent-PMSs (*Dossi/Patelli* (2010), pp. 507-511). However, a limitation of the study is the fact that it examines the design of the parent-PMS not by surveying the designers of parent-PMSs (i.e., employees from MNCs' head offices) but by surveying the users of parent-PMSs (i.e., employees from MNCs' foreign subsidiaries). This might distort survey answers since subsidiaries' employees might mix up local-PMSs and parent-PMSs when being asked on the performance measures that are included in parent-PMSs.

Similar to *Dossi/Patelli* (2010), *Abdallah/Alnamri* (2015) investigate the kind of performance measures that are included in parent-PMSs by surveying subsidiaries. In particular, by surveying Saudi Arabian subsidiaries of foreign MNCs, *Abdallah/Alnamri* (2015) show that the MNCs included in their sample **primarily rely on financial measures** to assess the performance of their subsidiaries. The most frequently used financial performance measures are total sales, unit production cost, and rate of return on investments while non-financial measures include number of customers' complaints, customer response time, or market share (*Abdallah/Alnamri* (2015), pp. 601-604). Since *Abdallah/Alnamri* (2015) survey subsidiaries' employees, their study underlies the same limitation as the study by *Dossi/Patelli* (2010).

In addition to studies executed in a single country, three studies compare the use of performance measures **across different countries**. First, *Choi/Czechowicz* (1983) analyze the survey responses of 88 head offices of MNCs to describe the performance measures that they use for evaluating subsidiary performance. Of these 88 MNCs, 64 stem from the US and 24 stem from other countries such as the UK, Sweden, and Switzerland (*Choi/Czechowicz*

(1983), p. 15). The authors find that head offices from both US and non-US MNCs consider **return on investment, sales, and profits** as most important financial performance measures. Concerning non-financial performance, the authors also do not find differences in the performance measures used by US and non-US MNCs. In fact, the authors document that head offices of both US and non-US MNCs consider **market share and productivity** as most important non-financial performance measures (*Choi/Czechowicz* (1983), pp. 16-17). However, the results should be interpreted cautiously as the questionnaire only contains a small number of financial and non-financial performance measures from which the head offices can choose. Furthermore, the authors do not address a potential response bias and do not provide evidence that the US and non-US MNCs are comparable with regard to fundamental characteristics such as firm size and industry.

Second, *Coates et al.* (1992) interview management accountants from 15 MNCs from Germany, the UK, and the USA. Although MNCs from all three countries place a **higher weight on financial performance measures**, the authors find some cross-national differences. Particularly, they find that MNCs' head offices from the UK and the USA rely more strongly on financial performance measures than German ones, which put relatively more emphasis on non-financial performance measures (*Coates et al.* (1992), pp. 137-143). However, a drawback of the study is that the authors do not describe how the 15 MNCs were selected, which makes it difficult to compare their findings with the results of other studies. Furthermore, the authors do not disclose which financial and non-financial performance measures the parent-PMSs include. Finally, the results of this study should be interpreted with caution due to the small sample size.

The third study on performance measures with a cross-country setting stems from *Chung et al.* (2006). Mainly concerned with the determinants explaining the selection of performance measures, the authors also provide descriptive evidence on the type of performance measures included in parent-PMSs from MNCs located in Japan, the USA, the UK, and Germany. *Chung et al.* document that head offices from all four countries **rely more strongly on financial performance measures** than on non-financial performance measures (*Chung et al.* (2006), pp. 159-161). Nevertheless, consistent with *Coates et al.'s* (1992) findings, the authors state that German and Japanese parent companies put relatively more emphasis on non-financial measures than MNCs from the US and UK. However, like *Coates et al.'s* (1992) study, *Chung et al.* (2006) are not specific on the financial and non-financial performance measures included in the parent-PMSs. Another limitation of this study is that it examines the design of the parent-PMS not by surveying the designers of these systems at head office level but by surveying employees from subsidiary level (*Chung et al.* (2006), p. 162).

All in all, financial performance measures seem to be more important for head offices to evaluate subsidiary performance. However, except for *Dossi/Patelli* (2010), prior studies are not specific on the question which performance measures are included in parent-PMSs. In particular, this holds for non-financial performance measures. Furthermore, the results of the prior studies should be interpreted cautiously due to several reasons. First, prior studies lack of representativeness due to small sample sizes (e.g., *Pausenberger* (1996), *Coates et al.* (1992)). Second, the questionnaires used in survey studies often include only few performance measures that the survey respondents can select (e.g., *Choi/Czechowicz* (1983), *Demirag* (1988)). It could be that the MNCs consider other performance measures as important that are not included in the questionnaires. Furthermore, two survey studies (*Dossi/Patelli* (2010), *Abdallah/Alnamri* (2015)) examine the design of the parent-PMSs not by surveying the designers of these systems but by surveying respondents from subsidiary level. This might distort the results since the subsidiaries' respondents might not have sufficient knowledge on the design of the parent-PMS or might mix up local-PMSs and parent-PMSs in their answers. Finally, the results of the studies using cross-country settings should be interpreted with caution since these studies do not match their sub-samples based on firm characteristics (e.g., firm size and industry). This makes it difficult to compare the results of the sub-samples among each other. Table 3–1 provides an overview of studies providing descriptive evidence on performance measures included in parent-PMSs.

Reference	Method and sample	Contribution to this study
Demirag (1988)	Questionnaire-based survey; responses from 105 head offices of MNCs from the UK.	Head offices consider cash flow potential, return on investment, and profits as most important performance measures for evaluating subsidiary performance.
Appleyard et al. (1991)	Interviews with head offices of eleven MNCs from the UK	Head offices perceive profits, return on capital employed, cash flows, and return on sales as most important financial performance measures. For evaluating non-financial performance, head offices consider market share, productivity, and growth as most important performance measures
Pausenberger (1996)	Questionnaire-based survey; responses from 19 head offices of German MNCs.	Head offices mainly use financial performance measures to evaluate the performance of foreign subsidiaries but often complement them with non-financial measures.
Kihn (2008)	Questionnaire-based survey; responses from 60 head offices of Finish MNCs.	Head offices put a higher emphasis on financial than on non-financial performance measures when evaluating performance of foreign subsidiaries.
Dossi/Patelli (2010)	Questionnaire-based survey; responses from 141 Italian subsidiaries of foreign MNCs.	In most cases, parent-PMSs contain more financial than non-financial performance measures. Concerning non-financial measures, all three examined perspectives (customers, employees and internal processes) are equally represented in parent-PMSs.
Abdallah/Alnamri (2015)	Questionnaire-based survey; responses from 72 Saudi-Arabian manufacturing subsidiaries of foreign MNCs.	Non-financial performance measures are less frequently included in parent-PMSs than financial indicators.

Table is continued on the next page

Choi/Czechowicz (1983)	Questionnaire-based survey; responses from head offices of 64 MNCs from the US and 24 non-US MNCs.	US and non-US MNCs do not differ in the choice of performance measures used for evaluating subsidiary performance. Head offices consider return on investment, sales, and profits (market share and productivity) as most important financial (non-financial) performance measures.
Coates et al. (1992)	Cross-sectional field study of 15 MNCs from Germany, the UK, and the USA. Interviews with employees from the firm's head office and interviews with employees from 30 domestic and foreign subsidiaries.	Head offices from the UK and USA put a higher weight on financial performance measures than German head offices. Overall, head offices from all three countries put a higher emphasis on financial than on non-financial performance measures.
Chung et al. (2006)	Questionnaire-based survey; Responses from 213 head offices from Germany, Japan, the UK, and the USA.	German and Japanese head offices place relatively more weight on non-financial performance measures than head offices from the USA and the UK. Overall, MNCs' head offices from all four countries rely more on financial performance measures than on non-financial ones.

Table 3–1: Overview of studies on performance measures in parent-PMSs

Targets

Studies describing parent-PMSs' targets are scarce. Some evidence on the kind of targets included in parent-PMSs stems from *Appleyard et al.'s* (1991) aforementioned study of eleven MNCs from the UK. The authors show that the head offices consider **budgets as most important standards of comparisons**, followed by the subsidiaries' past performance and external and internal benchmarks (*Appleyard et al.* (1991), p. 117). In a similar vein, *Pausenberger* (1996) finds in his survey study of 19 German multinationals that **budgets are most commonly used** as standards of comparisons by the sample firms, followed by past performance and internal benchmarks with other domestic and foreign subsidiaries (*Pausenberger* (1996), pp. 189-190). However, as noted above, the findings of both studies should be interpreted with caution due to the small sample sizes of the studies. Furthermore, the two studies do not provide evidence on the form and frequency of target evaluation.

Further evidence on parent-PMSs' targets stems from *van der Stede* (2003). Even though this study is primarily concerned with the question whether head offices adjust management control systems to local conditions, the author also provides some descriptive evidence on the types of targets and form of target evaluation. Particularly, by using survey data from 37 Belgian head offices and 153 domestic and foreign subsidiaries, the author shows that head offices put a **high emphasis on budgets** when evaluating the subsidiaries' achieved performance. Furthermore, he finds that formal performance evaluation based on written reports is equally important as review meetings and discussions between head offices and subsidiaries when evaluating performance (*van der Stede* (2003), pp. 276-279). However, *van der Stede* does neither reveal how the budget-based targets are determined (e.g., top-down planning, bottom-up planning, or counter-flow planning). Furthermore, he does not provide evidence whether target setting is different for financial and non-financial performance measures.

While originally being concerned with the determinants of targets included in parent-PMSs, *Du et al.* (2013) also provide some descriptive evidence. By surveying 82 Belgian subsidiaries of foreign MNCs the authors examine to what extent subsidiaries participate in setting targets and to what extent head offices consider factors that are not under the control of the subsidiaries' managers in evaluating performance. *Du et al.* document a **high level of subsidiary participation in setting targets,** which is even higher in cases of high mutual dependence between head offices and subsidiaries *(Du et al.* (2013), pp. 403-407). Furthermore, the authors show that head offices eliminate uncontrollable factors only to a small extent when evaluating subsidiary managers' performance *(Du et al.* (2013), p. 403). However, since *Du et al.'s* (2013) study is of explanatory nature, the authors only document the extent of participative target setting and subjective performance evaluation but do not describe how subsidiaries participate in setting targets or whether target setting is different for financial and non-financial performance measures.

In addition to the studies on parent-PMS's targets outlined above, numerous studies (e.g., *Roth/O'Donnell* (1996), *Groot/Lindahl* (2010))[42] examine the extent to which head offices rely on output controls compared to other control mechanisms such as behavioral controls or cultural controls *(Schmid/Kretschmer* (2010), pp. 222-224; *Sageder/Feldbauer-Durstmüller* (2018), p. 13). However, although these studies find that output controls (such as parent-PMSs) play an important role for head offices, the studies do not provide descriptive evidence on the targets that parent-PMSs include. Hence, these studies are not discussed here.[43]

Overall, there is little descriptive evidence on parent-PMSs' targets. Even though existing studies indicate that budget-based targets are an important standard of comparison for actual performance, they do not describe in detail how these targets are set or whether the type of targets differs for financial or non-financial performance measures. Furthermore, except *van der Stede* (2003), prior studies do not provide descriptive evidence on the form and frequency of performance evaluation. Table 3–2 provides an overview of studies shedding light on targets included in parent-PMSs.

Reference	Method and sample	Contribution to this study
Appleyard et al. (1991)	Interviews with head offices of eleven MNCs from the UK	Parent-PMSs primarily include budgets as targets, followed by past performance, external benchmarks, and internal benchmarks.
Pausenberger (1996)	Questionnaire-based survey; responses from 19 head offices of German MNCs.	Parent-PMSs primarily include budgets as targets, followed by past performance and internal benchmarks.

Table is continued on the next page

---

[42] Cf. also *Chang/Taylor* (1999); *Chung et al.* (2000); *Harzing/Sorge* (2003).

[43] For a comprehensive review of studies examining the extent and determinants of different control forms (e.g., output control, behavioral control and cultural control) in MNCs, cf. *Schmid/Kretschmer* (2010).

van der Stede (2003)	Questionnaire-based survey; responses from 37 head offices of Belgian MNCs and 153 of their domestic and foreign subsidiaries.	Budgets are most important for head offices to evaluate subsidiary performance. In addition to written reports, review meetings play an important role in determining subsidiary performance.
Du et al. (2013)	Questionnaire-based survey; responses from 82 Belgian subsidiaries of foreign MNCs.	Belgian subsidiaries are highly involved in the target-setting process. Head offices consider uncontrollable events only to a small extent when evaluating target achievement.

Table 3–2: Overview of studies on targets in parent-PMSs

Link to rewards

Concerning parent-PMSs' link to rewards, *Dossi/Patelli* (2008) provide some descriptive evidence, even though their study is mainly concerned with the determinants explaining how extensively subsidiaries use parent-PMSs.[44] The authors show that only 15% of their sample firms link performance results to reward systems, indicating that parent-PMSs are **seldom linked to rewards** (*Dossi/Patelli* (2008), p. 137). However, by using a binary variable to capture the link between parent-PMSs and rewards, *Dossi/Patelli's* study cannot provide detailed descriptive evidence on how parent-PMSs are linked to rewards (*Mahlendorf et al.* (2012), p. 708). In particular, the authors do not reveal what kind of performance measures are linked to subsidiary managers' rewards.

Similar to the aforementioned study, *Mahlendorf et al.* (2012) are mainly concerned with explaining the use of parent-PMSs by subsidiaries, but also provide some descriptive evidence on the link between parent-PMSs and rewards. As opposed to *Dossi/Patelli* (2008), *Mahlendorf et al.* (2012) do not use a dummy variable, but measure the link to rewards on a 7-point Likert scale. *Mahlendorf et al.* (2012) report that in 62 % of their sample firms, parent-PMSs are **important in determining the level of compensation** of subsidiary managers (*Mahlendorf et al.* (2012), p. 708). Since these results are in contrast to *Dossi/Patelli's* (2008) findings, it remains unclear whether parent-PMSs are linked to rewards. Furthermore, even though *Mahlendorf et al.* (2012) use a more granular measurement instrument, they do not describe how parent-PMSs and rewards are linked.

Van der Stede's (2003) earlier mentioned study on Belgian MNCs also provides descriptive evidence on the link of parent-PMSs to rewards. The author shows that the **compensation of the subsidiaries' managers is largely fixed** and therefore depends on performance measures of the parent-PMS only to a minor extent (13% on average). Furthermore, *van der Stede* (2003) documents that in half of the investigated MNCs, **the variable component is based on subjective judgement** of head offices' managers rather than being determined by strict rules. Moreover, the author shows that rewards are more often **linked to subsidiary performance** rather than to the performance of the whole MNC (*van der Stede* (2003),

---

[44] Since *Dossi/Patelli* (2008) mainly focus on the adoption of parent-PMSs at subsidiary level, it is discussed in more detail in section 3.2.

p. 273). However, the author does not reveal which performance measures are linked to the remuneration of the subsidiaries' managers.

To **conclude**, prior studies suggest a weak link between performance measures and targets from the parent-PMS on the one hand and the remuneration of subsidiaries' employees on the other hand. However, existing studies do not describe how performance measures are linked to rewards. In particular, it remains unclear whether rewards are connected to all performance measures or whether there are differences between financial and non-financial performance measures. Table 3–3 summarizes the studies providing evidence on the link between parent-PMSs and rewards of subsidiaries' managers.

Reference	Method and sample	Contribution to this study
Dossi/Patelli (2008)	Questionnaire-based survey; responses from 141 Italian subsidiaries of foreign MNCs.	Parent-PMSs are linked to the remuneration of subsidiary managers only in few cases.
Mahlendorf et al. (2012)	Questionnaire-based survey; responses from 148 Chinese subsidiaries of foreign MNCs.	Parent-PMSs are important for determining subsidiary managers' compensation.
van der Stede (2003)	Questionnaire-based survey; responses from 37 head offices of Belgian MNCs and 153 of their domestic and foreign subsidiaries.	Only a small component of subsidiary managers' compensation is variable. This variable component often relates to the performance of the subsidiary. Subjective judgement is as important as strict rules in determining the level of subsidiary managers' compensation.

Table 3–3: Overview of studies on the link of parent-PMSs to rewards of subsidiary managers

IT infrastructure

The IT infrastructure is a topic that is often neglected in studies examining the design of PMSs, especially in the context of MNCs (*Micheli et al.* (2011), p. 1118). Existing studies are mostly practitioner reports analyzing what **kinds of information systems are used in practice** for performance measurement (e.g., *Neely et al.* (2008), *Marr* (2005); cf. *Micheli et al.* (2011), p. 1118). However, these studies relate to PMSs in general, but do not examine the IT infrastructure of parent-PMSs used by head offices.

Evidence on the IT infrastructure in MNCs stems from *Micheli et al.'s* (2011) study on the introduction of a group-wide information system at Cisma, an Italian MNC. Particularly, by using a mixed-method approach, the authors describe how Cisma's head offices introduced a shared ERP system to support and align performance measurement within the group. *Micheli et al.* (2011) document that the parent company put a lot of effort into the implementation of this ERP, but failed to link this IT infrastructure to the other design elements of the parent-PMS such as performance measures. As pointed out by *Micheli et al.* (2011), this lack of guidance by the parent company resulted in a low uniform understanding of performance measurement practices within the group. Therefore, the study contributes to research by showing that the **IT infrastructure and the other design elements of parent-PMSs should be aligned** with each other. However, by examining only a single case, the authors are not able to describe if and how IT systems beyond ERP systems (such as spreadsheet applications or BI systems) are used as an IT infrastructure of parent-PMSs.

By using a case study approach, *Quattrone/Hopper* (2005) examine the implementation of an ERP system (SAP R/3) for performance measurement in two multinationals. The first MNC, a Japanese firm producing and selling sewing machines, uses SAP R/3 for real-time reporting. In doing so, the head office provides subsidiaries' management accountants with access to the ERP system and therefore uses SAP R/3 as a shared database within the MNC. The other MNC, an American manufacturer and supplier of composite materials, did not implement real-time reporting. In fact, the subsidiaries' management accountants still have to report performance measures to the head office after the end of each month. In the second MNC, only management accountants from the head offices have access to performance information on all subsidiaries. With their study, *Quattrone/Hopper* (2005) show that even though both MNCs implement the same ERP system (SAP R/3), **different configurations of this ERP system lead to different outcomes**. However, like *Micheli et al.* (2011), *Quattrone/Hopper* (2005) are only concerned with ERP systems and do not describe other IT systems in the infrastructure of parent-PMSs.

In **summary**, the two prior studies describe the use of ERP systems as IT infrastructure for parent-PMSs. More precisely, these studies indicate that ERP systems should be linked to the other design elements of parent-PMSs and that practitioners and researchers should also pay attention to the configurations of these systems. However, by focusing only on ERP systems, the two studies do not tell what other IT systems are used as IT infrastructure by MNCs. Table 3–4 provides an overview on studies providing evidence on parent-PMSs' IT infrastructure.

Reference	Method and sample	Contribution to this study
Micheli et al. (2011)	Mixed methods: Interviews at head office and subsidiary level and survey responses from 44 subsidiaries of an Italian MNC.	A parent-PMS's IT infrastructure should be closely linked to the other elements of the parent-PMS.
Quattrone/Hopper (2005)	Case studies of one American and one Japanese MNC. 35 interviews with employees from head offices and subsidiaries of the two MNCs.	In describing how information systems support parent-PMSs, researchers should not only consider the type of information system, but also different configurations of these systems.

Table 3–4: Overview of studies on the IT infrastructure of parent-PMSs

3.3   Adoption of parent-PMSs

While the previous section presented studies describing the design of parent-PMSs, this section reviews studies examining the adoption of parent-PMSs at subsidiary level, which is addressed by both quantitative and qualitative research. Since **quantitative and qualitative**

studies differ considerably in their approach of investigating subsidiaries' adoption of parent-PMSs, both types of studies are presented separately.[45]

Quantitative studies

The existing quantitative studies are mainly concerned with the determinants explaining **how extensively subsidiaries use parent-PMSs**. In addition, some of the quantitative studies also examine **whether and why subsidiaries develop local-PMSs**. Concerning their research design, the cited quantitative studies follow a similar approach. All studies rely on a questionnaire-based survey that is sent to employees of foreign subsidiaries. In all studies, the extent of use is measured by asking survey respondents to rate the impact of the parent-PMS on fifteen local decisions. [46] In addition, the questionnaires examine whether the subsidiaries develop a local-PMS or not.[47]

The first survey study on the adoption of parent-PMSs at subsidiary level stems from *Dossi/Patelli* (2008). Concerning the impact of the parent-PMS on local decisions, the authors find that subsidiaries use parent-PMSs more extensively if they have been involved in developing the parent-PMS's design. Furthermore, they find that subsidiary size, head offices' tolerance for uncertainty and perceived global pressure positively affect the **extent to which the subsidiaries use the parent-PMSs implemented by their head offices**. Contrary to the authors' hypotheses, neither the parallel use of both financial and non-financial performance measures in parents-PMSs nor the linkage of managers' rewards to performance measures from the parent-PMS increases the impact of parent-PMSs on subsidiaries' strategic decisions (*Dossi/Patelli* (2008), pp. 137-140). However, the finding concerning parent-PMSs' linkage to rewards should be interpreted cautiously for two reasons: First, *Dossi/Patelli* (2008) use a binary variable for measuring the link between parent-PMSs and rewards which might not adequately capture the complex reward structures that are present in MNCs. Furthermore, only a few head offices from the sample (15%) link the parent-PMS to rewards, which reduces the power of statistical analysis. These two aspects might explain the insignificant finding (*Dossi/Patelli* (2008), p. 136; *Mahlendorf et al.* (2012), p. 708).

In addition to examining the extent of use, *Dossi/Patelli* (2008) provide evidence on the existence of local-PMSs in Italian subsidiaries. In fact, they find that 86% of the surveyed subsidiaries implement local-PMSs. Furthermore, the authors show that subsidiaries' management accountants use these self-developed PMSs more extensively than the parent-PMSs, indicating a **high importance of local-PMSs for decision-making at subsidiary level** (*Dossi/Patelli* (2008), p. 140). To explore the reasons of developing local-PMSs, the authors complement their survey-based findings with a focus group discussion with nine

---

[45] In fact, quantitative studies examine the extent to which subsidiaries use parent-PMSs, while qualitative studies investigate how subsidiaries use the parent-PMSs. Furthermore, quantitative research deals with the prevalence of local-PMSs, while qualitative research describes how subsidiaries modify the design of parent-PMSs.

[46] These local decisions relate to the marketing and sales function, the area of production and research and development, and to the area of human resource management (*Dossi/Patelli* (2008), p. 136).

[47] This is examined by using a binary variable (0/1).

survey participants. They find that the **perceived inadequacy** of the parent-PMS by subsidiaries' management accountants and the **need for more detailed analysis** on the local level are more important for developing local-PMSs than administrative issues such as different accounting standards or the lack of integrative information systems. However, *Dossi/Patelli* (2008) do not consider other possible determinants that might influence the development of local-PMSs, such as different training and education of management accountants in different countries.

By building on *Dossi/Patelli* (2008), *Mahlendorf et al.* (2012) examine the adoption of parent-PMSs in China. Based on 148 questionnaires from Chinese subsidiaries, the authors show that the **influence of the parent-PMS on local decisions** is higher when subsidiaries are **embedded in the local business environment** and when the **head office provides rules and guidelines**. Furthermore, the authors find that subsidiaries use parent-PMS more extensively when the parent-PMS includes **financial and non-financial performance measures** derived from strategy and when the parent-PMS is **linked to rewards** (*Mahlendorf et al.* (2012), 703-705). These findings are in stark contrast to the findings of *Dossi/Patelli* (2008), who find that neither having both financial and non-financial measures nor linking parent-PMSs to rewards does affect how extensively subsidiaries use parent-PMSs.[48] Given these conflicting results, it remains unclear whether linking parent-PMSs to rewards and including both financial and non-financial measures positively affect the extent to which these systems are used at subsidiary level.

Based on the same dataset[49] as *Mahlendorf et al.* (2012), *Schäffer et al.* (2010) document the existence of local-PMSs in Chinese subsidiaries. They find that **about one quarter** of the surveyed Chinese subsidiaries develop local-PMSs (*Schäffer et al.* (2010), p. 312), which is considerably lower than the percentage of Italian subsidiaries developing own PMSs found by *Dossi/Patelli* (2008). Furthermore, the authors ask their survey respondents on the reasons for developing local-PMSs. Consistent with *Dossi/Patelli's* (2008) findings, *Schäffer et al.* (2010) report that the need for more detailed analysis, administrative problems, and a perceived inadequacy of the parent-PMSs are **more important** for developing local-PMSs than problems with the parent-PMS's IT infrastructure and different demands by different owners (*Schäffer et al.* (2010), p. 313). However, similar to *Dossi/Patelli* (2008), *Schäffer et al.* (2010) do not address other potential reasons for developing local-PMSs.

In another study in the Chinese context, *Wu/Schäffer* (2015) provide further evidence on the determinants that explain how extensively subsidiaries use parent-PMSs. The authors find that subsidiaries evaluate the parent-PMS more favorably and also use it more extensively the more they **identify themselves with their parent company** (*Wu/Schäffer* (2015), p. 123-129). Furthermore, consistent with *Dossi/Patelli* (2008), they find that involving subsidiaries in the design of the parent-PMS also increases the extent to which the parent-

---

[48] This might be due to the fact that both studies differ in the conceptualization and measurement of independent variables. For example, *Dossi/Patelli* (2008) use a binary variable to assess whether the parent-PMSs are linked to rewards, while *Mahlendorf et al.* (2012) measure the link to rewards by using a Likert scale.

[49] For more detailed information on this dataset, cf. *Mahlendorf et al.* (2012), pp. 698-699.

PMS is used at subsidiary level (*Wu/Schäffer* (2015), p. 125). However, *Wu/Schäffer* (2015) only examine the extent of use but do not distinguish different usage types.

In **summary**, the few existing quantitative studies contribute to the adoption of parent-PMSs at subsidiary level in two ways: First, concerning the **extent of use**, they provide evidence that involving subsidiaries in the design of parent-PMSs and monitoring the implementation of these systems increase the extent to which parent-PMSs are used at subsidiary level. Furthermore, a high identification of subsidiaries with the MNC might also positively affect the use of parent-PMSs. Concerning the **existence of local-PMSs**, the quantitative studies find a different prevalence of local-PMSs in MNCs' foreign subsidiaries. As pointed out by the previous studies, the most important reasons for developing local systems are a perceived inadequacy of the parent-PMS and the need for more detailed analyses.

However, the quantitative studies also share some **deficiencies** stemming from their research design. Concerning the **use of parent-PMSs** at subsidiary level, prior studies do not distinguish between different usage types. Particularly, the existing studies fail to examine whether parent-PMSs are used as intended by head offices or whether they are used in a ceremonial way only.[50] With respect to the **development of local-PMSs**, the quantitative studies can only provide first preliminary evidence.[51] This is the case for two reasons. First, by relying on a binary variable, prior quantitative studies examine the existence of local-PMSs in a vague way. In fact, this approach does not allow to describe differences between parent-PMSs and local-PMSs in detail. Second, when examining the reasons for developing local-PMSs, the prior quantitative studies neglect potential determinants such as a different education of management accountants in different countries or host countries' national laws. Table 3–5 summarizes the quantitative studies on the adoption of parent-PMSs at subsidiary level.

Reference	Method and sample	Contribution to this study
Dossi/Patelli (2008)	Questionnaire-based survey; responses from 141 Italian subsidiaries of foreign MNCs.	Involving subsidiaries' management accountants in the design of parent-PMSs positively affects the extent to which the system is used at subsidiary level. Local-PMSs are widespread in Italian subsidiaries.
Schäffer et al. (2010)	Questionnaire-based survey; responses from 148 Chinese subsidiaries of foreign MNCs.	About one quarter of Chinese subsidiaries develop local-PMSs, indicating that local-PMSs are less widespread than in *Dossi/Patelli's* (2008) study on Italian subsidiaries of MNCs.

Table is continued on the next page

---

[50] Furthermore, by only surveying MNC's subsidiaries (and not the corresponding head offices), the mentioned studies cannot assess the intended use by the designers of parent-PMSs.

[51] It has to be noted that the focus of the presented studies is on the use of parent-PMSs at subsidiary level and not on the development of local-PMSs. Therefore, it cannot be expected that they address this issue in depth.

Mahlendorf et al. (2012)	Questionnaire-based survey; responses from 148 Chinese subsidiaries of foreign MNCs (same sample as used by Schäffer et al. (2010)).	Monitoring and enforcing the imposition of parent-PMSs increases the extent to which parent-PMSs are used by subsidiaries' employees.
Wu/Schäffer (2015)	Questionnaire-based survey; responses from 110 Chinese subsidiaries of foreign MNCs.	Subsidiaries' employees evaluate the parent-PMSs more favorably and hence use the parent-PMS more extensively the more they identify themselves with the parent company. Involving subsidiaries' employees in the design of parent-PMSs also increases the extent of use.

Table 3–5: Overview of quantitative studies on the adoption of parent-PMSs

Qualitative studies

The following paragraphs review four case studies examining the adoption of parent-PMSs by subsidiaries and one cross-sectional field study investigating the adoption of budgeting systems at subsidiary level.

The first qualitative study on the adoption of parent-PMSs at subsidiary level stems from *Siti-Nabiha/Scapens* (2005). In a longitudinal single case study, the authors examine the imposition of a parent-PMS at Eagle, a domestic subsidiary of an East Asian state-owned oil company.[52] The state-owned parent company introduced a set of value-based performance measures that Eagle had to prepare and report to the parent company's head office on a monthly basis. As documented by the authors, the introduction of the value-based performance measures did not affect the decisions of Eagle. In fact, even though the subsidiary prepared and reported the financial measures to the head office, they did not actually use them for making local decisions. Eagle rather began to develop an own set of performance measures that was used for decision-making (*Siti-Nabiha/Scapens* (2005), p. 65). Through this study, *Siti-Nabiha/Scapens* show that subsidiaries' employees can **resist the implementation of parent-PMSs by ceremonially adopting it.** The authors explain the subsidiary's resistance against the parent-PMS by hinting at the production-oriented mindset of Eagle, which conflicted with the financial orientation of the value-based performance measures included in the parent-PMS. However, the study has several limitations. First, by examining only a single case, the authors cannot address other reasons for ceremonially adopting parent-PMSs than the contradiction between a production-oriented mindset of subsidiaries' employees and the financial-orientation of the parent-PMS. Furthermore, by examining a domestic subsidiary, the authors do not address issues that are relevant for foreign subsidiaries, such as cultural distance between the MNC's head office and subsidiaries. Finally, the authors do not describe the self-developed set of performance measures and therefore do not reveal how it differs from the performance measures included in the parent-PMS.

---

[52] For reasons of confidentiality, the authors do not display the company's real name (*Siti-Nabiha/Scapens* (2005), p. 67). This is a standard procedure in qualitative research (*Patton* (2015), p. 55) and applies for all reviewed qualitative studies.

Cruz et al. (2009) also deal with the imposition of a financially-oriented parent-PMS at subsidiary level. In their single case study, they examine the case of Hotelco, a Portuguese joint venture that is equally hold by a family-owned Portuguese company (Partner L) and a MNC (Partner G). Partner G implemented a standardized P&L on Hotelco and its other subsidiaries. Furthermore, Hotelco had to prepare yearly budgets according to standards provided by Partner G and to semi-annually report deviations between actual and budgeted performance. Opposed to *Siti-Nabiha/Scapens'* (2005) findings, *Cruz et al.* (2009) find **little resistance towards the parent-PMS** at Hotelco. Hotelco's employees rather acknowledged the efficiency gains stemming from adopting the standardized P&L and therefore actually used it in their daily work. Thus, the implementation of Partner G's parent-PMS was not ceremonial (*Cruz et al.* (2009), p. 107). However, Hotelco's **employees developed a local-PMS**, which contained some elements of the global system but also contained elements that existed only locally (such as a monthly deviation report). This local-PMS was necessary for Hotelco's employees to comply with requirements made by the other parent company, Partner L. For example, Partner L expected Hotelco to monitor deviations from the budget on a monthly basis. Overall, *Cruz et al.* (2009) show that joint ventures might develop local-PMSs – even if they do not resist and actually use parent-PMSs. However, *Cruz et al.'s* (2009) findings might not be transferable to this study for the following reason. In their case study, the local-PMS mainly arises because of the existence of two parent-PMSs, which is a special feature of joint ventures. Therefore, their findings might not hold for subsidiaries, which are subject to only one parent-PMS.[53]

In another study, *Cruz et al.* (2011) build on the empirical material from the abovementioned study, but scrutinize the local-PMS that existed at Hotelco in more detail. In particular, the authors examine those parts of the local-PMS that did not result from additional requirements by Partner L. The authors argue that the local-PMS helped Hotelco's employees to make Partner G's parent-PMS work at subsidiary level (*Cruz et al.* (2011), p. 419). *Cruz et al.* therefore conclude that subsidiaries do not necessarily develop local-PMSs to tackle the functionality of parent-PMSs, but also to **facilitate the implementation of parent-PMSs** at subsidiary level. However, the study underlies the same limitations as the study of *Cruz et al.* (2009). Therefore, the findings might not be transferable subsidiaries, which are subject to only one parent-PMS.

By using a single case study, *Cooper/Ezzamel* (2013) examine how foreign subsidiaries of Megacorp, a German MNC, adopt a parent-PMS implemented by Megacorp's head office. In particular, the authors investigate how production and sales units from the UK and China adopt a BSC implemented by the German head office. The authors find that two of the four foreign subsidiaries (sales units from China and the UK) **rejected to use the BSC**, while the production unit from the UK **negotiated with the head office to modify the**

---

[53] This is also acknowledged by the authors, who call for *"[m]ore qualitative studies on the adoption of externally imposed practices in other global/local settings [...] to refine the understanding of this phenomenon"* (*Cruz et al.* (2009), p. 91).

BSC.[54] As reasons for rejecting or renegotiating the BSC, interview partners from the examined foreign subsidiaries stressed that the implemented BSC did not fit national characteristics of the subsidiary (such as culture or geographical location). Thus, as opposed to *Siti-Nabiha/Scapens'* (2005) findings, Megacorp's subsidiaries did not ceremonially use the parent-PMS but were able to reject or renegotiate the introduction of the BSC. *Cooper/Ezzamel* (2013) hint at the relatively low pressure Megacorp's head office exerted on their subsidiaries to implement the BSC, which made it possible for foreign subsidiaries to renegotiate the implementation of the BSC with the head office. Thus, the **degree of pressure** exerted by head offices to implement parent-PMSs might influence how subsidiaries adopt these systems. In addition to examining the introduction of the BSC as a whole, the authors also focus more closely on specific performance measures included in the BSC, namely earnings before interest and taxes (EBIT) and number of suggestions per employee. *Cooper/Ezzamel* find that subsidiaries sometimes **interpret and calculate performance measures differently**, even if these performance measures are unambiguously defined. Overall, *Cooper/Ezzamel's* (2013) study shows that subsidiaries might openly reject or renegotiate parent-PMSs, especially if the pressure to adopt these systems is considerably low. However, this study also underlies two limitations: First, the authors only examine the adoption of one parent-PMS in one MNC. Therefore, the authors cannot observe whether and how different designs of parent-PMSs influence the adoption at subsidiary level. Second, their single case study only provides evidence on one particular determinant of the adoption of parent-PMSs, namely the degree of pressure exerted by MNCs' head offices when imposing parent-PMSs.

In addition to the four qualitative studies outlined above, this review also includes *Kornacker et al.'s* (2018) study on the **adoption of budgeting systems** by subsidiaries.[55] By conducting a cross-sectional field study of 28 German MNCs and their Chinese subsidiaries, the authors explore whether and why budgeting systems implemented by head offices are (not) used at subsidiary level. The authors find three different strategies that subsidiaries pursued to adopt budgeting systems: The first group of Chinese subsidiaries **reproduced** the budgeting practices of the German head offices, meaning that they accepted and used the given budgeting systems without modifying them. The second group of subsidiaries used the budgeting systems for decision-making but **modified** them when enacting them locally. In fact, similar to *Cruz et al.'s* (2011) findings, the second group modified the implemented budgeting systems to facilitate the adoption at subsidiary level. Finally, the third group of Chinese subsidiaries **ceremonially used** the budgeting systems (*Kornacker et al.* (2018), pp. 38-44). With respect to the determinants of the applied strategies, *Kornacker et al.* (2018) find that the local adoption of budgeting systems depends on the subsidiaries' **perceived predictability of future developments**. In fact, several interviewed management accountants (especially management accountants from subsidiaries that used the implemented

---

[54] At the Chinese production unit, evidence on the introduction of the BSC were mixed: Some of the local managers did not know the BSC, others claimed to use the BSC for their daily work (*Cooper/Ezzamel* (2013), p. 302).

[55] Even though this study does not deal with parent-PMSs, it can contribute to the topic of this study by shedding light on potential strategies of foreign subsidiaries (and their determinants) in adopting imposed management control systems.

budgeting systems ceremonially) argue that budgeting systems are less useful in China due to the high volatility of the Chinese market. Furthermore, the authors find that subsidiaries evaluate the budgeting system more favorably when head offices **adapt the budgeting system to local conditions**. However, it remains unclear whether the findings apply for parent-PMSs. As acknowledged by the authors,

> *"[...] the predictability of future developments [...] is likely to be of minor importance for the transfer of, for instance, other types of management controls or cost accounting structures."*

(*Kornacker et al.* (2018), p. 48)

Furthermore, the poor predictability of future events is a special feature of the Chinese market, which might not be transferable to other countries with a less volatile business environment (*Kornacker et al.* (2018), p. 47-48).

To **conclude**, the qualitative studies show that subsidiaries can pursue different strategies to cope with parent-PMSs implemented by head offices. Particularly, four different strategies can be differentiated: First, subsidiaries can simply use the parent-PMS without modifying its design.[56] Second, subsidiaries can develop local-PMSs that support the implementation of parent-PMSs (*Cruz et al.* (2009), *Cruz et al.* (2011)). As a third strategy, subsidiaries might ceremonially use parent-PMSs. When ceremonially adopting parent-PMSs, subsidiaries might rather use local-PMSs for decision-making (*Siti-Nabiha/Scapens* (2005)). Finally, subsidiaries might be sometimes able to convince the head office not to implement the parent-PMS (*Cooper/Ezzamel* (2013), p. 311).

However, the qualitative studies have some **shortcomings**. First, except *Kornacker et al.* (2018), the existing studies are single case studies and hence cannot examine the impact of different designs of parent-PMSs on the adoption at subsidiary level. Second, the findings might not be transferrable to this study since they examine budgeting systems rather than parent-PMSs (*Kornacker et al.* (2018)), joint ventures (*Cruz et al.* (2009) and *Cruz et al.* (2011)) or a domestic subsidiary (*Siti-Nabiha/Scapens* (2005)). Third, prior qualitative studies only distinguish between a ceremonial and a non-ceremonial use of PMSs but do not consider other usage types such as a monitoring or attention-directing use. Fourth, previous studies do not describe local-PMSs and hence do not reveal how local-PMSs differ from parent-PMSs. Finally, prior studies only examine few determinants explaining the adoption of parent-PMSs at subsidiary level.

Table 3–6 summarizes qualitative studies on the adoption of parent-PMSs and budgeting systems at subsidiary level.

---

[56] However, since *Kornacker et al.'s* (2018) study deals with budgeting systems, this first strategy has still to be shown for the adoption of parent-PMSs by subsidiaries' employees.

Reference	Method and sample	Contribution to this study
Siti-Nabiha/Scapens (2005)	Longitudinal single case study of an East Asian state-owned oil company. Interviews with 48 employees from the case firm's head office and a domestic subsidiary.	Subsidiaries' employees can resist the imposition of parent-PMSs by ceremonially adopting them. The reason for subsidiaries' employees' resistance towards the parent-PMS is the contraction between the parent-PMSs' financial orientation and the subsidiaries' employees' production-orientation.
Cruz et al. (2009)	Single case study of a Portuguese joint venture. Interviews with 24 management accountants and managers from the joint venture and the head offices of the two parent companies.	Employees from joint ventures might develop local-PMSs to comply with two different parent-PMSs (stemming from the two parent companies).
Cruz et al. (2011)	Single case study of a Portuguese joint venture. Interviews with 24 management accountants and managers from the joint venture and the head offices of the two parent companies (same empirical material as used by *Cruz et al.* (2009).	Local-PMSs might facilitate the adoption of parent-PMSs at subsidiary level.
Cooper/Ezzamel (2013)	Single case study of a German MNC. Interviews with 97 employees from the case firm's German head office and two production and sales units from China and the UK.	Subsidiaries' employees can openly reject parent-PMSs or renegotiate the design of these systems with the head office. This might be especially true if head offices only put low pressure on subsidiaries to adopt parent-PMS.
Kornacker et al. (2018)	Cross-sectional field study of 15 German MNCs and their Chinese subsidiaries. Interviews with 58 management accountants and managers from the German head offices and the Chinese subsidiaries.	Subsidiaries pursue different strategies of adopting budgeting systems. They might reproduce budgeting systems, ceremonially use them or modify them.

Table 3–6: Overview of qualitative studies on the adoption of parent-PMSs

3.4 Summary and research gaps

In essence, the studies describing the **design** of parent-PMSs indicate that financial performance measures are more prevalent in parent-PMSs than their non-financial counterparts. Furthermore, budgets seem to be an important standard of comparison for actual performance while at the same time targets are often only weakly linked to the remuneration of subsidiaries' employees. Concerning the IT infrastructure, prior studies mainly focus on the role of ERP systems.

However, the review of prior studies also reveals **two research gaps** concerning the design of parent-PMSs (see Figure 3–2). First, many of the studies presented in section 3.1 (e.g., *Kihn* (2008), *Dossi/Patelli* (2010); *Du et al.* (2013)) are explanatory studies providing **scant descriptive evidence** on the design of parent-PMSs. Consequently, there are several issues concerning the design of parent-PMSs that are not adequately addressed by prior studies. For instance, scarce descriptive evidence exists on the question which non-financial performance measures are included in parent-PMSs. Given that a large body of conceptual work advocates the inclusion of non-financial performance measures in PMSs (e.g., *Lynch/Cross* (1995), *Kaplan/Norton* (1996)), this lack of research is surprising and hinders to understand the role that head offices of MNCs attach to non-financial performance measures (*Dossi/Patelli* (2010), pp. 500-501). Furthermore, existing research gives a scant indication on how parent-PMSs are linked to the remuneration of subsidiaries' employees. This is especially true for survey studies measuring the link between parent-PMSs and rewards in a vague way (e.g., by using a dummy variable as done by *Dossi/Patelli* (2008)).[57]

Second, existing studies often address **only single design elements** of parent-PMSs, such as performance measures and targets. Thus, these studies cannot provide evidence on how the design elements are connected. For example, they do not examine which performance measures head offices link to rewards or whether head offices use different types of targets for financial and non-financial performance measures.

By using a case study approach, this study provides a detailed description of the design of parent-PMSs, which helps to reduce the first research gap. In particular, this approach allows to describe multiple design elements.

Concerning the **adoption** of parent-PMSs at subsidiary level, a paucity of research is evident. This is not surprising, however, since research examining the adoption at subsidiary level has just started in 2005. In fact, studies before 2005 did not address how parent-PMSs are adopted at subsidiary level or simply assumed that parent-PMSs are adopted by subsidiaries as intended by their head offices (*Cruz et al.* (2011), p. 414). The existing quantitative studies published after 2005 indicate that subsidiaries' employees tend to develop local-PMSs. The few existing qualitative studies indicate that subsidiaries pursue different strategies of adopting parent-PMSs.

However, due to the explorative stage of research on the adoption of parent-PMSs at subsidiary level, **several research gaps** remain unaddressed. First, only one qualitative study

---

[57] In addition to these content-related weaknesses, existing empirical findings on the design of parent-PMSs should be interpreted with caution for the following reasons. First, some studies (e.g., *Pausenberger* (1996), *Coates et al.* (1992) only examine small samples and are therefore not statistically generalizable (e.g., Pausenberger (1996), Coates et al. (1992)). Second, survey studies often only include few performance measures that the MNCs can select when answering the questionnaire (e.g., *Choi/Czechowicz* (1983), *Demirag* (1988)). Thus, these survey studies neglect performance measures that are important for the MNCs. Furthermore, survey studies sometimes examine the design of the parent-PMSs by surveying employees at subsidiary level (e.g., *Dossi/Patelli* (2010), *Abdallah/Alnamri* (2015)). This could distort the results of these studies since the subsidiaries' respondents might not have sufficient knowledge on the design of the parent-PMSs. Finally, the results of the studies using cross-country settings should be interpreted with caution since these studies use different samples in the different countries (e.g., *Coates et al.* (1992); *Chung et al.* (2006)).

(*Cooper/Ezzamel* (2013)) examines the adoption of parent-PMSs by **foreign subsidiaries**. All other studies focus on domestic rather than on foreign subsidiaries (*Siti-Nabiha/Scapens* (2005)), on joint ventures (*Cruz et al.* (2009); *Cruz et al.* (2011)), or on budgeting systems rather than parent-PMSs (*Kornacker et al.* (2018)). Therefore, the findings from these studies might not be transferable to the context of this study.

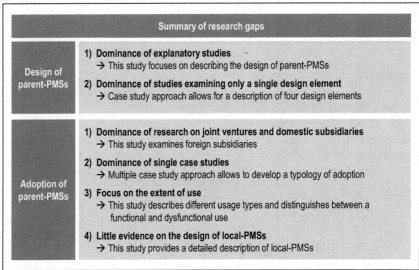

Figure 3–2: Summary of research gaps

Second, existing qualitative studies only examine single cases and therefore cannot compare and contrast different forms of adopting parent-PMSs by subsidiaries from different MNCs. By using a multiple case study approach, this study addresses the second research gap by **developing a typology** of the adoption of parent-PMSs at subsidiary level.

Third, prior studies focus on the **extent of use**. In this study, the functional use is further scrutinized by differentiating between four different functional usage types.[58] Furthermore, this study does not assume that parent-PMSs are used in a functional way but also considers the dysfunctional use of parent-PMSs. This procedure helps to shed further light on the use of parent-PMSs at subsidiary level.

Fourth, both quantitative and qualitative studies do not provide detailed descriptive evidence on the **design of local-PMSs** and the differences between parent-PMSs and local-PMSs. This hinders management accounting researchers and practitioners in understanding the role that local-PMSs play for MNCs.

Finally, little is known about the **factors that influence** how subsidiaries adopt the parent-PMSs. Although there are initial indications that the characteristics of parent-PMSs influ-

---

[58]   Cf. section 2.4.2 for a delineation of the functional and dysfunctional use of parent-PMSs.

ence the adoption, these have not yet been studied in detail. Furthermore, the existing literature provides scant evidence of the influence that characteristics of the subsidiaries and the host countries have on the adoption of parent-PMS.

4 Theory

This chapter presents the theoretical framework of this study, which is based on New Institutional Sociology. The first section introduces this theory by outlining its key assumptions and concepts. The subsequent sections (4.2, 4.3, and 4.4) describe the concepts of New Institutional Sociology in more detail. Finally, section 4.5 summarizes the theoretical framework.

4.1 Introduction to New Institutional Sociology

The New Institutional Sociology (NIS) belongs to a set of different institutional theories (*DiMaggio/Powell* (1991), p. 3; *Hussain/Hoque* (2002), p. 164). [59] It has been developed as a counterproposal to the notion of rational, efficiency-driven actors and organizations, which is assumed in other institutional theories such as new institutional economics (*Scott* (2001), pp. 2-5; *Moll et al.* (2006), p. 186). However, the NIS does not completely deny that organizations act according to efficiency criteria (*Westney* (1993), p. 54; *Walgenbach/Meyer* (2008), pp. 17-18). Instead, a core argument of the NIS is that organizations do not only consider efficiency concerns, but also seek **legitimacy** from the environment in which they operate (*Meyer/Rowan* (1977), pp. 352-353; *DiMaggio/Powell* (1983), pp. 148-149). According to *Suchman*, legitimacy can be defined as

> *"[...] a generalized perception or assumption that the actions of an entity are desirable, proper, or appropriate within some socially constructed system of norms, values, beliefs, and definitions."*

> (*Suchman* (1995), p. 574)

Receiving legitimacy from their environment – which is labeled as organizational field in NIS (*DiMaggio/Powell* (1983), p. 148; *Krücken* (2017), pp. 195-196) – is considered as a necessary condition for organizations. In fact, researchers following the NIS assume that the long-term survival of organizations is not possible without being considered as legitimate by the other actors of the organizational field (*Meyer/Rowan* (1977), p. 353). For example, companies that are not considered as legitimate by its industry will face difficulties in finding suppliers and customers and hence have bleak economic prospects (*Walgenbach/Meyer* (2008), p. 12). As pointed out by *Suchman*, organizations receive legitimacy by acting in a way that is perceived as appropriate within the organizational field (*Suchman* (1995), p. 574). Thus, the expectations of the organizational field influence how organizations and their members behave (*Walgenbach/Meyer* (2008), pp. 63-64). For example, organizations adapt their internal structures and practices to the expectations of their environment to gain legitimacy from this environment (*Moll et al.* (2006), pp. 186).

The **application field** of NIS has changed during the last decades in **two ways** (*Cruz et al.* (2009), p. 92-94). First, the NIS was initially developed for explaining the behavior of non-profit organizations (*Moll et al.* (2006), p. 196). In fact, early proponents of the NIS assumed that legitimacy is more important for non-profit organizations such as

---

[59] For an overview and comparisons of the different theories subsumed under the term "institutional theories" (e.g., new institutional economics and old institutional economics), cf. *Moll et al.* (2006), pp. 183-188.

public schools and hospitals than for profit-oriented organizations such as MNCs (*Powell* (1991), pp. 183-184; *Walgenbach/Meyer* (2008), p. 17). However, nowadays it is recognized that the latter also depend on the legitimacy of their environment (*Granlund/Lukka* (1998), pp. 159-160; *Cruz et al.* (2009), p. 92; *Kostova et al.* (2009), pp. 171-173). For example, a MNC has to comply with the laws of the host countries to get legitimacy from the local government and customers (*Westney* (1993), p. 59; *Walgenbach et al.* (2017), pp. 100-101). This extension in the field of application paves the way for applying NIS to profit-oriented organizations such as **MNCs** (*Cruz et al.* (2009), p. 92).

Second, in its early stage the NIS was primarily used for explaining why organizations, which operate in the same environment (e.g., firms of the same industry), tend to use similar practices (*Scott* (2001), pp. 43-44; *Moll et al.* (2006), pp. 186-187).[60] Nowadays, researchers also use the NIS for explaining why organizations deviate from common practices, especially in the context of MNCs (*Moll et al.* (2006), p. 193-195; *Cruz et al.* (2009), p. 92; *Lounsbury* (2008), p. 351). For example, researchers examine how and why subsidiaries **deviate** from the practices implemented by their head offices (e.g., *Kostova/Roth* (2002); *Siti-Nabiha/Scapens* (2005); *Rautiainen/Järvenpää* (2012)). Overall, due to its changed focus during the last decades, NIS is particularly suited to serve as a theoretical basis for this study.

The remaining chapter is organized as follows (see Figure 4–1).

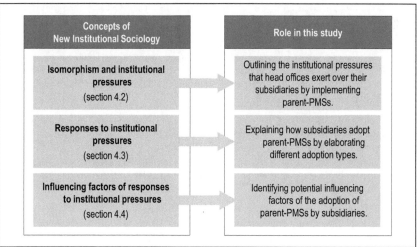

Figure 4–1: Concepts of New Institutional Sociology and their role in this study

First, section 4.2 outlines the concepts of isomorphism and institutional pressures, which are used to explain how head offices exert pressure on their subsidiaries to adopt parent-

---

[60] A classic example within management accounting research is the study of *Granlund/Lukka*, in which the authors use the NIS to explain the *"[...] tendency towards global homogenization of management accounting practices"* (*Granlund/Lukka* (1998), p. 153).

PMSs. Subsequently, section 4.3 presents how subsidiaries might respond to these institutional pressures. This serves to elaborate different adoption types of parent-PMSs. Section 4.4 uses the NIS to identify potential influencing factors of the adoption of parent-PMSs. In section 4.5, the theoretical framework is summarized.

4.2 Isomorphism and institutional pressures

As pointed out in the previous section, a key tenet of NIS is that the expectations of an organizational field influence how organizations and their members behave (*Walgenbach/Meyer* (2008), pp. 63-64). As a result, organizations become **isomorphic** with the environment in which they operate, meaning that they adopt the practices that are prevalent in this environment (*DiMaggio/Powell* (1983), pp. 150-153). Following this concept of isomorphism, organizations are subject to **three different kinds** of institutional pressures (*DiMaggio/Powell* (1983), pp. 150-153; *Zucker* (1987), p. 443; *Scott* (1995), p. 31), which often occur in combination (*van der Stede* (2003), p. 268):[61]

> 1) **Coercive pressures** base on unequal power in the organizational field (*Kostova/Roth* (2002), p. 216). A more powerful organization can mandate from subordinate organizations to behave in a certain way (*DiMaggio/Powell* (1983), pp. 150-151). For example, states can use their legislative power to issue laws and regulations that require a certain behavior from the MNCs in that country (*Walgenbach/Meyer* (2008), p. 35).
>
> 2) **Mimetic pressures** result from the fact that organizations imitate the practices of more successful organizations to reduce uncertainty (*DiMaggio/Powell* (1983), pp. 151-152; *Moll et al.* (2006), p. 187). For example, a MNC copies a practice of a competitor because that competitor is successful with this practice (*Walgenbach/Meyer* (2008), p. 36).
>
> 3) **Normative pressures** reflect the standards and best practices within an organizational field, which are postulated for example by consultancies and professional associations (*DiMaggio/Powell* (1983), pp. 150-151; *Moll et al.* (2006), p. 188). For example, a professional association defines what it considers as appropriate behavior by employees of the profession (*Walgenbach/Meyer* (2008), p. 38).

However, these institutional pressures do not only affect the organizations from the outside, but can also occur **within** organizations (*Walgenbach/Meyer* (2008), p. 35; *Kostova et al.* (2009), pp. 171-173; *Kajüter/Schröder* (2017), p. 75). In the NIS, this is referred to as *"intracorporate isomorphism"* (*van der Stede* (2003), p. 268). **Intracorporate isomorphism** is particularly relevant in MNCs, as they consist of a large number of entities (e.g., head offices and subsidiaries), which form a complex intraorganizational field (*Kostova* (1999), p. 320; *Kostova et al.* (2008), p. 998; *Cooper et al.* (2019), pp. 451-453). In this intraorganizational field, the subsidiaries' survival prospects depend on the legitimacy of their head offices (*Meyer/Rowan* (1977), pp. 352-353; *Kostova/Zaheer* (1999), pp. 67-68). For example, a

---

[61] For the description of the three types of institutional pressures, cf. also *Kostova/Roth* (2002), p. 216; *Moll et al.* (2006), pp. 187-188; *Walgenbach/Meyer* (2008), pp. 35-40.

MNC's head office decides on the resources of the subsidiaries and may decide to abandon a subsidiary if it does not meet the head office's expectations. Therefore, head offices are able to exert **intracorporate coercive pressures** on their subsidiaries (*Kostova/Roth* (2002), p. 219; *van der Stede* (2003), p. 268; *Yazdifar et al.* (2008), p. 406; *Cruz et al.* (2009), pp. 92-93). For example, head offices may require their subsidiaries to use certain management accounting practices that have been developed at the head office level:

> *"In company groups and multinational companies, it is evident that subsidiaries must adopt certain accounting, performance measurement, or budgeting practices [...] that are compatible with those of the parent company."*

> (*Walgenbach/Meyer* (2008), p. 35; translated from German)

Transferred to the topic of this study, head offices exert intracorporate coercive pressure on their subsidiaries by **developing and designing parent-PMSs** (*van der Stede* (2003), pp. 268-269; *Cruz et al.* (2009), p. 98. In fact, the management accountants in the head offices do not only design the parent-PMSs, but also impose them on their subsidiaries (*Kostova/Roth* (2002), p. 219; *Cruz et al.* (2009), p. 98). In this vein, the head offices expect their subsidiaries to follow the given design instructions and to use the parent-PMSs according to their intentions (*Walgenbach/Meyer* (2008), p. 35). The head offices' management accountants express their expectations, for example, by issuing internal guidelines, documentations, and presentations on the parent-PMS (*van der Stede* (2003), pp. 268-269). The following section outlines the different strategies that subsidiaries can follow to respond to these coercive pressures from their head offices.

4.3   Responses to institutional pressures

Early NIS writers (e.g., *Meyer/Rowan* (1977); *DiMaggio/Powell* (1983)) have taken **two organizational responses** to institutional pressures into account, namely acquiescence and decoupling (*Siti-Nabiha/Scapens* (2005), pp. 47-78; *Walgenbach/Meyer* (2008), p. 123). **Acquiescence** means that organizations comply with the coercive, mimetic, and/or normative pressures of their environment (*Oliver* (1991), pp. 152-153). For example, a subsidiary might adopt the practice implemented by their head office according to the head office's intentions (*Kostova/Roth* (2002), p. 220). In this vein, the subsidiary secures the legitimacy of the head office (*Meyer/Rowan* (1977), pp. 352-353; *Kostova/Zaheer* (1999), pp. 67-68). According to NIS, organizations' actors respond with acquiescence when the implemented practice is in accordance with their own expectations (*Oliver* (1991), p. 161; *Walgenbach/Meyer* (2008), p. 123). To continue the example stated above, a subsidiary acquiesces the practice implemented by the head office if it is in line with the goals and intentions of the subsidiaries (*Kostova/Roth* (2002), p. 220).

Decoupling[62] means that organizations adopt practices only on the surface without actually implementing and using them (*Meyer/Rowan* (1977), pp. 356-359; *Oliver* (1991), pp. 154-156; *Kostova/Roth* (2002), p. 220; *Cheng* (2012), p. 88). Thus, organizations pretend to

---

[62] Decoupling is often also referred to as ceremonial adoption (e.g., *Kostova et al.* (2008); *Collings/Dick* (2011); *Cheng/Yu* (2002)), especially in studies building on old institutional economics (*Dillard et al.* (2004), p. 536).

adopt the practice but actually continue with *"business as usual"* (*Boxenbaum/Jonsson* (2017), p. 78, cf. also *Ansari/Euske* (1987), p. 553; *Dillard et al.* (2004), p. 509).[63] For example, a subsidiary might decouple a head office's practice by pretending to comply with the rules of the practice, but without actually acting according to these rules (*Siti-Nabiha/Scapens* (2005), p. 58; *Rautiainen/Järvenpää* (2012), pp. 169-170). Organizations decouple practices if they do not consider the practices as useful or adequate for their organization (*Kostova/Roth* (2002), p. 220).[64] They secure the legitimacy from their environment, without experiencing the negative impact of the practice (*Pfeffer/Salancik* (1978), pp. 95-96; *Oliver* (1991), pp. 154-156; *Walgenbach/Meyer* (2008), pp. 81-83). However, this requires organizations to hide their non-conformity with the practice because otherwise they lose the legitimacy of their organizational field (*Oliver* (1991), p. 154; *Modell* (2001), p. 439).

In later work (e.g., *Oliver* (1991); *Lounsbury* (2008); *Ferner et al.* (2011)), researchers have extended organizations' responses to institutional pressures (*Siti-Nabiha/Scapens* (2005), pp. 46-48). These researchers argue that organizations cannot only acquiesce or decouple implemented practices, but that there is a *"gray area"* (*Rautiainen/Järvenpää* (2012), p. 165) of possible responses (*Oliver* (1991), pp. 151-152). Therefore, these researchers have developed **two additional response types**, namely modification and defiance (*Oliver* (1991), pp. 151-159; *Lounsbury* (2008), p. 351; *Ferner et al.* (2011), pp. 177-181).

First, **modification**[65] means that organizations adapt the implemented practices (*Lounsbury* (2008), p. 153; *Johansson/Siverbo* (2009), pp. 153-155; *Rautiainen/Järvenpää* (2012), pp. 168-169). They can do this in two opposing ways (*Ferner et al.* (2011), p. 180). On the one hand, there is **supportive** modification, which means that organizations adapt the practice according to their needs (*Ferner et al.* (2011), p. 178). In this vein, the organization adds, modifies, or removes elements from the implemented practice (*Cruz et al.* (2011), p. 414; *Ferner et al.* (2011), p. 178; *Cooper/Ezzamel* (2013), p. 292). On the other hand, there is **resistive** modification (*Ferner et al.* (2011), p. 180; *Oliver* (1991), pp. 157-159).[66] By resistive modification, organizations *"divert a practice from its normal function"* (*Ferner et al.* (2011), p. 178). Thus, organizations change a practice in such a way that the practice has no effect on the organization's processes or only an effect different from the original intention (*Ferner et al.* (2011), p. 178; *Boxenbaum/Jonsson* (2017), p. 85; *Cooper/Ezzamel* (2013), p. 292). Organizations can use resistive modification if they do not agree with the practice (*Oliver* (1991), pp. 157-158).

Second, organizations can **defy** implemented practices by openly rejecting them (*Oliver* (1991), p. 156; *Pache/Santos* (2010), p. 463). For example, a subsidiary might defy a practice implemented by their head office by openly criticizing and arguing against this practice (*Siti-Nabiha/Scapens* (2005), pp. 55-56). Defiance is the last resort for organizations and is

---

[63] In this vein, *Hannan/Freeman* refer to decoupling as a response of *"smoke and mirrors"* (*Hannan/Freeman* (1989), p. 94; cf. also *Westney* (1993), p. 61).

[64] Furthermore, organizations might engage in decoupling if the organizational field has diverse and conflicting expectations (*Zucker* (1987), p. 443; *Walgenbach/Meyer* (2008), pp. 28-32).

[65] *Ferner et al.* also use the terms *"hybridization"* and *"adaptation"* to refer to the modification response (*Ferner et al.* (2011), pp. 178-180).

[66] In *Oliver's* typology, supportive modification is labeled as *"compromise"* (*Oliver* (1991), pp. 153-154). For resistive modification, *Oliver* uses the term *"manipulation"* (*Oliver* (1991), pp. 157-159).

only used when the other response types are not possible or show no effects. This is because organizations endanger their legitimacy by openly rejecting a practice (*Oliver* (1991), pp. 156-157; *Modell* (2001), pp. 440-441).

Overall, NIS proposes **four types** of how organizations can react to institutional pressures (see Figure 4–2).[67] Which response type the organizations' members choose depends on the internalization of the practice, which can be considered as a continuum.[68] Following *Kostova/Roth*, internalization can be defined as

> *"[...] the state in which the employees at the recipient unit view the practice as valuable for the unit and become committed to the practice."*

> (*Kostova/Roth* (2002), p. 217)

Following this definition, a high (low) internalization means that the organization's employees agree (disagree) with the implemented practice. The more the organization's employees disagree with the practice, the more likely it is that they choose a response different from acquiescence (*Oliver* (1991), p. 146). In fact, the employees of an organization might then modify the practice or decouple it from the internal processes (*Oliver* (1991), p. 152). In case of extreme low internalization of the practice, the organization's employees might openly reject it. Since this endangers the organization's legitimacy within the organizational field, this is expected only in rare cases (*Oliver* (1991), p. 156-157; *Modell* (2001), p. 461).

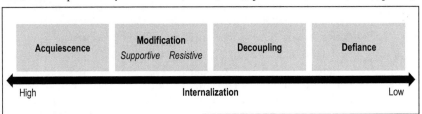

Figure 4–2: Overview of organizations' responses to institutional pressures
Based on *Oliver* (1991), p. 152; *Modell* (2001), p. 440; *Ferner et al.* (2011), p. 180.

With respect to **this study**, the considerations above imply that subsidiaries can adopt parent-PMSs in four ways. First, they might simply **acquiesce** the parent-PMSs and hence follow the head offices' intentions. This might be reflected in a functional use of the parent-PMS and the non-development of local-PMSs (*Kostova/Roth* (2002), pp. 229-230; *Cruz et al.* (2009), p. 95). Second, subsidiaries might **modify** the parent-PMSs (*Oliver* (1991), p. 152; *Ferner et al.* (2011), p. 180). In a **supportive** sense, this could mean that subsidiaries use parent-PMSs in a functional way and develop local-PMSs that play an enabling role for the parent-PMS (*Dossi/Patelli* (2008), p. 127; *Mahlendorf et al.* (2012), p. 700; *Cooper/Ez-*

---

[67] However, as pointed out by *Rautiainen/Järvenpää*, these response types might not always be clearly distinguishable in practice (*Rautiainen/Järvenpää* (2012), p. 169).

[68] *Oliver* and *Modell* use the term resistance, which is the antonym of internalization (*Oliver* (1991), p. 146; *Modell* (2001), p. 441. Thus, a high (low) internalization is equivalent to a low (high) resistance towards the practice.

zamel (2013), p. 292). In this vein, local-PMSs support the implementation and functioning of the parent-PMSs (*Cruz et al.* (2011), p. 413; *Rautiainen/Järvenpää* (2012), pp. 181-183; *Cooper/Ezzamel* (2013), p. 292). In a **resistive** sense, subsidiaries might develop local-PMSs that play a disabling role for the parent-PMSs (*Cooper/Ezzamel* (2013), p. 292). In this vein, the local-PMSs could dilute or counteract the intentions that the head offices have with the parent-PMSs (*Ferner et al.* (2011), p. 178; *Rautiainen/Järvenpää* (2012), pp. 181-183; *Cooper/Ezzamel* (2013), p. 292). Third, subsidiaries might **decouple** parent-PMSs. This could result in a situation in which the subsidiaries use these systems only ceremonially and hence only pretend to use them (*Oliver* (1991), pp. 154-156; *Kostova/Roth* (2002), pp. 220-221). Instead of using the parent-PMSs, the subsidiaries might develop their own local-PMSs that they use as an alternative to the parent-PMSs (*Siti-Nabiha/Scapens* (2005), p. 65). The subsidiaries could hide the non-use of the parent-PMS, for example, by reporting the performance measures of the parent-PMS (*Ansari/Euske* (1987), p. 559-561; *Siti-Nabiha/Scapens* (2005), p. 58). Finally, the subsidiaries could **defy** the parent-PMSs by openly complaining to their head offices about these systems. In this way, the subsidiaries could try to persuade their head offices to abolish the parent-PMSs (*Oliver* (1991), pp. 156-157; *Ferner et al.* (2011), p. 179).

However, these are only preliminary descriptions of how subsidiaries might adopt parent-PMSs. It is rather an objective of the empirical analyses to investigate which adoption types occur at the case companies' subsidiaries and to describe these adoption types in detail.[69]

4.4   Influencing factors of responses to institutional pressures

To derive factors that influence the adoption of parent-PMSs by subsidiaries, *Kostova/Roth's* concept of **institutional duality** is used (*Kostova/Roth* (2002), p. 216; *Roth/Kostova* (2003), p. 893). The basic idea of this concept is that MNCs' subsidiaries are not only affected by coercive pressures from their head offices, but also by institutional pressures from the host country in which they operate (*Kostova/Roth* (2002), p. 216-217; *Cheng/Yu* (2012), p. 82). This is based on the assumption that subsidiaries are anchored in **two organizational fields** rather than just one (*Hillman/Wan* (2005), p. 325; *Phillips/Tracey* (2009), pp. 169-170; *Kostova et al.* (2009), p. 172; *Walgenbach et al.* (2017), p. 105).

First, subsidiaries are anchored in an **intraorganizational field** with their head offices (*Westney* (1993), pp. 60-64; *Kostova/Roth* (2002), pp. 216). In this intraorganizational field, the subsidiaries are pressured by their head offices to adopt a certain practice (*Cheng/Yu* (2012), p. 82). For example, a head office exerts coercive pressure on the subsidiaries by requiring them to adopt parent-PMSs (*van der Stede* (2003), p. 268; *Cruz et al.* (2009), p. 103).[70] The characteristics of the implemented practice then determine how suitable the subsidiaries perceive the practice. Or to say it in the words of institutional theory, the characteristics of the practice determine the degree of internalization by the subsidiaries (*Oliver* (1991), pp. 161-162). In case the subsidiaries believe that the practice is suitable to increase the efficiency of the internal processes, they have a high internalization and hence acquiesce the practice (*Kostova/Roth* (2002), p. 229). If they perceive the practice or parts

---

[69]   The procedure of identifying adoption types based on NIS is outlined in detail in section 5.3.2.2.
[70]   See section 4.2.

of it as unsuitable, the resulting lower internalization will be reflected in response types such as modification, decoupling, or defiance (*Oliver* (1991), p. 152; *Modell* (2001), p. 440; *Ferner et al.* (2011), p. 165). Transferred to the topic of this study, the adoption of parent-PMSs at subsidiary level depends on how the subsidiaries perceive the **characteristics of these systems**. For example, the adoption of the parent-PMSs depends on how useful the subsidiaries perceive the design of these systems.

Second, subsidiaries are embedded in the **organizational fields of their host countries**, which consist of, for example, the host countries' governments, local competitors, and local customers (*Westney* (1993), pp. 60-64; *Kostova/Roth* (2002), p. 216). From this organizational field, the subsidiaries receive mimetic, normative, and coercive pressures to adopt certain practices (*Kostova et al.* (2009), p. 172; *Cheng/Yu* (2012), p. 82). For example, the host country's government exerts coercive pressure by issuing laws and regulations that require the subsidiaries to adopt certain practices (*Walgenbach/Meyer* (2008), p. 35). The institutional pressures of the host country might **conflict** with the pressures of the head office (*Roth/Kostova* (2003), p. 894; *Chen/Yu* (2012), p. 87). This is because the practices implemented by a head office often apply for all subsidiaries of that MNC in a standardized way and are hence not adapted to the local conditions of each subsidiary (*Roth/Kostova* (2003), p. 894; *Vance* (2006), pp. 42-44). Thus, characteristics of the host country and the subsidiary might be in conflict with the practice implemented by the head office (*Roth/Kostova* (2003), p. 894). For example, the practice might be in conflict with the laws and regulation in a certain host country (*Westney* (1993), p. 61). Conflicting expectations of the home and host country lead to a situation in which the subsidiary cannot simply acquiesce the head office's practice, since the subsidiary depends on the legitimacy from both organizational fields (*Westney* (1993), pp. 60-64; *Kostova/Roth* (2002), p. 216). Thus, the subsidiaries follow other response types such as modifying the head office's practices according to local conditions or decoupling them (*Oliver* (1991), p. 152; *Kostova/Marano* (2019), p. 112). Transferred to the topic of this study, **host country and subsidiary characteristics** influence how subsidiaries adopt parent-PMSs (*Vance* (2006), pp. 42-44).

Overall, the concept of institutional duality states that subsidiaries must strive for both internal (from the head office) and external (from the host country) legitimacy to ensure their long-term survival (*Kostova/Roth* (2002), p. 216; *Hillman/Wan* (2005), p. 325). Consequently, the adoption of parent-PMSs is influenced by factors from **two fields** (see Figure 4–3). These two fields are explored in the empirical analyses.

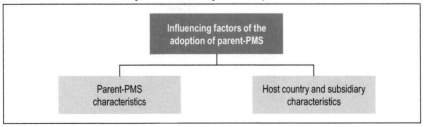

Figure 4–3: Overview of influencing factors

4.5   Summary of the theoretical framework

In summary, the theoretical framework relies on **three concepts** of NIS (see Figure 4–4). First, the concept of isomorphism and institutional pressures is used to outline how head offices exert **coercive pressures** on their subsidiaries to adopt parent-PMSs (*DiMaggio/Powell* (1983), pp. 150-153; *van der Stede* (2003), p. 268). Second, this study draws on response types to institutional pressures to develop **adoption types of parent-PMSs**. Based on NIS, subsidiaries can adopt parent-PMSs by acquiescing, modifying, decoupling, and defying them (*Oliver* (1991), p. 152; *Modell* (2001), p. 440; *Ferner et al.* (2011), p. 180). Finally, the concept of institutional duality is used to guide the empirical analyses on the **influencing factors** of the adoption of parent-PMSs (*Kostova/Roth* (2002), p. 216; *Roth/Kostova* (2003), p. 893). Following NIS, influencing factors stem from the characteristics of parent-PMSs and from local conditions of the host country and the subsidiary.

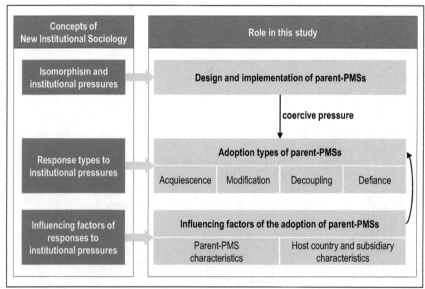

Figure 4–4: Summary of the theoretical framework

5   Empirical research approach

This chapter outlines the empirical research approach applied in this study. After justifying and explaining the choice of the research approach (section 5.1), section 5.2 describes the research design applied. Finally, section 5.3 sets out the research process.

5.1   Selection rationale

A research approach consists of both the followed research methodology and the chosen research method(s) (*Llewellyn* (1992), p. 18; *Ahrens/Chapman* (2006), p. 821). The research **methodology** entails general assumptions about how researchers can generate knowledge (*Llewellyn* (1992), p. 18). The choice of a research methodology in turn influences the availability of appropriate **research methods**, which are tools that allow researchers to collect data for empirical investigations (*Guba/Lincoln* (1994), p. 108).

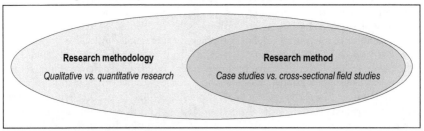

Figure 5–1: Overview of the research approach
Based on *Nienaber* (2020), p. 70.

The following paragraphs explain and justify the research approach followed in this study in two steps: In a first step, it is argued why a **qualitative** research methodology is more suitable than a quantitative methodology[71] for answering the research questions of this study. In a second step, the appropriateness of **case studies** as a research method is pointed out by comparing them to cross-sectional field studies.

5.1.1   Research methodology

The main objective of **quantitative research** is to develop **general laws** and **causal relationships** (*Chua* (1986), p. 607; *Lingnau* (1995), p. 124). Therefore, quantitative research is most suitable for examining average effect sizes or examining the prevalence of phenomena in a given population (*Yin* (2018), pp. 6-13). The search for general applicable laws is also reflected in the sampling procedures of quantitative research. In fact, quantitative research relies on the concept of **statistical generalizability** (*Chua* (1986), p. 611; *Lee* (1999), p. 8). The basic idea of this concept is to select and analyze a sample from which inferences

---

[71] In a broad sense, qualitative and quantitative research methodologies can be differentiated (*Brühl* (2017), p. 85). In addition, researchers can bridge both methodologies by using a mix of quantitative and qualitative research methods (*Modell* (2009), pp. 208; *Modell* (2010), pp. 126-128). For a discussion on mixed-method research in accounting research, cf. *Vaivio/Sirén* (2010), pp. 132-140, and *Grafton et al.* (2011), pp. 5-18.

can be drawn for the entire population (*Scapens* (1990), p. 269). A prerequisite for statistical generalizability is that researchers **randomly select** samples that are representative for the whole population (*Eisenhardt* (1989), p. 537). The main objective of quantitative research is also reflected in the role of theory and hypotheses. For generating general laws, quantitative researchers **develop and test hypotheses** derived from theory (*Chua* (1986), p. 607; *Tomkins/Groves* (1983), p. 362). Theory is therefore the starting point in quantitative research and shall be tested by empirical studies. The research process in quantitative research is linear and standardized and relies on **mathematical-statistical methods** such as linear regression models (*Denzin/Lincoln* (2011), p. 8). The standardization of methods for collecting and analyzing data helps to reduce the researcher's influence in order to make the results as **objective** as possible (*Wrona* (2006), p. 207).

In contrast to quantitative research, the main objective of **qualitative research** is to **understand phenomena** in their real-life context (*Lee* (1999), p. 7; *Lukka/Modell* (2017), p. 38). Qualitative researchers therefore zoom into specific phenomena to understand them in their entire complexity (*Ahrens/Chapman* (2006), pp. 825-827; *Yin* (2018), p. 15-16).[72] Therefore, qualitative research is especially appropriate for examining **how** and **why** questions (*Yin* (2018), p. 9; *Lukka/Modell* (2017), p. 42). The different objective of qualitative research compared to its quantitative counterpart also results in a different sampling approach. Since qualitative research does not aim to develop general laws, statistical sampling is not appropriate (*Eisenhardt* (1989), p. 537; *Scapens* (1990), p. 270). Qualitative researchers rather **purposefully** select cases that allow learning as much as possible about the phenomena under investigation (*Coyne* (1997), p. 624). Since qualitative researchers zoom into phenomena, sample sizes are typically small compared to quantitative large-scale studies. This is sometimes criticized by quantitative researchers (*Lukka/Kasanen* (1995), pp. 74-76; *Lewis/Ritchie* (2003), pp. 264-265). However, this criticism ignores that qualitative research does not intend to provide general laws for large populations (statistical generalization) but strives for **theoretical** generalization (*Parker/Northcott* (2016), p. 1101). The basic idea of theoretical generalization is to develop or refine theories that help to understand a phenomenon in the examined context and also in other, different settings (*Scapens* (1992), pp. 378-380; *Lukka/Modell* (2017), p. 43). Consequently, qualitative researchers do not formulate and test hypotheses but **develop and refine theories** to understand phenomena (*Siti-Nabiha* (2009), p. 43).[73] This is also reflected in the research process of qualitative research, which is characterized by **flexibility** and **openness** (*Breuer* (2010), p. 40; *Lamnek/Krell* (2016), p. 36). Indeed, in qualitative research, research questions are often adapted during data collection and analysis, which results in a circular rather than a linear research process (*Döring/Bortz* (2016), p. 67). For analyzing data, qualitative researchers do not apply mathematical-statistical methods but **interpret** empirical evidence (*Scapens* (1992), p. 371). Since the resulting interpretations depend on the skills and perceptions of the researcher, qualitative research is (at least to a certain extent) always a subjective task

---

[72] Therefore, a commonly used expression is that qualitative research yields in an *"in-depth understanding"* (*Ellingson* (2011), p. 605) of phenomena.

[73] In this vein, *Lukka/Modell* (2017) argue that theories serve as lenses for qualitative researchers through which they regard empirical data (*Lukka/Modell* (2017), p. 40).

(*Tomkins/Groves* (1983), p. 369; *Breuer et al.* (2011), p. 428).[74] Table 5–1 summarizes the differences between both research methodologies.

Criterion	Quantitative methodology	Qualitative methodology
Main objective	Identifying general laws and causal relationships	Understanding phenomena in their real-life context
Sampling and generalization	Random sampling for statistical generalization	Purposeful sampling for theoretical generalization
Role of theory and hypotheses	Theory shall be tested by formulating theory-based hypotheses	Theory is developed or refined; hypotheses are not formulated
Research process	Standardized research process; use of mathematical-statistical methods for analyzing data	Open and flexible research process; interpretation of empirical data

Table 5–1: Differences between quantitative and qualitative research methodologies
Based on *Patton* (2015), p. 91.

In this study, a **qualitative research methodology** is chosen for the following two reasons. First, this study examines how head offices design parent-PMSs and how and why subsidiaries adopt these systems.[75] Such **how** and **why** questions are best approached by a qualitative methodology (*Yin* (2018), p. 9). Second, this study describes and explains the design and adoption of parent-PMSs in an **explorative** way.[76] Given that qualitative research does not rely on predetermined hypotheses, it is especially useful for studying topics that lack a clear understanding (*Dickson-Swift et al.* (2007), p. 329; *Flick* (2019), pp. 26-28). The following section justifies the choice of case studies as a research method.

5.1.2   Research method

Within a qualitative research methodology, management accounting researchers usually choose between cross-sectional field studies and case studies (*Vaivio* (2008), pp. 73-75).

Cross-sectional field studies can be defined as

> "[...] limited-depth studies conducted at a nonrandom selection of field sites, thus laying somewhere between in-depth cases and broad-based surveys."

> (*Lillis/Mundy* (2005), p. 120)

As stated in the quote above, cross-sectional field studies usually exhibit sample sizes that are lower than in survey studies but higher than in studies using a case study method. As pointed out by *Kornacker*, the number of field sites typically ranges from 12 to 42 in cross-

---

[74] However, there is also some subjectivity in quantitative research, for example in choosing between different statistical methods for analyzing data (*Tomkins/Groves* (1983), p. 369; *Luft/Shields* (2014), pp. 552-557).

[75] For an overview and description of the research questions addressed in this study, cf. section 1.1.

[76] As outlined in chapter 3, little is known so far on how the subsidiaries adopt parent-PMSs.

sectional field studies. Per field site usually one semi-structured interview is conducted (*Kornacker* (2014), p. 132).[77] Given the large number of field sites (compared to case studies), cross-sectional field studies are only appropriate for **less complex** phenomena, which can be clearly defined before collecting data (*Lillis/Mundy* (2005), p. 131; *Piekkari et al.* (2009), p. 581). Furthermore, cross-sectional field studies are more suitable for **refining** theories or constructs than for exploring phenomena (*Lillis/Mundy* (2005), pp. 131-133; *Messner et al.* (2017), p. 437). Given their eligibility for refining theories and constructs, cross-sectional field studies are sometimes used as pilot studies for large-scale studies (*Lillis/Mundy* (2005), p. 121). For instance, cross-sectional field studies are used for carving out determinants, which are then examined and tested by a survey study.

A **case study** is defined by *Yin* as an

> *"[...] empirical method that investigates a contemporary phenomenon ('the case') in depth and within its real-life context, especially when the boundaries between phenomenon and context are not clearly evident."*

(*Yin* (2018), p. 15)

For examining phenomena in depth, case study research deeply engages with a **small number** of cases (*Messner et al.* (2017), p. 437). For these cases, researchers collect data from several sources such as interviews and internal documents. Furthermore, case study researchers gather data from multiple persons within each case (*Eisenhardt* (1989), p. 534). Consequently, while deeply engaging with the cases, case study research is especially meaningful for investigating **complex phenomena** (*Cooper/Morgan* (2008), p. 160; *Flyvbjerg* (2011), p. 301). In contrast to cross-sectional field studies, case studies are especially appropriate if the context in which the phenomenon occurs is important to consider or when there is no clear boundary between a phenomenon and its context (*Cooper/Morgan* (2008), p. 160; *Yin* (2018), p. 15). Concerning the role of theory, case studies are especially appropriate if there is **little extant** theory in advance of the research (*Wrona* (2005), p. 18). Table 5–2 summarizes the differences between cross-sectional field studies and case studies.

Criterion	Cross-sectional field study	Case study
Sample size	Medium to large	Small to medium
Data sources	Interviews as single data source	Triangulation of data sources
Complexity of phenomena	Phenomena of medium complexity; context is of little relevance	Complex phenomena; context is relevant and hence examined
Relation to theory	Refinement of theories and hypotheses	Development or refinement of theories

Table 5–2: Differences between cross-sectional field studies and case studies
Based on *Lillis/Mundy* (2005), p. 130.

---

[77] Researchers in cross-sectional field studies are often limited to interviews and cannot draw on other data sources such as internal documents (*Messner et al.* (2017), p. 437).

For this study, **case studies** seem to be more suitable than cross-sectional field studies. This is so for the following reasons: First, this study strives to shed light on **complex** phenomena, namely the design and adoption of parent-PMSs (*Cooper/Morgan* (2008), p. 160; *Yin* (2018), p. 15; *Nienaber* (2020), p. 74). As outlined in chapter 4, subsidiaries can adopt parent-PMSs in several ways that cannot be predicted in advance (*Johansson/Siverbo* (2009), p. 154; *Ferner et al.* (2011), p. 165). Furthermore, examining how the subsidiaries adopt parent-PMSs requires a research method that deeply engages with the field. As pointed out by *Scapens*, this is a special advantage of case study research, which allows to distinguish

> *"[...] between formal accounting systems which senior managers believe are used and the ways in which they are actually used."*

> (*Scapens* (1990), p. 264)

This is particularly important for this study as it considers the possibility that subsidiaries use parent-PMSs differently than intended by their head offices (*Siti-Nabiha/Scapens* (2005), p. 47).

Second, this study focuses on MNCs, which have a high internal **heterogeneity and complexity** due to their several locations in different countries (*Kostova/Roth* (2003), p. 888). As pointed out in chapter 4, the host country and subsidiary characteristics might influence how a subsidiary adopts the parent-PMS. Therefore, it is important to take into account the internal and external contexts in which MNCs are embedded (*Kostova/Roth* (2003), p. 889; *Kornacker* (2014), p. 130). As outlined before, this is another strong indication for a case study approach (*Yin* (2018), p. 15). Finally, by conducting interviews at head office and subsidiary level, this study examines parent-PMSs from **multiple perspectives** (*Nienaber* (2020), p. 74). For example, the subsidiaries might have a different opinion on the parent-PMS than the designers of these systems. The case study method is especially suitable for capturing different perspectives and opinions (*Scapens* (1990), p. 264; *Ahrens/Chapman* (2006), p. 822; *Cooper/Morgan* (2008), p. 163) and is hence applied in this study.

Overall, a qualitative case study approach seems to be reasonable and is therefore adopted for addressing the underlying research questions.

5.2   Research design

This section presents the research design of this study by outlining different design choices of case study research (section 5.2.1). Furthermore, section 5.2.2 presents the sampling strategy and provides an overview of the selected sample firms.

5.2.1   Case study design

When choosing a qualitative case study approach, researchers have to define what they consider as a case (**unit of analysis**) in their study (*Lee* (1999), pp. 59-60; *Yin* (2018), p. 53). Examples of cases are individuals, groups of persons, organizations, or events (*Stake* (2013), pp. 1-2; *Yin* (2018), pp. 52-53). This study considers **MNCs** as the unit of analysis. Thus, each MNC represents a separate case within this study.

After having defined the unit of analysis, researchers have to choose between different case study designs. Following *Yin*, the different design options can be summarized by a 2x2-matrix (*Yin* (2018), p. 48). As Figure 5–2 shows, researchers have to make **two** choices. They have to decide between single or multiple cases and between holistic or embedded case studies (*Yin* (2018), pp. 49).

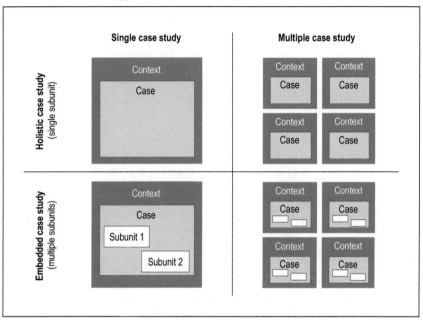

Figure 5–2: Design choices in case study research
Based on *Yin* (2018), p. 48.

The first decision relates to the **number of cases** (*Yin* (2018), p. 49). Particularly, case study researchers have to decide whether they want to examine a single case or multiple cases (*Scapens* (1990), p. 264; *Yin* (2018), p. 49). There are several rationales for examining a **single** case: Single cases can be used to confirm, reject, or modify a specific theoretical proposition (critical case) and for extending theory to a completely new context (extreme case) (*Scapens* (2004), p. 262; *Yin* (2018), pp. 49-50). Furthermore, a single case study design can be used for examining a case over a long time span (e.g., for examining the change of a management accounting system within a firm), which is called a longitudinal case study (*Patton* (2015), pp. 275-276). In addition, a single case can be revelatory, which describes a situation in which the researcher hits on a new phenomenon in the empirical field (*Yin* (2018), p. 50). Revelatory case studies often occur accidentally since it is difficult to know in advance, which case has the potential to provide novel evidence (*Berry/Otley* (2004), p. 235).[78]

A **multiple case study design** allows to compare and contrast different cases (*Eisenhardt* (1989), p. 534). The rationales for comparing and contrasting cases are twofold: First, similar cases can be selected to **replicate** findings. This is done to show that the findings hold true in more than one case, and hence to yield more robust results (*Yin* (2018), p. 55). Second, **contrasting** cases can be used to explore and understand how and why the phenomenon under investigation occurs under different circumstances (*Wrona/Gunnesch* (2016), pp. 734-735; *Yin* (2018), p. 55-56). Thus, by detecting patterns across cases, multiple case studies serve to develop and refine theoretical frameworks, which can then be applied in several contexts (theoretical generalization) (*Scapens* (2004), p. 263; *Buck* (2011), pp. 194-196). This study uses a **multiple case study design** because this allows analyzing case companies with different characteristics. Furthermore, analyzing similarities and differences between the case companies provides a better understanding of phenomena under investigation. In this vein, a multiple case study approach serves to refine the underlying theoretical framework.

The second decision relates to the question whether to use a holistic or embedded case study design (*Yin* (2018), pp. 49-54). **Holistic** case studies examine the cases as a whole without defining subunits. This is typically done if the cases cannot be divided into several parts (*Stake* (2013), p. 4; *Yin* (2018), pp. 51-52). In contrast, **embedded** case study designs consider different subunits within one case, which helps to consider specific aspects of the case (*Yin* (2018), p. 52-53; *Baxter/Jack* (2008), p. 550). Since MNCs naturally consist of several organizational units (*Daniel* (2009), p. 113), this study takes an **embedded** case study design. In this vein, this study distinguishes between MNCs' head offices and subsidiaries. At each case company, **two subsidiaries** are examined, which allows to compare the adoption of the MNC's parent-PMS between the two subsidiaries (*Yin* (2018), p. 52-53).[79]

The following section describes how the multiple cases and their subunits are selected and provides an overview of the sample firms.

5.2.2 Sample selection

5.2.2.1 Sampling strategy

Qualitative researchers are often criticized for not describing their sampling strategy, which limits the ability to interpret their findings and to replicate their studies (*Coyne* (1997),

---

[78] An example of such a revelatory case is *Siti-Nabiha/Scapens'* (2005) study on the adoption of a parent-PMS in a state-owned oil company. In this study, the focus of the research shifted from budgeting systems to parent-PMSs because the adoption of the parent-PMS turned out to be a revelatory topic (*Siti-Nabiha* (2009), p. 43).

[79] This study examines only two subunits within each case because a high number of subunits causes high personnel resources for the case companies and could therefore lower their willingness in participating in the research project.

p. 623; *Brühl et al.* (2008), p. 313). To avoid this pitfall, the following paragraphs outline how the cases and subunits are selected in this study.

Since qualitative researchers do not strive for statistical generalizability, they do not apply random sampling (*Eisenhardt* (1989), p. 537). They rather purposefully select **information rich** cases, i.e. cases that provide the researcher with relevant information for addressing the research questions at hand (*Coyne* (1997), p. 624; *Parker/Northcott* (2016), p. 1116). For purposefully selecting cases, qualitative researchers can rely on theoretical or selective sampling (*Patton* (2015), p. 264).

Theoretical sampling is mainly used in grounded theory approaches to develop new theories (*Glaser/Strauss* (1967), p. 45). Thus, in contrast to the supposed meaning of the term, theoretical sampling does not mean that a sound theoretical basis is used to select cases. Theory is rather the outcome of studies applying theoretical sampling. In theoretical sampling, the selection of cases is done based on the results from previous cases (*Glaser/Strauss* (1967), p. 45; *Wrona/Gunnesch* (2016), p. 734). The number and choice of cases is therefore not specified in advance but will be determined within the course of the empirical enquiry (*Patton* (2015), p. 301). When applying **selective** sampling, case selection is based on predetermined criteria derived from prior knowledge on the phenomenon under investigation (*Coyne* (1997), pp. 628-629; *Wrona/Gunnesch* (2016), p. 734).[80] In contrast to theoretical sampling, the final sample is therefore selected before entering the field. The selection criteria usually stem from prior literature, conceptual considerations, and/or theoretical frameworks (*Patton* (2015), p. 281).

This study uses **selective** sampling for two reasons: First, this study does not aim at developing a (complete) new theory as it is done in grounded theory approaches (*Glaser/Strauss* (1967), p. 45). It rather aims to **extend** and **refine** existing theory.[81] Second, this study can build on a conceptual and theoretical framework and on prior literature to choose **meaningful** selection criteria (*Patton* (2015), p. 281).

Selection criteria used in this study

As outlined in section 5.2.1, this study uses a multiple case study design to compare and contrast different cases. In such a multiple case study design, the selected cases should have both some **similarities** and some **differences** (*Palinkas et al.* (2015), p. 534; *Patton* (2015), pp. 305-306; *Flick* (2018), pp. 50-51). Therefore, this study defines some criteria that yield in similar cases as well as some criteria that result in differences between the cases.

On the one hand, **homogeneity** across cases is achieved by defining criteria on the MNC's nationality and business model. Furthermore, criteria are defined based on the ownership structure and age of subsidiaries. Concerning the nationality of MNCs, this study examines MNCs from **Germany**. Thus, all MNCs examined in this study have their corporate head office in Germany. This aims at excluding cultural effects at head office level, which might affect the design of parent-PMSs (*van der Stede* (2003), p. 270). Moreover, this study fo-

---

These criteria are sometimes also labeled as *"problem dimensions"* (*Wrona/Gunnesch* (2016), p. 734).
81 For the theoretical framework used in this study, cf. chapter 4.

cuses on **non-financial firms**. This is consistent with excluding finance and insurance companies since these firms have a completely different business model and hence might differ in the design of parent-PMSs. Furthermore, this study excludes subsidiaries that are subject to **more than one parent-PMS** because this might influence the adoption at subsidiary level (*Cruz et al.* (2009), p. 11; *Giacobbe et al.* (2016), p. 1043). This could be for instance the case in joint ventures, if both parent companies have their own parent-PMS. Finally, concerning a subsidiary's age, this study requires subsidiaries to belong to the MNC for at least **two years**. The rationale behind this decision is that the imposition and implementation of a parent-PMS at a subsidiary takes some time. Excluding recently acquired or developed subsidiaries therefore helps to eliminate effects arising from an incomplete implementation of parent-PMSs.

On the other hand, this study uses the size and industry of the MNC and the subsidiaries' nationality and function as criteria to create **heterogeneity** across cases. Concerning the **size**, this study selects MNCs representing a wide range of small to large firms. The size is operationalized by the MNC's worldwide number of employees and sales. The reason for selecting MNCs of different size is that firm size is a key determinant for the design of parent-PMSs (e.g., *Abdallah/Alnamri* (2015), pp. 601-604; *Kihn* (2008), pp. 162-164). Variations in the design of parent-PMSs allow to contrast and compare the impact of design choices on the adoption of parent-PMSs. For the same reason, this study chooses MNCs from different **industries** (e.g., agricultural and chemical industries). In addition, by examining foreign subsidiaries from **various countries**, the influence of different national cultures and host country environments on the adoption of parent-PMSs can be observed. Finally, this study selects subsidiaries fulfilling different **functions** for MNCs (e.g., production units and sales units), which might also influence the adoption of parent-PMSs by subsidiaries (*Cooper/Ezzamel* (2013), p. 311). Table 5–3 summarizes the selection criteria used in this study.

	Homogeneity across cases	Heterogeneity across cases
MNC and head office level	• German head offices (**MNC's nationality**) • Non-financial firms (**MNC's business model**)	• MNCs of different sizes, ranging from small to large companies (**MNC's size**) • MNCs operating in different industries (**MNC's industry**)
Subsidiary level	• Subsidiaries that are subject to only one parent-PMS (**number of parent-PMSs**) • Subsidiaries have to belong to the MNC for at least two years (**subsidiary's age**)	• Subsidiaries from various countries (**subsidiary's nationality**) • Subsidiaries having different functions (**subsidiary's function**)

Table 5–3: Selection criteria applied in this study

In addition to these selection criteria, the case firms also need to be **available** for the researcher. Case firms are available if the relevant firm members are willing to participate in the research project (*Palinkas* (2015), p. 535; *Flick* (2018), pp. 57-58). Since it is difficult to convince potential experts in participating in a research project, qualitative researchers often use case firms to which they have personal contacts. Such a sampling strategy (labeled as *convenience sampling*) is widely accepted in qualitative research (*Bédard/Gendron* (2004), p. 196). In this study, personal contacts of the researcher are used to identify and contact potential case firms.

5.2.2.2 Overview of the sample

Based on the selection criteria described in the previous section, the following **five**[82] case companies have been selected: CarSupCo, MaNuCo, AgriCo, ChemCo, and TechCo (for reasons of confidentiality the case companies' real names are disguised). At each of the five companies, **two subsidiaries** are examined.

As required by the selection criteria outlined above, all case companies stem from **Germany** and are **non-financial** companies. The case companies operate in different **industries**, ranging from automotive supply to the technology sector (see Table 5–4).[83] Furthermore, the case companies vary in **size**, which is determined here by the number of employees and the sales revenues.

Case firm	Industry	Number of employees	Sales (in € Mio.)	Sales generated abroad (% of sales)
CarSupCo	Automotive supply	> 2,500	> 250	> 55 %
MaNuCo	Insulating materials	> 2,500	> 500	> 75 %
AgriCo	Agriculture	> 10,000	> 2,500	> 75 %
ChemCo	Chemicals	> 100,000	> 50,000	> 65 %
TechCo	Technology	> 350,000	> 75,000	> 85 %

Table 5–4: Overview of the case companies

The **proportion of sales generated abroad** varies strongly between the five case companies (from 55% at CarSupCo to 85% at TechCo). However, all case companies generate more sales in foreign markets than in their domestic market.

All selected subsidiaries belong to the MNCs for at least **two years**. The subsidiaries fulfill different **functions** for the MNCs. Whereas the selected subsidiaries of ChemCo and TechCo are sales units, the subsidiaries from AgriCo are only responsible for manufacturing the MNC's products. At CarSupCo and MaNuCo, the selected subsidiaries are responsible for both selling and manufacturing products. Concerning their **nationality**, the subsidiaries stem from nine different countries and three different continents (see Table 5–5).

---

[82] The "right" number of cases in multiple case studies depends on the specific circumstances of the study (*Kornacker* (2014), p. 159). On the one hand, there should be enough cases to be able to detect patterns across cases (*Lillis/Mundy* (2005), p. 127). On the other hand, too many cases spur the risk that they cannot be examined in an appropriate depth due to limited resources and time constraints of the researcher (*Cheek* (2011), pp. 259-264). This study examines five cases in total, which allows both to make cross-case comparisons and to examine each case in depth.

[83] Source: Annual reports, interviews and external documents (financial year 2016).

Continent	Country	Case companies
	Denmark (North EMEA)	ChemCo
	France	AgriCo
Europe	Germany	ManuCo
	Italy (South EMEA)	ChemCo
	Poland	CarSupCo, ManuCo
	India	AgriCo
Asia	Oman	TechCo
	United Arab Emirates	TechCo
South America	Brazil	CarSupCo

Table 5–5: Geographical distribution of the subsidiaries

5.3 Research process

This section describes the research process by outlining how the data for this study is collected (section 5.3.1). Subsequently, section 5.3.2 deals with the data analysis. Finally, the research process is reviewed (section 5.3.3).

5.3.1 Data collection

5.3.1.1 Access to case firms

A prerequisite for conducting case study research is to secure access to case firms by obtaining approval from the case firms' **key actors** (*Devers/Frankel* (2000), p. 265; *Flick* (2018), pp. 57-58). These key actors serve as "gatekeepers", which help the researcher to identify and establish contact with relevant experts in the case firm (*Agndal/Nilsson* (2010), p. 154; *Poplat* (2013), pp. 107-108; *Ritchie et al.* (2014), p. 90-91).[84] In studies on MNCs, researchers can contact gatekeepers from head office or subsidiary level (*Kornacker* (2014), pp. 147-148; *Edwards et al.* (2011), pp. 411-412). Both approaches have advantages and disadvantages (see Table 5–6).

A main **advantage** of contacting gatekeepers from **MNCs' head offices** is that they usually possess **more power** than their counterparts at subsidiary level (*Devers/Frankel* (2000), p. 265). Therefore, gatekeepers from head offices are better placed to give a binding commitment for the MNC in participating in the research project. Furthermore, head offices' gatekeepers are also valuable in **identifying** relevant interview partners at subsidiary level

---

[84] Identifying and contacting experts is especially challenging in case studies on MNCs because these entities often have a large number of employees who are spread across several continents. Thus, the role of gatekeepers is even more important in case studies examining MNCs.

Devers/Frankel (2000), p. 265). This is an important advantage since it is difficult for researchers to obtain names and contact details of employees working in (foreign) subsidiaries through other channels (*Kornacker* (2014), p. 148; *Lervik* (2011), pp. 237-238). These advantages of contacting gatekeepers from the head office are also the main **disadvantage** of contacting gatekeepers from **subsidiary level**. In fact, gatekeepers from subsidiary level **might not have the power** to give a binding commitment for the research project and might be reluctant to contact the head office (*Devers/Frankel* (2000), p. 265).

Gatekeepers from...	Advantages	Disadvantages
...head offices	• Gatekeepers from head offices have the power to provide access to the subsidiaries. • Gatekeepers from head offices are able to identify relevant experts within the MNC.	• Gatekeepers from head offices might only provide access to unproblematic cases because they might be afraid of losing their face.
...subsidiaries	• Gatekeepers are directly contacted by the researcher, which reduces a potential bias of getting only unproblematic cases. • Gatekeepers from subsidiary level might also increase honesty and openness of the subsidiaries' interview experts because they do not have the impression that the researcher has been sent by the head offices.	• Gatekeepers might do not have the power or might be reluctant to secure access to the head office.

Table 5–6: Advantages and disadvantages of access strategies

A main **disadvantage** of contacting gatekeepers in head offices arises from the **general concerns** that gatekeepers have. Gatekeepers often fear to lose their face through unfavorable comments by other experts within the firm (*Denvers/Frankel* (2000), p. 267). This might be especially relevant to this study because it examines how the subsidiaries adopt parent-PMSs designed by the head offices. Thus, gatekeepers from head offices might fear that experts from subsidiaries openly criticize the parent-PMS. Consequently, gatekeepers from head offices might only be willing to establish contact to employees from the subsidiary level which are **favorable** of the parent-PMS. This could potentially bias the results of this study, especially if it is not noticed by the researcher. However, this is mitigated by the fact that gatekeepers are also interested in

> "[...] learning how others think and act [...] at other levels of their own organization (particularly of lower rank)."

> (*Denvers/Frankel* (2000), p. 267)

Following this argumentation, gatekeepers from head offices might also have an own interest in examining how subsidiaries actually adopt the parent-PMS. These disadvantages of contacting gatekeepers from head offices are also the main **advantages** of contacting gate-keepers from the MNCs' **subsidiaries**. In fact, contacting gatekeepers from subsidiaries **might reduce the potential bias** of getting only subsidiaries that are favorable of the parent-PMS (*Devers/Frankel* (2000), p. 265). Furthermore, the interview partners at subsidiary level might be more open and honest when using gatekeepers from subsidiary level as this reduces their impression that the research has been sent by the head office (*Devers/Frankel* (2000), p. 265).

Since both approaches have disadvantages, this study does not rely on a single strategy in securing access to case firms. This study rather leverages on **both approaches** and hence secures access by contacting gatekeepers at both head office and subsidiary level. Particularly, in two MNCs (AgriCo and CarSupCo), gatekeepers from the MNCs' head offices have been contacted. In the remaining three cases (TechCo, ChemCo, and ManuCo) access has been given by gatekeepers from subsidiary level. However, during the course of the research, no differences have been noticed between the two groups that could be attributed to one of the two access strategies.

Irrespective whether gatekeepers from head offices or subsidiaries were approached, each gatekeeper was provided with **detailed information on the research project** (e.g., an exposé outlining the content and course of the research project) to reduce uncertainty and to establish trust between the researcher and the gatekeeper (*Devers/Frankel* (2000), p. 266; *Turley* (2004), p. 456). After having clarified how access to case firms is obtained, the following section outlines the different data sources used in this study.

5.3.1.2 Overview of data sources

Following *Yin*, case study researchers should not only rely on a single data source, but should use **as many different data sources as possible** (*Yin* (2018), pp. 126-130). This so-called data triangulation helps the researcher to check the validity of empirical data (*Scapens* (1990), p. 275; *Patton* (2015), pp. 316-317). In this study, expert interviews serve as the main data source. The interview data is complemented by (internal and external) documents. The following paragraphs outline both data sources in more detail.

Expert Interviews

When using expert interviews as a data source, case study researchers have to define which persons count as experts for their study. In general, experts are those persons that are able to provide the researcher with relevant information on the research topic – either through factual knowledge or practical experience (*Kornacker* (2014), p. 2014). Furthermore, experts should be able and willing to reflect on their experiences and to communicate them to the researcher (*Whiting* (2008), p. 36). In this study, interview experts stem from both head office and subsidiary level.[85]

---

[85] Interviewing experts from both head offices and subsidiaries allows to distinguish between the design of parent-PMSs and the adoption at subsidiary level (*Dossi/Patelli* (2008), p. 127).

At **head office level**, the designers of parent-PMSs can be considered as experts, since they possess relevant knowledge of the design and implementation of these systems (*Kaplan/Norton* (1996), pp. 300; *Dossi/Patelli* (2008), p. 127). Consequently, for examining the design of parent-PMSs, **management accountants of the MNCs' head offices** serve as main interview partners in this study.

At **subsidiary level**, the experts need to have factual knowledge or practical experience with the adoption of parent-PMSs (*Kornacker* (2014), p. 2014). In selecting experts at subsidiary level, this study follows *Dossi/Patelli*, who argue that the **subsidiaries' management accountants** are appropriate experts on the adoption of parent-PMSs (*Dossi/Patelli* (2008), p. 134). This is for two reasons (*Euske et al.* (1993), pp. 288-289). First, the subsidiaries' management accountants **support the local management** (e.g., marketing managers, sales managers, and production managers) by taking an advisory role for decision-making (*Gleich* (2011), p. 317). Thus, they are deeply involved in decision-making processes at subsidiary level and can therefore provide detailed evidence on how subsidiaries use the parent-PMSs. Second, the subsidiaries' management accountants serve as **contact persons** for the management accountants at the head office. In this role, the subsidiaries' management accountants are expected to facilitate the implementation of the parent-PMSs at subsidiary level. Furthermore, the subsidiaries' management accountants are usually the designers of the local-PMSs (*Dossi/Patelli* (2008), p. 127; *Schäffer et al.* (2010), p. 312). Overall, the management accountants at subsidiary level can provide detailed evidence on how parent-PMSs are adopted.

Internal and external documents

In addition to conducting expert interviews, this study relies on internal and external documents. **Internal documents** comprise organizational charts, guidelines and presentations on performance measurement as well as performance reports (*Cruz et al.* (2011), p. 416). Organizational charts help the researcher to understand the reporting structure and responsibilities for performance measurement at the case firms. Guidelines and presentations on performance measurement reveal head offices' objectives in designing and implementing parent-PMSs at their subsidiaries. Moreover, they often include a comprehensive list and definition of performance measures included in the parent-PMS. Finally, performance reports provide the researcher with an overview of performance measures and the corresponding targets that are set for MNCs' subsidiaries. In many cases, the internal documents were not only provided to the researcher but were also reviewed and explained during the interviews.

External documents are those documents that are publicly available. They include MNCs' annual reports, company brochures, websites, and press releases. The external documents serve as background information for the researcher and as a preparation for the expert interviews. Figure 5–3 summarizes the data sources used in this study.

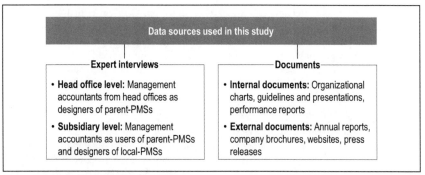

Figure 5–3: Data sources used in this study

5.3.1.3 Characteristics of expert interviews

Expert interviews can be conducted in several ways. Researchers therefore have to specify how they conduct expert interviews in their study. In particular, they have to decide on the

1) degree of structure,
2) interview medium, and on the
3) recording and transcription of expert interviews.

(*Brinkmann* (2014), p. 285)

The following paragraphs outline and justify how this study deals with these three issues of expert interviews.

Degree of structure

Concerning the degree of structure, expert interviews can be structured, semi-structured or unstructured (*Qu/Dumay* (2011), p. 238). However, these three types of interviews should be understood as a continuum rather than being separate concepts (*Brinkmann* (2014), p. 285; *Qu/Dumay* (2011), p. 239). At the one end of the continuum, **structured interviews** are characterized by a high degree of standardization[86], which shall increase the comparability of collected interview data. By being highly standardized and containing closed questions, structured interviews resemble questionnaire-based surveys in quantitative studies and are used to study facts of an organization (*Whiting* (2008), p. 35; *Döring/Bortz* (2016), pp. 358-359). At the other end of the continuum, **unstructured interviews** (or sometimes labeled narrative interviews) allow interviewees to tell their story (e.g., their experiences with a management accounting system) without being overly guided by the researcher (*Brinkmann* (2014), p. 286). The basic assumption of unstructured interviews is that it is impossible to specify all relevant interview questions in advance (*Qu/Dumay* (2011), p. 245). Therefore, the researcher identifies and picks up topics and themes that are raised by the

---

[86] Therefore, this type of expert interview is sometimes also labeled as standardized interview (*Qu/Dumay* (2011), p. 244).

interviewee during the interview (*Myers/Newman* (2007), p. 4).[87] Rather than using one of the two extreme types, qualitative researchers commonly use **semi-structured interviews** as a compromise (*Brinkmann* (2014), p. 286; *Flick* (2019), pp. 203-205). Semi-structured interviews usually rely on an interview guideline that contains both closed and open questions. This interview guideline shall help the researcher to cover all relevant topics in the interviews (*Qu/Dumay* (2011), pp. 246-247; *Myers/Newman* (2007), p. 14). However, the interviewer is not restricted to the questions contained in the interview guideline but is encouraged to take up topics that are raised by the interviewees (*Brinkmann* (2014), p. 286).

In this study, **semi-structured interviews** are used for the following reasons: First, in contrast to unstructured interviews, interview guidelines increase the comparability of answers between different interviews, which is especially important in multiple case studies (*Scapens* (2004), p. 266; *Qu/Dumay* (2011), p. 244; *Maxwell* (2013), pp. 88-89). Additionally, in contrast to completely structured interviews, semi-structured interviews allow the researcher to pick up topics that emerge during the interview, which is consistent with the explorative nature of this study (*Myers/Newman* (2007), p. 14).

Interview medium

In addition to deciding on the degree of structure, case study researchers have to choose the medium through which the interviews shall be conducted. While face-to-face interviews are still the most common way to conduct interviews in management accounting research, interviews by phone or videoconferencing tools also receive an increased attention (*Tucker/Parker* (2014), p. 7; *Weinmann et al.* (2012), p. 959). When deciding on the interview medium, researchers should take the advantages and disadvantages of the different media into account (*Tucker/Parker* (2014), p. 10).

A major advantage of **face-to-face interviews** is that the interviewer can assess the interviewee's emotions and facial expressions, which might help in interpreting the empirical material (*Brinkmann* (2014), p. 290). Furthermore, face-to-face interviews help to develop trust between the researcher and the interviewee and therefore might increase the commitment of the interviewee (*Christmann* (2009), p. 212; *Gläser/Laudel* (2010), p. 154). Finally, a face-to-face setting provides the opportunity to discuss and review additional documents (such as performance reports) with the interview partner (*Gläser/Laudel* (2010), pp. 153-154). However, a drawback of face-to-face interviews is that they are time consuming and costly due to travelling time and travel costs. For this reason, interviews conducted by **phone** or **videoconferencing tools** can serve as alternatives that are less costly for the researcher (*Weinmann et al.* (2012), p. 959; *Janghorban et al.* (2014), pp. 1-2). Moreover, phone and videoconferencing interviews are sometimes perceived as being more anonymous by interviewees, which might be helpful for interviews on sensitive topics (*Sturges/Hanrahan* (2004), p. 108; *Tucker/Parker* (2014), p. 12). Similar to vis-à-vis interviews, videoconferencing tools also allow interview participants to see each other and to share additional doc-

---

[87] However, even unstructured interviews should not be understood as having no structure at all since researchers always have in mind an initial idea about the main topics of the interview. Otherwise it would be a casual conversation rather than an expert interview (*Brinkmann* (2014), p. 285).

uments (*Weinmann et al.* (2012), p. 959; *Sedgwick/Spiers* (2009), p. 2). However, videoconferencing tools are susceptible to technical problems and require certain technological skills by both the interviewer and the interviewee (*Tucker/Parker* (2014), p. 13).

Whenever possible, this study uses **face-to-face** interviews since they increase the commitment of the interviewee and provide the researcher with a high level of detail for interpreting the data. Those vis-à-vis interviews were complemented by interviews conducted by **phone** and **videoconferencing tools**, especially in interviews with participants from foreign subsidiaries or in case of time constraints of the interviewee.

Recording and transcription

Finally, case study researchers have to decide **how** to **record** the interviews and **how** to **transcribe** these recordings (*Hayes/Mattimoe* (2004), p. 361). Recording and transcribing are essential elements in qualitative research since they enable the researcher to analyze and interpret data after the interviews have been conducted (*Gläser/Laudel* (2010), pp. 157-158).

In general, interviews can be **recorded** by using a tape-recorder or manually, i.e. by taking notes and memos during the interview (*Hayes/Mattimoe* (2004), p. 359). Both approaches have some advantages and disadvantages, which should be considered by the interviewer. A disadvantage of tape-recording compared to manual recording is that interviewees are often not familiar with being tape-recorded, which creates an **unnatural setting** for the interview (*Gläser/Laudel* (2010), pp. 157). Furthermore, interview partners might be reluctant to disclose **sensitive information** in case of tape-recording (*Bédard/Gendron* (2004), pp. 197-198). However, this is only a weak argument against tape-recording since interviewees might also be reluctant to give sensitive information when notes are taken by the researcher (*Gläser/Laudel* (2010), p. 158).[88] Finally, tape-recording requires some technical know-how by the interviewer and bears the risk of losing interview data due to **technical problems** (*Hammond* (2017), p. 205). A main advantage of tape-recording is that it allows the researcher to listen to the interview for **several times** and to transcribe the interview ex-post (*Rubin/Rubin* (2012), pp. 98-100). This ensures that the transcript **correctly reflects** the statements made by the interviewee – without the risk of losing or changing some of the statements which might happen in case of manual recording (*Rubin/Rubin* (2012), pp. 98-100). Moreover, when using a tape-recorder, the interviewer is not **distracted** by making notes (*Gläser/Laudel* (2010), pp. 157; *Hayes/Mattimoe* (2004), p. 364). Given these advantages of tape-recording, interviews are recorded by the researcher of this study whenever possible and permitted by the interviewee.[89]

---

[88] Moreover, *Gläser/Laudel* (2010) argue that interview partners who follow a strategy of giving distorted answers would do so, irrespective of the kind of recording by the research (*Gläser/Laudel* (2010), p. 158).

[89] Except for one interview, all interview partners allowed to tape-record the interviews.

In addition to stating how interviews are recorded, researchers should be specific on how the **interview transcripts** are created. Interview transcripts should reflect what the interviewee says, without omitting or altering statements (*Poland* (1995), p. 293). In this study, all interviews are transcribed based on the following transcription rules:[90]

- Interviews are transcribed verbatim (as spoken) without modifying or summarizing statements.
- Non-verbal expressions such as laughing are typed in squared brackets (e.g., "[laugh]").
- Filler words such as "ähm", "aha" are deleted unless they are necessary for understanding the statements.
- Pauses in speech are indicated in round brackets.
- Punctuation and language are slightly smoothed (e.g., local dialects are converted to standard language).
- For each interview statement, a separate paragraph is introduced and labeled with an abbreviation to identify the different interview partners and the interviewer.
- Interview partners' names and other confidential information are anonymized.
- Words that were particularly accentuated by the interviewer or the interviewee are underlined.

Based on these rules, all interviews are anonymized and then transcribed in the language of the interview (*Flick* (2018), p. 91). Interviews were held in German and English. The initial transcription was done by student assistants and later reviewed by the researcher of this study. In this review, the researcher checked the correctness of the transcription (*Gläser/Laudel* (2010), p. 190; *Nienaber* (2020), p. 90). Furthermore, the researcher deleted the audio tapes after reviewing the transcripts to secure the anonymity of interview partners (*Helfferich* (2011), pp. 190-192; *Flick* (2018), p. 91; *Nienaber* (2020), p. 90). The following section presents the interview guideline serving as a basis for the semi-structured interviews.

5.3.1.4 Interview guideline

Semi-structured expert interviews – as used in this study – typically rely on an interview guideline that is prepared by the researcher (*Qu/Dumay* (2011), p. 245; *Flick* (2019), pp. 194-195). The basic idea of using an interview guideline is to collect all questions that are necessary for the interviewer to answer his research questions. This shall ensure that relevant data is obtained in all interviews in a comparable way (*Gläser/Laudel* (2010), p. 42 and pp. 142-143). However, in contrast to a standardized questionnaire, the interviewer is not restricted to these questions but shall be open to touch upon points made by the interviewee (*Brinkmann* (2014), p. 286).[91] Furthermore, the interviewer can change the sequence of questions during the interview if necessary (*Döring/Bortz* (2016), pp. 358-359).

In **developing** the interview guideline, this study follows four steps (see Figure 5–4).

---

[90]   These transcription rules were developed based on *Kuckartz* (2018), pp. 164-171. For an application of similar transcription rules, cf. *Poplat* (2013), p. 112, *Schulz* (2018), p. 88, and *Nienaber* (2020), p. 90.
[91]   This openness is especially relevant in exploratory research like this study.

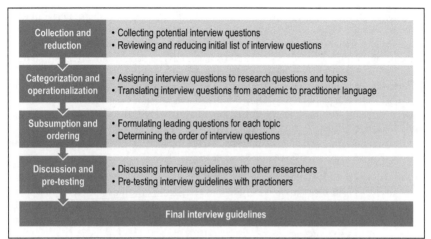

Figure 5–4: Development of interview guidelines
Based on *Nienaber* (2020), p. 87.

In a first step, the researcher **collects** a large number of potential interview questions and subsequently reduces the number of questions (*Nienaber* (2020), p. 87). Collecting potential interview questions aims at obtaining as many questions as possible without being overly concerned about the importance or wording of these questions (*Helfferich* (2011), p. 182). For coming up with potential interview questions, the researcher draws on the conceptual and theoretical framework of this study (e.g., design elements of parent-PMSs or influencing factors derived from NIS) and on prior literature (*Wrona/Gunnesch* (2016), p. 735). The resulting initial list of interview questions is then **shortened** by deleting questions. Particularly, four types of questions are eliminated from the initial list of questions:

• factual questions for which answers can be obtained in other ways (e.g., by referring to external or internal documents),
• questions that evoke short answers and that are hence not suitable for encouraging discussions,
• questions for which answers are already known by the interviewer and that do not directly relate to the research questions, and
• questions that are potentially manipulative by influencing interviewees' perceptions or emotions.

(*Helfferich* (2011), pp. 182-184; *Schnell et al.* (2018), pp. 306-307; *Nienaber* (2020), p. 87)

In a second step, the remaining questions are categorized and translated from academic to practitioner language (*Nienaber* (2020), pp. 87-88). Concerning the **categorization**, questions are assigned to the two overarching research questions of this study (*Bogner et al.* (2014), p. 33; *Nienaber* (2020), p. 87). Thus, questions are classified as relating either to the design of parent-PMSs or to the adoption of parent-PMSs at subsidiary level. This procedure results in **two different interview guidelines** – one for interview partners at the case firms' head offices and one for interviewees from subsidiary level.[92] Furthermore, within the two interview guidelines, interview questions are categorized into different topics (e.g., performance measures, targets, etc.). The **operationalization** and translation of questions from academic to business language is important since interview partners are often not familiar with the concepts and terms that underlie the research questions – or even worse, they understand concepts and terms differently than the researcher (*Gläser/Laudel* (2010), p. 113; *Qu/Dumay* (2011), p. 239). Thus, while research questions are formulated to address other researchers, interview questions are tailored to the people that are interviewed in this study (*Maxwell* (2013), p. 101; *Wrona/Gunnesch* (2016), p. 736). Consequently, all questions are rephrased into simple and understandable interview questions to yield detailed and specific answers from interviewees (*Gläser/Laudel* (2010), p. 145).

In a third step, interview questions are subsumed and sequenced (*Nienaber* (2020), p. 88). The basic idea of **subsuming** interview questions is to reduce the number of interview questions, which is presented to the interviewee. Therefore, for each topic a leading interview question is formulated, which is presented to the interviewee, while more detailed questions are held ready by the interviewer (*Kaufmann* (2015), p. 51). This is done to give the interview guideline a clearer layout and to avoid that the interview guideline is understood by interview partners as a checklist or questionnaire (*Helfferich* (2011), p. 180; *Nienaber* (2020), p. 88). The leading questions are then **ordered** by starting with simple questions, which can be easily answered by interview experts. This ensures a smooth starting of the interview conversation and helps the interviewee to get familiar with the interview situation.

Finally, the (preliminary) interview guidelines are discussed with other researchers and pre-tested with practitioners (*Nienaber* (2020), p. 88). Concerning the former, the preliminary guidelines were **discussed** with the supervisor of this study and other researchers from the corresponding chair. For the interview guideline aiming at the case firms' head offices, the pre-test was conducted with the Chief Financial Officer (CFO) of a German conglomerate, which owns domestic and foreign subsidiaries. The interview guideline containing questions for employees from the case firms' subsidiaries was tested with a management accountant working in the Australian subsidiary of a German MNC. Resulting feedback from academia and practice was used to alter the wording of questions and to further reduce the number of questions. The final interview guidelines are presented in Appendix A.

5.3.1.5 Interview data

This section describes the interview data, as interviews are the main data source of this study (see section 5.3.1.2). The interviews were conducted between **November 2017 and June 2018**. Over this period, **33 experts** from five case firms were interviewed yielding about **37 hours** of interview material (see Figure 5–5). The interviews lasted approximately 68 minutes on average.[93]

In qualitative research, there is no predetermined "right" number of interviews (*Beitin* (2012), pp. 243-244). Instead, the number of interviews is often decided during the course

---

[92] For a similar procedure, cf. *Cooper/Ezzamel* (2013), pp. 293-294.
[93] An exhaustive list of all interview partners is presented in appendix B.

of the research project based on **theoretical saturation** (*Beitin* (2012), pp. 243-244; *Messner et al.* (2017), p. 434). The basic idea of this concept is to stop contacting additional interview experts if the collected empirical data is sufficient to answer the research questions and if new interviews to not lead to new insights to this topic (*Khalifa/Mahama* (2017), p. 255). In addition, the adequateness of the number of interviews can be assessed by comparing it with the number of interviews in prior studies addressing similar research questions. In this vein, conducting interviews with 33 experts as it is done in this study is comparable with other studies examining the adoption of parent-PMSs (e.g., 37 interview partners in *Siti-Nabiha/Scapens* (2005) and 24 interview partners in *Cruz et al.* (2009)).

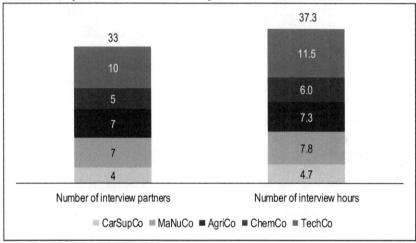

Figure 5–5: Overview of number of interview partners and interview hours

The number of interview experts at the case companies ranges from four (CarSupCo) to ten (TechCo). The picture is similar for the number of interview hours, which ranges from 4.7 (CarSupCo) to 11.5 (TechCo) interview hours. The data shows that both the number of interview partners and the number of interview hours is considerably higher for TechCo than for the other four case firms. This can be explained by the large size of TechCo and the resulting **complexity** of the case firm's organizational structures.

Interviews were conducted at head office level and subsidiary level. As can be seen from Figure 5–6, **15 experts** from the head office level and **18 experts** from the subsidiary level were interviewed. These interviews resulted in about 18 hours (19 hours) of interview data at the head office level (subsidiary level). As indicated by these figures, there are only small differences in the number of interview partners and interview hours between the head office and subsidiary level. This is important since this study examines both the design of parent-PMSs at head office level and the adoption of these systems at subsidiary level.

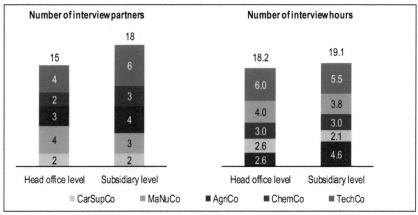

Figure 5–6: Number of interview partners and interview hours per sublevel

5.3.2   Data analysis

5.3.2.1   Data coding

This section turns the focus from the collection to the analysis of data. The collected empirical material (interview transcripts, internal documents, and external documents) is structured, summarized, and interpreted (*Messner et al.* (2017), p. 435). Through this process of **coding**, researchers can identify important and recurring topics from the cases, which allow them to interpret the data and to draw conclusions from it (*Ahrens/Chapman* (2006), pp. 831-833; *Flick* (2018), p. 126). Consequently, data coding can be seen as the basis of analyzing qualitative data and therefore can be compared with doing statistical analyses in quantitative research (*Dey* (2005), p. 3; *Ayres et al.* (2003), p. 880). Similar to quantitative researchers who reveal how they conduct their statistical analyses, qualitative researches should explicitly disclose how the data is coded. This is especially important for securing that results from qualitative studies are inter-subjectively traceable (*Ahrens/Chapman* (2006), p. 835). For coding, different approaches exist:

- theoretical coding,
- qualitative content analysis, and
- thematic coding.

(*Malina/Selto* (2001), pp. 61-62; *Lamnek/Krell* (2016), pp. 482-483)

These three coding approaches can be ordered by their **degree of strictness** (*Flick* (2019), pp. 386-387). On one end of the scale, **theoretical coding** is used in studies developing and generating theories for phenomena that lack convincing or consistent theoretical explanations (*Alberti-Alhtaybat/Al-Htaybat* (2010), pp. 209-211).[94] Consistent with its strong

---

[94]   Consequently, theoretical coding is often used by studies following grounded theory approaches and is
         sometimes labeled as *"grounded theory coding"* (*Charmaz* (2011), p. 363).

focus on exploration, categories for coding are not specified in advance but are developed within the process of reading and coding data case by case (*Malina/Selto* (2001), p. 62). Identified categories within one case are then constantly compared to categories derived from the other cases (*Walker/Myrick* (2006), p. 553). This so-called axial coding allows to identify both relationships and commonalities and differences across the identified categories (*Corbin/Strauss* (1990), p. 13). Within the course of research, theoretical coding strives to select the key themes and topics that are prevalent across all cases (selective coding) (*Corbin/Strauss* (1990), p. 14-16; *Parker/Roffey* (1997), pp. 228-229). Theoretical sampling is often criticized for not providing specific criteria, signaling to the researcher that a theoretical saturation of identifying, comparing, and selecting categories is reached (*Coyne* (1997), p. 625). Furthermore, researchers applying theoretical coding face the challenge to creatively identify new categories by interpreting data while at the same time securing that findings are traceable for researchers (*Flick* (2019), pp. 401-402).

On the other end of the scale, **qualitative content analysis** introduced by *Mayring* provides strict rules and procedures for coding data (*Mayring* (2016), pp. 114-120; also cf. *Flick* (2019), pp. 409-410). This approach is especially useful for reducing and comparing large amounts of qualitative data, which is for instance necessary in studies examining narrative disclosures in firms' financial reports (*Kuckartz* (2018), pp. 64-71; *Flick* (2019), p. 409). In contrast to theoretical coding, categories are developed and specified in advance. These categories are mainly deductively derived from prior literature, theory, or a study's conceptual basis (*Flick* (2019), p. 409-410). The resulting content analysis catalogue is then applied in a consistent and standardized manner to the empirical data collected by the researcher (*Kuckartz* (2018), pp. 98-99). A drawback of qualitative content analysis is that it needs clearly defined phenomena and categories, which can be determined before starting with coding data. Therefore, qualitative content analysis is less useful for explorative studies (*Gläser/Laudel* (2010), pp. 198-199; *Flick* (2019), pp. 416-417).

Thematic coding[95] is in the middle of the spectrum since it combines elements of both theoretical coding and qualitative content analysis (*Kuckartz* (2018), p. 77). It is especially useful for identifying common themes and topics in multiple case studies and comparing categories across cases (*Flick* (2019), p. 402). In contrast to theoretical coding, categories are not only inductively derived but also deduced from prior knowledge (*Messner et al.* (2017), p. 435). Consequently, pre-defined categories are refined, adjusted and advanced during the process of coding empirical data. Thus, thematic coding also differs from qualitative content analysis since the former only defines broad categories prior to coding (*Kuckartz* (2018), pp. 77-78). As the other two approaches, thematic coding has some limitations. First, the application of thematic coding is limited in very explorative settings such as grounded theory since it requires previous conceptual and theoretical knowledge for defining broad categories (*Flick* (2019), pp. 408-409). Second, different from theoretical coding, thematic coding requires the selection of cases prior to coding data (*Flick* (2019), pp.

---

[95] Thematic coding is sometimes named structuring-thematic coding, which goes back to the German term *"Inhaltlich strukturierende qualitative Inhaltsanalyse"* used by *Kuckartz* (2018), p. 97. This study uses the more common term *"thematic coding"* (e.g., *Charmaz* (2011), p. 370; *Flick* (2019), p. 402).

408-409).[96] Finally, a drawback of thematic coding is that it is time consuming because the researcher elaborates on the categories during the course of coding data. This makes thematic coding less useful for coding very large amounts of empirical material (*Kuckartz* (2018), p. 88).

In this study, **thematic coding** is applied for the following reason: This study can build on prior literature, theory and a conceptual basis (e.g., design and use of parent-PMSs) to **develop broad categories**, which serve as a starting point for coding data. Therefore, on the one hand, a grounded theory approach that mainly inductively derives categories from empirical material is not suitable for this study. On the other hand, this study **explores** how subsidiaries adopt parent-PMSs implemented by their head offices. This explorative stage hinders the research in defining detailed categories in advance and requires adjusting the (broad) categories when coding data. Therefore, as a middle ground between both extreme approaches, thematic coding provides the flexibility to develop and refine categories by both deduction and induction (*Kuckartz* (2018), pp. 77-78).

There are several different ways of conducting thematic coding.[97] This study follows an approach for thematic coding developed by *Kuckartz*. The basic idea of this approach is to start with broad categories, which are further refined during the course of coding data (*Kuckartz* (2018), p. 77). As Figure 5–7 shows, several process steps are followed.

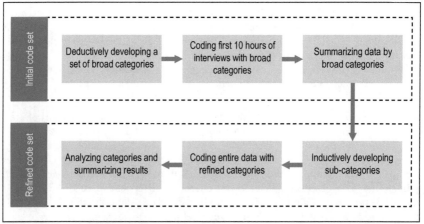

Figure 5–7: Process of thematic coding
Based on *Kuckartz* (2018), p. 100.

The first step is to **develop a broad set of categories** that is derived from a study's research questions, conceptual and theoretical basis and from prior literature (for this paragraph cf. *Kuckartz* (2018), p. 78-93). These categories should also be reflected in the interview

---

[96] In grounded theory approaches, cases are not determined in advance but are selected step-by-step during the course of research. Thus, subsequent cases are selected based on findings from previous cases (*Charmaz* (2011), p. 364; *Wrona/Gunnesch* (2016), p. 734).

[97] For an overview of the different forms of thematic coding, cf. *Flick* (2019), pp. 402-407.

guideline used for collecting data. Examples of broad categories used in this study are the four design elements of PMSs (performance measures, targets, link to rewards, and IT infrastructure). In the second step, a **sub-sample (10 hours of interviews) of the empirical material is coded** by using the initial code set developed in the previous step. Based on this initial coding, the broad categories were adjusted and extended. Subsequently, the entire empirical material was coded by using the set of broad categories. As a next step, **summaries for the categories** were prepared. After writing summaries, **sub-categories** were inductively derived from the empirical material. In a next step, the resulting refined code set was used for **re-coding** the entire data set. Finally, all coded segments were **summarized** and **analyzed** both within the cases and across the five case firms.

During the entire process of the thematic coding outlined above, the coding of empirical data was supported by the qualitative data analysis (QDA) software **MAXQDA**.[98] Using QDA software has two main advantages: First, QDA software increases the **efficiency** of coding compared to paper-and-pencil-based coding and hence decreases the time needed for coding (*Miles et al.* (2014), pp. 46-48). This is especially important when many interviews have to be coded or when thematic coding is used, which is inherently time-consuming (*Ji* (2017), p. 457). Second, using QDA software increases the **transparency** of the data analysis and hence the traceability of a study's findings (*Messner et al.* (2017), p. 435). This is the case because the researcher can export the coding system from QDA software to share it with other researchers (*Anderson-Gough et al.* (2017), p. 421). Given these advantages[99], MAXQDA is used for coding data in this study.

5.3.2.2 Typology development

This study aims at identifying different types of the adoption of parent-PMSs at subsidiary level. Developing a typology is often referred to as the ultimate goal of qualitative research (*Kuckartz* (2018), pp. 143-144). In particular, typologies serve two purposes in qualitative research. First, developing a typology contributes to the **theoretical generalization** of a study (*Wrona* (2006), p. 207). This is because future studies can build on the developed types to conduct further analyses on the phenomenon addressed by the typology (*Scapens* (1992), pp. 378-380). For example, a quantitative large-scale study could examine the prevalence of the different types of the adoption of parent-PMSs. Second, typologies contribute to the practice by providing **illustrative descriptions** on the types and their relations (*Doty/Glick* (1994), p. 230; *Kuckartz* (2018), p. 117). For example, a typology

---

[98] More precisely, MAXQDA 2018 was used for coding data (https://www.maxqda.com/). Following Anderson-Gough, MAXQDA *"offers coding, memo writing and working with a framework of categories"* (*Anderson-Gough et al.* (2017), p. 409).

[99] Even though QDA software is commonly used in qualitative research, some authors criticize the use of such software. For instance, it is argued that QDA software might seduce qualitative researchers to collect more data than necessary and that learning to use QDA software is time-consuming. Furthermore, it is sometimes argued that QDA software could lead to an excessive categorization of data that adversely affects the interpretation of data (*Anderson-Gough et al.* (2017), p. 421). Taking these considerations into account, particular emphasis was given to achieve a reasonable balance between categorizing, summarizing, and interpreting data.

might support the management accountants of MNCs' head offices to better understand how their subsidiaries adopt the parent-PMS.

Following *Weber*, a typology consists of *"ideal types"* (*Weber* (1949), p. 90), which are **simplified representations** of a real existing phenomenon (*Kelle/Kluge* (2010), pp. 83-84). These types describe the underlying phenomenon by outlining their key characteristics (*Doty/Glick* (1994), pp. 230-231), but *"without claiming that actual cases fit exactly with the typology generated"* (*Kilfoyle et al.* (2013), p. 386). For elaborating the typology of the adoption of parent-PMSs at subsidiary level, **four steps** are necessary (*Kelle/Kluge* (2010), p. 92; *Kuckartz* (2010), pp. 556-558; see Figure 5–8).

The first step is to **identify relevant characteristics** that can be used to describe the types (*Kelle/Kluge* (2010), pp. 93-96). These characteristics can be derived deductively from prior literature and theory and/or inductively from the empirical data (*Kuckartz* (2018), pp. 125-126). In this study, the four adoption types (acquiescence, modification, decoupling, and defiance) discussed in the NIS serve as a starting point for identifying relevant characteristics. Furthermore, additional characteristics are derived from the empirical material. These additional characteristics relate to both the use of parent-PMSs and the existence and design of local-PMSs.

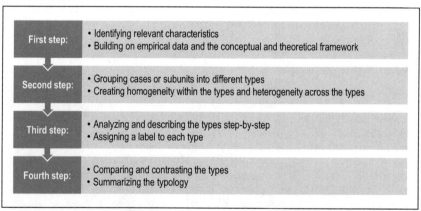

Figure 5–8: Steps of typology development
Based on *Kelle/Kluge* (2010), p. 92; *Kuckartz* (2010), p. 557.

The second step is to **group the cases or subunits into different types** based on the identified characteristics (*Kelle/Kluge* (2010), pp. 96-101). In this study, the typology refers to subunits, namely to the case companies' subsidiaries. The classification of the subsidiaries into the different types follows the idea that the subsidiaries within each type should be as homogeneous with regard to the identified characteristics. Furthermore, subsidiaries that are grouped into different types should be as different as possible concerning these characteristics (*Kelle/Kluge* (2010), p. 93; *Kuckartz* (2018), p. 118).

In the third step, the resulting types are **analyzed and described in detail** (*Kelle/Kluge* (2010), pp. 105-107; *Kuckartz* (2018), p. 119). In particular, each type is described based on the characteristics identified in the first step and examples from the empirical material (*Kuckartz* (2018), p. 119). In addition, a label is assigned to each type (*Kelle/Kluge* (2010), p. 105).

The final step is to **compare and contrast** the different types to point out the similarities and differences between them (*Kuckartz* (2018), p. 119). Furthermore, the final step is to summarize the typology and to explain how it contributes to literature, theory, and practice (*Kelle/Kluge* (2010), pp. 106-107).

5.3.2.3 Structure of analyses

The coded data is analyzed both within and across the five cases (see Figure 5–9).

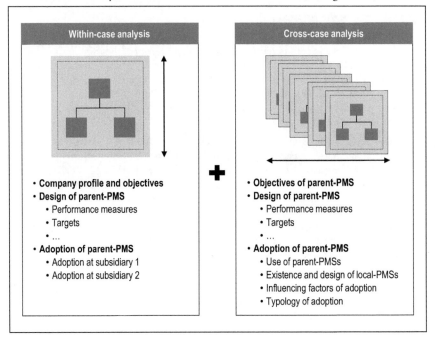

Figure 5–9: Structure of analyses

The aim of the **within-case** analyses is to deeply engage with each case to grasp the key themes of the cases (*Voss et al.* (2002), pp. 213-215; *Ayres et al.* (2003), p. 873). In this vein, each case is examined and outlined separately, i.e. without reference to the other cases (*Yin* (1981), pp. 58-65). In this study, the structure of the within-case analysis is identical for each case company and consists of three parts. The first part introduces the case company by providing a short description of the **company's profile** and the **objectives** that the case company's head office pursues with designing and implementing the parent-PMS. The second part deals with the **design of the parent-PMS** and is structured along the four design elements outlined in chapter 2. This leads to a thick description of the parent-PMS's design. Finally, the third part presents how the case company's subsidiaries **adopt** the parent-PMS. In particular, the third part deals with the use of the parent-PMS and the existence and design of a local-PMS.

The **cross-case** analysis is structured in a similar way and comprises the head offices' objectives of developing parent-PMSs, the design of the parent-PMSs, and the adoption of parent-PMSs at subsidiary level. The cross-case analysis aims to detect and discuss patterns across the cases and to develop a typology on the adoption of parent-PMSs (*Kornacker et al.* (2018), pp. 34-35). The findings of the cross-case analyses are discussed in the light of prior literature and the theoretical framework.

5.3.3   Review of the research process

Irrespective of writing a PhD study or papers for academic journals, empirical researchers should always assess and communicate the quality and integrity of their findings (*Messner et al.* (2017), pp. 432-440). To do so, empirical researchers typically draw on **quality criteria**, which are then transferred and applied to the specific research study at hand (*Lincoln et al.* (2011), p. 98; *Flick* (2018), pp. 74-75). While there is a commonly agreed set of quality criteria for quantitative research[100], qualitative research does not have a commonly accepted approach of using quality criteria (*Lincoln* (1995), p. 275; *Messner et al.* (2017), p. 433).

Qualitative researchers mainly use **two opposing approaches.**[101] On the one hand, some researchers argue that qualitative research should be assessed by **different quality criteria** than quantitative research (*Morse et al.* (2002), p. 15; *Mayring* (2016), pp. 140-143). Thus, proponents of this approach develop own quality criteria that are specifically developed for qualitative research (*Goddard* (2017), pp. 104-105). The main argument of researchers following this approach is that the criteria used in quantitative research do not address the particularities of qualitative research (*Lukka/Modell* (2010), p. 468-470). However, there is no commonly accepted set of criteria that qualitative researchers should use (*Morse et al.* (2002), p. 15; *Goddard* (2017), pp. 104-105).

On the other hand, some researchers propose to **adapt the quality criteria of quantitative research** to the needs of qualitative studies (*Morse et al.* (2002), pp. 15-19). The main advantage of this approach is that it increases the comparability of qualitative and quantitative studies (*Wrona/Gunnesch* (2016), p. 739; *Messner et al.* (2017), pp. 433-440). This study uses the **second approach**, since there is no consensus in the literature on quality criteria for qualitative research. Therefore, this study takes the quality criteria of quantitative research (internal validity, external validity, reliability, and objectivity) and adapts them to the qualitative nature of this study (*Wrona* (2006), pp. 204-208).

---

[100]   Quality criteria for quantitative research are the internal and external validity, reliability, and objectivity of research (*Wrona* (2006), pp. 204-208).

[101]   Some qualitative researchers even propose not to use quality criteria at all (*Wrona* (2006), p. 203). However, since this approach can be criticized for not being transparent on the quality of the research (*Wrona* (2006), p. 203), this is approach is not discussed here.

Internal validity

In qualitative research, internal validity is approached by ensuring a high credibility of the research, which can be achieved by being close to the empirical data and by communicative validation (*Messner et al.* (2017), p. 433). For **being close to the data**, several measures are applied in this study: First, this study relies on triangulation of both interview partners and data sources (*Lincoln/Guba* (1985), p. 305; *Patton* (2015), pp. 316-317). In fact, this study does not only capture the views of management accountants working in MNCs' head offices but also the perspective of local management accountants (triangulation of informants). This is especially important for this study since management accountants in head offices might have a biased view on the adoption of their self-designed PMSs (*Messner et al.* (2017), pp. 434-435). Furthermore, this study does not only interpret interview transcripts but also internal and external documents such as organizational charts or performance reports. This approach of data triangulation helps to reduce biases arising from intentionally and inadvertently distorted answers made by interview partners (*Voss et al.* (2002), p. 211; *Wrona* (2006), p. 205). Second, closeness to the data is achieved by creating interview transcripts based on recorded interview conversations. Recording interviews allows to create verbatim accounts of interviewees' responses, without modifications or gaps in the text due to a lack of the researcher's memory (*Gläser/Laudel* (2010), pp. 157). Finally, the empirical findings of this study are underlined by power and proof quotes. While power quotes are used to illustrate and tell the story of each case, proof quotes are used to demonstrate the correct reproduction of organizational facts (*Pratt* (2008), p. 501). Overall, using power and proof quotes increases the transparency of interpretations made by the researcher (*Messner et al.* (2017), p. 436).

Communicative validation means that interview partners are provided with the written transcripts after each interview in order to check whether interviewees' statements are correctly reproduced by the researcher (*Voss et al.* (2002), p. 209). Furthermore, the researcher shared parts of the empirical findings with the interviewed experts (*Wrona* (2006), p. 205). To account for communicative validation, interview transcripts were made available in this study to the interviewees (*Voss et al.* (2002), p. 209). However, none of the interview partners requested to change or delete passages from the transcripts, indicating that responses were correctly transcribed.

External validity

In qualitative research, external validity is not evaluated in terms of statistical representativeness as done in quantitative studies. It is rather important for qualitative researchers to demonstrate that their findings are theoretically generalizable, which can be achieved by an appropriate sampling strategy and the development of typologies (*Wrona* (2006), pp. 206-207). Concerning the **sampling strategy**, this study applies selective sampling based on criteria derived from prior literature and the theoretical framework. In this vein, this study ensures that information-rich cases are selected, which can be used to refine and extend existing theory. For instance, by exploring determinants on the use and enactment of parent-PMSs by subsidiaries, this study draws on and refines propositions derived from NIS. These findings can be then incorporated by further studies on the adoption of parent-PMSs at subsidiary level. In addition to an appropriate sampling strategy, theoretical generalization can be enhanced by **developing a typology** from empirical data (*Wrona* (2006), p. 207). In this study, ideal types of adopting parent-PMSs were identified based on the theoretical framework. These ideal types were then compared to the empirical data and refined based on the findings of this study. These refined types of adopting PMSs can be used by further qualitative and quantitative studies on this topic. For example, a survey study could examine the prevalence of these types in a certain sample.

Reliability

In quantitative studies reliability relates to the consistency and stability of empirical findings. Thus, a high reliability means that the findings of a study can be reproduced by other researchers when following the same procedures as in the original study (*Wrona* (2006), p. 207). In qualitative research, the reproduction of findings is limited for two reasons: First, it is not possible for other researchers to conduct the same interviews with the same participants as done in the first study. Second, qualitative research relies on the interpretative skills of the researcher, which are subjective by nature. Consequently, reliability cannot be evaluated in qualitative studies by referring to the stability of findings but rather be assessed by the reliability of the research process (*Wrona* (2006), p. 207). The reliability of the research process can be increased by disclosing the research process (especially the interview guideline) and by using QDA software for coding and analyzing the empirical material (*Messner et al.* (2017), p. 440).

A detailed **documentation** of the research process enables other researchers to comprehend how the data for a study has been collected and analyzed. In this study, the research process is disclosed in detail to the reader, which is a strength of a monograph compared to academic papers (*Messner et al.* (2017), p. 440).[102] In particular, the researcher explains how the interview guideline was prepared and discloses the resulting document to the reader.

By electronically documenting codes and summaries, the use of **QDA software** makes the research process more transparent (*Anderson-Gough et al.* (2017), p. 421). In this study, thematic coding was executed with the coding software **MAXQDA**. In particular, all interview transcripts and additional documents were imported to the software package and subsequently coded, summarized, and analyzed.

Objectivity

In quantitative research, much emphasis is placed on securing that a study's findings are independent from the researcher who has conducted the study. Therefore, objectivity can be increased in quantitative studies by appropriately applying (standardized) research methods (*Wrona* (2006), p. 207). In qualitative research, the role of the researcher is noticeably different. Indeed, (subjective) interpretations made by the researcher are an important feature of qualitative research (*Tomkins/Groves* (1983), p. 369). Thus, qualitative research always contains a certain degree of subjectivity. Following *Wrona*, qualitative researchers

---

[102] As pointed out by *Messner et al.* (2017), *"a monograph allows for more space than a journal paper to present empirical data and to explain the methods of data collection and analysis"* (*Messner et al.* (2017), p. 440).

should therefore clearly document the research process, which helps other researchers to understand how the interpretations have been derived (*Wrona* (2006), p. 207). Table 5–7 summarizes the quality criteria and the procedures that are followed in this study to address them.

Criteria	Evaluation in qualitative research	Procedures followed in this study
Internal validity	Credibility of research (closeness to empirical field and communicative validation)	• Triangulation of interview partners and data sources • Creating interview transcripts as verbatim accounts • Providing the interviewees with the written transcripts • Using power and proof quotes in presenting the empirical results
External validity	Theoretical generalization	• Selecting case companies purposefully based on prior literature and theoretical framework • Developing a typology of the adoption of parent-PMSs at subsidiary level
Reliability	Consistency and stability of empirical findings	• Documenting and disclosing the research process • Using MAXQDA for data analysis
Objectivity	Objectivity is not the aim of qualitative research	• Documenting and disclosing the research process

Table 5–7: Summary of the quality criteria and procedures followed in this study

6   Empirical results

This chapter presents the empirical results of this study. Section 6.1 depicts the results of the within-case analyses. The within-case analyses describe the case companies' profiles and the objectives of the parent-PMSs. Furthermore, the within-case analyses illustrates the design and adoption of the parent-PMSs. Section 6.2 provides cross-case analyses of the five MNCs with regard to the objectives, design, and adoption of the parent-PMSs.

6.1   Within-case analyses

6.1.1   CarSupCo case

6.1.1.1   Company profile and objectives of the parent-PMS

CarSupCo is a family-owned supplier for the **automotive industry**. The MNC produces and sells products such as air filters and oil cleaners to internationally leading car manufacturers and to the independent aftermarket. It employs approximately 3,000 people around the globe and generates revenues of about € 300 million. During the last two decades, the case company has grown strongly and has established and purchased several new locations. In 2018, it had more than 15 foreign subsidiaries in about ten countries. These foreign locations contribute to more than half of CarSupCo's total revenues, indicating the high importance of foreign markets for the MNC.

The small size of CarSupCo is reflected in a **lean organizational structure** (see Figure 6–1). This structure includes a direct reporting link between the corporate management accounting department located at the German head office and the domestic and foreign subsidiaries.[103] While the German head office includes corporate functions such as R&D and management accounting, the subsidiaries are responsible for producing and selling CarSupCo's products in the respective markets.

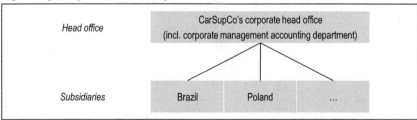

Figure 6–1: CarSupCo's organizational structure

At CarSupCo, interviews were conducted at the German head office and two foreign subsidiaries. At the head office, the researcher conducted interviews within the corporate management accounting department, which is responsible for designing the MNC's parent-PMS and for overseeing its implementation at the subsidiaries. In particular, the **Head of**

---

[103] Thus, there are no other organizational levels between CarSupCo's head office and the subsidiaries such as a regional head office.

corporate management accounting and his employee were interviewed.[104] At the subsidiary level, the researcher conducted interviews within the Brazilian and Polish subsidiary. The subsidiary in Brazil was established more than ten years ago and employs approximately 140 people. It is responsible for producing and selling CarSupCo's products in the Brazilian and other South American markets. The Polish subsidiary was founded in 2014 and employs more than 100 people. In addition to producing and selling goods to the Polish market, the subsidiary produces intermediate products that are shipped to Germany. At each of the two subsidiaries, the respective **Head of management accounting** was interviewed, who is in charge of the local management accounting department and serves as a contact person for the head office. Table 6–1 summarizes the interview partners at CarSupCo.

Title	Organizational level
Head of corporate management accounting	Head office
Corporate management accountant	Head office
Head of management accounting	Subsidiary Brazil
Head of management accounting	Subsidiary Poland

Table 6–1: Interview partners at CarSupCo

Objectives of CarSupCo's parent-PMS

The development of CarSupCo's parent-PMS was initiated by the CFO, who joined the MNC at the turn of the year 2010/2011:

> *"The development of our system started in 2010/2011. At that time, we got our first CFO [...]. He came from a large automotive supplier, which had already implemented such a reporting system. He came along with a set of key performance measures that we then looked at [...]."*

> *CarSupCo – Head of corporate management accounting*

The new CFO asked the corporate management accountants to develop a parent-PMS based on the above-mentioned initial set of performance measures. The resulting parent-PMS has then been implemented at the subsidiaries as a **standardized system**. Thus, the parent-PMS applies to all subsidiaries in the same way, irrespective of their size, geographical location or other characteristics.

In designing and implementing the parent-PMS, the corporate management accountants pursue two objectives, which they consider as equally important. The first objective is receiving information on the performance of the subsidiaries for **facilitating decisions**. Due to the increase in the number of foreign locations over the last two decades, receiving performance information is important for CarSupCo's corporate management accountants. In particular, the parent-PMS shall help them to identify negative developments at the subsid-

---

[104] There are no other employees in this department involved in performance measurement of foreign subsidiaries.

iaries. In case of such unfavorable developments, the employees from the head office propose countermeasures that have to be implemented by the foreign subsidiaries. In this way, negative trends shall be identified and corrected at an early stage.

Second, CarSupCo's corporate management accountants intend to provide the subsidiaries' employees with performance measures that they can use to manage their daily tasks:

> *"The different department heads shall use the performance measures to manage the respective areas that they are in charge of. For example, a quality manager uses performance measures such as "failure costs" or "number of customers that we have discussions with". This is his [the quality manager's; added by the author] daily business."*
>
> *CarSupCo – Corporate management accountant*

By providing the subsidiaries' employees with performance measures, the corporate management accountants intend to **influence their behavior**. In fact, the subsidiaries' employees are expected to consider the performance measures from the parent-PMS in their daily work. As pointed out by the interviewed corporate management accountants, this is important to achieve a common understanding within CarSupCo and to focus on the same objectives.

6.1.1.2 Design of the parent-PMS

Performance measures

CarSupCo's corporate management accountants have selected **18 performance measures** for evaluating the subsidiaries' performance. As Table 6–2 shows, these performance measures stem from four measurement perspectives.

Measurement perspective	Performance measures
Financial perspective:	Sales revenues, gross margin, operating margin, EBITDA, EBIT, days sales outstanding, days payables outstanding, days inventory outstanding, capital expenditures, free cash flow
Customer perspective:	Order backlog, order intake
Internal process perspective:	Failure rate of production, R&D project processing quota
Employee perspective:	Headcount, absenteeism rate, accident rate, employee fluctuation

Table 6–2: Performance measures included in CarSupCo's parent-PMS

The **financial perspective** accounts for most of the performance measures in the parent-PMS (ten out of 18 performance measures). The performance measures from this perspective relate to the subsidiaries' profitability (e.g., gross margin and EBIT), their working capital management (e.g., days inventory outstanding and days sales outstanding), their capital expenditures, and to the free cash flows. The financial perspective does not only include most of the performance measure in terms of quantity, but also **receives the highest attention** from CarSupCo's corporate management accountants. The importance of the financial perspective was already taken into account when selecting the performance measures for the parent-PMS:

> *"We started to develop a set of performance measures that should be reported by our subsidiaries. It was very clear to us that we have to look at subsidiaries' P&L (turnover, margins, profits etc.), at changes in working capital (days sales outstanding for example) and on capital expenditures. These measures are the basis. And of course, we have some additional measures from the operational side."*

> *CarSupCo – Head of corporate management accounting*

As pointed out by the Head of corporate management accounting, CarSupCo' parent-PMS additionally includes **non-financial performance measures**[105] relating to subsidiaries' customers, employees, and internal processes. Concerning the perspective of **customers**, the order intake and the number of orders in backlog are measured. The corporate management accountants selected these two performance measures because they consider them as useful for predicting the subsidiaries' future revenues. The performance measures relating to subsidiaries' **internal processes and employees** were selected in accordance with the MNC's corporate production & quality department and the corporate R&D department. In fact, employees from these two departments were asked what they consider as important performance measures for their specific areas. This consultation resulted in a set of two performance measures dealing with subsidiaries' internal processes and five performance measures dealing with subsidiaries' employees. Concerning the subsidiaries' **internal processes**, the failure rate of fabricated products and the success of R&D projects are evaluated. With respect to the subsidiaries' **employees**, the case company's head office pays attention to the absence of employees due to illness, accidents, and notices of termination.

The rationale for including these non-financial performance measures into CarSupCo's parent-PMS is that they are expected by the corporate management accountants to explain the subsidiaries' financial performance. In fact, the non-financial performance measures shall **enable a more detailed analysis of the causes of financial performance** – especially if the subsidiaries' financial results remain below expectations. Therefore, the corporate management accountants selected non-financial performance measures that are strongly related to the subsidiaries' financial performance:

> *"When selecting operational performance measures, we paid attention that they have a clear link to the P&L and cash flow statement. Because in the end, we have to earn money and we have to pay our bills."*

> *CarSupCo – Head of corporate management accounting*

---

[105] Within CarSupCo, non-financial performance measures are called "operational performance measures".

Targets

Targets are defined for all 18 performance measures included in CarSupCo's parent-PMS. In setting targets, the MNC's corporate management accountants distinguish between financial and non-financial performance measures. For financial performance measures, targets are derived from the **yearly budgeting process**, in which the targets are negotiated between CarSupCo's head office and the foreign subsidiaries. In this counter-flow planning, the subsidiaries' management accountants make the first proposal on target levels. Subsequently, the MNC's corporate management accountants review these proposals. In case the corporate management accountants consider the proposed target values to be too low, they make counterproposals for individual or all financial performance measures. These counterproposals are then discussed in budget meetings (via phone or web conferences) with the Head of management accounting of the respective subsidiary and the subsidiary's management. In these meetings, both sides attempt to reach a consensus.[106] After the targets have been agreed on between CarSupCo's head office and each subsidiary, the corporate management accountants consolidate the targets over all subsidiaries. In a next step, the consolidated target levels are presented to the MNC's management board (especially to the CFO).[107]

In contrast to the financial performance measures, target levels for the non-financial performance measures are not derived from the annual budgeting process. For these performance measures, target levels are rather set **based on an assessment of past performance**. In fact, the corporate management accountants rather carry forward the target levels from the previous year. Changes to the target levels are only made in case of new conditions such as the introduction of a new product type, which might increase, for example, the number of production failures during the first months of production.

For both – financial and non-financial performance measures – target levels are only determined for the subsidiary **as a whole**, but are not broken down into sub-targets for individual employees or for groups of employees. For example, a target for the absenteeism rate exists only at subsidiary level, but not for certain departments or teams (e.g., production teams).

The corporate management accountants evaluate the target achievement based on written performance reports and review meetings. The **monthly performance reports**, which are prepared by the subsidiaries' management accountants, consist of three sections. In the first section, the management accountants summarize the performance of the subsidiary by making statements on the highlights and lowlights of the previous month. The second section shows the actual and planned performance for all financial performance measures. Finally, achieved and targeted performance for all non-financial performance measures is outlined in the third section. Each financial and non-financial performance measure is marked with either a green, yellow, or red color in the report. By representing a traffic light system (*Bititci et al.* (2002), p. 700), these colors indicate whether subsidiaries achieve their targets or not.

---

[106] In the rare event that no agreement is reached in the budget meetings, CarSupCo's management board is involved to take a final decision.

[107] The management board might then initiate further changes to the target values, which are then discussed again between corporate and local management accountants.

Whenever a performance measure is marked in red, the subsidiaries' management accountants have to comment on this performance measure as a lowlight in the summary of the report. This shall help the management accountants in the head office and the subsidiaries to easily identify areas that need improvement.

In addition to the written performance report, target evaluation takes places in review meetings. These **monthly meetings** are held as web conferences with participants from CarSupCo's head office and the respective subsidiary. From the head office, one corporate management accountant (either the Head of corporate management accounting or his subordinate) and the CFO or Chief Operating Officer (COO) participate in this meeting. The subsidiary is represented by its General Manager and Head of management accounting. In the review meetings, the participants discuss the subsidiary's performance of the previous month. Attention is particularly paid to the performance measures marked in red. For these performance measures, the corporate management accountants expect an explanation for the negative target deviation. Figure 6–2 summarizes the target setting and target evaluation at CarSupCo.

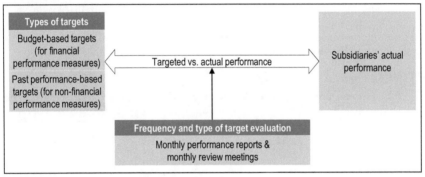

Figure 6–2: Target setting and target evaluation at CarSupCo

Link to rewards

At CarSupCo, the subsidiaries' management is eligible for bonus payments. The payment of the bonus depends on **two aspects**, as explained by the Head of corporate management accounting:

> "*The bonus scheme is designed in such a way that obtaining a bonus depends on the one hand on the success of the company – I mean the financial result of the whole company – and on the other hand on personal goals of the respective employees [...].*"

> *CarSupCo – Head of corporate management accounting*

CarSupCo's **financial performance** is operationalized by the performance measure EBITDA. However, for determining the bonus payment, the **group's** EBITDA instead of the subsidiaries' EBITDA is considered. The **personal targets** for the subsidiaries' management are determined by CarSupCo's management board and the corporate HR department. However, this only applies to the subsidiaries' top management (i.e., General manager and Finance manager). For the department heads, the personal targets are not set by the head office, but by the subsidiaries' management. For example, the General manager sets the personal goals for the Head of local management accounting. The following quote illustrates examples of how personal goals can be defined:

> "[...] For example, the Head of management accounting in Brazil might have the personal goal to support reducing inventory on hand by X days or he might have softer targets such as being project leader for the implementation of a new ERP system [...]. These personal targets are defined by the local management based on what they consider as important for the upcoming year."

> CarSupCo – Head of corporate management accounting

The personal goals do not need to be linked to performance measures from the parent-PMS. Instead, the management of each subsidiary **is free to decide on the personal targets** of the department heads.

Concluding, only one performance measure from the parent-PMS (EBITDA) is linked to the remuneration of the subsidiaries' management and executive employees. However, the payment of the bonus depends on the performance of the entire MNC and not on the performance of the respective subsidiary.

IT infrastructure

As an IT infrastructure, the parent-PMS builds on ERP systems and spreadsheet software (see Figure 6–3).[108]

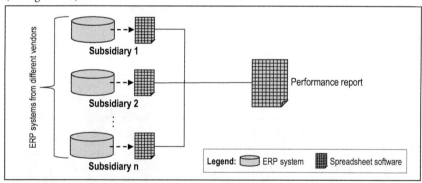

Figure 6–3: IT infrastructure of CarSupCo's parent-PMS

ERP systems are implemented at each subsidiary. These ERP systems serve as data collection and storage tools and contain all necessary information for calculating the 18 performance measures of the parent-PMS. However, CarSupCo does not have a group-wide, integrated

---

[108] For a similar depiction of a PMS's IT infrastructure, cf. *Hyvönen et al.* (2008), p. 52. This reference applies to all figures on the parent-PMSs' IT infrastructure within section 6.1.

ERP system. Instead, each subsidiary has its own ERP system. Therefore, **various ERP systems stemming from different ERP vendors** (e.g., SAP, Microsoft, and Sage) are in place at the case company:

> *"In principle, we have different ERP systems in our group. At our head office, we use SAP, as well as in the US. China will switch to SAP in next year but still has Sage. All other locations – such as Brazil – have other ERP Systems than SAP. Our Danish subsidiary, which we have bought in 2016/2017, uses Microsoft Dynamics Navision."*
>
> *CarSupCo – Head of corporate management accounting*

This fragmented ERP landscape is the result of CarSupCo's many acquisitions during the last two decades. The acquired subsidiaries often have their own ERP systems, which are not necessarily from the German ERP vendor SAP. Even though the head office is trying to migrate all subsidiaries to SAP (as the example of the Chinese subsidiary shows), there are still many different ERP systems within the group.

In addition to ERP systems, the case company uses spreadsheet software (Microsoft Excel) that serves as IT infrastructure for the written performance report. For this performance report, the corporate management accountants created a **standardized Excel template** that must be filled in by the subsidiaries' management accountants on a monthly basis. To do so, the subsidiaries' management accountants extract the required data from the local ERP systems and copy it into the Excel template. The template is designed in a way that the performance measures' values are calculated automatically by formulas.

6.1.1.3 Adoption of the parent-PMS

6.1.1.3.1 Adoption at CarSupCo Brazil

At the Brazilian subsidiary, the management accountants use the parent-PMS for several purposes. First, they use this system for **monitoring** whether the subsidiary achieves its targets. In particular, the management accountants analyze the performance report of the parent-PMS, which shows deviations between actual and targeted performance:

> *"The information from the performance report tells us 'Hey look, we are here, but we were supposed to be there', or it tells us that our performance is much better than expected [...]. When you walk, you always need to know where you need to arrive. That's why we compare our results with the targets."*
>
> *CarSupCo – Head of management accounting (Brazil)*

For negative target deviations, the management accountants try to identify the causes by looking for information that is more detailed in the ERP systems. Furthermore, they discuss possible reasons with the managers that are responsible for the respective performance measure. The target deviations and their causes are then presented each month to the subsidiary's management in a regular meeting. For this meeting, the management accountants prepare a presentation showing the major target deviations of the previous month.

Second, the management accountants use the parent-PMS to **develop countermeasures** by building on the deviation analyses and the discussions with the responsible managers. In these discussions, the managers have to explain whether the too low performance stems from an exceptional event or not. If the responsible event is not exceptional, the management accountants prompt the responsible manager to develop corrective actions. In case of too high employee fluctuation, for example, the management accountants ask the HR department to take countermeasures.

Third, the Brazilian management accountants use the parent-PMS for **evaluating decision alternatives**, which is done upon the request of the subsidiaries' managers. The management accountants then estimate how the different decisions would affect the financial and non-financial performance measures. For these estimates, the management accountants draw on two factors. First, they look at the outcomes of past decisions by obtaining past performance data from the ERP systems. Second, they get an opinion from the responsible manager, who has asked the management accountants to estimate the impact on the subsidiary's performance.

Finally, the management accountants use the parent-PMS to **motivate the subsidiaries' employees**:

> *"Everyone in our subsidiary is responsible for achieving his or her goals – otherwise we cannot achieve the EBITDA. It [the parent-PMS; added by the author] is some way of motivating our employees – it symbolizes several things."*

> *CarSupCo – Head of management accounting (Brazil)*

The management accountants require the managers to discuss the performance measures and targets with their subordinates. For example, the production managers shall frequently discuss the failure rate with the production workers and the sales managers shall discuss turnover figures with the sales force. Through these discussions, the subsidiaries' employees shall be aware of their targets and shall be motivated to reach them.

At the Brazilian subsidiary, the management accountants have **not developed a local-PMS**. Thus, they solely use the parent-PMS implemented by their head office. The following section analyzes the adoption of the parent-PMS at the Polish subsidiary.

6.1.1.3.2 Adoption at CarSupCo Poland

The Polish management accountants use the parent-PMS to **gain a deeper understanding of the subsidiary's business situation**. They regularly discuss the performance report of the parent-PMS before sending it to the head office. Furthermore, they discuss the report with the subsidiary's management in regular meetings. In these meetings, the management accountants and the managers discuss, for example, the highlights and lowlights of the previous month. These discussions help them to determine the drivers of the subsidiary's performance.

Furthermore, the management accountants use the parent-PMS for **monitoring** whether the Polish subsidiary achieves its targets or not. In particular, they look at the monthly performance report of the parent-PMS, which shows actual and targeted values for all performance measures:

> *"Month for month the system provides us with a standardized picture of what is going on in our company. And very important, it shows us the deviations from the plan."*
>
> *CarSupCo – Head of management accounting (Poland)*

In case of negative deviations from the budget, local management accountants are instructed to **identify the causes of the deviations**. For example, in case of too high manufacturing expenses, the local management accountants are asked to find out which types of expenses or which invoices cause the deviation from the targeted values. Furthermore, the management accountants shall work out concrete measures that help to achieve the targets in the following months. However, the management accountants are not supposed to do this on their own, but with the support of the managers that are in charge of the performance measures. For example, in case of too high manufacturing expenses, the management accountants discuss possible counteractions with the production managers.

Finally, the Polish management accountants also use the parent-PMS for **projecting the subsidiary's future performance**. The management accountants create a rolling forecast that is updated semi-annually. Furthermore, the management accountants update the forecast in case of unexpected developments (e.g., the gain or loss of an important customer). The forecast is done for all performance measures of the parent-PMS. It serves planning purposes (e.g., hiring new production workers or increasing warehouse capacity) and is used to get an early signal whether the yearly target levels will be met.

Existence and design of local-PMS

The Polish management accountants have developed a **local-PMS**. This local-PMS consists of **21 performance measures** that relate to four measurement perspectives (see Table 6–3). The majority of these 21 performance measures are also included in the parent-PMS. In fact, the Polish management accountants have taken all 18 performance measures of the parent-PMS because they consider them as relevant at subsidiary level. In addition, the Polish management accountants selected **three performance measures** that they are missing in the parent-PMS. These three additional performance measures relate to the subsidiary's internal processes and employees.

With respect to the subsidiary's **internal processes**, the management accountants additionally look at two performance measures, namely the fulfillment of production plans and the scrap rate. They argue that these two internal process measures are necessary because the subsidiary mainly produces intermediate products that are shipped to CarSupCo's head office. For these intermediate products, the subsidiary receives production schedules that the subsidiary has to follow. It is very important for the MNC that the Polish subsidiary delivers the preliminary products on time, as they still have to be processed in Germany. However, the production schedules can change at short notice, which makes it difficult for the Polish subsidiary to adhere to these schedules. Therefore, the Polish management accountants add a performance measure to track whether the **production follows the planned schedule**:

*"What is really important for us is the measurement of the fulfillment of our produc-
tion plan. It means we measure the percentage of the production orders that we complete in time."*

CarSupCo – Head of management accounting (Poland)

Furthermore, the Polish management accountants measure the **scrap rate** of each production line, which indicates the extent to which material is wasted during production. This is
necessary since the short-term changes of production schedules can lead to a waste of materials.

Measurement perspective	Performance measures
Financial perspective:	Sales revenues (LP), gross margin (LP), operating margin (LP), EBITDA (LP), EBIT (LP), days sales outstanding (LP), days payables outstanding (LP), days inventory outstanding (LP), capital expenditures (LP), free cash flow (LP)
Customer perspective:	Order backlog (LP), order intake (LP)
Internal process perspective:	Failure rate of production (LP), R&D project processing quota (LP), *fulfillment of production plan (L), scrap rate (L)*
Employee perspective:	Absenteeism rate (LP), accident rate (LP), employee fluctuation (LP), headcount (LP), *employee productivity (L)*
Legend:	
(L):	Performance measures included in the local-PMS only (highlighted in italics)
(LP):	Performance measures included in both the local-PMS and the parent-PMS

Table 6–3: Performance measures included in the local-PMS (CarSupCo Poland)

Concerning the **employee perspective**, the management accountants additionally examine
the productivity of the production workers:

*"We measure the employee productivity, it means we compare the hours that were
actually worked with the hours that were planned in the routing."*

CarSupCo – Head of management accounting (Poland)

The Polish management accountants consider employee productivity as important because
wages are a substantial cost item. By measuring employee productivity, they encourage the
production workers to work as efficiently as possible. This is especially important for the
Polish subsidiary as CarSupCo's head office decided to produce the intermediate produc-
tions in Poland to save production costs.

For all 21 performance measures of the local-PMS, **targets** are defined. For the 18 performance measures that are included in **both** the parent-PMS and the local-PMS, the Polish
management accountants take the target levels from the parent-PMS. Thus, for the financial
performance measures budget-based targets and for the non-financial performance

measures past performance-based targets are used. For the three performance measures that are **only part of the local-PMS**, the management accountants set local target levels that are only used within the Polish subsidiary. They determine the target levels for these three performance measures based on **past performance**. In particular, they carry forward the target levels from the previous year without requiring an improvement in these target levels.

For **evaluating the target achievement**, the management accountants use two performance reports. First, for evaluating the 18 performance measures that are included in both the parent-PMS and the local system, they use the performance report of the parent-PMS. Second, for evaluating the target achievement of the three additional performance measures, they have created a local report that shows the actual and targeted values for these three performance measures. All 21 performance measures of the local-PMS are discussed in a local review meeting, which is held every month. Figure 6–4 summarizes the target setting and target evaluation at CarSupCo Poland.

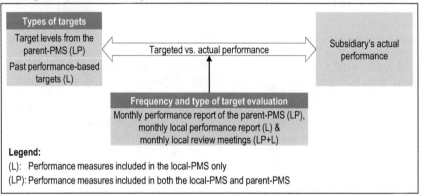

Figure 6–4: Target setting and target evaluation at CarSupCo Poland

The Polish management accountants **do not** link the performance measures of the local-PMS to the **rewards** of the subsidiary's employees. Thus, the three performance measures that are only included in the local-PMS and the corresponding target levels are not used for determining the bonus payments of the subsidiary's management or production workers.

The **IT infrastructure** of the local-PMS builds mainly on the IT systems of the parent-PMS (see Figure 6–5). In fact, the data for the 21 performance measures comes from the ERP system implemented by the head office. From this ERP system, the management accountants extract the data and transfer it to a **self-created spreadsheet template**, which only exists in the local-PMS. They use this spreadsheet template to calculate the three additional performance measures and to report them within the subsidiary. Different from the Excel-based performance report of the parent-PMS, the local performance report is not sent to the case company's head office.

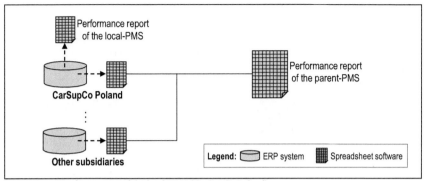

Figure 6–5: IT infrastructure of the local-PMS (CarSupCo Poland)

6.1.1.4 Summary

To **summarize**, CarSupCo's parent-PMS consists of 18 performance measures stemming from four measurement perspectives. For all of these performance measures, the management accountants set targets. For financial performance measures, budget-based targets are used, which are negotiated in counter-flow planning between CarSupCo's head office and the subsidiaries. For the non-financial performance measures, the corporate management accountants set targets based on past performance. The evaluation of the target achievement is based on a monthly performance report and monthly review meetings between Car-SupCo's head office and the subsidiaries. The case company uses the EBITDA of the group and personal goals for rewarding the subsidiaries' management. Regarding the IT infrastructure, the corporate management accountants have implemented ERP systems from different vendors and an Excel-based performance report.

At both the Brazilian and Polish subsidiary, the management accountants use the parent-PMS in a functional way. For example, they use the parent-PMS for evaluating decision alternatives, for monitoring performance, and for projecting the subsidiary's future performance. While a local-PMS does not exist at the Brazilian subsidiary, the Polish management accountants have developed such a local system. This difference might be due to the fact that the Polish subsidiary receives short-dated production schedules from the German head office, which is not the case for the Brazilian subsidiary. These short-dated production schedules require the Polish management accountants to examine three additional performance measures that they include in the local-PMS (fulfillment of production plan, scrap rate, and employee productivity). For these additional performance measures, the local-PMS includes targets based on past performance, which are evaluated through a local performance report and review meeting. The Polish management accountants do not link the local-PMS to the remuneration of the subsidiary's management and staff. As an IT infrastructure, the local-PMS is based on the IT systems of the parent-PMS and on a local spreadsheet template, which has been prepared by the Polish management accountants.

6.1.2 MaNuCo case

6.1.2.1 Company profile and objectives of the parent-PMS

MaNuCo is a global manufacturer and supplier of **insulation and foams for the construction industry**. The case company has approximately 3,000 employees worldwide and generates sales of about € 600 million. The about 25 foreign production and sales sites contribute to more than two-third of MaNuCo's total sales. This shows the high importance of foreign markets for the MNC. During the last two decades, the ownership of the sample firm has changed several times. In fact, before becoming an independent company in the beginning of the 2000s, MaNuCo was a division of a global manufacturing company based in the United States. Later, between 2010 and 2018, different private equity investors bought the case company.

MaNuCo is organized in a **regional structure**. This regional structure comprises a corporate head office, regional head offices for geographical regions such as Asia or EMEA, and subsidiaries. Each subsidiary consists of at least one production plant for manufacturing different product types and a sales office for distributing the products to the respective markets. Figure 6–6 summarizes MaNuCo's organizational structure.

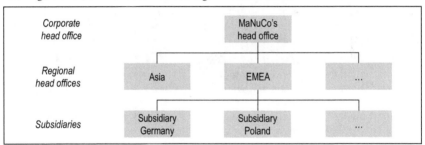

Figure 6–6: MaNuCo's organizational structure

At MaNuCo, interviews were conducted at the corporate and regional head offices and two subsidiaries (see Table 6–4).

Title	Organizational level
Corporate management accountant	Corporate head office
Corporate management accountant	Corporate head office
Management accountant for production & logistics	Corporate head office
Management accountant for production & logistics	Corporate head office
Finance manager	Regional head office of EMEA
Head of management accounting	Subsidiary Germany
Head of management accounting	Subsidiary Poland

Table 6–4: Interview partners at MaNuCo

At the corporate head office, interviews were conducted with **four management accountants**. Two of them have a special focus on production and logistics. At the regional head office for EMEA, the respective **Finance manager** was interviewed. For exploring the adoption of the parent-PMS at the MNC's subsidiaries, interviews were conducted at the German and the Polish subsidiary. By employing about 600 people and by comprising three plants, the German subsidiary is one of the largest subsidiaries. The Polish subsidiary has about 200 employees and comprises one factory. At both subsidiaries, the **Head of management accounting** was interviewed.

Objectives of MaNuCo's parent-PMS

MaNuCo's parent-PMS was implemented together with a company-wide, standardized production system ("World-Class Manufacturing Mindset", WMM). This production system, which was developed by a global consulting firm, aims at improving and standardizing the production processes at the case company's worldwide plants. Consistent with the idea of the WMM, the parent-PMS was implemented as a **standardized system**. With developing this parent-PMS, MaNuCo's management accountants pursued several objectives. They consider these objectives as equally important. First, the corporate management accountants use the parent-PMS to receive information on the performance of the subsidiaries for **facilitating decisions**. In particular, the parent-PMS allows them to check whether the subsidiaries achieve their targets. Furthermore, it signals the management accountants whether countermeasures have to be taken:

> "[...] We developed the reports, the tools and so on to check whether we are good or whether we are bad. We are sailing the boat in order to get to the objective, for example to an EBITDA target. During the trip, there are some storms, heavy rains, bad winds. We might lose one of our engines on our boat and so on. And our duty is actually to navigate the boat. And whenever we are not good, we have to know what to do to get the boat back to the right track."

> *MaNuCo – Finance manager (EMEA)*

Examples of countermeasures are projects to improve production processes, such as redesigning the factories' workstations to increase the utilization of the machines.

Second, the parent-PMS is used to evaluate which of the initiatives and countermeasures are successful. This helps the management accountants **to identify and share best practices** within the MNC. In this vein, the parent-PMS helps to accumulate knowledge.

Finally, MaNuCo's parent-PMSs is intended to **influence the behavior** of the employees in the subsidiaries. Or to say in other words, it *"shall bring a message"* (*MaNuCo, Finance manager EMEA*) to the subsidiaries' employees. Thus, the parent-PMS shall serve as a tool for managers and team leaders to manage their respective areas. For example, the subsidiaries' plant managers shall use the performance measures to assess how the production teams are performing.

6.1.2.2 Design of the parent-PMS

Performance measures

MaNuCo's parent-PMS comprises **twelve performance measures** that are used to evaluate the performance of the subsidiaries. As Table 6–5 shows, these performance measures stem from three measurement perspectives.

Measurement perspective	Performance measures
Financial perspective:	Net sales, manufacturing variances, days inventory outstanding, free cash flow, EBITDA
Customer perspective:	-
Internal process perspective:	Production output, overall equipment effectiveness, scrap rate
Employee perspective:	Absenteeism rate, accident rate, headcount, overtime hours

Table 6–5: Performance measures included in MaNuCo's parent-PMS

The **financial perspective** includes **five performance measures**. First, the amount of net sales generated by the subsidiaries' sales offices is measured. Since the subsidiaries are responsible for selling the MNC's products to external customers, this performance measure is important for MaNuCo's corporate and regional management accountants to assess the subsidiaries' sales efforts. The second performance measure relates to the costs of production and stems from the case company's costing system. In fact, the manufacturing variances show the differences between the planned and actual costs incurred for producing the products.[109] Third, the days inventory outstanding are examined to ensure that the subsidiaries keep inventories to a minimum. In addition, the subsidiaries' liquidity is monitored by looking at the free cash flows and the EBITDA. However, there is not only one EBITDA, but different versions of it:

> *"[...] Whenever someone wants to see an EBITDA, the first question is what EBITDA the person wants. We have the EBITDA from a legal point of view, as it will be shown in our external financial reporting. But then we also have information that we call 'unusual items'. The unusual items include all expenses that are extraordinary. We remove these unusual expenses from our EBITDA. That means we improve our EBITDA by the extraordinary expenses to see how our results would have been if we hadn't had the broken machine, for example."*
>
> *MaNuCo – Corporate management accountant*

As expressed by the quote above, MaNuCo uses two different types of the EBITDA: An unadjusted EBITDA and an EBITDA, which is adjusted for extraordinary expenses. Extraordinary expenses can arise, for example, from mergers and acquisitions or from job

---

[109] The overall manufacturing variances are further subdivided into variances of material costs, labor costs and other variances.

cuts.[110] For evaluating the subsidiaries' cash flows, the corporate and regional management accountants use both the adjusted and the unadjusted EBITDA.

In addition to financial performance measures, MaNuCo's parent-PMS consists of performance measures relating to the subsidiaries' internal processes and employees. The **three performance measures** from the **internal process perspective** relate only to production processes. Thus, other processes or activities at the subsidiaries such as research and development or administrative processes are not considered. The first performance measure relates to the subsidiaries' production output, which is measured in cubic meters of produced tubes. Second, the overall equipment effectiveness indicates the utilization of the machines (*Muchiri/Pintelon* (2008), p. 3518). Finally, the scrap rate reflects the extent to which material is wasted during production.

Concerning the subsidiaries **employees**, the corporate and regional management accountants employ **four performance measures**. First, the absence of subsidiaries' employees due to illness is investigated, which is expressed by the absenteeism rate. Second, the safety rate quantifies the number of accidents per 1000 worked hours.[111] Thus, this performance measure reflects safety concerns, which have a high priority at the case company:

"Within our world class manufacturing approach, the first pillar is safety. Safety has a top priority here. And there is a very important reason for that: If everybody is safe, we can all work."

MaNuCo – Management accountant for production and logistics

Finally, MaNuCo's parent-PMS includes the subsidiaries' headcount and the number of overtime hours of subsidiaries' employees. The corporate and regional management accountants use these two performance measures to examine whether the subsidiaries use their human capital efficiently.

Targets

At MaNuCo, targets are defined for all twelve performance measures of the parent-PMS. In **setting targets**, the management accountants of the case company's head offices distinguish between financial and non-financial performance measures. For **financial performance measures**, the targets are derived from an **annual budgeting process**, which starts in August each year.[112] The budgeting process begins on subsidiary level, at which the local management accountants have to make a first proposal on the target levels for the twelve performance measures. The proposed target levels for the financial performance measures stem from a calculation of the products' standard costs. The subsidiaries' proposals are consolidated by the responsible regional head offices and are forwarded from there to Ma-

---

[110] What counts as an extraordinary expense is defined in an internal guideline issued by the MNC's corporate management accounting department.

[111] The safety rate is further subdivided into an accident rate for minor accidents (accidents that cause a lost time of less than one working day) and an accident rate for major accidents (accidents that cause a lost time of more than one working day).

[112] MaNuCo's business year corresponds with the calendar year.

NuCo's corporate management accounting department. The corporate management accountants discuss the budget with the MNC's management board, especially with the CFO and COO. The management board and the corporate management accountants compare the budget to a three-year sales plan, which the management board prepares and updates each year.[113] In case the management board requests changes to the proposed budget, the changes are discussed with the regional head offices. The final proposal is then presented to MaNuCo's private equity investor, who might demand changes to the proposal. Afterwards, the management board and the corporate management accountants must incorporate these changes. Often several discussion rounds are necessary before the MNC's investor approves the final budget:

> *"We always need to defend our budget proposal to the investor and explain if we can do better or not better for this and that reason. Because the investor wants to get the maximum. And most of the time we have two or three budget rounds and finally by the 10th or 15th of September we basically get the approval from our investor for the budget of the year after."*

> *MaNuCo – Finance manager (EMEA)*

For the **non-financial performance measures**, the targets are derived from the **past performance** of the subsidiaries. MaNuCo's corporate and regional management accountants consider the subsidiaries' performance of the previous six months. Consistent with the idea of continuous improvement initiated by the WMM, the subsidiaries' have to increase the performance of the non-financial performance measures by a fixed percentage each year (compared to the average performance of the last six months). This percentage is negotiated between the management board and the private equity investor every few years.

For both – financial and non-financial performance measures – target levels are not only determined for each subsidiary as a whole but are also broken down on **product level** (for financial performance measures) and on the **level of production teams** (for non-financial performance measures).

MaNuCo's corporate and regional management accountants **evaluate the target achievement** based on written performance reports and review meetings. There are **four monthly** performance reports. The first report includes all financial performance measures of the parent-PMS. However, it only shows the overall manufacturing variances of the subsidiaries but does not go into detail. Thus, the first report does not show which proportion of the overall manufacturing variances stem from material cost variances or labor cost variances. For a more detailed analysis of the manufacturing variances, MaNuCo has a second report, which is labeled "Manufacturing variances report". In this report, the manufacturing variances are broken down into the different types of variances such as labor cost variances or material cost variances. The third report is called "Manufacturing report". It contains actual and planned values for the seven non-financial performance measures. Furthermore, it includes a column in which the subsidiaries have to comment on outstanding deviations from

---

[113] This three-year sales plan contains planned sales figures per country and product and is based on macroeconomic trends such as the forecasted growth of the construction industry.

the budgeted values. Finally, the "Project report" lists the projects proposed by the subsidiaries and shows their implementation status. In addition, it compares actual and planned effects of the projects.

The four reports are discussed in two different kinds of **monthly review meetings**. First, there is a review meeting between the regional head offices and the subsidiaries. This meeting, which is held as a phone conference, takes place in the second week of each month. The meeting is attended by the respective regional finance manager (e.g., finance manager EMEA), the subsidiaries' management accountants, and plant managers. During the phone conference, the participants discuss the four performance reports. In fact, the subsidiaries must justify and explain deviations from the budget. Furthermore, in case the projects listed in the "Project report" do not have the desired effects, additional projects shall be proposed by the subsidiaries. A second review meeting takes place between the regional head offices and MaNuCo's corporate head office. In this meeting, the responsible regional finance manager, the chief executive officer (CEO), the COO, and corporate management accountants discuss about the performance of the respective region. The finance manager of each region has to present the performance of his region and to explain any deviations from the targets. In addition, the finance managers must give an outlook on the region's future performance. Figure 6–7 summarizes the target setting and target evaluation at MaNuCo.

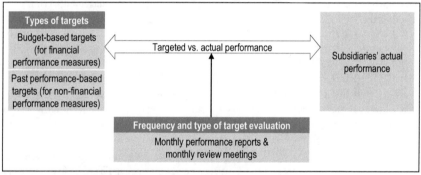

Figure 6–7: Target setting and target evaluation at MaNuCo

Link to rewards

At MaNuCo, the subsidiaries' management and production staff have a variable component in their remuneration. For the **subsidiaries' management**, the payment of the variable component depends on the following **three aspects:**

- EBITDA excl. unusual expenses of MaNuCo,
- EBITDA excl. unusual expenses of the subsidiary, and
- personal targets.

The first two aspects refer to a performance measure from MaNuCo's parent-PMS, namely the EBITDA excl. unusual expenses. The third aspect, namely the personal targets, are linked to qualitative targets rather than to performance measures from the parent-PMS. Given that the first two aspects relate to a performance from the parent-PMS, it becomes obvious that there is a link between the remuneration of the subsidiaries' management and MaNuCo's parent-PMS. However, the first aspect relates to the EBITDA excl. unusual expenses of the whole MNC, which can only be influenced to a limited extent by the subsidiaries' management. Furthermore, the use of the EBITDA excl. unusual expenses instead of the unadjusted EBITDA also means that the subsidiaries' management has an incentive to declare as many expenses as possible as "unusual". To prevent this, MaNuCo's corporate management accountants have developed a guideline that defines what an unusual expense is and what it is not. At the end of each month, the subsidiaries have to submit a list of expenses that they consider as unusual, which has to be approved by the corporate management accounting department. Despite the guideline and the associated rules, there are sometimes discussions about the unusual expenses between the subsidiaries' management and the corporate management accounting department:

> *"In fact, there are subsidiaries that are very inventive and try to declare a lot of expenses as unusual. Sometimes they move in a grey area and try to take advantage of it. Then we have discussions with them. But there are also many subsidiaries that simply stick to the guidelines [...]."*

> *MaNuCo – Corporate management accountant*

For the **staff involved in production processes**, the variable compensation depends on the **success of the projects** listed in the Project report of each subsidiary. If the projects have the desired impact, it effects the bonus payment positively. Since the projects usually aim to improve the performance measures of the **internal process perspective**, the bonus of the production workers and their team leaders is connected to the performance measures of the parent-PMS.

Concluding, the compensation of the subsidiaries' management is linked to performance measures of the parent-PMS, since the bonus payment for these employees depends on the EBITDA of the respective subsidiary. For the subsidiaries' staff involved in production processes, the bonus payments depend on the success of the projects listed in the Project report, which are usually linked to internal process measures of MaNuCo's parent-PMS.

IT infrastructure

MaNuCo's IT infrastructure for the parent-PMS consists of a combination of ERP systems, BI systems, and spreadsheet software (see Figure 6–8). An **ERP system** is implemented at each of MaNuCo's subsidiaries. These ERP systems are used to collect data for both the financial and non-financial performance measures. Exceptions are subsidiaries that were recently acquired by MaNuCo. Furthermore, small subsidiaries do not receive SAP for cost reasons:

> *"95% of our subsidiaries use SAP. But we also have a few subsidiaries – mostly new acquisitions – that are not yet using SAP. They still have their local data system."*

> *MaNuCo – Corporate management accountant*

"At EMEA, SAP is installed in all entities except of Denmark. This is because the subsidiary is too small and SAP implementation is a cost driver. There is no payback because Denmark is a too small entity."

MaNuCo – Finance manager (EMEA)

From the ERP systems, the data flows into further systems. The data for the financial performance measures (excluding the detailed manufacturing variances) is forwarded to a **BI system** from Oracle (Hyperion Financial Management).[114] This performance measurement tool serves two purposes. First, it **automatically** calculates the values of the financial performance measures. Thus, MaNuCo's management accountants only have to worry about data maintenance and consistency in the SAP systems, but not about the calculation of the financial performance measures. Second, it serves as a **shared information tool** for management accountants at the subsidiaries and at the regional and corporate head offices. In fact, MaNuCo's management accountants can extract reports on the financial performance measures from this tool.

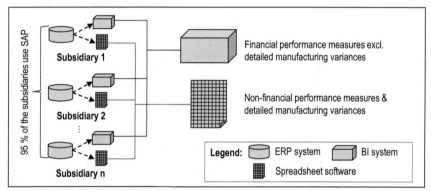

Figure 6–8: IT infrastructure of MaNuCo's parent-PMS

For the non-financial performance measures and the detailed manufacturing variances, the local management accountants extract data from the ERP system and transfer it to a **spreadsheet** template (Microsoft Excel). This Excel template, which is provided by the corporate management accounting department, calculates values for the non-financial performance measures automatically by formulas.

6.1.2.3 Adoption of the parent-PMS

6.1.2.3.1 Adoption at MaNuCo Germany

MaNuCo's German management accountants use the performance reports of the parent-PMS to **monitor the subsidiary's performance.** For the non-financial performance

---

[114] Information on the detailed manufacturing variances is not provided by the BI system due to technical reasons.

measures, the past performance-based targets are used. For the financial performance measures, the management accountants compare the actual performance with the budget-based targets that are negotiated with the regional and corporate head office:

> *"We compare our financial performance with the budget, which is defined once a year together with our parent company. This budget is the basis for us to evaluate whether our performance is satisfying or not. We do not only use the budget within our subsidiary, but we also discuss it in review meetings with the head office."*

> *MaNuCo – Head of management accounting (Germany)*

In the next step, the management accountants create deviation analyses based on these comparisons to **identify the reasons for positive and negative target deviations**. The results of the deviation analyses are communicated to the subsidiary's managers to give them feedback on their performance. For example, the production manager receives feedback on performance measures such as production output or scrap rate. However, the target deviations are not only communicated to the managers. The managers must also comment on and explain deviations towards the management accountants. This applies not only to negative deviations, but also to positive ones:

> *"We discuss the reasons for the deviations with the managers. Not only the negative developments, but also the positive results. The findings are then also communicated so that they can spread quickly and that they can also be used by other teams. And in the case of negative deviations, so that corrective action can be taken rapidly."*

> *MaNuCo – Head of management accounting (Germany)*

Furthermore, as expressed in the quote above, these discussions are the basis for **developing and implementing actions** to improve the subsidiary's performance. The purpose of these actions is twofold. First, in case of negative target deviations, countermeasures shall be developed to steer the performance in the right direction. This is to ensure that negative developments are corrected as early as possible. Second, positive target deviations shall result in best practices that are then shared with other teams. For example, the successful redesign of a work-station at one production team might help the other production teams to design their work-stations.

Existence and design of local-PMS

At MaNuCo Germany, a **local-PMS** exists. This local-PMS contains **thirteen performance measures** relating to three measurement perspectives. As Table 6–6 shows, twelve of the thirteen performance measures stem from MaNuCo's parent-PMS. Thus, the German management accountants consider all performance measure of MaNuCo's parent-PMS as important at subsidiary level. However, they also miss **one performance measure** in the parent-PMS, namely the production surplus, and hence include it in the local-PMS. They use this performance measure in the production of tubes. It indicates how many cubic meters of material are used in the production that exceed customers' requested sizes. Thus, the performance measure shows how much material can be saved during production.

Measurement perspective	Performance measures
Financial perspective:	Net sales (LP), manufacturing variances (LP), days in inventory (LP), cash flow (LP), EBITDA (LP)
Customer perspective:	-
Internal process perspective:	Production output (LP), overall equipment effectiveness (LP), scrap rate (LP), *production surplus (L)*
Employee perspective:	Absenteeism rate (LP), accident rate (LP), headcount (LP), overtime hours (LP)
Legend:	
(L): Performance measures included in the local-PMS only (highlighted in italics)	
(LP): Performance measures included in both the local-PMS and the parent-PMS	

Table 6–6: Performance measures included in the local-PMS (MaNuCo Germany)

Targets exist only for the twelve performance measures that are included in both the parent-PMS and the local-PMS. For these performance measures, the German management accountants use the target levels of the parent-PMS. Thus, for the financial performance measures, budget-based targets are used. The target levels for the non-financial performance measures are derived from past performance. For the production surplus, which is included only in the local-PMS, the subsidiary does not set targets. This is because the optimal level of the production surplus cannot be predicted in advance due to unstable chemical processes during production. For **evaluating the target achievement** of the twelve performance measures, the German management accountants use the performance report of the parent-PMS. They discuss these reports in monthly local review meetings. Figure 6–9 summarizes the target setting and evaluation at MaNuCo Germany.

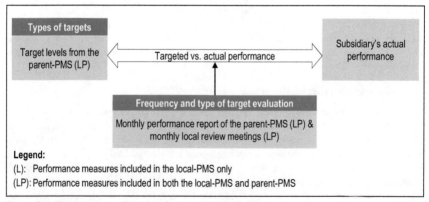

Figure 6–9: Target setting and target evaluation at MaNuCo Germany

The management accountants of MaNuCo Germany **do not** link the performance measures of the local-PMS to the **rewards** of the subsidiary's employees. Thus, the production surplus is not used for determining the bonus payments of the subsidiary's management or production workers.

As an **IT infrastructure** of the local-PMS, the German management accountants mainly build on the IT systems of the parent-PMS (see Figure 6–10).

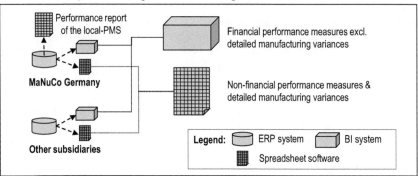

Figure 6–10: IT infrastructure of the local-PMS (MaNuCo Germany)

In fact, the data for the thirteen performance measures of the local-PMS comes from the ERP system of the parent-PMS. The management accountant extract the data from this ERP system and transfer it to a **self-created spreadsheet template**, which is only part of the local-PMS. The German management accountants use this spreadsheet template to calculate the production surplus and to report it within the subsidiary.

6.1.2.3.2   Adoption at MaNuCo Poland

At MaNuCo's Polish subsidiary, the management accountants use the parent-PMS for several purposes. First, they use it to **monitor the performance** of the subsidiary by checking for each of the twelve performance measures whether the target levels are met. Thus, the past performance-based targets of the parent-PMS are used for the non-financial performance measures. However, the Polish management accountants do not compare the actual results of the financial performance measures with the budget-based targets of the parent-PMS:

> *"In the budgeting process, we propose realistic target levels. However, we always get the information from our regional head office that our targets are too low. You have to know, that there is a lot of pressure from our investor – that is why the head offices require these unrealistic high target levels. Are we able to reach these targets? No, we are not."*
>
> *MaNuCo – Head of management accounting (Poland)*

As expressed by the quote above, the Polish management accountants consider the budgeted target levels as **too high**. In fact, they argue that the head offices make top-down adjustments in the budgeting process, which are not achievable by the subsidiary. Since Ma-NuCo's head offices have the last word on the target levels, the Polish management accountants cannot prevent these top-down adjustments. Rather than using the budget-based target levels of the parent-PMS, the management accountants compare the financial results with the performance of the previous year.

Second, the parent-PMS is used to **determine the causes of the negative target deviations**. For this purpose, the subsidiary's managers have to comment on and explain negative deviations to the management accountants. The managers also have to explain whether the deviations stem from continuous problems or from non-recurring events:

> *"Very important is that you know if you have a continuous problem or a single, unusual event that causes the problem. I give you an example: We have a continuous problem with scrap on a production line and we do not meet our targets. Then we need to find out if it is related to the product, the chemical formula, or whatsoever. This is something which is important for us."*

> *MaNuCo – Head of management accounting (Poland)*

Third, based on the assessment of the causes of target deviations, the parent-PMS is used to **develop and implement actions and initiatives** that improve the subsidiary's performance. This includes corrective actions that aim to improve the performance on performance measures that are falling below the target levels. In addition, actions and initiatives shall also be developed independently of poor performance. This is in line with the idea of continuous improvement, which is anchored in the parent-PMS. Therefore, the local management accountants encourage the responsible managers to propose potential improvements and to translate them into concrete projects. These projects are then added to the project report of the parent-PMS.

At MaNuCo's Polish subsidiary, the management accountants have **not developed a local-PMS**. Thus, the Polish management accountants solely use the parent-PMS.

6.1.2.4 Summary

Overall, MaNuCo's corporate management accountants include twelve performance measures in the parent-PMS, which relate to the subsidiaries' financial performance, internal processes, and employees. For all performance measures of the parent-PMS, targets are set. The financial performance measures' targets are negotiated in a yearly budgeting process between the head offices and subsidiaries. The targets of the non-financial performance measures are based on an assessment of the subsidiaries' past performance. For evaluating the achievement of the financial and non-financial performance measures, the corporate management accountants use several performance reports and monthly review meetings. The performance measures and targets of the parent-PMS are linked to the remuneration of the subsidiaries' management production workers. For the former, the bonus payment depends on the EBITDA of the respective subsidiary. For the latter, it depends on internal process measures of the parent-PMS. As an IT infrastructure, the head offices have implemented a BI system for the financial performance measures and spreadsheet templates for the non-financial performance measures.

ManuCo's German and Polish subsidiaries use the parent-PMS in a functional way such as monitoring and identifying causes of negative target deviations. However, the Polish management accountants do not use the entire parent-PMS in a functional way. In fact, they use the targets of the parent-PMS only ceremonially as they consider them too high. This might be explained by the high uncertainty avoidance in Poland and the resulting preference for lower target levels (*Chow et al.* (1999), p. 448; *Schuler/Rogovsky* (1998), pp. 165-166; *van der Stede* (2003), p. 268; *Paik et al.* (2011), p. 651). In contrast to the Polish subsidiary, the German management accountants have developed a local-PMS. This is because they miss a performance measure in the parent-PMS indicating the amount of material that can be saved during production. However, since an optimal level cannot be specified in advance, the German management accountants do not set targets for this performance measure.

6.1.3   AgriCo case

6.1.3.1   Company profile and objectives of the parent-PMS

AgriCo is a world-leading producer and distributer of high-quality **agricultural machinery and equipment** such as harvesters and tractors. The family-owned MNC employs about 10,000 people worldwide and has production sites and sales offices in more than 15 countries. These foreign locations contribute to more than two thirds of AgriCo's total revenues of more than € 2.5 billion. This substantial share indicates a high importance of foreign markets for the MNC. When entering foreign markets, AgriCo relies mainly on acquiring or establishing wholly-owned subsidiaries rather than creating joint ventures with external partners.

AgriCo's organizational structure is characterized by a **direct reporting link** between the MNC's corporate management accounting department located at the German head office and AgriCo's subsidiaries (see Figure 6–11). The subsidiaries are further classified into production units and sales units. Production units are responsible for purchasing raw materials, research and development, and for manufacturing the MNC's various product types. Sales offices are responsible for selling the finished goods to external customers.

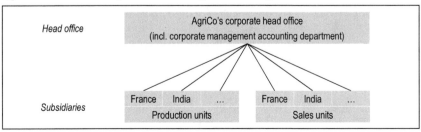

Figure 6–11: AgriCo's organizational structure

The interviews at AgriCo were conducted with experts from AgriCo's corporate head office and two foreign subsidiaries. At the head office level, interviews were conducted within the corporate management accounting department, which is in charge of developing and designing AgriCo's parent-PMS. In particular, the **Head of corporate management accounting** and **two of his employees** were interviewed. At the subsidiary level, interviews were conducted at the French and Indian subsidiaries.[115] The French subsidiary was acquired in the early 2000s from a French automotive producer and employs about 1,500 people. **Two French management accountants** were interviewed for examining the adoption of AgriCo's parent-PMS at this subsidiary. The Indian subsidiary was founded in 2008 and has about 400 employees. The adoption of the parent-PMS at the Indian subsidiary was explored by interviewing **the subsidiary's head of management accounting**. Table 6–7 summarizes the interview partners at AgriCo.

Title	Organizational level
Head of corporate management accounting	Head office
Corporate management accountant	Head office
Corporate management accountant	Head office
Local management accountant	Subsidiary France
Local management accountant	Subsidiary France
Head of local management accounting	Subsidiary India

Table 6–7: Interview partners at AgriCo

Objectives of AgriCo's parent-PMS

AgriCo's head office introduced the parent-PMS in 2004 as one part of a group-wide **"Production excellence system" (PES)**. The goal of the PES is to assure a high-quality production at low costs by continuously improving and standardizing the subsidiaries' production processes. The **standardized** parent-PMS serves two purposes. First, the parent-PMS shall provide the head office with information on the subsidiaries' performance for **facilitating decision-making**. In particular, the corporate management accountants use the information of the parent-PMS to evaluate the subsidiaries' target achievement and for resource allocation. Furthermore, by being a standardized system, the parent-PMS shall provide comparable information that allows to benchmark the subsidiaries.

Second, and even more important, the parent-PMS shall **influence the decisions** of the subsidiaries' employees:

---

[115] The interviews were conducted solely in production units. The rationale behind this is that AgriCo did not have a parent-PMS for sales units in place when the interviews were conducted. In fact, AgriCo's corporate management accountants have started to develop a parent-PMS for sales units in 2017. Given that this study focuses on parent-PMSs that are already fully implemented at subsidiaries, AgriCo's sales units are excluded from further analysis. This is in line with the selection criteria of this study (see chapter 5) and helps to eliminate effects arising from not (fully) implemented parent-PMSs.

"We want to achieve that our system [parent-PMS; added by the author] contains performance measures that can be used by local management to improve production [...]. Not only to look back by saying that was good or that was bad – the subsidiaries should be able to use the performance measures to steer production."

AgriCo – Corporate management accountant

Following the quote above, the corporate management accountants' intention is to design a parent-PMS that can be used by the subsidiaries' employees to control the effectiveness and efficiency of production processes. The subsidiaries' employees shall use the performance measures from the parent-PMS, for example, to monitor whether the production processes are executed in an optimal way.

6.1.3.2 Design of the parent-PMS

Performance measures

AgriCo's parent-PMS consists of **thirteen performance measures** that are used to evaluate the subsidiaries' performance (see Table 6–8). These performance measures stem from two measurement perspectives.

AgriCo's parent-PMS **does not include any financial performance measures**. For example, it does not contain performance measures on the cost of production (e.g., operational expenditures) or on the financial success of the subsidiaries (e.g., EBITDA). Thus, the corporate management accountants do not use the parent-PMS to assess the subsidiaries' financial performance. This is due to the fact that AgriCo's parent-PMS was implemented as part of the group-wide PES, which aims to standardize and improve production processes.

Concerning the subsidiaries' **non-financial performance**, AgriCo's parent-PMS includes performance measures from the internal process and employee perspective. The **internal process perspective** is covered by a total of **nine performance measures**. The first five performance measures (early hour failures, failures per audit, defective machine rate, rework rate, and rework time) reflect the MNC's self-image as a quality leader in agricultural machinery. Consequently, the first five performance measures relate to the number of failures that are made during the production and the time that is needed to fix them. As the sixth performance measure in this perspective, the standard-time reduction is examined, which is in accordance with the PES' idea of continuously improving production processes. In addition, the parent-PMS includes the stock coverage, which indicates how many days the production can continue with the current stock level. Finally, two performance measures are related to the delivery punctuality and failure rate of external suppliers. Since AgriCo's subsidiaries are dependent on deliveries from external partners (e.g., special parts or raw materials), these two performance measures shall ensure that incoming materials are of good quality and that they are delivered on time:

"External Supplier Reliability is important for the stability of processes and the quality of production. Missing parts lead to failures and rework what causes avoidable costs."

AgriCo – Internal guideline on the parent-PMS

When looking at the performance measures from the internal process perspective, it is evident that the performance measures relate only to production processes. Thus, the parent-PMS does not cover any other processes that are conducted within the subsidiaries (e.g., research and development or administrative processes).[116]

Measurement perspective	Performance measures
Financial perspective:	-
Customer perspective:	-
Internal process perspective:	Early hour failures, failures per audit, defective machine rate, rework rate, rework time, standard-time reduction, stock coverage, suppliers' defect rate, suppliers' delivery punctuality
Employee perspective:	Absenteeism rate, accident rate, suggestions from employees, employee productivity

Table 6–8: Performance measures included in AgriCo's parent-PMS

The reason for including performance measures from the **employee perspective** is that the corporate management accountants assume that a successful production can only be achieved with motivated employees:

> *"Production can only be successful, if employees are motivated and if they help to continuously improve and optimize processes at their work place."*

AgriCo – Internal presentation on the parent-PMS

The corporate management accountants selected **four performance measures**, which address the employee perspective. The first two performance measures (absenteeism rate and accident rate) relate to the number of days per month that the subsidiaries' employees are not at work. While the absenteeism rate refers to the absence due to illness, the accident rate measures absent days that are caused by work-related accidents. The third performance measure covers the number of suggestions that are made by the subsidiaries' employees per month. To collect this performance measure, each subsidiary is required to install a proposal system that allows the employees to make suggestions for process improvements. Finally, the productivity of production workers is measured by relating the number of productive hours (hours of maintenance, travel, training, or breaks are not counted as productive) to the total hours of attendance.

---

[116] This is due to the fact that the parent-PMS has been implemented as one part of the group-wide PES, which focuses on improving and standardizing production processes within AgriCo.

Targets

AgriCo defines **budget-based targets** for each of the thirteen performance measures. These targets are derived from the group-wide annual budgeting process, in which AgriCo's overall targets are defined. As part of this budgeting process, AgriCo's head office negotiates target levels for the non-financial performance measures of the parent-PMS with the subsidiaries. These target levels serve as the basis for defining the MNC's overall targets. The target levels for the performance measures of the parent-PMS are negotiated by **counter-flow planning** between the head office and the subsidiaries. In this counter-flow planning, the subsidiaries' management accountants make the first proposal in June of each year.[117] These proposals include suggested target levels and explanations to justify the target levels. The targets are only determined on an aggregated level for the whole subsidiary, but not on product or team level. The subsidiaries' proposals are subsequently reviewed at AgriCo's head office. Based on this review, the head office creates counter-proposals that are discussed with the subsidiaries in budget meetings:

> *"When we are receiving the proposals from our subsidiaries, we review them with our corporate production and quality management departments. Based on these considerations, we create a counter-proposal that is then discussed in budget meetings with each subsidiary. In these meetings, we agree on target levels for those performance measures for which both sides have different opinions."*
>
> *AgriCo – Corporate management accountant*

The budget meetings are held either at the head office or as web conferences. In these meetings, the management accountants from the head office and the subsidiaries agree on **target levels for each performance measure**. If no consensus is reached, a committee, which is responsible for the PES, is involved to take a final decision on target levels.

After the final target levels are determined, the subsidiaries' management accountants are expected to define **sub-targets** for production managers, team leaders, and production workers. For example, a team leader might receive target levels for performance measures such as employee productivity or early-hour failures within his area of responsibility. It is very important for the corporate management accountants that the target levels are clearly communicated within the subsidiaries. Therefore, the subsidiaries' management accountants shall discuss the performance measures and corresponding targets with their managers:

> *"In order to involve all employees, results on the performance measures should be communicated on all levels within the production sites. [...] [T]he local management should encourage the usage of the performance measures in order to achieve long term-oriented efficiency. That's why the results of the performance measures should be integrated in existing team meetings as one discussion point. For example, the foreman should regularly talk with his people about the absenteeism rate or productivity."*
>
> *AgriCo – Internal guideline on the parent-PMS*

---

[117] AgriCo's business year deviates from the calendar year and covers the period from October 1st to September 30th of the following year.

In addition, AgriCo's head office recommend the subsidiaries' management accountants to show the actual and budgeted results on movable walls at the production halls. This shall further increase the visibility of targets and shall ensure that the subsidiaries' employees try to achieve the budgeted targets.

AgriCo's corporate management accountants **evaluate the achievement** of the budget-based targets by written reports, review meetings, and an award ceremony (see Figure 6–12). Two types of written reports exist, a performance report and a benchmarking report. The **monthly performance report** shows positive and negative deviations between actual performance and target levels. In fact, it displays both the relative target achievement for each performance measure and the average target achievement for all performance measures. The **benchmarking report**, which is prepared by AgriCo's corporate management accountants on a monthly basis, compares the relative target achievement for each performance measure among the subsidiaries. Furthermore, the benchmarking report contains a ranking of the subsidiaries based on their relative target achievements. Thus, the subsidiary's employees can easily assess how their subsidiary performed vis-à-vis the other subsidiaries.

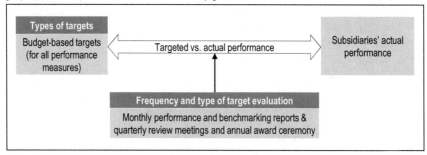

Figure 6–12: Target setting and target evaluation at AgriCo

In addition to these monthly performance reports, the budget-based targets are evaluated in **quarterly review meetings.** In these review meetings, the Head of the corporate production & quality management, the Head of corporate management accounting, the subsidiaries' management, the subsidiaries' management accountants, and members of AgriCo's owning family take part. The subsidiaries' management must comment on the best and worst three performance measures (based on relative target achievement of budgeted targets). The attendance of members of AgriCo's owning family in the quarterly review meetings shows the high importance that is devoted to budget-based targets at the MNC. Furthermore, AgriCo's head office organizes an **annual award ceremony,** which is attended by corporate and local management accountants, the management board, and members of AgriCo's owning family. In this ceremony, the three subsidiaries with the highest relative target achievements are awarded. This award ceremony shall further motivate the subsidiaries' employees to reach a high relative target achievement:

> "In this ceremony, we award the best three subsidiaries. [...]. The opportunity to get on the podium shall motivate them to achieve the best performance."
>
> AgriCo – Corporate management accountant

Link to rewards

Two groups of AgriCo's subsidiaries' employees have a variable component in their remuneration: The subsidiaries' management and employees involved in production processes (e.g., production managers, team leaders of production teams, and production workers).

For the **subsidiaries' management**, the payment of the variable component depends on achieving the following **three** targets:

- CFROI target of AgriCo,
- ROS target of the respective subsidiary, and
- personal targets.[118]

As this list shows, the performance measures of the parent-PMS are not used for determining the bonus of the subsidiaries' management. In fact, the first two targets are not included as performance measures in the parent-PMS. Thus, AgriCo's head office uses other performance measures than those contained in the parent-PMS for determining the bonus of the subsidiaries' management. This is also true for the individual targets, which are linked to qualitative targets rather than to performance measures from the parent-PMS. Therefore, there is **no link** between the performance measures and targets from the parent-PMS and the remuneration of the subsidiaries' management.

For the subsidiaries' **employees involved in production processes**, the bonus payment depends on performance measures from the **internal process perspective** of the parent-PMS (e.g., early hour failures, defective machine rate, and rework rate). Thus, the performance measures of the parent-PMS are linked to the remuneration of these employees. However, not all performance measures of AgriCo's parent-PMS are relevant for determining the bonus payments, but only the performance measures of the internal process perspective.

Concluding, the compensation of the subsidiaries' management is not linked to AgriCo's parent-PMS. The bonus of these employees rather depends on performance measures, which are not included in the parent-PMS, such as the CFROI of the MNC. For the subsidiaries' employees involved in production processes, the parent-PMS is linked to the compensation. In fact, the bonus of these employees depends on the internal process measures of AgriCo's parent-PMS.

IT infrastructure

The IT infrastructure of AgriCo's parent-PMS consists of ERP systems and BI systems (see Figure 6–13). ERP systems are implemented at each subsidiary. These ERP systems serve to collect and store data on the thirteen performance measures. Even though all ERP systems stem from the same EPR vendor (SAP), the ERP systems implemented at AgriCo's

---

[118] The extent to which these three targets are included in the bonus calculation depends on the position of the employees in the subsidiary's organization chart. The first two targets tend to become more important the higher the employee ranks in this hierarchy. The personal goals therefore play a greater role for a subsidiary's department head than for the management team. This is to reflect the fact that employees of lower hierarchical ranks can only indirectly influence AgriCo's CFROI and the ROS of their subsidiary.

subsidiaries are not identical. Instead, each subsidiary has **its own configuration of SAP**. Thus, AgriCo does not have a single, integrated ERP system that is used by all entities of the MNC. There are two reasons for this. First, some subsidiaries were acquired from other companies. In this case, AgriCo has often simply taken the SAP configuration that has already been in place at the acquired company. Second, the subsidiaries have different sizes. For cost reasons, smaller production companies have received simplified versions of SAP.

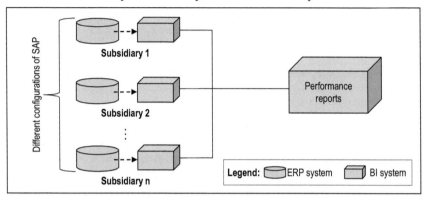

Figure 6–13: IT infrastructure of AgriCo's parent-PMS

The data from the ERP systems flows into a uniform BI system. This BI system serves two purposes. The first purpose is the **calculation of performance measures**. Based on the data from the ERP systems, the BI system automatically calculates values for AgriCo's performance measures. However, this automatic calculation of performance measure values only works for about two-thirds of the thirteen performance measures. For the remaining performance measures, the subsidiaries' management accountants must calculate the values manually.[119] As explained by the Head of corporate management accounting, this is due to missing data in the ERP systems:

> *"We are trying to define performance measures that can directly and automatically be calculated by our BW tool based on our SAP database. This is what we would like to have for all our performance measures. However, there are also some performance measures that have to be calculated manually by our subsidiaries because some data is not available from the SAP database."*

> *AgriCo – Head of corporate management accounting*

The second purpose of the BI system is to serve as a **shared information tool** that can be used by both corporate and local management accountants. In fact, the BI system automatically creates performance reports on each subsidiary. Therefore, both corporate and local management accountants can use the BI system to obtain performance information on the

---

[119] Examples of performance measures that have to be calculated manually are employee productivity, re-work time, and standard time reduction.

subsidiaries.[120] Furthermore, corporate management accountants use the BI system as a basis for creating the monthly benchmarking report.

6.1.3.3 Adoption of the parent-PMS

6.1.3.3.1 Adoption at AgriCo France

The management accountants at the French subsidiary acknowledge the importance of AgriCo's parent-PMS for the head office. In fact, they stress that the parent-PMS is necessary and useful for AgriCo's head office to get a consolidated picture of the subsidiaries' performance und to benchmark the subsidiaries among each other. Consequently, the subsidiary's management accountants do not reject to provide performance information to the head office. For example, they report the thirteen performance measures on a monthly basis to the head office and attend the quarterly review meetings. In addition, the French management accountants take part in the budgeting process, for example by proposing target levels for the thirteen performance measures:

> *"There are thirteen performance measures that we have to report to our head office. [...] We use them to build the budget and for discussing our results with our head office."*
>
> *AgriCo – Management accountant (France)*

However, the parent-PMS plays only a minor role in controlling the French subsidiary. This is demonstrated by the fact that the French management accountants do not discuss the performance measures of the parent-PMS with the subsidiary's managers. For example, the management accountants do not discuss the number of suggestions from employees with the HR manager or the defective machine rate with the production manager. Thus, the subsidiary's management accountants collect data and report the performance measures of the parent-PMS, but they do not use them at their subsidiary. This is because they perceive the parent-PMS as a mere benchmarking tool that is useful for AgriCo's head office but that is **not useful** to control the subsidiary:

> *"The performance measures defined by our head office are more a way to make comparisons between different subsidiaries – but they are not a way to make some progress. That is why we have our own initiative [Manufacturing Balanced Scorecard; added by the author]."*
>
> *AgriCo – Management accountant (France)*

Existence and design of local-PMS

Since the French management accountants do not perceive the parent-PMS to be useful for controlling their subsidiary, they have developed a **local-PMS**. They refer to this self-developed system as "Manufacturing Balanced Scorecard". The local-PMS consists of **ten performance measures**, which relate to all four measurement perspectives (see Table 6–9).

---

[120] Whereas corporate management accountants have access to performance data from all subsidiaries, the subsidiaries' management accountants can only see the data of their own subsidiary.

In contrast to the parent-PMS, the local-PMS addresses the subsidiary's **financial performance** by including **one financial performance measure**, namely the operational expenditures. The French management accountants include this performance measure to increase the cost awareness of the production managers and production workers.

With regard to the subsidiary's **non-financial performance**, the local-PMS includes performance measures regarding the customer, internal process, and employee perspectives. The **customer perspective** of the local-PMS contains **two performance measures**. First, the order backlog indicates how many ordered machines still have to be produced and delivered to the sales units. The French management accountants include the order backlog in the local-PMS to have an early indicator for the subsidiary's future sales revenues. Second, the management accountants examine the delivery punctuality, which shows how many of the produced machines are delivered to the sales units on time.

Measurement perspective	Performance measures
Financial perspective:	*Operational expenditures (L)*
Customer perspective:	*Order backlog (L), delivery punctuality (L)*
Internal process perspective:	Standard-time reduction (LP), rework rate (D), stock coverage (D), *non-personnel production costs (L), costs of scrap (L),* *costs of product launching (L)*
Employee perspective:	Employee productivity (LP)
Legend: (L): Performance measures included in the local-PMS only (highlighted in italics) (LP): Performance measures included in both the local-PMS and the parent-PMS (D): Different definition in the local-PMS than in the parent-PMS	

Table 6–9: Performance measures included in the local-PMS (AgriCo France)

The **internal process perspective** is covered by **six performance measures** in the local-PMS. One of these six performance measures, the standard-time reduction, is also included in the parent-PMS. Two further performance measures (rework costs and stock coverage) are based on performance measures from the parent-PMS but are **changed in their definitions**. For example, in the local-PMS, the stock coverage is not expressed in the number of machines, but in the machines' monetary value (in € million; valued by the costs of goods sold). The remaining three performance measures of the process perspective (non-personnel production costs, costs of scrap, and costs of product launching) are contained exclusively in the local-PMS. By determining the non-personnel production costs, the subsidiary's management accountants try to create awareness among the production managers and production workers for the efficient use of materials. The same intention is pursued with the costs of scrap, which indicates the waste of material in production (in € million). In addition, the local-PMS contains the costs of product launching, which the management accountants use to determine how cost-effectively new products are developed by the local R&D department. Unlike AgriCo's parent-PMS, the local-PMS therefore not only relates to production processes, but also to product development executed by the local R&D department.

As regards the **employee perspective**, the local-PMS contains **one performance measure**, namely employee productivity. The subsidiary's management accountants have taken this performance measures from the parent-PMS. Other employee measures from the parent-PMS (absenteeism rate, accident rate, and suggestions from employees) are not included in the local-PMS of the French subsidiary.

The subsidiary's management accountants set **targets** for all ten performance measures of the local-PMS. The types of targets that are set differ for performance measures that are included in both the parent-PMS and the local-PMS and for ones that are only included in the local-PMS. For the former, the budget-based targets of AgriCo's parent-PMS are used. Thus, the target levels for the employee productivity and standard time reduction are derived from AgriCo's annual budgeting process. The targets for the remaining eight performance measures are set locally by the French subsidiary. This is done in **yearly budget meetings** between the subsidiary's management accountant and the subsidiary's management. In this budget meeting, the participants discuss and agree on target levels for the eight performance measures. After the meeting, a manager is assigned to each performance measure, who is then responsible that the target level is reached. For example, the head of the R&D department is responsible for the product launching costs.

The **target achievement** is evaluated based on a local, written performance report and monthly review meetings. Thus, the French management accountants do not use the performance reports of the parent-PMS but **create their own performance report**. This monthly performance report contains the actual values for the ten performance measures and highlights deviations to the target levels. In addition, the report contains a column in which the responsible person has to describe actions plans that aim to improve the performance. The written report is also the basis for **monthly review meetings**, in which the subsidiary's management accountants and the managers who are responsible for the performance measures participate. In these meetings, the managers have to comment on and explain negative deviations from the target levels. Figure 6–14 summarizes the target setting and target evaluation.

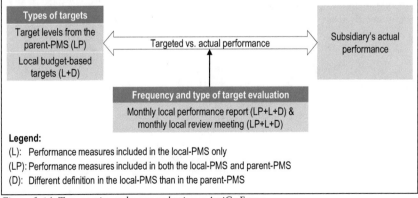

Figure 6–14: Target setting and target evaluation at AgriCo France

The French management accountants **do not** link the performance measures of the local-PMS to the **rewards** of the subsidiary's employees. Thus, the performance measures of the local-PMS are not used for determining the bonus payments of the subsidiary's management or production workers.

The **IT infrastructure** of the local-PMS bases on the ERP system and the BI system of the parent-PMS (see Figure 6–15). From these two systems, the subsidiary's management accountants extract the required data for calculating the performance measures of the local-PMS. Based on this data input, the performance measures are then calculated in a **spreadsheet template** (Microsoft Excel), which the French management accountants have created additionally. This spreadsheet template is also used for reporting the performance measures within the subsidiary.

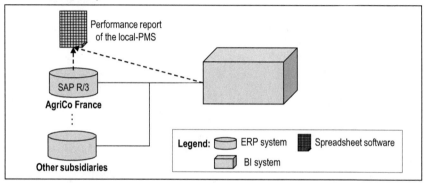

Figure 6–15: IT infrastructure of the local-PMS (AgriCo France)

6.1.3.3.2   Adoption at AgriCo India

At the Indian subsidiary, the management accountants stress the high importance of AgriCo's parent-PMS within the group:

> *"The PES and the relating performance measures have a very strong significance in the group and are also very strongly pushed by our head office. Not only from the corporate management accounting department, but also from corporate production. And there are also review meetings with the head office, at which the owner of the group is present. Thus, this system has an outstanding position within our group."*

> *AgriCo – Head of management accounting (India)*

Given the high standing of the parent-PMS within the group, the management accountants do not refuse to report performance information to AgriCo's head office, for example by regularly reporting the performance measures. Furthermore, the Indian management accountants use the performance information of parent-PMS for the following two purposes. First, they use them to **monitor** whether the subsidiary meets its targets. In case of negative target deviations, the management accountants prepare deviation analyses, which are discussed with the responsible managers. Furthermore, the management accountants present the major target deviations to the subsidiary's management.

Second, the subsidiary's management accountants use the parent-PMS to **draw the managers' attention** to the performance measures and targets. For this purpose, the management accountants assign a manager for each performance measure, who is then responsible that the targets of the parent-PMS are achieved. For example, the head of the local production department is responsible for the rework rate and standard-time reduction.

However, the Indian management accountants **do not use all performance measures** of the parent-PMS for monitoring and raising the managers' attention:

"In general, we use all performance measures. However, some of them with more and others with less emphasis. The absenteeism rate makes no sense for India. In Germany, if a lot of people are ill, I know something is wrong. But in India, people don't stay at home unless they really can't come to work because they broke a leg or something. There is no such thing as paid holidays in India. Thus, the absenteeism rate makes no sense here. We only report it to Germany, because we have to."

AgriCo – Head of management accounting (India)

As expressed by the quote above, the subsidiary's management accountants do not consider the absenteeism rate to be meaningful at the Indian subsidiary. They argue that this performance measure is meaningless, because employees in India are hardly absent from work. Furthermore, labor costs are much lower in an emerging economy such as India than in, for example, Germany. Consequently, the subsidiary's management accountants pay less attention the absenteeism rate. For example, they do not create deviation analyses for this performance measure and do not discuss it with the subsidiary's managers.

Existence and design of local-PMS

The Indian management accountants have developed a **local-PMS**, which they call "Cockpit report". This local-PMS consist of **15 performance measures** stemming from all four measurement perspectives (see Table 6–10). In contrast to AgriCo's parent-PMS, the local-PMS covers the subsidiary's **financial performance** by including **one financial performance measure**, namely the subsidiary's sales revenues. The management accountants have selected this performance measure to be able to monitor the sales revenues that are generated by selling the finished machines to AgriCo's sales units.

Concerning the subsidiaries' **non-financial performance**, the local-PMS addresses the customer, internal process, and employee perspectives. Concerning the **customer** perspective, the management accountants examine the delivery punctuality, which indicates the percentage of machines that is delivered on time to the sales units. For the **internal processes**, the subsidiary's management accountants look at nine performance measures that are also included in the parent-PMS.

With respect to the **employee** perspective, **three** performance measures are taken from the parent-PMS (accident rate, suggestions from employees, and employee productivity).[121] Of

---

[121] Since the Indian management accountants do not perceive the absenteeism rate to be useful at subsidiary level, they do not include this performance measure in the local-PMS.

these three performance measures, the **definition** of one performance measure **was changed**, namely the employee productivity:

> *"For employee productivity, there is always a discussion about what are productive hours and what are not. We therefore prefer to look at the attendance hours that we have to produce a machine."*

AgriCo – Head of management accounting (India)

As expressed by the quote above, the Indian management accountants do not compare the productive with the non-productive hours for determining the employee productivity, but simply add up the hours that it takes to produce the machines.

Measurement perspective	Performance measures
Financial perspective:	*Sales revenues (L)*
Customer perspective:	*Delivery punctuality (L)*
Employee perspective:	Accident rate (LP), suggestions from employees (LP), employee productivity (D)
Internal process perspective:	Early hour failures (LP), failures per audit (LP), defective machine rate (LP), rework rate (LP), rework time (LP), standard-time reduction (LP), stock coverage (LP), suppliers' defect rate (LP), suppliers' delivery accuracy (LP)
Legend:	
(L): Performance measures included in the local-PMS only (highlighted in italics)	
(LP): Performance measures included in both the local-PMS and the parent-PMS	
(D): Different definition in the local-PMS than in the parent-PMS	

Table 6–10: Performance measures included in the local-PMS (AgriCo India)

For all 15 performance measures of the local-PMS, the subsidiary's management accountants set **targets**. For the performance measures that are taken from the parent-PMS, the **target levels from the parent-PMS** are used. For the two additional performance measures (sales revenues and delivery punctuality) and the modified employee productivity, the subsidiary's management accountants define **own, local targets**. These local targets are defined in a yearly budget meeting between the subsidiary's management, the Head of management accounting, the Head of production, and the Head of HR. In this meeting, the participants agree on target levels for the 15 performance measures of the local-PMS.

The **target achievement** is evaluated based on a local, written performance report and monthly review meetings. The subsidiary's management accountants create the local **performance report** at the beginning of each month. It contains actual values of all performance measures of the local-PMS. Furthermore, the report shows the deviations to the target levels. The written report is also used in the **monthly review meetings** between the subsidiary's management accountants and managers. In these meetings, the managers have to comment and explain negative deviations from the target levels. Figure 6–16 summarizes the types of targets and the target evaluation of the French local-PMS.

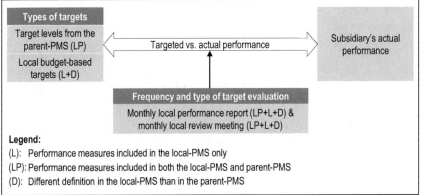

Figure 6–16: Target setting and target evaluation at AgriCo India

At the Indian subsidiary, the management accountants **do not** link the performance measures of the local-PMS to the **rewards** of the subsidiary's employees. Thus, the performance measures of the local-PMS are not used for determining the bonus payments of the subsidiary's management or production workers.

As an **IT infrastructure** for the local-PMS, the Indian management accountants build on the IT systems of the parent-PMS (see Figure 6–17). In fact, the subsidiary's management accountants use the ERP system and the BI system to extract the input data for the performance measures of the local-PMS. Afterwards, they transfer this data into a **self-developed, additional spreadsheet template**. This template is used to calculate the performance measures and serves as a basis for the local performance report. Furthermore, the management accountants use this template to report the performance measures of the local-PMS within the subsidiary.

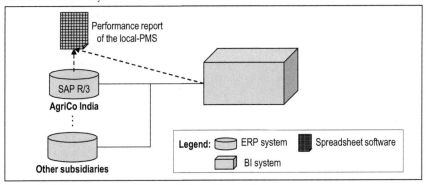

Figure 6–17: IT infrastructure of the local-PMS (AgriCo India)

6.1.3.4 Summary

In **summary**, AgriCo's parent-PMS consists of thirteen performance measures, which relate to the subsidiaries' employees and internal processes. For these thirteen performance measures, the budget-based targets are set, which are negotiated between the corporate head office and the subsidiaries. For evaluating the target achievement, the corporate management accountants rely on a monthly performance report, a benchmarking report, and quarterly review meetings between AgriCo's head office and the subsidiaries. The performance measures and targets of the parent-PMS are not linked to the remuneration of the subsidiaries' management, but to the remuneration of production managers and production workers. In fact, the bonus of the employees involved in production processes depends on the internal process measures of the parent-PMS. Concerning the IT infrastructure, AgriCo's corporate management accountants have implemented ERP systems from different vendors and a group-wide BI system.

The parent-PMS is differently adopted at the French and Indian subsidiaries. The French management accountants contest the relevance of the parent-PMS at subsidiary level and therefore do not use it for internal purposes. In contrast, the Indian management accountants generally see the value of the parent-PMS. They only use one performance measure (absenteeism rate) ceremonially by arguing that it is irrelevant at India due to the low level of labor costs. Both the French and Indian management accountants have developed a local-PMS. However, the local-PMS of the French subsidiary differs to a greater extent from the parent PMS than the local system of the Indian subsidiary. For example, the French local-PMS consists of several performance measures that are not included in the parent-PMS. This is due to the fact that the French management accountants do not see the value of the parent-PMS while the Indian management accountants only miss some performance measures in the parent-PMS.

6.1.4 ChemCo case

6.1.4.1 Company profile and objectives of the parent-PMS

ChemCo operates in the **chemical** industry. The case company is listed at a major German stock exchange. It has several business units, ranging from agricultural solutions, chemicals, coatings for the automotive industry to nutrition and health care solutions.[122] By employing over 100,000 people worldwide and generating more than € 70 billion revenues, ChemCo is a large player in the chemical industry. The MNC has production and sales sites in over 80 countries. These foreign locations contribute to about two third of ChemCo's total revenues.

ChemCo's **organizational structure** includes different types of head offices (see Figure 6–18). At the top of the organizational structure is the corporate head office, which includes the MNC's management board. At the second level, each business unit has its own head office. The business unit Automotive coatings has regional head offices at the third level

---

[122] In this study, the focus is on business unit Automotive coatings. This business unit contributes to about five percent of ChemCo's overall revenues.

that are responsible for specific geographical regions (e.g., EMEA and North America). At the bottom of this organizational structure are the subsidiaries, which are responsible for selling the different product types in their respective region.

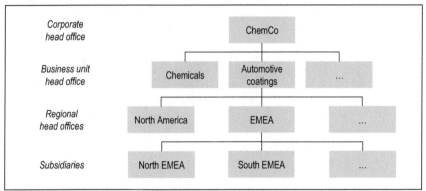

Figure 6–18: ChemCo's organizational structure

At ChemCo, interviews were conducted with experts from the head office of Automotive coatings, the regional head office of EMEA, and from two foreign subsidiaries. At the head office level, **three management accountants** were interviewed – one from the business unit head office and two from the regional head office. At the subsidiary level, interviews were conducted within the subsidiary North EMEA and the subsidiary South EMEA. The subsidiary North EMEA is responsible for selling ChemCo's products into the Nordic countries and the UK, while the subsidiary South EMEA sells the products into twelve countries from South-East Europe. At both subsidiaries, the respective **Head of management accounting** was interviewed. Table 6–11 summarizes the interview partners at ChemCo.

Title	Organizational level
Management accountant	Business unit head office of Automotive coatings
Head of management accounting	Regional head office EMEA
Management accountant	Regional head office EMEA
Head of management accounting	Subsidiary North EMEA
Head of management accounting	Subsidiary South EMEA

Table 6–11: Interview partners at ChemCo

Objectives of ChemCo's parent-PMS

The parent-PMS of ChemCo is **standardized**. Therefore, it applies to all business units and subsidiaries in the same way and does not differentiate, for example, between domestic and foreign subsidiaries or between different geographical regions such as EMEA or North America. In every newly founded or acquired subsidiary, the parent-PMS is implemented at that subsidiary to ensure that all subsidiaries of the business unit are subject to the same system. With the standardized parent-PMS, ChemCo's management accountants pursue **two objectives**, which are equally important.

First, the management accountants of ChemCo's head offices use the parent-PMS to obtain performance information from their subsidiaries to **facilitate decision-making**. In the head offices of the business units, the management accountants use this information to create a consolidated picture of their business unit's performance. Furthermore, the parent-PMS serves as a basis or supporting the operational and strategic decisions of the business unit's management. In addition, the head offices of the business units use the parent-PMS to benchmark the performance of the different regions. At ChemCo's corporate head office, the management accountants use the performance reports of the parent-PMS to obtain a picture on the group performance.

Second, the management accountants of ChemCo's head offices use the parent-PMS also for creating a consistent understanding of performance measurement within the group:

"We all want to march in one direction. Therefore, it is necessary that we talk about the same things. If you think of the senior managers, who are in country A for one week and in country B the other week – we always talk about the same things."

ChemCo – Head of regional management accounting

As expressed by the quote above, the standardized parent-PMS shall ensure that the employees of all subsidiaries and head offices use the same performance measures. In this vein, the parent-PMS shall facilitate the communication between the different entities of the MNC and shall ensure that all entities and employees work towards the same goals. Thus, ChemCo's head offices uses the parent-PMS also to **influence the subsidiaries' decisions**.

6.1.4.2 Design of the parent-PMS

Performance measures

The parent-PMS of ChemCo comprises **eight performance measures** that are used for evaluating the subsidiaries' performance. As Table 6–12 shows, these performance measures relate to two measurement perspectives.

Measurement perspective	Performance measures
Financial perspective:	Gross sales, net sales, gross profit, fixed SG&A expenses, travel expenses, advertisement expenses, EBITDA
Customer perspective:	-
Internal process perspective:	-
Employee perspective:	Accident rate

Table 6–12: Performance measures included in ChemCo's parent-PMS

ChemCo's parent-PMS **contains almost exclusively financial performance measures.** In fact, **seven** out of eight performance measures relate to the subsidiaries' financial performance. First, by including the gross sales and net sales, ChemCo's head offices evaluate the subsidiaries' success in selling products to external customers. Furthermore, the management accountants of the head offices examine the subsidiaries' gross profit, which is determined by deducting the cost of goods sold and the variable SG&A expenses from the net sales. In addition, they look at the subsidiaries' fixed SG&A expenses to make the subsidiaries aware of their generated expenses. Since travel and advertisement expenses account for a large amount of the fixed SG&A expenses, these two aspects are included as two separate performance measures in the parent-PMS. Finally, the parent-PMS includes the EBITDA for indicating the subsidiaries' profits.

The **employee** perspective is addressed by **one performance measure,** namely the accident rate. This performance measure is defined as the number of accidents which cause lost time per one million worked hours. The inclusion of the accident rate in the parent-PMS is due to the fact that at ChemCo a high importance is assigned to occupational safety. This is the case, because the MNC operates in the chemicals sector, where occupational safety is monitored by governmental and non-governmental organizations.

Targets

ChemCo sets **budget-based targets** for the seven financial performance measures.[123] These budget-based targets are the result of an annual budgeting process, in which the target levels are negotiated by **counter-flow planning.** This counter-flow planning starts with the management board releasing basic assumptions on future sales and profit trends of the MNC. Based on these basic assumptions, the management accountants of each subsidiary have to propose target levels for the seven financial performance measures. Since 2017, they are no longer required to propose target levels on customer or product level. They only have to submit an aggregated target level for each financial performance measure on subsidiary level. This change in the budgeting process was introduced because of several top-down adjustments in the budgeting process that thwarted the detailed local planning:

> *"[...] In the past, it was a very detailed bottom-up approach. Very intensive questions were asked about what the subsidiaries expect, in some cases even at customer level [...]. A great deal of energy was put into this from both sides [head offices and subsidiaries; added by the author]. However, a top-down budget was almost given by the business unit head office, which was then returned to the subsidiaries and partly ensured that the entire local planning process was actually no longer tenable, so that the subsidiaries had to start from scratch again."*

> *ChemCo – Management accountant for regional business units*

Based on the subsidiaries' proposed target levels, the regional head offices prepare a consolidated picture for their region and forward it to business unit's head office. There, the management accountants critically review the proposed target levels and either approve these

---

[123] For the accident rate, target levels are not determined for each subsidiary. Instead, a target level for this performance measure exists only at the level of the whole MNC.

targets or make a top-down adjustment. In case of a top-down adjustment, the regional head offices have to decide how to distribute the additionally required target contributions among the subsidiaries. If the management accountants from the business unit's head office approve the proposed target levels, they forward them to ChemCo's corporate head office. There, the corporate management accountants consolidate the target levels and present the consolidated picture to the MNC's management board. The management board approves the overall budget or makes top-down adjustments. In case of the former, the corporate management accountants communicate the final target levels to the business units' head offices, the regions' head offices and the subsidiaries.

The **achievement of the budget-based targets** is evaluated based on monthly performance reports, a benchmarking report, and ad-hoc review meetings. ChemCo uses **two different performance reports**. The first report is jointly created by the business unit's head offices and the regional head offices and is sent on a monthly basis to the subsidiaries. It shows actual and targeted values for five financial performance measures, namely gross sales, net sales, consolidated gross profit, fixed SG&A expenses, EBITDA.[124] The second report, which is called travel and advertisement (T&A) report, is prepared on a monthly basis by one of ChemCo's shared service centers.[125] It includes the actual and targeted values on the two remaining financial performance measures, namely travel expenses and advertising expenses. In addition to these performance reports, the business unit's management accountants prepare a **monthly benchmarking report** and send it to all regional head offices and to all subsidiaries. In this report, the performance of the different regions (e.g., EMEA or North America) concerning the financial and non-financial performance measures of the parent-PMS is compared. In fact, the benchmarking report shows the actual values for all performance measures for all regions. Furthermore, it contains a ranking of regions based on the achieved gross profit for the respective month:

> *"We compare the regions based on the achieved gross profit and share this information within the whole business unit. Everyone can then see very transparently, as with a Bundesliga [German soccer league; added by the author] table, where things are going well and where there are difficulties."*

> *ChemCo – Head of regional management accounting*

Besides these written reports, target evaluation is also carried out trough **ad-hoc review meetings**. These review meetings, which are held by phone or web conferences, are scheduled by the head offices' management accountants in case they have questions or comments on the subsidiaries' performance. Figure 6–19 summarizes the target setting and target evaluation at ChemCo.

---

[124] This report only shows the aggregated values for the five performance measures on subsidiary level and no values on customer or product level. There is another report for these details, which is also provided to the subsidiaries on a monthly basis. However, since targets are not set based on customer or product level, this detailed report is not used to evaluate subsidiaries' target achievements but is intended to provide the subsidiaries with a more detailed insight on their performance.

[125] The report is prepared by the shared service center to reduce the workload on management accountants in the head offices.

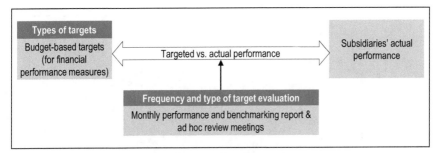

Figure 6–19: Target setting and target evaluation at ChemCo

Link to rewards

At ChemCo, two groups of the subsidiaries' employees are eligible to bonus payments. The subsidiaries' management and the subsidiaries' sales staff. The bonus payment of the **subsidiaries' management** depends on **two aspects**:

- ROI of ChemCo and
- personal targets.

The first aspect captures the financial success of the whole MNC, which is expressed by the performance measure ROI, which is not included in ChemCo's parent-PMS. The second aspect relates to the personal success of the subsidiaries' management, which are determined by ChemCo's management board. These personal targets are also not linked to performance measures from the parent-PMS. Consequently, there is no link between the performance measures and the case company's parent-PMS and the remuneration of the subsidiaries' management and executive employees.

The bonus payment of the **sales staff** depends on subsidiaries' **net sales.** Since this performance measure is included in the parent-PMS, there is a link between the remuneration of the sales staff and ChemCo's parent-PMS. However, for rewarding the sales staff, only one performance measure of the parent-PMS is used. Thus, the other seven performance measures are not used to determine the bonus payment for the sales staff.

Concluding, the compensation of the subsidiaries' management is not linked to ChemCo's parent-PMS. The bonus payment to these employees rather depends on performance measures that are not included in the parent-PMS, such as the ROI. For the subsidiaries' sales staff, there is a link between the parent-PMS and the compensation. In fact, the bonus payment of the sales staff depends on the net sales of the respective subsidiary.

IT infrastructure

The IT infrastructure of ChemCo's parent-PMS consists of ERP systems, BI systems, and spreadsheets (see Figure 6–20).

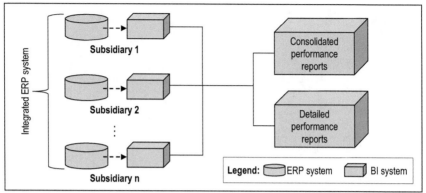

Figure 6–20: IT infrastructure of ChemCo's parent-PMS

ChemCo uses an **integrated ERP system** (SAP R/3) that is implemented in a standardized way throughout the whole MNC:

> *"At [ChemCo; added by the author], we have a uniform SAP system, a single ERP system. This is the single source of truth and is then transferred into different business warehouse systems."*

> *ChemCo – Head of regional management accounting*

This integrated ERP system serves as a shared database and contains all data necessary for calculating values for the eight performance measures included in ChemCo's parent-PMS.

From the ERP system, the data is transmitted to two different BI systems. These BI systems **automatically** generate the values for the eight performance measures. ChemCo's management accountants therefore do not have to calculate performance measure values manually but can retrieve them from the BI systems. The two BI systems differ with regard to the level of detail of performance measure values. The first BI system ("aggregated system") displays **aggregated** performance values on subsidiary level. For example, it shows the net sales or advertising expenses per subsidiary. This aggregated BI system is the basis for preparing the excel-based reports such as the performance report and the benchmarking report. The second BI system ("detailed system") displays the values not only at subsidiary level but also at customer and product level. It was primarily developed for the subsidiaries and is intended to provide the subsidiaries' management accountants with a **detailed insight** into the performance of the subsidiary. The subsidiaries' management accountants can use the detailed BI system, for example, to see which customers or products have contributed to the net sales.

6.1.4.3   Adoption of the parent-PMS

6.1.4.3.1   Adoption at ChemCo North EMEA

At the subsidiary North EMEA, the parent-PMS is used for several purposes. First, the subsidiary's management accountants use the performance reports to **monitor** the achievement of the target levels from the parent-PMS. This is done at the beginning of each month, when the management accountants receive the results of the previous month. They highlight positive and negative deviations from the target levels in the reports.

Second, the subsidiary's management accountants **examine the reasons for the positive and negative target deviations.** For this purpose, the subsidiary's management accountants look into the detailed BI system of the parent-PMS:

> *"We can see the overall development of the performance measure values from the performance report. However, if I want to understand why something has developed in another direction, we have to go into the detailed BI system. There we can filter the results by customer or product. For example, we can see whether the good results are due to a single customer or whether this is a general market trend."*

> *ChemCo – Management accountant (North EMEA)*

Furthermore, the management accountants discuss possible reasons with the subsidiary's department heads. Subsequently, the management accountants present the major target deviations and their reasons to the country managers. Each of them is responsible for one of the ten countries that are subsumed under North EMEA.

Third, the parent-PMS is used to **decide between decision alternatives.** For each decision alternative, the management accountants simulate the effects on the performance measures of the parent-PMS and discuss the effects with the responsible manager. In case of product discounts, for example, the simulations are discussed with the Head of marketing & sales.

Finally, the subsidiary's management accountants **draw the managers' attention** to the performance measures of the parent-PMS. In fact, the management accountants regularly discuss the performance results with the managers. Furthermore, for each performance measure, a responsible manager is defined that has to ensure that the target levels from the parent-PMS are achieved. For example, the Head of operations is responsible for the accident rate and the Head of marketing & sales for the subsidiary's net sales.

At the subsidiary North EMEA, the management accountants **have not developed a local-PMS.**

6.1.4.3.2   Adoption at ChemCo South EMEA

The management accountants of ChemCo South EMEA use the parent-PMS to **monitor** the subsidiary's actual performance and to compare it with the budgeted targets. This is done at the beginning of each month when the performance reports of the parent-PMS are available to the local management accountants:

"Every month we receive performance reports. They are prepared by our head office and by the shared service center in Berlin. They give us the first shot of the month and allow us to check how the month was in comparison to the last year and the budget."

ChemCo – Head of management accounting (South EMEA)

If the subsidiary's actual performance is below expectations, it is the task of the management accountants to analyze the reasons for the deviations. In particular, they obtain additional information from the BI systems of the parent-PMS. In addition, the management accountants discuss the variances with the responsible managers. For example, a sales decline in a certain product category is discussed with the responsible sales manager to investigate the reasons for the sales drop.

Furthermore, the performance reports of the parent-PMS are also discussed by the subsidiary's management team on a monthly basis. In these meetings, the management accountants present and explain the subsidiary's performance over the previous month. This is done to give the management a **better understanding of the subsidiary's business situation.** Furthermore, the performance reports of the parent-PMS also serve as a basis for operational and strategic decision-making. For example, the information from the performance reports is used to decide whether and to what extent further sales and marketing measures have to be taken for the subsidiary's products.

In addition, the parent-PMS is used to **influence the behavior** of the subsidiary's employees. This applies in particular to the sales area, as this is the main task of the subsidiary. The behavior of the sales employees (i.e. the sales managers and the sales stuff) shall be influenced by regularly presenting them the target achievement for performance measures such as gross sales and net sales:

"The performance reports are also the basis to control the sales guys of the Region South. For example, the reports show our regional sales managers the sales targets that they have to achieve each month."

ChemCo – Head of management accounting (South EMEA)

The comparison of the actual sales figures with the targets shall motivate the employees from the sales area to contribute to the achievement of the budgeted targets.

Existence and design of local-PMS

At ChemCo South EMEA, a **local-PMS** exists. This local-PMS includes **ten performance measures** from two measurement perspectives. Eight of these ten performance measures stem from the parent-PMS. This is due to the fact that the management accountants at ChemCo South EMEA consider all performance measures of the parent-PMS as useful at subsidiary level. In addition, the subsidiary's management accountants have selected **two performance measures** that are only included in the local-PMS. These two performance measures relate to the financial and employee perspective.

Concerning the **financial** perspective, the management accountants add **one performance measure**, namely the sales volume. This allows the local management accountants to assess at a glance whether changes in the gross and net sales are driven by price changes or due to an increase in the sales volume. With respect to the **employee perspective**, the subsidiary's management accountants added the headcount. They regard this performance measure as important because it allows a more fine-grained analysis of the subsidiary's expenses. This applies in particular to travel expenses, which depend on the number of people working at the subsidiary. Since the parent-PMS does not include the headcount, the management accountants are not able to determine whether an increase in the travel expenses is due to an increase in the subsidiary's headcount or due to other factors. Apart from the two performance measures, the local-PMS does not contain any different or additional performance measures than the parent-PMS.

Measurement perspective	Performance measures
Financial perspective:	Gross sales (LP), net sales (LP), *sales volume (L)*, gross profit (LP), fixed SG&A expenses (LP), travel expenses (LP), advertisement expenses (LP), EBITDA (LP)
Customer perspective:	-
Internal process perspective:	-
Employee perspective:	Accident rate (LP), *headcount (L)*
Legend:	
(L): Performance measures included in the local-PMS only (highlighted in italics)	
(LP): Performance measures included in both the local-PMS and the parent-PMS	

Table 6–13: Performance measures included in the local-PMS (ChemCo South EMEA)

For all ten performance measures of the local-PMS **targets** are set. The target setting differs between the performance measures taken from the parent-PMS and the additional performance measures. For the former, the target levels from the parent-PMS are used. For the latter, the subsidiary's management accountants set targets based on the **past performance** of the subsidiary. In fact, they compare the results of the sales volume and headcount with the performance of the previous year. Concerning the **target evaluation**, the management accountants have created two additional performance reports. First, they have created a local sales report, which includes actual and targeted values for the net sales, gross sales, and the sales volume. Second, the subsidiary's management accountants have created a local T&A report, which is based on the T&A report of the parent-PMS:

"We have one report provided by our head office, which is called T&A report. This is a good basis, but unfortunately, it is not in too much detail. [...] The report does not count how many people we are. Last year we were five people and this year we are eight people, for example. Then it seems that the costs are increasing. But it is increasing just because of the fact that we have three people more than last year.

That's why we have reproduced this T&A report on a local view. We want to have additional data that are missing in the official report."

ChemCo – Head of management accounting (South EMEA)

Both local reports are prepared on a monthly basis by the management accountants and then shared with the subsidiary's managers. Figure 6–21 summarizes the target setting and target evaluation of the local-PMS.

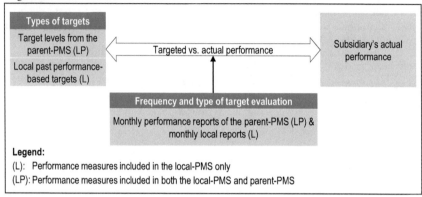

Figure 6–21: Target setting and target evaluation at ChemCo South EMEA

The performance measures of the local-PMS are **not used for rewarding** the subsidiary's employees. Thus, the sales volume and the travel expenses are not used for determining the bonus payments of the subsidiary's management or production workers.

The **IT infrastructure** of the local-PMS is based on the ERP system and the BI systems of the parent-PMS (see Figure 6–22).

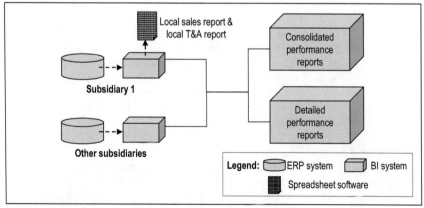

Figure 6–22: IT infrastructure of the local-PMS (ChemCo South EMEA)

From these systems, the management accountants extract performance data that is then transferred to **self-developed spreadsheet templates**. These templates form the basis for the two additional performance reports of the local-PMS.

6.1.4.4 Summary

To **conclude**, ChemCo's parent-PMS consists of eight performance measures. Of these eight performance measures, seven relate to the financial perspective and one to the subsidiaries' employees. For the financial performance measures, the budget-based targets are set, which are negotiated between ChemCo's several head offices and the subsidiaries. The evaluation of the target achievement is based on monthly performance and benchmarking reports and ad-hoc review meetings between the head offices and the subsidiaries. The performance measures and targets of the parent-PMS are not relevant for deciding on the bonus payments of the subsidiaries' management. Instead, the corporate management accountants use a ROI that is not included in the parent-PMS. For the subsidiaries' sales staff, the bonus payments depend on the net sales of the respective subsidiary. Regarding the IT infrastructure, ChemCo's parent-PMS builds on an integrated ERP system and two types of BI Systems.

At both ChemCo North and South EMEA, the management accountants use the parent-PMS in a functional way. In particular, they use the parent-PMS for decision-making, monitoring, and drawing the managers' attention to the performance measures. In contrast to North EMEA, the management accountants at South EMEA develop a local-PMS. This local-PMS differs from the parent-PMS mainly by including two additional performance measures. The management accountants argue that these performance measures are necessary to conduct a more fine-grained analysis of the subsidiary's travel expenses. In fact, since the parent-PMS does not include the headcount, the management accountants are not able to determine whether an increase in the travel expenses is due to an increase in the subsidiary's headcount or due to other factors.

6.1.5 TechCo case

6.1.5.1 Company profile and objectives of the parent-PMS

TechCo is a global player operating in the **technology sector**. The MNC, which is listed at the German stock exchange, has several divisions offering products and services such as power generation solutions and mobility applications. TechCo employs more than 350,000 people and operates in more than 200 countries. The MNC achieves about € 75 billion revenues, from which more than 85 % are generated at foreign markets.

TechCo has implemented a **matrix structure** consisting of a corporate head office, divisions, regions, and subsidiaries. At the top of the matrix structure, the corporate head office is home to the MNC's management board and corporate functions such as management accounting and finance. TechCo's several divisions have their own divisional head offices, which are responsible for the worldwide activities of the divisions.[126] Different from the divisional head offices, the regional head offices are responsible for the success of TechCo's operations in certain geographical areas. These geographical areas typically cover several countries. For example, the regional head office for Middle East is responsible for countries such as the United Arab Emirates (UAE) or Oman. By being imbedded in the matrix of divisions and regions, TechCo's subsidiaries have to report to both divisional head offices and regional head offices. Figure 6–23 summarizes TechCo's organizational structure.

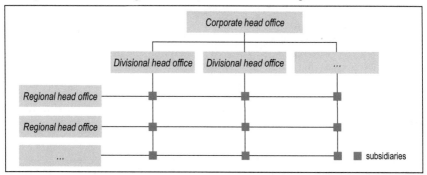

Figure 6–23: TechCo's organizational structure

At TechCo, interviews were conducted at the corporate head office, two divisional head offices, the regional head office of Middle East and two foreign subsidiaries (see Table 6–14).

Title	Organizational level
Corporate management accountant	Corporate head office
Divisional management accountant	Divisional head office
Divisional management accountant	Divisional head office
Divisional management accountant	Divisional head office
Head of regional management accounting	Regional head office Middle East
Regional management accountant	Regional head office Middle East
Regional management accountant	Regional head office Middle East
Management accountant	Subsidiary UAE
Local CFO	Subsidiary Oman
Commercial manager	Subsidiary Oman

Table 6–14: Interview partners at TechCo

---

[126] Some divisions are further divided into different business units. In this case, each business unit has its own business unit head office, which reports to the divisional head office.

At the head office level, **six management accountants** were interviewed – one from the corporate head office, three from divisional head offices, and three from the regional head office Middle East. For examining the adoption of the parent-PMS at subsidiary level, interviews were conducted at two foreign subsidiaries, namely the UAE and the Oman. Both subsidiaries are sales units. The subsidiary in the UAE was founded more than two decades ago and employs about 1,000 people. From this subsidiary, **two management accountants** were interviewed. The Omani subsidiary was established in 2006 and has approximately 50 employees. At the Omani subsidiary, interviews were conducted with the **local CFO** and **one management accountant.**

Objectives of TechCo's parent-PMS

TechCo' corporate management accountants have developed the parent-PMS more than five years ago as a **standardized** system:

> *"We follow an 'one-fits-all' approach for the performance measurement of our subsidiaries. For all our subsidiaries, we use the same set of performance measures."*
>
> *TechCo – Divisional management accountant*

The objectives of TechCo's parent-PMS are twofold. The corporate management accountants consider both objectives as equally important. The first objective is receiving information on the performance of the subsidiaries for **facilitating decisions**. The management accountants of TechCo's head offices use this information mainly to examine whether the subsidiaries achieve their targets. In this vein, the management accountants are able to identify undesirable development at an early stage:

> *"Our understanding is that we look at the performance measures to see if something is going wrong and to find out what goes wrong. It is always our task to recognize as early as possible whether there is a problem."*
>
> *TechCo – Divisional management accountant*

In case such undesirable developments are identified, the MNC's head offices intervene and impose measures and initiatives that the respective subsidiary must implement. Furthermore, the parent-PMS is also used to forecast future performance of the subsidiaries. These forecasts are not only important for TechCo's internal planning (e.g., capital budgeting), but also for providing forecasts to the capital market:

> *"As a listed company, we need to deliver reliable data on performance measures such as sales revenues or order intake. Not only for the current financial year, but also in the forecasts for our investors."*
>
> *TechCo – Regional management accountant*

Second, the parent-PMS is used to **influence the behavior** of the subsidiaries. In fact, the management accountants of TechCo's head office implement the parent-PMS to provide a common set of performance measures that is used within the whole MNC. The employees of each subsidiary shall be aware of these performance measures and shall consider them in making decisions. Furthermore, the standardized set of performance measures shall lead to a common understanding of performance measurement within the MNC.

6.1.5.2 Design of the parent-PMS

Performance measures

TechCo's parent-PMS includes **eight performance measures** that are used to evaluate the subsidiaries' performance. As Table 6–15 shows, these performance measures mainly refer to the **subsidiaries' financial perspective**. Only three of the eight performance measures relate to the subsidiaries' non-financial performance.

Measurement perspective	Performance measures
Financial perspective:	Sales revenue, gross profit, SG&A expenses, EBIT, free cash flow
Customer perspective:	Order backlog, order intake
Internal process perspective:	-
Employee perspective:	Headcount

Table 6–15: Performance measures included in TechCo's parent-PMS

Concerning the subsidiaries' **financial performance**, TechCo's parent-PMS contains **five performance measures**. First, the parent-PMS includes the subsidiaries' sales revenues, which are important for TechCo's head offices to evaluate the subsidiaries' sales efforts. Second, the parent-PMS includes the gross profit, which is calculated by deducting the cost of goods sold from the net sales. In addition, the head offices' management accountants pay attention to the SG&A expenses of the subsidiaries. Reducing the SG&A expenses is an important issue for TechCo, since the case company faces strong cost pressure from shrinking markets. Fourth, the parent-PMS includes the subsidiaries' EBIT, which indicates the subsidiaries' profitability. Finally, the management accountants from TechCo's head offices look at the subsidiaries' free cash flows. This performance measure enables the management accountants to determine the amount of cash that is available for dividend payments to the case company's shareholders.

Concerning the subsidiaries' non-financial performance, the parent-PMS captures the customer and employee perspective. For addressing the **customer** perspective, TechCo's head offices have selected **two performance measures**, namely the order backlog and order intake. By indicating the volume of the project stock and the volume of incoming orders, these two performance measures serve as early indicators for the future sales revenues of the subsidiaries. The **employee perspective** is addressed by **one performance measure**, namely the subsidiaries' headcount.

Targets

For all eight performance measures of TechCo's parent-PMS, **budget-based targets** are defined. These targets are derived from the annual budgeting process in which the subsidiaries and the corporate, divisional, and regional head offices are involved. The budgeting process starts with the management board setting the key strategic assumptions for the group. Based on these assumptions, the local management accountants make initial proposals on the target levels of the eight performance measures in June of each year. [127] For some of the performance measures, the subsidiaries' management accountants coordinate with the local sales department (for the order intake, order backlog, and sales revenues) and with the local HR department (for the headcount). The target levels are determined on **subsidiary level** and are not further broken down into, for example, customer, or product level.

After determining the target levels, the subsidiaries' management accountants send their proposals in a first step to the regional head offices. At the regional head offices, the regional management accountants and the respective CFO critically discuss the subsidiaries' proposals. In case the regional head offices do not agree with single or multiple target levels, the regional management accountants go into discussions with the subsidiaries' management accountants. Based on these discussions, which must be completed by mid-June at the latest, the management accountants of the subsidiaries adjust the target levels if necessary. In a second step, the subsidiaries send the agreed target levels to the divisional head offices, where the target levels are discussed from the division's point of view. The divisional management accountants have time until end of July to critically review the subsidiaries' proposals. The divisional management accountants compare the proposed target levels with the division's strategic goals. These strategic goals are agreed every two years between the divisions and TechCo's corporate head office. They serve as a benchmark for the divisional management accountants to assess whether the proposed target levels are appropriate or not. If the divisional management accountants do not consider the proposed target levels to be adequate, they discuss the proposals with the subsidiaries' management accountants in order to reach an agreement. After these discussions, the divisional management accountants send the proposals to the corporate head office, where the target levels are consolidated and discussed by the case company's management board. Based on these discussions, the corporate head office makes top-down adjustments, which in turn have to be implemented by the divisional and regional head offices and the subsidiaries. The final target levels for the eight performance measures will then be available in October/November of each year, i.e. shortly after the start of the new business year.

The **target achievement** is evaluated based on a monthly performance report and monthly and annual review meetings. The **performance report**, which is extracted from a BI system, can be accessed by the management accountants from the subsidiaries and head offices on the third working day of each month. It shows actual and targeted values for all performance measures of TechCo's parent-PMS. The performance report is the basis for the **monthly review meetings**. In these meetings, which are held as phone or web conferences, local, regional and divisional management accountants discuss about the subsidiaries' performance:

> "At the beginning of each month we have a call with the subsidiaries. For this call, we invite the locations and make a target/actual analysis of the monthly results. We

---

[127] TechCo's business year deviates from the calendar year and covers the period from October 1st to September 30th of the following year.

*then go through the figures and check whether what happened was planned or not
and what effect unplanned events have on our performance measures."*

TechCo – Divisional management accountant

For these meetings, the subsidiaries' management accountants must prepare an overview
and comments on the highlights and lowlights of the previous month, which are also discussed in the meetings. In addition to the monthly meetings, there is an **annual meeting**
at the corporate head office. In this annual meeting, the target achievement of the whole
MNC is presented and discussed between TechCo's CFO, the divisional and regional CFOs
and the CFOs of the subsidiaries. Figure 6–24 summarizes the target setting and target
evaluation at TechCo.

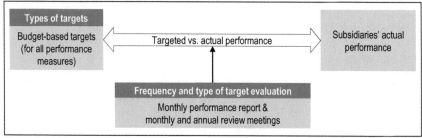

Figure 6–24: Target setting and target evaluation at TechCo

Link to rewards

At TechCo, two groups of subsidiaries' employees are eligible to bonus payments: The subsidiaries' management and the subsidiaries' sales staff. The bonus payment for the **management** depends on the overall performance of TechCo and the achievement of personal targets:

> *"The bonus for the management and non-tariff employees of the subsidiaries depends
> on our group's overall performance rather than on the performance of the subsidiary.
> Our non-tariff employees also have personal goals that are relevant for the bonus
> payment."*

TechCo – Divisional management accountant

The **overall performance** of TechCo is operationalized by two performance measures,
namely earnings per share and EVA. Thus, TechCo uses performance measures that are not
included in the parent-PMS for determining the bonus payments for the subsidiaries' management. The **personal targets** are set by TechCo's regional and divisional head offices.
These individual targets refer only to qualitative aspects and are hence not linked to performance measures from the parent-PMS.

The bonus payments for the **subsidiaries' sales staff** depend on the **sales revenues** of the
respective subsidiary and on personal targets. Since the sales revenues are included as a performance measure in the parent-PMS, there is a link between the parent-PMS and the compensation of the subsidiaries' sales staff. However, the bonus payment for the subsidiaries'

sales staff also depends on **personal targets**. These personal targets are of qualitative nature and therefore do not relate to performance measures from the parent-PMS.

Concluding, the compensation of the subsidiaries' management is not linked to TechCo's parent-PMS. The bonus payment for these employees rather depends on performance measures not included in the parent-PMS, such as the EVA. For the subsidiaries' sales staff, there is a link between the parent-PMS and the compensation. In fact, the bonus payment of the sales staff depends, among other things, on the sales revenues of the respective subsidiary.

IT infrastructure

The IT infrastructure of TechCo's parent-PMS consists of ERP systems and BI systems (see Figure 6–25).

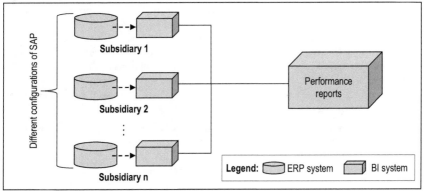

Figure 6–25: IT infrastructure of TechCo's parent-PMS

At each subsidiary, an ERP system is implemented. The ERP systems serve to collect and store input data that is necessary for calculating actual values for the eight performance measures of TechCo's parent-PMS. Since TechCo aims to reduce the number of different ERP systems in the company, each subsidiary has to use an ERP system from SAP (SAP R/3 or SAP HANA). This also applies to newly acquired subsidiaries, which have to switch to SAP in case they had a different ERP system before the acquisition. Although all subsidiaries have an ERP system from SAP, the ERP landscape is still heterogeneous. This is because the subsidiaries often adapt the ERP systems to their own needs:

> *"Each SAP system is different, more or less, because each location, as soon as they get the standard solution, starts to individualize it. This means that you lose a bit of the global unity in the ERP systems, because each location then does things a bit differently."*
>
> TechCo – Divisional management accountant

From the ERP systems the data flows into a BI system (SAP BW). Different from the ERP systems, this BI system is a uniform system that is used throughout the entire MNC. At TechCo, the BI system serves two purposes: First, it uses the data from the ERP systems to

calculate actual values for the eight performance measures. This calculation is performed automatically by the BI system, without the need for manual data collection, adjustment, or calculation by the subsidiaries' management accountants. The management accountants of the subsidiaries only have to upload the budget-based target levels manually once a year. Second, the BI serves as a **shared information tool** for the management accountants in the case company's head offices and subsidiaries. In fact, the management accountants can access the BI system to create standardized performance reports showing actual and targeted values for all eight performance measures.

6.1.5.3   Adoption of the parent-PMS

6.1.5.3.1   Adoption at TechCo Oman

At TechCo Oman, the management accountants use the performance reports of the parent-PMS for **monitoring** the target achievement. This is done for the different divisions that are located within the subsidiary and for the subsidiary as a whole. Within each division, the management accountants compare the division's actual performance with the budgeted targets and communicate the deviations to the responsible managers. For example, the sales manager receives feedback on target deviations for performance measures such as order intake and order backlog. At the level of the entire subsidiary, the target deviations are presented to the subsidiary's CFO.

Second, the subsidiary's management accountants use the parent-PMS to **determine the causes of negative target deviations**. This is done in a monthly meeting between the local CFO, the subsidiary's management accountants, and the managers of the different divisions. In these meetings, which are held shortly before review meetings of the parent-PMS take place, the participants discuss the reasons for the target deviations. In fact, the managers have to comment and explain the negative target deviations for the performance measures for which they are responsible.

Third, based on the identification of the causes of target deviations, the managers **develop and initiate countermeasures:**

> *"If we deviate from the budgeted targets, we investigate the causes and see, for example, where the additional costs of projects lie. It is important to draw conclusions and learn from it to avoid that similar extra costs arise again in future projects."*
>
> *TechCo – CFO (Oman)*

For example, in case of a too low gross profit due to higher project costs, the responsible project managers have to propose countermeasures to stop the cost increase.

Finally, the parent-PMS is used to **forecast the future performance** of the subsidiary. For this purpose, the local CFO and the management accountants prepare a quarterly forecast for the eight performance measures included in TechCo's parent-PMS. This forecast consists of three scenarios, representing the best case, worst case, and average case. The scenarios are used for planning purposes (e.g., hiring new employees or planning project capacities) and for predicting if the budget-based targets will be met in the following months.

Existence and design of local-PMS

The Omani management accountants have developed a **local-PMS**, which contains **nine performance measures**. Of these nine performance measures, eight are also included in the parent-PMS (see Table 6–16). In addition, the subsidiary's management accountants selected **one performance measure** relating to the employee perspective.

Measurement perspective	Performance measures
Financial perspective:	Sales revenue (LP), gross profit (LP), SG&A expenses (LP), EBIT (LP), free cash flow (LP)
Customer perspective:	Order backlog (LP), order intake (LP)
Internal process perspective:	-
Employee perspective:	Headcount (LP), *omanization rate (L)*
Legend:	
(L): Performance measures included in the local-PMS only (highlighted in italics)	
(LP): Performance measures included in both the local-PMS and the parent-PMS	

Table 6–16: Performance measures included in the local-PMS (TechCo Oman)

This so-called "Omanization rate" indicates the percentage of Omani employees that are working in the subsidiary. The subsidiary selected this performance measures since the local government requires a minimum percentage of domestic employees for certain professions:

> *"Here in Oman, we have another performance measure that is very important to us. The point is that we have to hire a certain percentage of domestic employees. That sounds banal, but it was in today's newspaper that 161 companies might lose their licenses to operate in Oman because they do not meet this quota."*

> *TechCo – Commercial manager (Oman)*

For all nine performance measures of the local-PMS **targets** exist. For the performance measures that are included in both the parent-PMS and the local-PMS, the Omani management accountants take the target levels of the parent-PMS. Thus, for these eight performance measures budget-based targets are used. For the Omanization rate, the subsidiary sets the target level based on the requirements of the Omani government. This is to avoid sanctions resulting from a too low percentage of local employees. For **evaluating the target achievement** of the eight performance measures that are included in both the parent-PMS and the local-PMS, the subsidiary uses the performance report of the parent-PMS. For the Omanization rate, a monthly local performance report exists. All nine performance measures of the local-PMS are discussed each month in a local review meetings. Figure 6–26 summarizes the target setting and target evaluation at TechCo Oman.

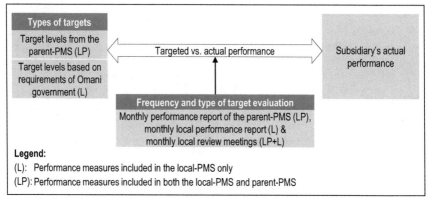

Figure 6–26: Target setting and target evaluation at TechCo Oman

The Omani subsidiary does **not** use the local-PMS for **rewarding** the subsidiary's management or sales staff. Thus, the Omanization rate is not used for determining the bonus payments of the subsidiary's employees.

The **IT infrastructure** of the local-PMS mainly builds on the IT systems of the parent-PMS. In fact, the data for the seven performance measures that are also included in the parent-PMS comes from the ERP system of the parent-PMS. For the Omanization rate, the Omani management accountants have created a spreadsheet template. They use this template for calculating the Omanization rate and for reporting it within the subsidiary (see Figure 6–27).

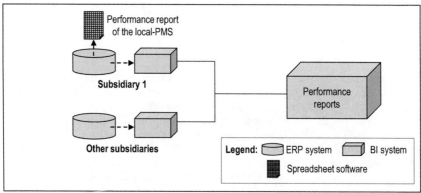

Figure 6–27: IT infrastructure of the local-PMS (TechCo Oman)

6.1.5.3.2 Adoption at TechCo UAE

At the subsidiary in the UAE, the management accountants use the parent-PMS in three ways. First, they use the parent-PMS for **monitoring the performance of the subsidiary**.

In particular, the management accountants use the monthly performance reports from the parent-PMS and compare the subsidiary's actual performance with the budgeted targets:

"We always compare the performance of our subsidiary with the targets. Each month we check whether we meet the budget."

TechCo – Management accountant (UAE)

Second, the parent-PMS is used to determine the **reasons for negative target deviations**. Based on the comparison of the actual performance with the targets, the subsidiary's management accountants analyze from which projects or areas the target deviations originate. For this purpose, they extract detailed performance data from the BI system. For example, they examine the gross profit at project level. In this vein, the management accountants are able to quickly identify which projects or areas are underperforming and can afterwards inform the responsible manager.

Finally, the parent-PMS is used to **forecast the subsidiary's future performance**. In particular, the management accountants forecast the order intake of the subsidiary. They create three different scenarios (best case, worst case and average case) each quarter. By developing these scenarios, the management accountants work together with the sales managers, who keep an internal project list of pending orders. In this list, probabilities are assigned to upcoming tenders, which indicate the probability that the tender will be won by the subsidiary. These probabilities serve as the basis for developing the best case, worst case, and average case scenario. The scenarios are only used within the subsidiary and support the management accountants in planning, for example, the subsidiary's headcount.

At TechCo UAE, the management accountants **did not develop a local-PMS** but solely use the parent-PMS.

6.1.5.4 Summary

To **summarize**, TechCo's parent-PMS consists of eight performance measures. These performance measures address the subsidiaries' financial perspective and the subsidiaries' customers and employees. For all eight performance measures budget-based targets are set, which are negotiated between TechCo's different head office and the subsidiaries. The evaluation of the target achievement bases on a monthly performance report and monthly and annual review meetings. The performance and targets of the parent-PMS are not linked to the compensation of the subsidiaries' management and executive employees, but to the compensation of the subsidiaries' sales staff. In fact, the bonus payment for the sales staff depends on the sales revenues of the respective subsidiary. As an IT infrastructure, TechCo's parent-PMS builds on ERP systems and BI systems.

The management accountants from the Oman and the UAE use the parent-PMS in a functional way. For example, they use the parent-PMS for identifying causes of negative target deviations and for projecting the subsidiary's future performance. While a local-PMS does not exist at the subsidiary from the UAE, the Omani management accountants have developed a local-PMS. This local-PMS differs from the parent-PMS mainly by including an additional performance measure (Omanization rate), which is not part of the parent-PMS.

This performance measure is necessary as the Omani government requires companies to employ a certain percentage of domestic employees.

6.2   Cross-case analyses

This section presents the results of the cross-case analyses. The results are structured into the objectives, design, and adoption of the parent-PMSs.

6.2.1   Objectives of the parent-PMSs

The objectives that the case companies' head offices pursue with parent-PMSs coincide with the two objectives outlined in the conceptual basis of this study, namely facilitating decisions and influencing the decisions of the subsidiaries (*Austin* (1996), pp. 21-28; *Horváth/Seiter* (2009), p. 396; *Speklé/Verbeeten* (2014), p. 134). At all case companies, the head offices address not only one of the two objectives, but **both** of them.[128]

Facilitating decisions

The case companies use the parent-PMS for **facilitating decisions** at head office level. In particular, parent-PMS support decision-making by providing information on the subsidiaries' performance. In this vein, the head offices' management accountants stress that the parent-PMSs are important for getting an **overview** of the subsidiaries' performance. For example, the management accountants of CarSupCo's head office introduced the parent-PMSs because they had an increased demand for information due to establishing and acquiring several new foreign subsidiaries:

> "The structure of the Group has changed over the last ten to fifteen years. We got new locations that all had sales and production tasks in the beginning. Later they also took on research and development tasks. We also founded small subsidiaries that only have sales tasks. The new locations made it necessary to introduce a group-wide reporting to have an ongoing flow of information."
>
> *CarSupCo – Head of corporate management accounting*

Furthermore, the parent-PMSs support the head offices in **identifying undesirable developments**. For this purpose, the management accountants compare the subsidiaries' actual performance with pre-defined targets:

> "When the results of the subsidiaries are available, we compare them with the budgeted figures. To do so, we go through the different reports."
>
> *MaNuCo – Corporate management accountant*

> "Our books are closed at the end of the month. Then on the second or third working day of the next month, we compare the results with the targets. We then see whether the results are satisfactory."

---

[128] This is consistent with *Austin*'s observation that it is difficult to design parent-PMSs that address only one of the two objectives (*Austin* (1996), pp. 29-31; cf. also section 2.2).

TechCo – Corporate management Accountant

In case of undesirable developments, the head offices ask the subsidiaries' management accountants to explain the reasons for the negative target deviations, for example in regular review meetings or ad-hoc phone calls.

Finally, at one sample firm (MaNuCo) information on the subsidiaries' performance help to build **company knowledge**. In fact, the management accountants of MaNuCo's head office point out that both the employees from the head office and the subsidiaries can learn from the performance information of the parent-PMS. For example, the information can be used to evaluate whether actions and initiatives (e.g., redesigning the workstation within a subsidiary's factory) are successful. The head office's management accountants share the outcome of this evaluation with the other subsidiaries so that they can benefit from this experience.

Influencing decisions of the subsidiaries

The case companies' head offices try to influence the decisions of the subsidiaries in several ways. First, the head offices of all case companies try to make the subsidiaries **aware of the performance measures**. For increasing awareness, the heads offices' management accountants discuss the performance measures and the corresponding targets in the regular review meetings. In these meetings, the subsidiaries' management accountants have to explain and justify poor performance results. This is to ensure that the subsidiaries do not ignore or forget the performance measures and targets:

> "Through the discussions in the review meetings, the performance measures and related topics come up repeatedly. The performance measures are therefore so present that it can be assumed that the employees of our subsidiaries consider them in their daily work. However, this does not mean that they forget individual performance measures over the course of the year. As long as we do not ask about the performance measures, the subsidiaries probably do not look at the performance measures. They just report them and if nobody asks, that is it. Only when we say this or that performance measure is red or when say there is a problem, then the subsidiaries take a closer look at the performance measures."

CarSupCo – Head of corporate management accounting

Furthermore, the head office of one case company (AgriCo) tries to increase the awareness of the performance measures by proposing the subsidiaries to display the performance measures and targets on movable walls within the subsidiaries' buildings. This shall make the performance measures and targets visible for the subsidiaries' employees and shall ensure that everyone can see whether the subsidiary achieves its targets. In addition, the case company's head office offers trainings on the parent-PMS, in which the head offices' management accountants explain the importance of the performance measures:

> "We recommend to the subsidiaries to make the performance measures visible by displaying them in the different parts of the subsidiaries. If you go for a walk, for example, in a factory of a subsidiary, you will see movable walls displaying the most important performance measures and the current target achievement. By looking at

these walls, the employees of the subsidiaries can quickly see where there are problems."

AgriCo – Corporate management accountant

Finally, the head offices of two sample firms (AgriCo, ChemCo) attempt to influence the subsidiaries through **internally benchmarking** the performance results of the subsidiaries. This aims to stimulate competition between the subsidiaries and thus to motivate the subsidiaries to achieve their targets. For this purpose, the subsidiaries are ranked based on their performance so that everyone can see at a glance which position each subsidiary has within the group.

Although all case companies address both objectives, they differ according to the **importance** that they attach to the two objectives. As presented in Table 6–17, two opposing approaches exist.

	CarSupCo	ManuCo	AgriCo	ChemCo	TechCo
Importance of objectives	Both objectives are equally important	Both objectives are equally important	Focus on influencing decisions	Both objectives are equally important	Both objectives are equally important

Table 6–17: Objectives of parent-PMSs

Most case companies (CarSupCo, ManuCo, ChemCo, TechCo) attach equal importance to the two objectives. The management accountants of these head offices either emphasize that it is difficult to determine which objective is more important (TechCo) or attach the same importance to both objectives (CarSupCo, ChemCo). Only at AgriCo the corporate management accountants consider it more important to influence the decisions of the subsidiaries with the parent-PMS:

> *"Researcher: You have mentioned two objectives: To see what is happening in the subsidiaries and to direct the behavior of the employees. What is more important from your point of view?*
>
> *Interview partner: Influencing their behavior. That is what we want in the end. We want to give them tools to manage their day-to-day business."*

AgriCo – Head of corporate management accounting

The high importance that AgriCo's head office attaches to influencing the decisions of the subsidiaries is explained by the history of the parent-PMS as one part of AgriCo's PES. This PES was developed with the idea of providing the subsidiaries with tools to control their production processes.

To achieve the objectives described above, all five case companies rely on **standardized** parent-PMSs. The head offices' management accountants therefore do not adapt the parent-PMSs to the subsidiaries' specific needs that arise, for example, out of the size or geographical location of the subsidiary. The following section analyzes the design of these standardized parent-PMSs.

6.2.2 Design of the parent-PMSs

6.2.2.1 Performance measures

This section analyzes the performance measures included in the parent-PMSs. The analysis is split into two parts. The first part addresses the number, kind, and importance of the four measurement perspectives. The second part provides detailed evidence on the performance measures that are included in these measurement perspectives.

Measurement perspectives

The case companies differ according to the **number** of measurement perspectives that they use for evaluating the subsidiaries' performance. Similar to the findings in prior studies (e.g., *Pausenberger* (1996), p. 189; *Dossi/Patelli* (2010), pp. 507-511), the case companies have in common that they evaluate the performance of their subsidiaries not only from a single but from **multiple perspectives** (see Figure 6–28). In fact, the lowest number of perspectives used is two perspectives (AgriCo, ChemCo). Only one MNC (CarSupCo) uses all four perspectives to assess the performance of its subsidiaries.

	Financial perspective	Customer perspective	Internal process perspective	Employee perspective
CarSupCo	✓	✓	✓	✓
ManuCo	✓		✓	✓
AgriCo			✓	✓
ChemCo	✓			✓
TechCo	✓	✓		✓

Figure 6–28: Measurement perspectives addressed by the parent-PMSs

At CarSupCo, the high measurement diversity might be explained by the fact that the parent-PMS relates to both production and sales units. Furthermore, the corporate management accountants have not developed the parent-PMS on their own. Instead, other departments and functions, such as the corporate production and the corporate HR department, have also been involved in selecting the performance measures. Since management accountants often have a financial focus (*Seal* (2001), pp. 493-494; *Schäffer/Weber* (2015), p. 3), employees from other departments and functions might view the performance of the subsidiaries from a different angle.

When looking at the **kind** of measurement perspectives, it is evident that four sample firms (CarSupCo, ManuCo, ChemCo, TechCo) consider the subsidiaries' **financial perspective**. Only AgriCo does not use financial performance measures to evaluate the performance of the subsidiaries:

"The system does not include any financial performance measures. Of course, many of the performance measures in the system have an influence on the financial performance, but the financial performance measures are not explicitly included."

AgriCo – Corporate management accountant

AgriCo only indirectly addresses the financial perspective through assumed cause-and-effect relationships. Different from the other sample firms, AgriCo's head office therefore does not use the parent-PMS for evaluating the subsidiaries' financial performance. This is in contrast with prior literature, which indicates that non-financial performance measures complement but do not replace their financial counterparts (e.g., *Dossi/Patelli* (2010), pp. 507-511; *Abdallah/Alnamri* (2015), pp. 601-603). The omission of financial performance measures might be explained by the fact that AgriCo's parent-PMS was implemented as one part of the group-wide Production Excellence System, which primarily focuses on the efficiency of production processes. In this vein, the parent-PMS only applies to production units. Consequently, AgriCo's head office has selected performance measures that are suitable for measuring the efficiency of the subsidiaries' production processes.

Concerning the **non-financial perspectives**, all case companies address the employee perspective. Therefore, they have in common that they consider the employee perspective as an essential part for evaluating the subsidiaries' performance. The internal processes and customers of the subsidiaries receive less attention. These two measurement perspectives are only considered by three (AgriCo, CarSupCo, MaNuCo) and two case companies (CarSupCo, MaNuCo), respectively. The dominance of the employee perspective is in contrast to prior empirical evidence, which indicates that the three non-financial perspectives are equally represented in parent-PMSs (*Dossi/Patelli* (2008), p. 137). The exclusion of the internal process perspective at TechCo and ChemCo might be explained by the fact that the parent-PMSs of these two case companies refer only to sales units, which do not carry out production activities. In fact, prior literature has shown that performance measures on internal processes are more relevant for production than for sales units (*Abdel-Maksoud et al.* (2005), pp. 269-27). However, parent-PMSs could also include performance measures addressing the internal processes of sales units such as the mean time that it takes to generate an order (*Kirsch-Brunkow* (2017), p. 8). At AgriCo, the parent-PMS only refers to production units, which do not sell products to external customers. This might explain the exclusion of performance measures on the customer perspective at this MNC.

In addition to the number and kind of measurement perspectives, this study analyzes whether the sample firms attach more **importance** to the subsidiaries' financial or non-financial performance. For AgriCo, this question does not arise, because the parent-PMS does not address the financial perspective. At the other sample firms, the head offices pay particular attention to **financial performance measures**. This becomes obvious by the following two points. First, the underlying importance is reflected in the **number of performance measures** addressing the subsidiaries' financial performance. At all four case companies, which address the subsidiaries' financial perspective, financial performance measures are represented to a larger extent than performance measures from the three non-financial perspectives. In fact, the proportion of financial performance measures in the parent-PMSs varies from 42% at MaNuCo to 88% at ChemCo. Second, the high perceived importance of the financial perspective becomes apparent when looking at the **selection process** of the performance measures:

> *"When selecting operational performance measures, we paid attention that they have a clear link to the P&L and cash flow statement. Because in the end, we have to earn money and we have to pay our bills."*
>
> *CarSupCo – Head of corporate management accounting*

> *"At our group, we have one report that we understand to be the heart of our reporting. For this report we selected financial performance measures such as net sales and profits."*
>
> *ChemCo – Head of regional management accounting*

As expressed by these two quotes, selecting financial performance measures receives high attention by the sample firms (except AgriCo). In fact, the head offices consider the financial performance as the ultimate goal of the MNC. The financial performance measures are then supplemented by non-financial performance measures, which shall help to explain the outcomes of the financial perspective. This result is line with extant prior conceptual (*Ittner/Larcker* (2003), pp. 1-3; *Kaplan/Norton* (1996), pp. 17-18) and empirical research (e.g., *Coates et al.* (1992), p. 137-143; *Chung et al.* (2006), p. 159-161; *Kihn* (2008), pp. 162-164).

Performance measures included in each of the measurement perspectives

Prior studies do not provide detailed evidence on the performance measures that are included in parent-PMSs.[129] To reduce this gap, the following paragraphs describe the financial and non-financial performance measures that the case companies use. As depicted in Figure 6–29, the **financial perspective** includes performance measures relating to six aspects. First, the subsidiaries' **sales** are examined by all four case companies that address the financial perspective of the subsidiaries (CarSupCo, MaNuCo, ChemCo, TechCo). For examining the subsidiaries' sales, the head offices consider the sales revenues. At ChemCo, the sales revenues are further subdivided into net sales and gross sales to have a detailed overview of the price reductions that the subsidiaries allow towards their customers. Second, the financial perspective includes performance measures on the subsidiaries' **cost situation**. At MaNuCo and CarSupCo, the performance measures relate to the subsidiaries' production costs. At ChemCo and TechCo, the SG&A costs are in the focus of the head offices of these two case companies:

> *"A major focus for us at present is on SG&A costs. Above all, we want to reduce travel costs, which are included in these SG&A costs. We are therefore trying to do much more with phone and video conferencing and we have already replaced a number of personal events – including full-day events – with phone and video conferencing."*

---

[129] In particular, this holds for non-financial performance measures (see the review of prior research in chapter 3).

TechCo – Divisional management accountant

"Of course, we also include SG&A costs when assessing the performance of our subsidiaries. At our company, SG&A costs primarily include selling costs and, above all, freight costs."

ChemCo – Head of management accounting for regional business units

By including the SG&A costs in the parent-PMSs, the head offices of the two case companies intend to increase cost awareness of the local management accountants. This is particularly important since the two case companies face cost pressure due to competition and investors' expectations.

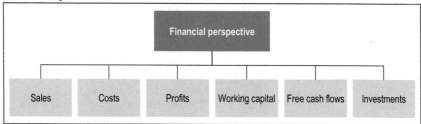

Figure 6–29: Financial perspective of the parent-PMSs

Third, for evaluating the subsidiaries' **profits**, the case companies rely on both absolute and relative profit measures (*Gladen* (2014), p. 15). As absolute profit measures, the case companies use EBIT (TechCo), EBITDA (MaNuCo, ChemCo), or both EBIT and EBITDA (CarSupCo). As relative profit measure, the case companies draw on the subsidiaries' gross margin. It is remarkable that the sample firms do not make use of value-based performance measures such as EVA or ROCE. Although the literature emphasizes the advantages of value-based performance measures (e.g., *Ittner/Larcker* (1998), pp. 209-210; *Knauer et al.* (2018), pp. 43-44), they are not used by the sample firms. However, these results are in line with prior empirical evidence, which indicates that value-based performance measures are included only to a small extent in parent-PMSs (*Dossi/Patelli* (2010), p. 509).

Fourth, the **working capital** of the subsidiaries is addressed by performance measures such as days inventory outstanding and days payables outstanding. This is the case for CarSupCo and MaNuCo, whose subsidiaries carry out capital-intensive production tasks. Fifth, by including the free cash flows, some of the case companies (CarSupCo, MaNuCo, TechCo) use their parent-PMSs for monitoring the subsidiaries' **cash situation**. By aggregating the free cash flows over all subsidiaries, the head offices can determine how much cash is available for dividend payments and loan repayments. Finally, CarSupCo also draws attention to the subsidiaries' **investments** by examining the level of capital expenditures. This is to ensure that the subsidiaries invest in their machines, which CarSupCo's head office considers highly important.

Concerning the **customer perspective**, the case companies address only one aspect, namely the subsidiaries' **order situation** (see Figure 6–30).

Figure 6–30: Customer perspective of the parent-PMSs

CarSupCo and TechCo examine the order intake and the order backlog. Both performance measures serve as early indicators for the subsidiaries' future sales revenues. In contrast to findings in the literature (*Dossi/Patelli* (2010), p. 511), the case companies do not use customer satisfaction and market share as performance measures. At CarSupCo, ManuCo, and ChemCo, the reason for not-considering customer satisfaction might be that these case companies operate in the business-to-business segment, which makes it more difficult to obtain information on the customers' satisfaction (*Molinari et al.* (2008), pp. 369-370).[130] At TechCo, the market share is calculated by the corporate sales department, but is not included as a performance measure in the parent-PMS. The performance of the subsidiaries is therefore not evaluated based on their achieved market shares. Accordingly, the subsidiaries do not receive targets for the market share and the market is not discussed in the review meetings between TechCo's head offices and the subsidiaries. TechCo's management accountants explain the exclusion of the market share in the parent-PMS by the subjectivity inherent in the calculation of this performance measure:

> "We do not consider the market share to be suitable for performance measurement. Even though we can estimate the market share better here in the project business than, for example, in the product business, there is always a certain subjectivity in how the entire market is calculated. There is simply too much scope for discretion in determining the size of the entire market."

> TechCo – Divisional management accountant

Regarding the **internal process perspective**, the case companies address four issues (see Figure 6–31). The first two aspects refer to the subsidiaries' production processes. In particular, the parent-PMSs include performance measures on the **production quality** (AgriCo, CarSupCo) and **production efficiency** (AgriCo, ManuCo).[131] At AgriCo and CarSupCo, the focus of the parent-PMS is more on production quality than on production efficiency. This might be due to the fact that these two MNCs position itself as quality leaders in their markets. Therefore, the head offices of these two MNCs pay particular attention to the subsidiaries' production quality by using performance measures such as early-

---

[130] At AgriCo, the exclusion of customer performance measures might be explained by the fact that the parent-PMS only refers to production units, which do not sell products to external customers.

[131] The parent-PMSs of ChemCo and TechCo do not include performance measures on the subsidiaries' production processes as the parent-PMSs only relate to sales units.

hour failures, failures per product audit, defective machine rate, and rework rate. In contrast, MaNuCo's head office is more concerned with production efficiency. This might be because the MNC is exposed to tremendous cost pressure from its competitors. In addition, MaNuCo is facing pressure from its private equity investor, who expects high returns. To address the production efficiency, MaNuCo's head offices examine the production output, machine utilization, and scrap level.

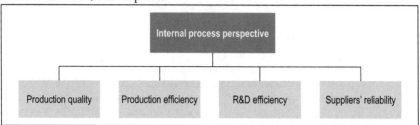

Figure 6–31: Internal process perspective of the parent-PMSs

Third, one case company (CarSupCo) addresses the **efficiency of the R&D department**, which is done by including the R&D-project processing quota in the parent-PMS. This performance measure points out how many of the projects initiated by the R&D department make it to market maturity. At MaNuCo, ChemCo, and TechCo, the parent-PMSs do not include performance measures on R&D efficiency, as subsidiaries of these case companies are not responsible for R&D. At AgriCo, the exclusion of performance measures dealing with R&D can be explained by the narrow focus of AgriCo's parent-PMS on production processes:

> *"One weakness is definitely that we do not evaluate all functional areas with our PMS [...]. For the future, we want to see if we also include other areas, such as administrative processes. Or research and development, which is something we have completely ignored so far."*

> *AgriCo – Head of corporate management accounting*

Finally, one case company (AgriCo) uses two performance measures on the **reliability of the suppliers**. These performance measures relate to the error rate of the supplied preliminary products (suppliers' defect rate) and to the punctuality of the deliveries (suppliers' delivery punctuality). These performance measures are important for AgriCo in order to ensure a smooth flow of production and to sustain the high product quality.

Concerning the subsidiaries' **employees**, the sample firms consider four aspects (see Figure 6–32). First, three sample firms (CarSupCo, MaNuCo, TechCo) monitor the subsidiaries' **headcount** and **employee fluctuation**. The headcount is used to ensure that the subsidiaries operate with as few employees as possible to save costs. In addition to the headcount, CarSupCo's head office examines the employee fluctuation to keep the direct costs associated with personnel changes at a low level.

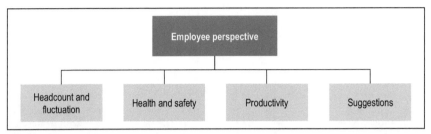

Figure 6–32: Employee perspective of the parent-PMSs

Second, all case companies except TechCo consider **occupational health and safety**. They address this aspect by using the accident rate, which measures the number of accidents per certain number of worked hours. Furthermore, the head offices of the sample firms also pay attention to the absenteeism rate, which measures the number of days lost due to illness or accidents. Fourth, AgriCo and CarSupCo address the **employee productivity**. However, both sample firms only measure the productivity of the production workers. Thus, their head offices do not monitor the productivity of employees from other divisions or departments. Finally, AgriCo's head office pays attention to the **number of suggestions** made by the subsidiaries' employees. By including this performance measure, the subsidiaries' employees shall be encouraged to make suggestions aiming at improving the performance of the subsidiary. Table 6–18 summarizes the issues addressed by the five parent-PMSs.

	CarSupCo	ManuCo	AgriCo	ChemCo	TechCo
Financial perspective	Sales, profits, working capital, costs, investments, cash flows	Sales, profits, working capital, costs, cash flows	-	Sales, profits, costs	Sales, profits, costs, cash flows
Customer perspective	Order situation	-	-	-	Order situation
Internal process perspective	Production quality, R&D efficiency	Production efficiency	Production quality, production efficiency, Suppliers' reliability	-	-
Employee perspective	Headcount, health and safety, productivity	Headcount, health and safety	Health and safety, productivity, suggestions	Health and safety	Headcount

Table 6–18: Overview of issues addressed by the parent-PMSs

6.2.2.2 Targets

This section analyzes the targets included in the parent-PMSs. Consistent with the conceptual framework of this study, both target setting and target evaluation are examined.

Target setting

For setting targets, the case companies use different **types of targets**. In line with the findings of prior research (*Pausenberger* (1996), pp. 189-190; *van der Stede* (2003), pp. 276-279), **budget-based** targets play an important role in target setting. In fact, all of the case companies derive targets from the annual budgeting process, as depicted by the following quotes:

> *"Within the annual budgeting process, for each performance measure a target has to be defined. [...] These targets are the basis for the target achievement calculation during the business year."*

> *AgriCo – Internal guideline*

> *"We report and compare the performance of our subsidiaries month by month with the budget. The deviations between actual performance and the budget must then always be explained by the colleagues from the subsidiaries."*

> *CarSupCo – Corporate management accountant*

> *"Every month there is a discussion with the subsidiaries about the budget deviations. The budget is important and indicates where the subsidiary should end up at the end of the year."*

> *TechCo – Divisional management accountant*

The head offices do not simply set the budgets by top-down planning, but negotiate them with the subsidiaries by **counter-flow planning**. At the two largest case companies (ChemCo, TechCo), this counter-flow planning starts at **head office level**, where management board presents their key assumptions on the MNC's performance in the following year. Based on these assumptions, the subsidiaries make first proposals on the target levels. At the other case companies (CarSupCo, MaNuCo, AgriCo), the counter-flow planning starts at **subsidiary level**, at which the subsidiaries' management accountants propose target levels to their head offices. However, at these case companies the subsidiaries' management accountants do not only have to propose target levels but also have to explain and justify them in written statements. At MaNuCo, the subsidiaries even have to propose concrete projects that help to achieve the budgeted target levels. After submitting their proposals, the subsidiaries discuss them with their head offices in budget meetings.[132] These results support prior scant evidence (*Du et al.* (2013), pp. 403-407), which suggests that subsidiaries are involved in setting budget-based targets.

---

[132] At those MNCs having multiple head offices (MaNuCo, ChemCo, and TechCo) there are also several rounds of negotiations between the various head offices (e.g., between divisional and regional head offices or between regional head offices and the corporate head office).

However, prior literature does not examine how the **final target levels are agreed on** in case of different expectations between head offices and subsidiaries. For defining the final target levels, the case companies pursue two contrasting approaches. On the one hand, the head offices take the final decision, which mitigates the subsidiaries' scope in setting target levels. All sample firms, except AgriCo, follow this approach. On the other hand, the final target levels at AgriCo are decided by a committee, which includes participants from both the head office and the subsidiaries. In addition, the committee includes members of AgriCo's owning family, which creates pressure on both sides to reach an agreement. Consequently, both the local and corporate management accountants try to reach an agreement without involving the committee:

> "For the performance measures for which we still have different opinions, we try to agree on a target level. This is a typical negotiation – as on the farmer's market [laughs]. If we could not agree on a target level, we would go to the next higher level, to the committee. However, we avoid that as far as possible, so it is more of a hypothetical approach."

> *AgriCo – Corporate management accountant*

In addition to budget-based targets, two sample firms (CarSupCo, MaNuCo) also use targets based on **past performance**, which is also in line with the findings in the literature (*Pausenberger* (1996), pp. 189-190; *van der Stede* (2003), pp. 276-279). The two sample firms proceed differently in setting these past performance-based targets. At CarSupCo, the corporate management accountants carry forward the performance of the previous business year, without requiring the subsidiaries to increase this performance. In contrast, MaNuCo's head offices demand from the subsidiaries to increase the performance by a fixed percentage each year. This percentage is agreed on every few years between the management board of MaNuCo and the private equity investor.

None of the case companies set targets based on **external** or **internal benchmarking**. The absence of **external benchmarking** might be due to a lack of data availability and high costs of external benchmarking, especially if carried out by an external consultancy firm (*Drew* (1997), p. 429). This is also in line with prior research, which finds that MNCs do not use external benchmarking for target setting (*Pausenberger* (1996), p.189-190). **Internal benchmarking** exists at two case companies (AgriCo, ChemCo), but is not used for determining the subsidiaries' target levels:

> "We have a benchmarking report in which we compare the relative target achievement of our subsidiaries. We show both the relative target achievement for each performance measures and the average target achievement. We also make a ranking to increase competition among our subsidiaries."

> *AgriCo – Corporate management accountant*

> "We benchmark the different geographical regions by comparing and sharing their actual performance results."

> *ChemCo – Corporate management accountant*

Instead, AgriCo's head office uses the internal benchmarking only to increase competition among the subsidiaries. In fact, AgriCo's head office intends to reinforce the subsidiaries' efforts in achieving the budgeted targets. Consequently, the benchmarking report compares the subsidiaries' achievement of the budgeted targets. At ChemCo, the internal benchmarking is not used for setting the subsidiaries' target levels as the benchmarking is done on a more aggregated level only. In fact, ChemCo's head office does not carry out the benchmarking on subsidiary level, but only on the level of the geographical regions (e.g., EMEA, North America, and South America). ChemCo's corporate management accountants explain this with the size of the MNC and the resulting high number of subsidiaries. Furthermore, ChemCo's head office carries out the internal benchmarking for informational purposes only and does not use it to motivate the subsidiaries.[133] Figure 6–33 summarizes the types of targets that the case companies use.

	Budget-based targets	Past performance-based targets	Benchmarking-based targets
CarSupCo	✓	✓	
ManuCo	✓	✓	
AgriCo	✓		
ChemCo	✓		
TechCo	✓		

Figure 6–33: Overview of types of targets

Prior studies do not provide evidence whether the different types of targets are **associated with different measurement perspectives**. For performance measures from the financial and customer perspective, the case companies use budget-based targets. Thus, the target levels for these two measurement perspectives are derived by detailed and formal budgeting processes. For the employee and internal process measures, the case companies set target levels rather based on the past performance of the subsidiaries:

> *"For our operational performance measures, we do not have such a detailed planning as for the financial and customer-related measures. In setting targets for the operational performance measures – such as failure rate – it is mainly relevant how the subsidiaries have performed during the recent months."*

> *CarSupCo – Corporate management accountant*

The case companies choose a less formal and less detailed planning of target levels for the employee and internal process measures. This might be because the case companies consider these two perspectives as less important than the financial and customer perspective.

---

[133] Cf. section 6.1.4.1.

The case companies also differ in terms of the **aggregation level** of the targets (see Figure 6–34). Two case companies (AgriCo, CarSupCo) determine targets only for the subsidiary as a whole. Thus, these MNCs do not define sub-targets for products or production teams. However, AgriCo's head office recommends towards the local management accountants to define sub-targets for the different production teams, for example:

> *"The subsidiaries take the targets that we have agreed with them and allocate them to the various departments and areas. An area manager can then in turn allocate the target levels to the various team leaders and teams. The targets should be passed through from top to bottom, as in a pyramid."*

> *AgriCo – Corporate management accountant*

However, this is only a recommendation and not a binding directive.[134] Consequently, AgriCo's corporate management accountants do not verify whether the local management accountants define sub-targets or not. Furthermore, the sub-targets are not reported to AgriCo's head office. The high aggregation level at AgriCo and CarSupCo could be due to the small size of these MNCs and the related lean organizational structures. In fact, both MNCs do not have regional head offices. For the corporate head office, it would therefore be very labor-intensive to set and monitor the targets at the level of production teams, for example. At the two largest case companies (ChemCo, TechCo), the head offices define the subsidiaries' target levels on a more detailed level by setting targets on product level. However, they do not define sub-targets for the sales teams.

At ManuCo, the target levels are planned in most detail. The MNC determines target levels on product and sales team level (for financial and customer performance measures) and on production-line level (for internal process and employee performance measures). ManuCo's corporate management accountants see the main advantage of detailed target levels in monitoring the subsidiaries' performance. In particular, they stress that detailed target levels allow them to better understand target deviations. For example, if a subsidiary does not meet the budgeted target for the scrap rate, ManuCo's head offices can see from which production line the deviations stem. This detailed monitoring of the subsidiaries might be possible due to ManuCo's organizational structure, which is complex for the company size. In fact, despite its small size, the MNC has regional head offices that are responsible for controlling the subsidiaries in a certain region.

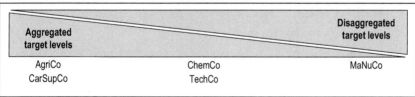

Figure 6–34: Aggregation level of targets

---

[134] This recommendation is included, for example, in an internal guideline on the parent-PMS. Defining sub-targets is intended to make the target levels more tangible and visible for the subsidiaries' employees. For example, each production team should know what results it should achieve in order for the subsidiary to achieve the overall target level.

Target evaluation

Concerning the **type** of target evaluation, the sample firms use both written performance reports and review meetings (see Figure 6–35). This is in line with prior evidence (*van der Stede* (2003), p. 276-279), which suggests that written performance reports and review meetings are equally important for head offices in evaluating the subsidiaries' performance.

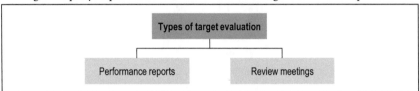

Figure 6–35: Types of target evaluation

Two different types of **written performance reports** exist at the sample firms. First, **internal benchmarking reports** are prepared by AgriCo's and ChemCo's head office. These reports show the actual performance of the subsidiaries (AgriCo) or geographical regions (ChemCo). In addition, the benchmarking reports of the two sample firms contain a ranking of the subsidiaries and regions based on their performance.[135] The second kind of written performance reports are **deviation reports**, which all case companies use. These deviation reports include the subsidiaries' actual performance and show deviations to the target levels. In the deviation reports of CarSupCo and MaNuCo, differences between actual and targeted performance are marked with color (e.g., negative deviations are marked in red). These optical accentuations shall help their corporate management accountants to identify weak points in the subsidiaries' performance at a first glance. Moreover, the colors shall also draw the attention of the local management accountants to performance measures for which the performance is below expectations. In addition to target deviations, the reports of some case companies (AgriCo, CarSupCo, MaNuCo) also include a section for comments and explanations by the local management accountants:

> *"The report starts with the performance measures and target levels. Then there is space for comments by the subsidiaries. The subsidiaries have to briefly comment on the three worst and three best performance measures of the month. It should be particularly explained why there are deviations to the target levels and what actions the subsidiaries are taking to improve the performance."*

> *AgriCo – Corporate management accountant*

> *"At the beginning of the report, there is an executive summary with all highlights and lowlights of the month. We always want to give the subsidiaries the opportunity to comment on the performance measures. Nothing is worse than having a report with the same comment or no comment at all every month. If the traffic light is green,*

---

[135] At AgriCo, the ranking is based on the relative target achievement of the budgeted targets. At ChemCo, the ranking is based on the regions' actual performance.

that's okay, but as long as the traffic light is yellow or red, there should be a comment by the subsidiaries."

CarSupCo – Head of corporate management accounting

The comment fields in the reports fulfill two functions. First, they help the management accountants in the head offices to interpret the subsidiaries' actual performance. By receiving the subsidiaries' comments, the head offices become aware of, for example, problems with the production facilities at the subsidiaries or the entry of a new competitor into the foreign market. Second, the comment fields shall ensure that the subsidiaries investigate and address the reasons for negative target deviations.

In addition to the written performance reports, the head offices evaluate the target achievement in **review meetings,** which are held at all five sample firms. In the review meetings, management accountants from both head offices and subsidiaries take part. In addition, employees from the subsidiaries' production department (CarSupCo), parts of the MNCs' management boards (AgriCo, CarSupCo, MaNuCo) and owners of the MNC (AgriCo) attend the review meetings. The attendance of the MNCs' management boards and owners shows the high importance the sample firms attach to the review meetings. The topics of the review meetings are based on information from the written performance reports, i.e., target deviations and comments from the subsidiaries. The head offices use the review meetings to clarify unclear issues in the comments and to challenge the local management accountants. At MaNuCo, the local management accountants also have to propose projects that are able to improve the performance of the subsidiaries – especially for those performance measures with negative target deviations. The status of the proposed projects is then discussed in further review meetings.

The **frequency** of target evaluation differs for performance reports and review meetings (see Figure 6–36). The performance reports are consulted monthly by the head office to evaluate the subsidiaries' performance. The frequency of the review meetings differs between the case companies. At all case companies except ChemCo, the review meetings are held on a regular basis – either quarterly (AgriCo) or monthly (CarSupCo, MaNuCo, TechCo). At ChemCo, in contrast, review meetings are held only on an ad-hoc basis. In fact, ChemCo's head offices demand explanations from the subsidiaries and ask them to take appropriate actions if necessary. As opposed to the other four case companies, ChemCo's head offices therefore do not use the review meetings to be regularly informed about relevant topics at the subsidiaries. Instead, the review meetings are used exclusively to react quickly to negative developments of the subsidiaries' performance.

Performance reports	Review meetings		
Regular, monthly basis	Regular basis		Ad hoc basis
	Quarterly	Monthly	
All five MNCs	AgriCo	CarSupCo MaNuCo TechCo	ChemCo

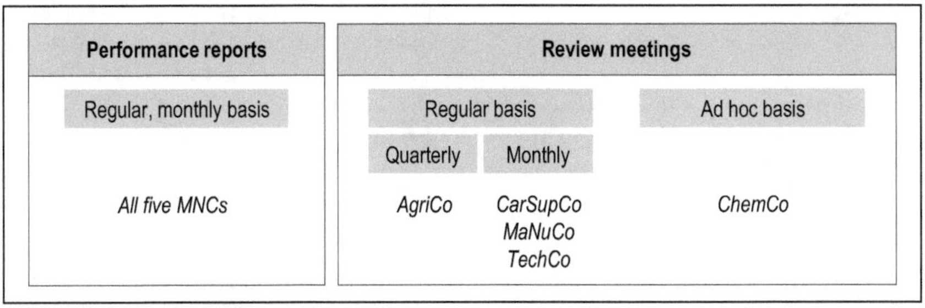

Figure 6–36: Frequency of target evaluation

6.2.2.3 Link to rewards

This section compares and contrasts whether and how the case companies link the parent-PMSs to the remuneration of the subsidiaries' employees. In a first step, it is analyzed which groups of subsidiaries' employees are eligible to bonus payments. The second step is to examine the types of rewards (individual vs. group rewards) that the case companies use. Finally, this section analyzes whether and which performance measures of the parent-PMSs are linked to the two types of rewards.

Existence of bonus payments

The few existing studies (*Dossi/Patelli* (2008); *Mahlendorf et al.* (2012); *Coates et al.* (1995)) dealing with the link of parent-PMSs to rewards only examine the link to the remuneration of the subsidiaries' management. This study adds to the literature by also including the subsidiaries' staff (e.g., production workers) in the analyses.

At all case companies, the subsidiaries' **management** has a variable component in the re-muneration (see Figure 6–37). The management includes, for instance, the CFO and CEO of the subsidiaries.

	Subsidiaries' management	Subsidiaries' staff
CarSupCo	✓	
ManuCo	✓	✓
AgriCo	✓	✓
ChemCo	✓	✓
TechCo	✓	✓

Figure 6–37: Subsidiaries' employees eligible for bonus payments

In addition, all case companies except CarSupCo also provide bonus payments for the **subsidiaries' staff**. ChemCo and TechCo use the parent-PMSs for rewarding the subsidiaries' sales staff, while ManuCo and AgriCo do so for the subsidiaries' production workers. These differences stem from the fact that the parent-PMSs refer to subsidiaries with different func-tions (sales units at ChemCo and TechCo, production units at ManuCo and AgriCo). CarSupCo's head office does not provide bonus payments for the subsidiaries' staff but for the management of the subsidiaries. This might be due to the small size of CarSupCo. In fact, prior research finds that smaller companies tend to have less elaborated reward systems than larger companies have (*Ferner/Almond* (2012), p. 248). The following paragraphs an-alyze the types of the rewards that the case companies use for the subsidiaries' management and staff.

Types of rewards

Consistent with the conceptual basis (chapter 2), individual and group rewards are distinguished. All case companies reward the subsidiaries' **management** based on both their individual and group performance. The case companies' head offices define the **individual targets** for the subsidiaries' management in written target agreements. In particular, the case companies' management boards and HR departments set these individual targets on a yearly basis. In addition to individual rewards, all case companies provide **group-based incentives** for the subsidiaries' management. The level of these group rewards differs between the case companies. At three of them (CarSupCo, ChemCo, TechCo), the bonus payments depend on the performance of the whole MNC. Thus, the rewards of a subsidiary's CFO, for example, depend on the performance of the MNC. The other two case companies (AgriCo, MaNuCo) reward the management not only based on the performance of the MNCs as a whole but also on the performance of the respective subsidiary.

For the **sales staff** of the subsidiaries, ChemCo and TechCo use group-based incentives. At both MNCs, the bonus payments depend on the performance of the sales team and the subsidiary. For the **production workers**, MaNuCo and AgriCo provide rewards solely based on the performance of the production teams. For example, at MaNuCo the production workers are grouped into different production teams according to the different production lines of the plants. Thus, the case companies tend to use **lower levels of group rewards** for the subsidiaries' staff (e.g., team level) than for the subsidiaries' management (e.g., subsidiary or MNC level). These differences might be explained by the controllability principle (*Drury/Tayles* (1995), pp. 267-268; *Merchant/van der Stede* (2007), p. 33; *Burkert et al.* (2011), p. 143).[136] In fact, the subsidiaries' staff is often only able to influence the performance of their teams rather than the performance of the whole subsidiary. For example, production workers can only influence the scrap rate of their production line (*Langfield-Smith et al.* (2006), p. 674). In contrast, the subsidiaries' management is responsible for the performance of the whole subsidiary. This might be the reason that all case companies determine the bonus payments for the subsidiaries' management based on subsidiary rather than on team performance. Three case companies (CarSupCo, ChemCo, TechCo) additionally reward the subsidiaries' management on the basis of the MNC's overall performance. The reason for this could be that the head offices of these case companies attempt to create a culture of ownership (*Hansen* (1997), pp. 37-38; *Ferreira/Otley* (2009), p 273). Figure 6–38 summarizes the types of rewards that the case companies use.

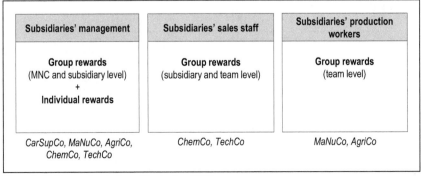

Subsidiaries' management	Subsidiaries' sales staff	Subsidiaries' production workers
Group rewards (MNC and subsidiary level) + Individual rewards	Group rewards (subsidiary and team level)	Group rewards (team level)
CarSupCo, MaNuCo, AgriCo, ChemCo, TechCo	ChemCo, TechCo	MaNuCo, AgriCo

Figure 6–38: Types of rewards used by the five MNCs

Performance measures used in reward systems

The following paragraphs analyze the performance measures that the MNCs include in the reward systems for the subsidiaries' management and staff. Attention is particularly paid to whether these performance measures originate from the parent-PMSs or not.

For the **subsidiaries' management**, a distinction must be made between individual and group rewards. At all sample firms, the **individual rewards** refer only to qualitative targets. For example, a department head might receive the individual target to oversee the implementation of a new ERP system at the subsidiary or to attend training activities. As can be seen from this example, the individual rewards are not connected to quantitative targets. Consequently, the individual rewards are not linked to performance measures of the parent-PMSs. For the **group rewards**, the situation is different. At the sample firms, the group rewards refer to quantitative targets. In fact, at all sample firms the group rewards refer to profit measures. However, the sample firms choose two contrasting approaches in selecting these profit measures. On the one hand, two MNCs (CarSupCo, MaNuCo) use profit measures from the parent-PMSs (see Table 6–19). At CarSupCo, the bonus payments depend on the EBITDA target of the MNC. At MaNuCo, the bonus payment bases on both the EBITDA of the MNC and the EBITDA of the respective subsidiary.

	Performance measures	Included in the parent-PMSs
CarSupCo	EBITDA of the MNC	
MaNuCo	EBITDA of the MNC EBITDA of the subsidiary	**Yes**
AgriCo	CFROI of the MNC ROS target of the subsidiary	
ChemCo	ROI of the MNC	**No**
TechCo	EPS of the MNC EVA of the MNC	

Table 6–19: Performance measures used for rewarding the subsidiaries' management

On the other hand, the other sample firms (AgriCo, ChemCo, TechCo) use profit measures that are not included in their parent-PMS. At AgriCo, the bonus payments depend on the MNC's CFROI and the subsidiaries' ROS. ChemCo uses the ROI of the MNC for rewarding the subsidiaries' management. At TechCo, the bonus depends on the EPS and EVA of the MNC.

Concluding, the link between the parent-PMSs and the remuneration of the subsidiaries' management **differs among the case companies**. Two case companies use a performance measure (EBITDA) from the parent-PMS for deciding on the bonus payments for the subsidiaries' management. In contrast, the other three case companies (AgriCo, ChemCo, TechCo) do not include any performance measures of their parent-PMS in their reward system. Instead, these case companies use other performance measures. Therefore, at these three case companies, the performance measures of the parent-PMSs do not have an impact on the level of bonus payments for the subsidiaries' management. These differences among the case companies might arise from the different sizes of the MNCs and the relating sophistication of reward systems (*Ferner/Almond* (2012), p. 248). In this vein, the larger case companies (AgriCo, ChemCo, TechCo) could include other performance measures in reward systems than contained in parent-PMSs to broaden the focus of the subsidiaries' management *"into other areas of managerial tasks"* (*Coates et al.* (1995), p. 128). Furthermore, the larger case companies might particularly focus on selecting performance measures for reward systems that are hard to manipulate (*Atkinson et al.* (1997), p. 34; *Günther/Grüning* (2002), p. 8).[137] Since this is not necessarily the case for all performance measures of their parent-PMS, TechCo uses other performance measures for rewarding such as EPS:

> *"For the reward system, we consider performance measures than are contained in the annual report. Thus, we take only those performance measures that are officially reported and verified by auditors. This is to prevent any manipulation."*

TechCo – Divisional management accountant

Different than for the subsidiaries' management, the case companies use performance measures of their parent-PMS for determining the bonus payments of the **subsidiaries' staff**. At ChemCo and TechCo, the bonus of the sales staff depends on the subsidiaries' sales revenues, which are included as a performance measure in the parent-PMS:

> *"In the sales area, rewarding does not work without a sales target. Therefore, the bonus for our sales staff depends on the sales revenues."*

ChemCo – Regional management accountant

At AgriCo und MaNuCo, the bonus of the production workers depends on internal process measures of the parent-PMS. For example, the two case companies include the number of production failures or the overall equipment effectiveness in the reward systems of the production workers. The differences between the remuneration of the subsidiaries' management and staff could be again explained by the controllability principle (*Drury/Tayles* (1995), pp. 267-268; *Merchant/van der Stede* (2007), p. 33; *Burkert et al.* (2011), p. 143). The staff is only responsible for certain parts of the subsidiary performance (e.g., production workers are responsible for the failure and scrap rate). Therefore, it does not seem reasonable to use other performance measures for rewarding the subsidiaries' staff

---

[137] While this also applies to parent-PMSs (see section 2.3.2.1), it is even more important for reward systems to avoid that the subsidiaries' managers can influence the level of their bonus payments (*Choudhury* (1986), p. 190).

that they cannot influence (*Hopwood* (1972), p. 158; *Langfield-Smith et al.* (2006), p. 674; *Merchant/van der Stede* (2007), p. 33).

Overall, only the two smallest MNCs (CarSupCo, MaNuCo) use performance measures of their parent-PMS for rewarding the subsidiaries' management. The other three case companies (AgriCo, ChemCo, TechCo) rather determine the bonus payments to the subsidiaries' management based on performance measures that are not included in the parent-PMSs. This supports prior research that finds that performance measures of parent-PMSs are not important for determining the bonus payments of the subsidiaries' management (*Dossi/Patelli* (2008), p. 137; *Mahlendorf et al.* (2012), p. 708). The situation is different regarding the subsidiaries' staff (sales staff and production workers). At four case companies (MaNuCo, AgriCo, ChemCo, TechCo), the subsidiaries' staff is eligible for bonus payments. The head offices of these case companies use performance measures of their parent-PMS for rewarding the subsidiaries' staff.

6.2.2.4 IT infrastructure

This section examines the IT infrastructure of the parent-PMSs in two steps. In the first step, the types of IT systems are analyzed. The second step is to carve out how the case companies combine the different IT systems and to analyze the advantages and disadvantages of these combinations.

Types of IT systems

As pointed out in the review of prior research (chapter 3), there are so far no studies examining the **types of IT systems** that are used as an IT infrastructure of parent-PMSs. The case companies use ERP systems, BI systems, and spreadsheet software. All case companies implement **ERP systems**, which serve to collect and store performance data. However, the case companies differ in the extent to which they use an integrated, uniform ERP system throughout the group. At the one end of the scale are ChemCo and MaNuCo. ChemCo has implemented one integrated ERP system. At MaNuCo, the situation is similar as approximately 95% of the subsidiaries use the same ERP system. At the other end of the scale, the other case companies have a more heterogeneous landscape of ERP systems. This can be seen from the following quotes:

> *"Our SAP systems are not standardized worldwide. Instead, the subsidiaries have different configurations of SAP – partly for historical reasons. We therefore have a high degree of heterogeneity in our ERP systems."*
>
> *AgriCo – Corporate management accountant*

> *"We try to push forward the integration of our SAP systems worldwide. Because if every region or subsidiary has its own version of SAP, it is not really efficient. But that is an ongoing process because we are continuously acquiring companies that often have different ERP systems than we have."*
>
> *TechCo – Corporate management accountant*

"We have a colorful bouquet of ERP systems in our group. For example, we have ERP systems from ERP vendors such as SAP, Navision, and Sage."

CarSupCo – Corporate management accountant

As expressed in the quotes above, AgriCo and TechCo have implemented different systems and configurations of the same ERP vendor. At CarSupCo, the ERP systems are even more diverse since the MNC uses ERP systems from several different ERP vendors. The reasons for this heterogeneity are twofold. First, **acquisitions** of subsidiaries contribute to heterogeneity as the acquired companies often have their own ERP systems that are not necessarily identical to the ERP system implemented in the MNC (*Sheu et al.* (2004), p. 362). Since the subsidiaries are sometimes reluctant to use a new ERP system, the head offices sometimes do not require the subsidiaries to implement the established ERP system of the group. Second, the case companies underline the **high level of resources** required to implement an integrated ERP system:

"Harmonizing ERP systems is not always so easy. The subsidiaries often have other priorities than changing their ERP system. In addition, a rollout of a globally harmonized ERP system is nothing you can do overnight. This usually costs a lot of resources."

TechCo – Corporate management accountant

Particularly in the case of small subsidiaries, the high level of resources might not be justified by the benefits of an integrated ERP system. Therefore, the case companies refrain from rolling out an integrated ERP system at smaller subsidiaries. Figure 6–39 summarizes the continuum of homogeneity and heterogeneity in the ERP systems.

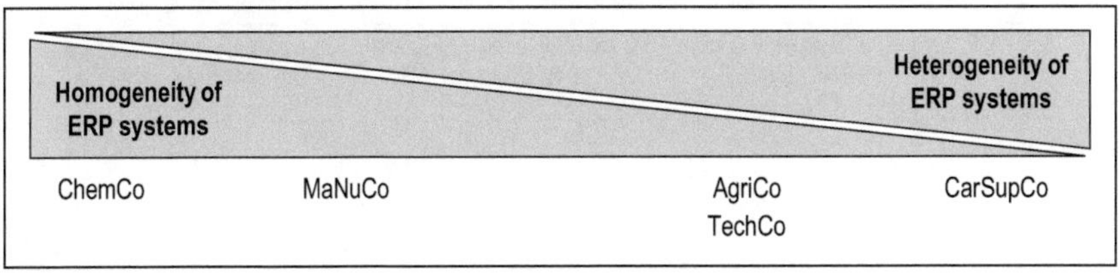

Figure 6–39: Continuum of homogeneity and heterogeneity of ERP landscape

In addition to ERP systems, four sample firms (AgriCo, MaNuCo, ChemCo, TechCo) also use **BI systems**, which serve to prepare and report performance data throughout the groups. The sample firms show different approaches in implementing BI systems. On the one hand, some case companies (AgriCo, MaNuCo, TechCo) use the same BI system at head offices and subsidiaries. ChemCo, on the other hand, has two different types of BI systems – one for the head offices and one for the subsidiaries. The BI system for the subsidiaries includes the performance data in a higher **level of detail**. For example, while the BI system for the head offices only contains data on the revenues per subsidiaries, the detailed BI system also provides the sales revenues on product level. This enables the local management accountants to prepare detailed analyses of the current performance of their subsidiaries.

Finally, two sample firms (CarSupCo, ManuCo) use **spreadsheet software**. At CarSupCo, the spreadsheet software is used instead of a BI system. Thus, the spreadsheets are used to prepare the performance data and to report it to the head offices:

> *"The subsidiaries can more or less automatically download the data from the ERP systems and then transfer it to an Excel file. This Excel file then contains the formulas that we [the corporate management accountants; added by the author] have defined for calculating the performance measure values. The Excel file contains about 15 sheets and is sent to us every month."*

> *CarSupCo – Head of corporate management accounting*

At ManuCo, the spreadsheets supplement the existing BI system. While the BI system is only used for the financial performance measures of the parent-PMS, the spreadsheets are used for preparing and reporting non-financial performance data. This is due to the fact that ManuCo's existing BI system is designed solely for financial performance measures and has no interfaces to the IT systems in the production plants. Therefore, non-financial performance measures cannot be displayed in the BI systems. At both case companies, the head offices have developed a standardized Excel-template that is provided to the subsidiaries.

These results contribute to the literature by indicating that ERP systems seem to be an integral part of the parent-PMSs' IT infrastructure. In fact, ERP systems are used at all sample firms for collecting and storing performance data. However, the sample firms differ widely in the homogeneity of the ERP systems. In addition to ERP systems, the sample firms use BI systems and spreadsheet applications. Figure 6–40 summarizes the types of IT systems used as an IT infrastructure for the parent-PMSs of the five sample firms.

	ERP systems	BI systems	Spreadsheet software
CarSupCo	✓		✓
ManuCo	✓	✓	✓
AgriCo	✓	✓	
ChemCo	✓	✓	
TechCo	✓	✓	

Figure 6–40: Types of IT systems used as IT infrastructure for the parent-PMSs

Combinations of IT systems

Building on the previous analysis, it is examined how the case companies **combine** different IT-systems. **Two approaches** of combining IT systems are evident at the case companies (see Figure 6–41).

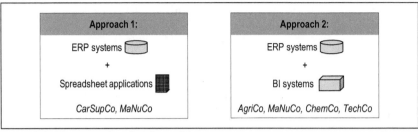

Figure 6–41: Two approaches of combining IT systems

The two approaches have in common that they include ERP systems to collect and store performance data. In the first approach, the ERP systems are combined with spreadsheet applications such as Microsoft Excel. This approach is used by CarSupCo and partly by ManuCo.[138] The second approach, which is used by AgriCo, ManuCo, ChemCo, and TechCo, combines ERP systems with BI systems. Both approaches can be compared according to their implementation time and costs, the degree of automatization, and data quality (e.g., *Borchers* (2000), p. 98; *Bititci et al.* (2002), p. 1280; *Bange et al.* (2004), pp. 11-13; *Allen et al.* (2017), p. 4).

Concerning the **implementation time and costs**, the case companies following the first approach (CarSupCo, ManuCo) emphasize the **short time** it takes to set up the Excel-based reports compared to implementing a BI system. Furthermore, the two case companies prefer this approach because they had already implemented the necessary software (Microsoft Excel). Therefore, there was no need for a time-consuming implementation of new IT systems. In addition to the short implementation time, the two case companies also emphasize the **low implementation costs** for the Excel-based solution, since no additional software has to be purchased. Furthermore, the Excel-templates were developed by the head offices without the need for external consultants. These results are in line with conceptual studies on IT systems in general (*Horváth/Seiter* (2009), p. 402; *Allen et al.* (2017), p. 4), which suggest that spreadsheets are faster and cheaper to implement than, for example, BI systems.

The two approaches also differ with regard to the **degree of automatization** in preparing and reporting the performance data. Concerning the **data preparation**, the first approach is associated with a high degree of manual work for the management accountants in subsidiaries and head offices. In the subsidiaries, the management accountants have to transfer the data from the ERP systems manually into the Excel-template:

> *"The subsidiaries have to find a way to get the data from their local ERP systems into our Excel-template. This cannot be done completely automatically – the subsidiaries rather have to manually merge the data in Excel."*

> *CarSupCo – Head of corporate management accounting*

---

[138] ManuCo used both the first and the second approach. While the first approach is used for all non-financial performance measures, the second approach is employed for all financial performance measures.

The management accountants in the head offices have to spend a lot of time and effort for consolidating the performance data over all subsidiaries. This is done every month after the local management accountants have sent the completed Excel-templates. The consolidation is hampered by the fact that the Excel-based solutions are not designed for large amounts of data:

> *"In our reporting, we are getting to the Excel limit. Therefore, we will slim down the reports in the next year and split the report into different files because they are then simply smaller and more manageable."*

CarSupCo – Head of corporate management accounting

In the second approach, data preparation is more automated. In fact, the management accountants in the subsidiaries do not have to transfer the data from the ERP system to an Excel-template. Instead, the data is automatically transferred and prepared by the BI systems. The local management accountants only have to manually enter the budgeted target values in the BI systems once a year. However, one exception is AgriCo. At AgriCo, only two thirds of the performance measures of the parent-PMS can be calculated automatically by the BI system. For the remaining third, this is impossible because the ERP systems do not contain the data for these performance measures. Therefore, the local management accountants have to manually prepare the data for one third of performance measures. In addition to the data preparation, the second approach also involves less manual effort for the management accountants when it comes to **reporting**. This is due to the fact that BI systems automatically create the reports – without the manual consolidation from the corporate management accountants. The results concerning the degree of automatization support conceptual studies on IT systems (e.g., *Bititci et al.* (2002), p. 1280; *Bange et al.* (2004), pp. 11-13), which indicate that spreadsheet solutions are less automated than BI systems and therefore more work-intensive for the management accountants in data preparation and reporting.

Finally, the two approaches differ in terms of the **quality of the performance data**. With the first approach, errors can easily occur due to the manual preparation of the data in Excel. For example, the local management accountants might intentionally or unintentionally change the formulas in the Excel-templates:

> *"One challenge is that the subsidiaries sometimes destroy the formulas in the Excel files. As a result, in review meetings it takes half an hour or one hour to go through the file to find it if everything is ok or whether there are mistakes in the formulas. Only then we can look at the content of the Excel files."*

CarSupCo – Head of corporate management accounting

To mitigate the problem of unintended errors, some head offices (CarSupCo, MaNuCo) provide guidelines and trainings on the use of the Excel-templates for the local management accountants. With the second approach, the risk of incorrect data is lower because the BI systems prepare and report the performance data automatically. However, the data quality can also be limited with the second approach, due to the **heterogeneity of the ERP systems**. This can lead to a situation where the performance measures in different subsidiaries are calculated based on different input data:

"The problem or challenge that sometimes arises is that the basis for calculating certain performance measures is not the same in all locations. The reason is that we do not have the same ERP system at all locations. I give you an example, namely failure costs: Failure costs are clustered and calculated based on different categories stemming from SAP. And we do have locations that do not have SAP and that hence do not have the same categories. Thus, when I am looking at different locations, it might be the case that what is called failure costs is not 100 % congruent between these locations. I think the only way out of this dilemma is to use the same ERP system with the same configurations in all locations."

CarSupCo – Corporate management accountant

The results concerning the data quality are in line with conceptual studies on IT systems (e.g., *Bititci et al.* (2002), p. 1280; *Bange et al.* (2004), pp. 11-13), which suggest that spreadsheet applications are more prone to errors than BI systems.

Overall, these results contribute to the literature by carving out **two different approaches** of combining IT systems in parent-PMSs. In the first approach, the case companies combine ERP systems and spreadsheets. Consistent with the argumentation in conceptual studies on IT systems (e.g., *Bititci et al.* (2002), p. 1280; *Bange et al.* (2004), pp. 11-13), this approach is quick and inexpensive to implement, but work-intensive and prone to errors. The low implementation effort of the first approach might explain why the two smallest case companies (CarSupCo, MaNuCo) use this approach. In fact, this might be because smaller companies tend to have a smaller IT budget than larger companies and therefore a less sophisticated IT infrastructure (*Möller* (2000), p. 335). In the second approach, ERP systems are implemented together with BI systems. This approach, which is used by the larger MNCs, is characterized by a higher degree automation and higher data quality but also by higher implementation effort. Figure 6–42 summarizes the advantages and disadvantages of the two approaches.

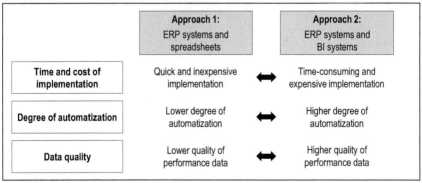

Figure 6–42: Advantages and disadvantages of the two approaches

6.2.2.5 Summary

This section summarizes the descriptive results of the design of the parent-PMSs (see Table 6–20). Concerning the **performance measures**, the cross-case analyses indicate that the five MNCs use multiple perspectives to evaluate the performance of their subsidiaries, which is in line with prior evidence (*Dossi/Patelli* (2008), p. 137). In contrast to evidence from prior literature (e.g., *Pausenberger* (1996), pp. 187-189; *Dossi/Patelli* (2010), pp. 507-511), the financial perspective is not addressed by all case companies. In fact, the parent-PMS of AgriCo does not contain any financial performance measures. This might be explained by the fact that AgriCo's parent-PMS has been implemented as part of a Production Excellence System, which focuses primarily on production processes. At the other four case companies, the financial perspective is not only represented, but is also perceived as more important than the non-financial perspectives by the MNCs' head offices, which is line with findings in prior literature (e.g., *Kihn* (2008), pp. 162-164; *Abdallah/Alnamri* (2015), pp. 601-604). The high importance that the head offices attach to financial performance can be seen, for example, in the high number of financial performance measures in the parent-PMSs. The case companies mainly consider the subsidiaries' internal processes and employees as non-financial perspectives. The internal process perspective mainly refers to production processes and contains performance measures on, for example, production quality and production efficiency. The employee perspective includes aspects such as headcount, health and safety of the employees, and employee productivity. The customer perspective addresses the order situation. These results complement prior literature, which does not provide detailed evidence on which non-financial performance measures are used by MNCs.

With respect to the **targets**, a distinction is made between target setting and target evaluation. For **setting targets**, all sample firms use budget-based targets, which are negotiated by counter-flow-planning. These results are in line with prior evidence (*Du et al.* (2013), p. 403), which indicates that subsidiaries' employees are involved in the target setting process. Besides budget-based targets, some sample firms also use targets based on past performance, which supports the findings in the literature (e.g., *Pausenberger* (1996), pp. 189-190). The case companies use neither internal nor external benchmarking-based targets. External benchmarking might be neglected because of a lack of data and high costs (*Drew* (1997), p. 429). Two case companies (AgriCo, ChemCo) benchmark their subsidiaries, but do not use this internal benchmarking for determining target levels. Instead, they use the internal benchmarking for informational purposes (ChemCo) or for motivating the subsidiaries (AgriCo). The target setting differs for the measurement perspectives. Budget-based targets are primarily used for performance measures from the financial and customer perspective. For the performance measures relating to the subsidiaries' employees and internal processes, targets are set based on past performance. **For evaluating targets**, the sample firms use both performance reports and review meetings. This supports scant prior evidence (*van der Stede* (2003), pp. 276-279), which suggests that written performance reports and review meetings are equally important for head offices in evaluating the subsidiaries' performance. The performance reports and review meetings are used by the head offices more on a regular basis (monthly and quarterly) rather than on an ad-hoc basis.

	CarSupCo	MaNuCo	AgriCo	ChemCo	TechCo
Performance measures					
Measurement Perspectives	Financials, customers, internal processes, employees	Financials, internal processes, employees	Internal processes, employees	Financials, employees	Financials, customers, employees
Financial vs. non-financial orientation	Financial	Financial	Non-financial	Financial	Financial
Targets					
Types of targets	Budgets, past performance	Budgets, past performance	Budgets	Budgets, past performance	Budgets
Type and frequency of target evaluation	Regular performance reports and review meetings	Regular performance reports and review meetings	Regular performance reports and review meetings	Regular performance reports and ad-hoc review meetings	Regular performance reports and review meetings
Link to rewards					
Bonus payments	Management	Management and staff	Management and staff	Management and staff	Management and staff
Performance measures included in reward systems	From the parent-PMS (for management)	From the parent-PMS (for management and staff)	Other performance measures (for management) and from the parent-PMS (for staff)	Other performance measures (for management) and from the parent-PMS (for staff)	Other performance measures (for management) and from the parent-PMS (for staff)
IT infrastructure					
Types and combination of IT systems	Combination of ERP systems and spreadsheets	Combination of ERP and BI systems, and spreadsheets	Combination of ERP and BI systems	Combination of ERP and BI systems	Combination of ERP and BI systems
Integration of ERP systems	Low	High	Low	Full	Low

Table 6–20: Summary of the parent-PMSs' design

Concerning the **link of parent-PMSs to rewards**, the cross-case analyses find that all case companies except CarSupCo do not only use bonus payments for the subsidiaries' management, but also for the subsidiaries' staff. In line with the results of prior studies (*Dossi/Patelli* (2008), p. 137; *Mahlendorf et al.* (2012), p. 708), three case companies (AgriCo, ChemCo, TechCo) do not use performance measures of their parent-PMS for rewarding the subsidiaries' management. Only the two smallest case companies (CarSupCo, MaNuCo) include a performance measure of the parent-PMS in their reward system. Furthermore, the bonus payments tend to be based on the performance of the entire MNC rather than on the performance of the subsidiary, which can be influenced only very indirectly by the individual manager. For rewarding the subsidiaries' sales staff and the production workers, four case companies (MaNuCo, AgriCo, ChemCo, TechCo) use performance measures of their parent-PMS. For example, the bonus of production workers depends on performance measures from the internal process perspectives of the parent-PMSs. These results complement prior literature (e.g., *Coates et al.* (1995); *Dossi/Patelli* (2008); *Mahlendorf et al.* (2012)), which exclusively deals with the rewards of the subsidiaries' management.

As regards the **IT infrastructure**, the cross-case analyses find that the case companies use ERP systems for storing and collecting performance data. However, the integration level of these ERP systems is rather low, which is in line with prior evidence (*Quattrone/Hopper* (2005), pp. 760-761). Only ChemCo uses a fully integrated ERP system for the whole group. The other four case companies either use ERP systems from different ERP vendors or use different systems from the same ERP vendor. The case companies combine the ERP systems with either spreadsheets or BI systems. In the latter approach, the degree of automatization and the data quality tend to be higher than in the former approach. However, the former approach can be implemented faster and cheaper by the head office, which might explain why this approach is primarily used by smaller MNCs. These results add insights to prior literature (e.g., *Quattrone/Hopper* (2005); *Micheli et al.* (2011)), which does not examine which types of IT systems head offices include and combine in their parent-PMSs.

6.2.3 Adoption of the parent-PMSs

6.2.3.1 Use of parent-PMSs

This section analyzes how the case companies' subsidiaries use the parent-PMSs. Consistent with the conceptual basis of this study, a distinction is made between a functional and dysfunctional use.[139]

Functional use

The functional use of the case companies' subsidiaries can be classified into the **four usage types** outlined in the conceptual basis of this study (*Simons* (1995); *Atkinson et al.* (1997); *Henri* (2006), *Schäffer et al.* (2010); *Speklé/Verbeeten* (2014):

- decision-making use,
- monitoring use,

---

[139] Cf. section 2.4.2.

- attention-focusing use, and
- learning use.

At most case companies (CarSupCo, MaNuCo, ChemCo, TechCo), the subsidiaries use the parent-PMSs for **decision-making**, which manifests itself in two ways. First, the decision-making use enables the subsidiaries' managers to **decide between decision alternatives** for both operational and strategic decisions. For this purpose, the management accountants provide the managers with performance data (e.g., performance results at product level of the previous years) from the ERP and BI systems. In addition, they simulate the effects of the decision alternatives on the performance measures of the parent-PMSs. For example, ChemCo's local management accountants simulate how different levels of product discounts affect the profit margins. This serves the sales managers as a basis for price negotiations with the customers. At CarSupCo and MaNuCo, the local management accountants calculate for instance, how the redesign of a workstation impacts performance measures such as production time and manufacturing expenses. Second, the subsidiaries **develop actions to improve their performance**. In particular, the subsidiaries use two contrasting approaches. On the one hand, the subsidiaries of some case companies (CarSupCo, ChemCo, TechCo) only develop countermeasures in case of poor performance for single or multiple performance measures. The basis for developing these countermeasures are the deviation analyses that the local management accountants prepare. The deviation analyses show which of the managers need to take countermeasures. On the other hand, MaNuCo's subsidiaries continuously develop actions and initiatives to improve performance. In fact, the managers and management accountants discuss and develop project ideas in monthly meetings:

"We are constantly developing projects to improve performance. These projects are then prioritized and a resource plan is made. And of course, the progress of these projects is regularly reviewed. To check whether the projects are successful, we use our performance measures. For example, for a project aiming at the production we use performance measures such as overall equipment effectiveness or scrap rate."

MaNuCo – Head of management accounting (Germany)

The management accountants use performance measures from MaNuCo's parent-PMS to check whether the implemented actions and initiatives have the desired effects. Figure 6–43 summarizes the two forms of the decision-making use.

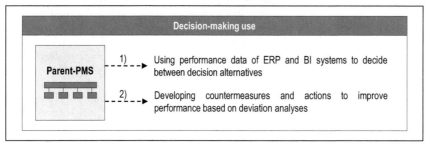

Figure 6–43: Decision-making use of parent-PMSs

The **monitoring use**, which is evident at all case companies, has three different forms. First, the subsidiaries' management accountants use the performance reports of the parent-PMSs to **evaluate whether the subsidiary achieves its targets**. In case the sample firms plan the target levels in detail, the management accountants also evaluate whether the different products, brands, and teams meet the targets. The timing of this target evaluation differs between the case companies. For case companies in which the subsidiaries have to create the reports manually in spreadsheet software (CarSupCo, MaNuCo), the target evaluation takes place before the reports are sent to the head offices. In fact, immediately after preparing the reports, the management accountants check for each performance measure whether the target level is reached. At the other case companies (AgriCo, ChemCo, TechCo), the management accountants examine the achievement of targets instantly after the reports are available in the BI systems of the parent-PMSs.

Second, the subsidiaries' management accountants **analyze the causes of target deviations**:

> *"When we have deviations to our targets, we dig deeper into the data. Imagine we have a problem in the costs of production. We can then easily check which type of cost created this deviation and then we can drill down to the invoice and so on."*

CarSupCo – Head of management accounting (Poland)

> *"We look at the reasons for the deviations from the budget. For example, we break down the manufacturing variances into different parts such as purchase price variations or manufacturing overhead. By doing this, we can examine in detail where the deviations come from."*

MaNuCo – Head of management accounting (Germany)

> *"To understand how our performance measures have developed, we look at the reports in the BI system. There we can filter a lot, for example by brand, customer, or product. If I see that our sales have dramatically improved or declined, I can check whether this is, for example, due to grinding paper or ink pots."*

ChemCo – Management accountant (North EMEA)

To detect the causes of target deviations, the subsidiaries' management accountants follow three steps. In a first step, they look for detailed information in the ERP and BI systems. For example, they examine the invoices of purchased material to analyze whether exceptional manufacturing variances stem from increased material costs. In a second step, the management accountants prepare deviation analyses based on this information. Subsequently, they share and discuss these deviation analyses with the subsidiaries' managers (e.g., sales managers or production managers). This serves to inform the managers about target deviations. Furthermore, it helps both the subsidiaries' management accountants and the managers to better understand the reasons of the deviations. As a final step, the management accountants present the deviations to the CFOs and CEOs of the subsidiaries. However, in contrast to the discussions with the production and sales managers, only major target deviations are discussed. This serves to provide the management with a brief overview of the performance results. Furthermore, it intends to prepare the management for the review meetings, in which the head offices ask them to explain the performance results and the reasons for target deviations.

Finally, the subsidiaries of two case companies (CarSupCo, MaNuCo) use the parent-PMSs as **early-warning systems**. In particular, the subsidiaries' management accountants analyze the results of the non-financial performance measures, as they assume cause-and-effect relationships between non-financial and financial performance. This is in line with the literature, which argues that non-financial performance measures can provide early indications of deteriorating financial performance (*Ittner/Larcker* (1998), p. 2; *Dossi/Patelli* (2010), p. 502). For example, a poor performance in the failure rate might be an early indicator for future product recalls, which might influence the subsidiary's future financial performance negatively (*de Haas/Kleingeld* (1999), p. 251). Figure 6–44 summarizes the three forms of the monitoring use that are evident at the case companies' subsidiaries.

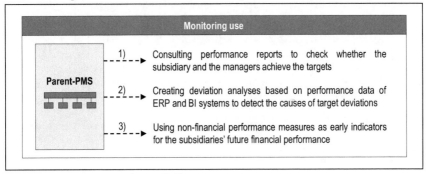

Figure 6–44: Monitoring use of parent-PMSs

At three case companies (AgriCo, CarSupCo, ChemCo), the subsidiaries' management accountants use the parent-PMSs for **focusing the managers' attention** on the performance measures and targets of the parent-PMS. The purposes behind this are twofold. First, the subsidiaries' management accountants intend to increase the **managers' awareness** for the performance measures and targets. For this purpose, they regularly discuss the performance with the managers, for example by presenting the results of the deviation analyses. In addition, they directly confront the managers with negative target deviations, which shall ensure that the managers keep an eye on their target achievement. At AgriCo's Indian subsidiary, the management accountants also present the monthly performance results on movable walls in the production halls and in the office building.[140] This is to confront the managers with their achieved performance during their daily work:

> *"We have DIN A3 sheets showing the performance. We hang them up at various points in the factory and at several other departments so that everyone can see them."*

> *AgriCo – Head of management accounting (India)*

---

[140] The idea to present the monthly performance results on movable walls stems from AgriCo's corporate management accountants. They propose this for example in an internal guideline on the parent-PMS.

Second, focusing the managers' attention shall increase the **motivation** of the managers:

> *"Everyone at our subsidiary is responsible for achieving his or her targets, otherwise we cannot achieve the EBITDA. It [the parent-PMS; added by the author] is a way of motivating our employees – it symbolizes what we need to achieve."*
>
> *CarSupCo – Head of management accounting (Brazil)*

Presenting the performance results shall stimulate the managers to achieve their targets. At two case companies (CarSupCo, ChemCo), the subsidiaries' management accountants do that mainly by explaining to each manager how he contributes to the overall performance of the subsidiary. At AgriCo, the local management accountants mainly use the monthly benchmarking reports to arouse the managers' ambition. Each manager can compare the relative target achievement of his area with those of the other subsidiaries with these reports. Figure 6–45 summarizes the two purposes of the attention-focusing use.

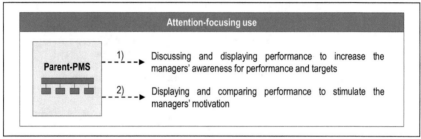

Figure 6–45: Attention-focusing use of parent-PMSs

Finally, at four case companies (CarSupCo, ManuCo, ChemCo, TechCo), the subsidiaries use the parent-PMSs for **learning** purposes. The learning use has three manifestations. First, the managers and management accountants use the performance reports to improve their **understanding of the business situation** of the subsidiaries:

> *"It [the parent-PMS; added by the author] reflects the basic understanding of the company and is a good tool to understand what is going on in such a small entity as our Polish subsidiary [...]. So overall, this allows us to understand a little bit more what is going on in our company."*
>
> *CarSupCo – Head of management accounting (Poland)*

> *"We use the performance reports in meetings with the regional managers. For example, today we have a meeting with the first line of the regional management. We put the reports on the screen and discuss the results of the month. This helps us to understand the results."*
>
> *ChemCo – Head of management accounting (South EMEA)*

A better understanding of the business situation is mainly achieved through regular discussions between the managers and management accountants. Furthermore, the management accountants of some subsidiaries (CarSupCo, ManuCo, ChemCo) also carve out and present the highlights and lowlights of the previous month to the managers. Second, the regular discussions and deviation analyses enable the subsidiaries' managers to better understand how preceding decisions have affected the performance. This allows the subsidiaries to **build knowledge and develop best practices:**

> "*The performance reports show us whether our initiatives have been successful or not. Maybe they were not as successful as we wanted, but then we learn from them. In this way, we build company-know-how. We build company-know-how that stays in the company. This is going to sound a little bit harsh, but we build know-how that stays in the company regardless whether people leave the company.*"

> *ManuCo – Head of local management accounting (Germany)*

Finally, the subsidiaries use the performance data of the parent-PMSs to **project the subsidiaries' future financial and non-financial performance.** In fact, the local management accountants prepare scenarios that represent different developments (e.g., best case, worst case, and average case). Subsequently, they present these scenarios to the subsidiaries' managers, which allows the managers to better assess future developments. Figure 6–46 summarizes the three forms of the learning use.

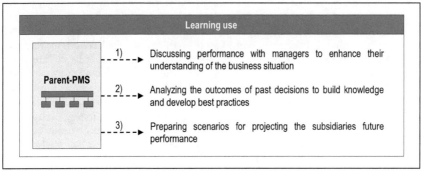

Figure 6–46: Learning use of parent-PMSs

In **summary**, the subsidiaries of the case companies use the parent-PMSs in all four potential ways outlined in the conceptual basis (see chapter 2). For decision-making, the parent-PMSs support the subsidiaries' managers in selecting between decision alternatives and in developing countermeasures and actions to improve performance (see Figure 6–47). The monitoring use is characterized by comparing actual and planned performance, identifying causes of target deviations, and by identifying negative developments as early as possible. Increasing the managers' awareness for performance measures and targets and enhancing their motivation is part of the attention-focusing use. Finally, the subsidiaries use performance data for learning purposes, which includes gaining a better understanding of the business situation, building knowledge and best practices, and projecting the subsidiaries' future performance. These results complement prior literature, which has mainly examined only the extent to which the subsidiaries use parent-PMSs (e.g., *Dossi/Patelli* (2008); *Mahlendorf et al.* (2012)).

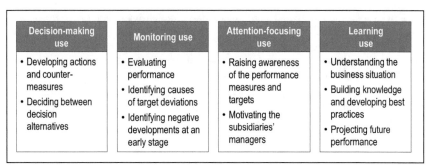

Figure 6–47: Summary of functional usage types of parent-PMSs

Dysfunctional use

Three subsidiaries (AgriCo's French and Indian subsidiary, ManuCo's Polish subsidiary) use the parent-PMSs in a **ceremonial** way (*Ansari/Euske* (1987), pp. 561-564; *Siti-Nabiha/Scapens* (2005), p. 54). At **AgriCo's French subsidiary**, the management accountants do not perceive the parent-PMS as useful for managing and controlling their subsidiary. They rather argue that it is a benchmarking tool for the head office, which has no relevance at subsidiary level. In particular, the French management accountants stress the lack of financial performance measures. However, they do not openly complain to the head office, for two reasons: First, they want to avoid conflicts with the head office, which requires all subsidiaries to use the system. Second, they understand the head office's need for having a parent-PMS, which enables the corporate management accountants to compare the performance of the subsidiaries. Consequently, the French management accountants do not demand from their head office to abolish it. They rather pretend to use it, for example by reporting performance measures, taking part in budget and review meetings, and attending the yearly award ceremony. However, the management accountants do not actually use the parent-PMS in a functional way. For example, they do not analyze reasons for target deviations or discuss the results with the production managers:

> *"Interview partner: We have what we call a shop floor management workshop every day. During this workshop, I talk with the production management about the performance measures, especially about the financial results.*
>
> *Researcher: But financial results are not included in the parent-PMS?*
>
> *Interview partner: Yes, you are right. However, for us it is very important to have a clear link to the P&L, even if financial results are not part of the system. Therefore, we have our own system [Manufacturing Balanced Scorecard; added by the author].*
>
> *Researcher: So, in these meetings, are you discussing the performance measures from the parent-PMS or from the Manufacturing Balanced Scorecard?*
>
> *Interview partner: I would say we definitely focus more on the Manufacturing Balanced Scorecard."*
>
> *AgriCo – Head of management accounting (France)*

As expressed by the discussion above, the French management accountants rather discuss the performance measures of a local-PMS. Thus, they only pretend to use the parent-PMS (e.g., by reporting performance measures and attending review meetings), but do not actually do so.

At **AgriCo's Indian subsidiary**, the management accountants generally appreciate the parent-PMSs. Consequently, they do not only pretend to use it, but also actually use it in a functional way, namely for monitoring and directing the managers' attention. For example, the management accountants discuss the performance measures with the managers of the subsidiary and analyze the causes of target deviations. However, this does not apply for all performance measures:

> *"In general, we use all performance measures. However, some of them with more and others with less emphasis. The absenteeism rate makes no sense for India. In Germany, if a lot of people are ill, I know something is wrong. But in India, people don't stay at home unless they really can't come to work because they broke a leg or something. There is no such thing as paid holidays in India. Thus, the absenteeism rate makes no sense here. We only report it to Germany, because we have to."*

> *AgriCo – Head of management accounting (India)*

The Indian management accountants argue that this performance measure is meaningless, because employees in India are hardly absent from work. Furthermore, labor costs are much lower in an emerging economy such as India than in, for example, Germany. Consequently, the management accountants do not pay much attention to the results of the absenteeism rate and do not conduct deviation analyses for this performance measure. Furthermore, the absenteeism rate does not play a role in discussions with the subsidiary's managers. Thus, the management accountants use the absenteeism rate in a ceremonial way – they report this performance measure to the head office, but do not use it in a functional way.

At **ManuCo's Polish subsidiary**, the management accountants perceive all performance measures of the parent-PMS as meaningful. Therefore, they do not only report the performance measures to the head office, but also use them in a functional way. However, the Polish management accountants reject the target levels of the parent-PMS because they consider them as too high. Therefore, the management accountants at the Polish subsidiary use the target levels only in a ceremonial way. In fact, the management accountants do not examine and discuss deviations to the budget-based targets with the subsidiary's managers. Instead, they use the performance of the previous year as a target level.

The three subsidiaries have in **common** that they do not actually use the parent-PMS (or at least parts of it) in a functional way. For example, the subsidiaries' management accountants do not discuss the performance measures or target deviations with the subsidiaries' managers. Even though the management accountants do not perceive (parts of) the parent-PMS as useful, they do not openly complain to their head offices. Instead, they pretend to use the parent-PMSs, for example by reporting the performance measures to the head offices or by attending review and budget meetings. Thus, they use the parent-PMSs only ceremonially. Following NIS, the subsidiaries do so to maintain the legitimacy of the head offices in order to secure their long-term survival (*Meyer/Rowan* (1977), pp. 343-347; *Siti-*

Nabiha/Scapens (2005), p. 50). Figure 6–48 summarizes the characteristics of the ceremonial use.

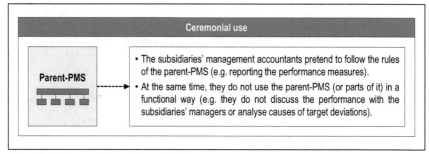

Figure 6–48: Ceremonial use of parent-PMSs

However, the three subsidiaries differ in the **extent** to which they use the parent-PMSs in a ceremonial way. At the one end of the scale is AgriCo's French subsidiary. The French management accountants use the entire parent-PMS ceremonially, because they do not perceive it as useful at subsidiary level. At the other end of the scale are AgriCo's Indian and ManuCo's Polish subsidiary. At both subsidiaries, the management accountants only use parts of the parent-PMSs in a ceremonial way. The management accountants of AgriCo's Indian subsidiary only use one performance measure (absenteeism rate) ceremonially. At ManuCo's Polish subsidiary, the management accountants use all performance measures in a functional way, but use the budget-based targets only ceremonially, because they perceive the target levels as too high.

Except *Siti-Nabiha/Scapens* (2005), prior literature only examined the extent of use, but does not provide descriptive evidence on how subsidiaries can use parent-PMSs in a dysfunctional way. Therefore, these results add to the literature in **two ways**. First, the results show that the ceremonial use can have different manifestations. Subsidiaries might not only use performance measures in a ceremonial way (as in the case study of *Siti-Nabiha/Scapens* (2005), but also **other elements** of parent-PMSs (e.g., targets) if they do not consider these elements as useful. Second, the results indicate that the ceremonial use is not an either-or-issue, but should be considered as a **degree**. In fact, subsidiaries might use only a single performance measure or the entire parent-PMS in a ceremonial way.

In **summary**, the subsidiaries of the case companies use the parent-PMSs in both a functional and dysfunctional way (see Figure 6–49). Concerning the functional use, the subsidiaries show a decision-making, monitoring, attention-focusing, and learning use. With regard to the dysfunctional use, three subsidiaries reveal a ceremonial use.

	Decision-making use	Monitoring use	Attention-focusing use	Learning use	Ceremonial use
CarSupCo	✓	✓	✓	✓	
ManuCo	✓	✓		✓	✓
AgriCo		✓	✓		✓
ChemCo	✓	✓	✓	✓	
TechCo	✓	✓		✓	

Figure 6–49: Summary of functional and dysfunctional use

6.2.3.2 Development of local-PMSs

This section analyzes the second aspect of the adoption of parent-PMS, namely the existence and design of local-PMSs.

6.2.3.2.1 Existence

As the following exemplary quotes show, several of the case companies' subsidiaries develop **local-PMSs**:

"We also have our own board – our cockpit report – on which we report our most important performance measures [...]."

AgriCo – Head of management accounting (India)

"We are evaluated on the basis of the consolidated reports. However, local reports also play an important role for us. Our local reports help us sometimes to provide explanations for deviations to our head office."

ChemCo – Head of management accounting (South EMEA)

"We have some performance measures in our local reports that are missing from the manufacturing report. These performance measures are very important for us – that is why we include them in our daily report."

MaNuCo – Head of management accounting for production (Germany)

In fact, at all case companies at least one of the two examined subsidiaries develops a local-PMS (see Table 6–21). At one case company (AgriCo), both subsidiaries have a self-developed PMS. These results substantiate previous studies (e.g., *Siti-Nabiha/Scapens* (2005), *Dossi/Patelli* (2008), *Schäffer et al.* (2010)), which have shown that subsidiaries tend to develop their own PMSs.

	CarSupCo		ManuCo		AgriCo		ChemCo		TechCo	
	Poland	Brasilia	Germany	Poland	France	India	North EMEA	South EMEA	Oman	UAE
Existence of local-PMS	Yes	No	Yes	No	Yes	Yes	No	Yes	Yes	No

Table 6–21: Existence of local-PMSs

As indicated by the quotes above, the subsidiaries differ in how they label the local-PMSs. At AgriCo's subsidiaries, the local-PMSs have their own terminology and are labeled as "*Manufacturing Balanced Scorecard*" (AgriCo France) and "*Cockpit Report*" (AgriCo India). At the subsidiaries (CarSupCo Poland, ManuCo Germany, ChemCo South EMEA, TechCo Oman), the employees simply speak of, for example, "*local reports*" (ChemCo Italy) or "*local performance measures*" (TechCo Oman).

So far, little is known about the **characteristics** of local-PMSs.[141] In particular, the literature lacks understanding which objectives the subsidiaries pursue with the local-PMSs, which departments within the subsidiaries are responsible for developing the local-PMSs, and whether the head offices know about the existence of the local-PMSs. Consequently, the following paragraphs discuss these three aspects.

First, the literature provides conflicting results regarding the **objectives** that the subsidiaries pursue with the local-PMSs. Some studies find that local-PMSs support the functioning of the parent-PMSs (*Cruz et al.* (2009); *Cruz et al.* (2011), *Cooper/Ezzamel* (2013)). In contrast, another study (*Siti-Nabiha/Scapens* (2005) provide evidence that local-PMSs serve as an alternative to the parent-PMSs. At the case companies' subsidiaries, both objectives are evident. The objective of **supporting the functioning of the parent-PMSs** is evident at most subsidiaries that have developed a local-PMS (CarSupCo Poland, ManuCo Germany, AgriCo India, ChemCo South EMEA, TechCo Oman). The employees of these subsidiaries develop the local-PMSs because they see **weaknesses in the parent-PMSs**. For example, the management accountants at TechCo Oman argue that the parent-PMSs lacks a performance measure addressing the number of local employees. The management accountants at AgriCo India question for instance the relevance of a performance measure (absenteeism rate) for the local context. To provide another example, the management accountants at ChemCo South EMEA argue that one performance report of the parent-PMS (T&A report) is not useful because it comprises too aggregated information.[142] As shown by these examples, the local-PMSs shall support the functioning of the parent-PMSs that are implemented by the head offices:

> "*For getting an overall overview of our performance, the corporate report is okay. But for analyzing it in a more detailed way, the local report is required. In this more detailed report, we can see for instance the performance of each production line. In*

---

[141] Cf. section 2.4.3.
[142] Cf. the within-case analyses in section 6.1.

my opinion, the combination of the corporate report and our own reports is really the perfect solution. "

MaNuCo – Head of management accounting (Poland)

By using both systems in combination, the subsidiaries' management accountants receive the information that they consider as important for controlling the subsidiary.

The objective of **replacing the parent-PMS** is evident at one subsidiary (AgriCo France). At this subsidiary, the management accountants develop the local-PMSs as an **alternative** to the parent-PMS. In contrast to the management accountants of the other subsidiaries, AgriCo's management accountants do not only see individual weaknesses in the parent-PMS but also perceive the entire parent-PMS as not useful for controlling the subsidiary. Therefore, the management accountants of this subsidiary exclusively use the local-PMS.[143]

These results on objectives of local-PMSs support preliminary evidence in the literature. In fact, the results of this study indicate that the local-PMSs can play **two contrary** roles for the subsidiaries. On the one hand, the local-PMSs can support the functioning of the parent-PMSs. This substantiates the findings of prior studies (e.g., *Cruz et al.* (2009); *Cooper et al.* (2013)), which argue that local-PMSs can sometimes be necessary for the parent-PMSs to work at subsidiary level (*Cruz et al.* (2009), p. 113). This might explain the results of *Dossi/Patelli*, who find that parent-PMSs and local-PMS often concurrently influence the decisions of the subsidiaries (*Dossi/Patelli* (2008), p. 114). By interpreting their findings, the authors speculate that the simultaneous use of two PMSs might indicate a lack of communication and goal incongruence between head offices and subsidiaries (*Dossi/Patelli* (2008), p. 114). However, the findings of the present study provide evidence that the simultaneous use of parent-PMSs and local-PMSs might be due to the fact that local-PMSs can be necessary for compensating the weaknesses of parent-PMSs. Thus, the existence and use of local-PMSs does not necessarily mean that the subsidiaries pursue other goals than those of the MNC.

On the other hand, the local-PMSs can replace the parent-PMSs. This is consistent with the findings in *Siti-Nabiha/Scapens*. In their study, the authors find that the employees of a domestic subsidiary develop an alternative set of performance measures that they use instead of the parent-PMS. Given these contradictory objectives of local-PMSs, it is not sufficient for researchers and practitioners (e.g., management accountants of MNCs' head offices) to examine the existence of these systems. Instead, a closer look at the roles that these systems play at subsidiary level is required.

Second, little is known about the **departments at subsidiary level** that are responsible for developing the local-PMSs. At all subsidiaries of the sample, the responsibility for developing and maintaining the local-PMSs lies with the **local management accounting department**. The subsidiaries' management accountants are responsible, for example, for selecting performance measures and setting targets. Furthermore, the management accountants of three subsidiaries (AgriCo France and India, ChemCo Italy) create internal documents such

---

[143] The parent-PMS is only used ceremonially (cf. section 6.2.3.1).

as guidelines and presentations on the local-PMSs. These documents, which exist in addition to the official documents of the parent-PMSs, contain information on, for example, the performance measures contained in the self-developed PMSs or the target setting process. In contrast to the official documents, the guidelines and presentations on the local-PMSs are not approved by the head office and are only used within the respective subsidiaries.

At four subsidiaries (AgriCo France and India, ManuCo, TechCo), **other departments** are also involved in developing the local-PMSs. At AgriCo's French and Indian subsidiaries and MaNuCo's German subsidiary, production managers support the management accountants by proposing performance measures that they consider as relevant. Furthermore, they support the management accountants in defining the performance measures. At TechCo Oman, the HR department is involved in developing the local-PMS by suggesting a performance measure. Even though employees from other departments are involved in developing the local-PMSs at these three subsidiaries, the responsibility for the local-PMSs still lies within the subsidiaries' management accounting departments.

Finally, the literature has not yet examined whether **MNCs' head offices are aware that their subsidiaries develop local-PMSs.** At the case companies, two different perspectives are evident. On the one hand, the head offices of the two largest case companies (ChemCo, TechCo) state that they **do not know** whether their subsidiaries develop local-PMSs. They simply expect that their subsidiaries do not develop their own PMSs but solely use the parent-PMSs. This is explained by the fact that these two case companies have a very large number of subsidiaries. Therefore, it is more difficult for the head offices of these two case companies to know whether a single subsidiary develops a local-PMS or not.

On the other hand, the head offices of the other case companies (CarSupCo, MaNuCo, AgriCo) are **aware that some of their subsidiaries develop local-PMSs:**

> *"Yes, such local systems exist definitely in our group. [...] This is because we at the head office have a different perspective than our subsidiaries. In the subsidiaries everything is much more operational – and do I want to interfere in operational matters of the subsidiaries? Not really. That is why our subsidiaries need to have their own, separate systems. Nevertheless, there should of course be a certain level of uniformity in our group. Therefore, we offer our performance measures and our system to the subsidiaries. We select performance measures that we believe are meaningful for operational matters at the subsidiaries. And of course, we hope that our system has a certain relevance in the subsidiaries."*

AgriCo – Head of corporate management accounting

> *"The subsidiaries also have additional information that they use, especially more detailed information. If, for example, the quality manager talks to his team, he will not only discuss our performance measures, but feed them with more detailed information. Perhaps there are also performance measures in our system that he does not care about – then he will probably not discuss them. However, it is not the case that our subsidiaries have a 'shadow world' or something like that."*

CarSupCo – Corporate management accountant

As expressed by the quotes above, the management accountants in the head offices do not perceive the existence of local-PMSs solely as negative. They rather understand the subsidiaries' need for developing their own PMSs. In particular, they argue that the subsidiaries need additional information that might be not included in the parent-PMSs.

6.2.3.2.2 Design

So far, the literature has not provided descriptive evidence on how subsidiaries design their local-PMSs. The following paragraphs analyze the design of the local-PMSs by describing their performance measures, targets, and IT infrastructure. Since none of the subsidiaries link the local-PMS to the rewards of the subsidiary's employees, this design element is not depicted here.

Performance measures

At the case companies' subsidiaries, **three** approaches of selecting performance measures for the local-PMS prevail:

1) Performance measures from the parent-PMS are transferred to the local-PMS.

2) Performance measures from the parent-PMS are changed in their definition when being transferred to the local-PMS.

3) Performance measures are selected that are not included in the parent-PMS.

First, all subsidiaries having a local-PMS take performance measures from the parent-PMS and transfer them to their local-PMS. However, the subsidiaries **differ in the extent** to which they build on performance measures from the parent-PMS. At the one end of the scale, most subsidiaries (CarSupCo Poland, MaNuCo Germany, ChemCo South EMEA, TechCo Oman) transfer all performance measures from the parent-PMS to the local-PMS (see Table 6–22). Thus, at these subsidiaries, the performance measures of the parent-PMSs are fully reflected in the subsidiaries' self-developed PMSs. For example, the local-PMS of CarSupCo's Polish subsidiary comprises all 18 performance measures that are also included in the head office's parent-PMS.

	CarSupCo		MaNuCo		AgriCo		ChemCo		TechCo	
	Poland	Brazil	Ger-many	Poland	France	India	North EMEA	South EMEA	Oman	UAE
Selected from the parent-PMS	18	n.a.	12	n.a.	4	12	n.a.	8	8	n.a.
Omitted from the parent-PMS	0	n.a.	0	n.a.	9	1	n.a.	0	0	n.a.
n.a.: not applicable because the subsidiary does not have a local-PMS										

Table 6–22: Number of performance measures selected and omitted from the parent-PMSs

At the other end of the scale, the management accountants of one subsidiary (AgriCo France) only select **few performance measures** from the parent-PMS. In fact, they omit nine performance measures from the parent-PMS that they do not consider as relevant (e.g., absenteeism rate, accident rate, suggestions from employees, and early hour failures). Thus, at this subsidiary, there is little overlap between the local-PMS and the parent-PMS regarding the performance measures.

Second, the management accountants of two subsidiaries (AgriCo France, AgriCo India) **change the definitions** of some performance measures that they take from the parent-PMS:

> "What could be improved about the performance measurement is the definition of performance measures. We still have our own definitions for individual performance measures. We have already made suggestions to our head office on how the definitions could be improved."

> AgriCo – Management accountant (France)

Since the performance measures that changed in definition are also reported in the parent-PMS, the subsidiaries' management accountants calculate the performance measures in two different ways. First, they calculate them according to the instructions and guidelines of the parent-PMS. These calculations are then reported to the head office. Second, the subsidiaries' management accountants calculate the performance measures according to their own definition. This is because they consider the definitions that are used in the parent-PMS as too complex. For example, the Indian management accountants do not distinguish in their definition of employee productivity between productive and non-productive hours. Instead, they only examine the total number of hours that is needed for manufacturing a product. These calculations in the local-PMSs are not sent to the head office but remain within the subsidiary.

Finally, the subsidiaries' management accountants select **own performance measures** that are not included in the parent-PMSs. How many and which performance measures the management accountants select on their own varies between the subsidiaries. As shown in Table 6–23, the **number** of own performance measures varies between one (ManuCo Germany and TechCo Oman) and six (AgriCo France).

| | CarSupCo | | ManuCo | | Agrico | | ChemCo | | TechCo | |
	Poland	Brazil	Germany	Poland	France	India	North EMEA	South EMEA	Oman	UAE
Added by the subsidiaries	3	n.a.	1	n.a.	6	2	n.a.	2	1	n.a.

n.a.: not applicable because the subsidiary does not have a local-PMS

Table 6–23: Number of performance measures added by the subsidiaries

Concerning the **type**, the additional performance measures stem from all four measurement perspectives (see Figure 6–50). At three subsidiaries (AgriCo France, AgriCo India, ChemCo South EMEA), the management accountants add **financial** performance measures. In fact, they include the subsidiaries' sales volume (ChemCo South EMEA), sales revenues (AgriCo India), and operational expenses (AgriCo France). Since AgriCo's parent-PMS does not address the subsidiaries' financial perspective, the local-PMSs of the French and Indian subsidiaries contain an additional measurement perspective. At two subsidiaries (AgriCo France, AgriCo India), the management accountants select their own **customer** performance measures. In particular, both subsidiaries add the delivery punctuality, which indicates the number of machines that are delivered on time to the sales units.

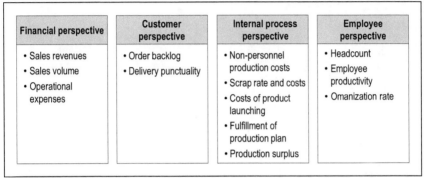

Financial perspective	Customer perspective	Internal process perspective	Employee perspective
• Sales revenues • Sales volume • Operational expenses	• Order backlog • Delivery punctuality	• Non-personnel production costs • Scrap rate and costs • Costs of product launching • Fulfillment of production plan • Production surplus	• Headcount • Employee productivity • Omanization rate

Figure 6–50: Overview of performance measures exclusively contained in the local-PMSs

At three subsidiaries (AgriCo France, CarSupCo Poland, MaNuCo Germany) the management accountants select their own **internal processes** measures. These performance measures relate to the efficiency of the production processes, such as scrap rate (CarSupCo Poland, MaNuCo Germany) and the fulfillment of production plans (CarSupCo Poland). In addition, the management accountants of one subsidiary (AgriCo France) select the costs of product launching to evaluate the efficiency of the R&D department. The management accountants of three subsidiaries (CarSupCo Poland, ChemCo South EMEA, TechCo Oman), select own performance measures addressing the **employee** perspective. They add three performance measures in total, namely employee productivity (CarSupCo Poland), headcount (ChemCo South EMEA), and omanization rate (TechCo Oman).

Overall, the local-PMSs contain different performance measures than the parent-PMSs (see Table 6–24). However, the extent of the differences varies considerably between the case companies' subsidiaries. At the one end of the scale, the management accountants of most subsidiaries (AgriCo India, CarSupCo Poland, ChemCo South EMEA, MaNuCo Germany, TechCo Oman) **build heavily** on the parent-PMS in selecting performance measures for their local-PMS. In fact, the management accountants of these subsidiaries transfer (almost) all performance measures of the parent-PMS to the local-PMS. In addition, they add performance measures that are not included in the parent-PMS. However, the number of added performance measures is rather low at these subsidiaries and varies between one (MaNuCo Germany, AgriCo India, TechCo Oman) and three (CarSupCo Poland).

	CarSupCo		ManuCo		AgriCo		ChemCo		TechCo	
	Poland	Brazil	Germany	Poland	France	India	North EMEA	South EMEA	Oman	UAE
Performance measures in parent-PMS	18	n.a.	12	n.a.	13	13	n.a.	8	8	n.a.
Performance measures in local-PMS	21	n.a.	13	n.a.	10	14	n.a.	10	9	n.a.
Thereby selected from parent-PMS	18	n.a.	12	n.a.	2	11	n.a.	8	8	n.a.
Thereby changed in definition	0	n.a.	0	n.a.	2	1	n.a.	0	0	n.a.
Thereby added by the subsidiaries	3	n.a.	1	n.a.	6	2	n.a.	2	1	n.a.

n.a.: not applicable because the subsidiary does not have a local-PMS

Table 6–24: Number of performance measures in parent-PMSs and local-PMSs

At the other end of the scale, the management accountants of one subsidiary (AgriCo France) only transfer few performance measures from the parent-PMS. Instead, they select several additional performance measures that are not included in the head office's parent-PMS. This is consistent with the notion that AgriCo's French subsidiary intends to develop the local-PMS to replace the parent-PMS. The resulting local-PMS contains two additional measurement perspectives (financial and customer perspective). Figure 6–51 summarizes the extent of differences/similarities of local-PMSs and parent-PMSs regarding the included performance measures.

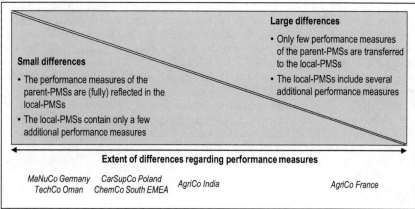

Figure 6–51: Extent of similarities and differences regarding performance measures

Targets

The **types of targets** that the subsidiaries set differ for performance measures that are taken from the parent-PMSs and for ones that are changed in definition or added by the subsidiaries (see Figure 6–52). For the former, the subsidiaries take the **target levels from the parent-PMSs**. Thus, the target levels for these performance measures refer to the budget-based and past performance-based targets of the parent-PMSs.

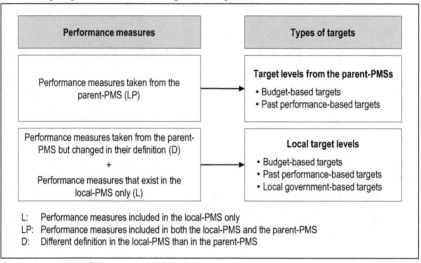

Figure 6–52: Types of targets in the local-PMSs

For the latter, the subsidiaries set **local targets**. However, one exception is MaNuCo Germany. At this subsidiary, the management accountants do not set target levels for the production surplus, which is only included in the local-PMS. This is due to the fact that an optimal level of the production surplus is difficult to determine. At the other subsidiaries, three different types of targets are used for the performance measures that are changed in definition and that are added by the subsidiaries. First, **budget-based** targets are used at two subsidiaries (AgriCo France, AgriCo India). At these subsidiaries, the target levels are derived from a local budgeting process. In this process, the subsidiaries' management accountants and the management team agree on target levels. A first proposal is made by the management accountants, which is then reviewed by the managers. In case both sides do not find a consensus, the subsidiaries' management teams take a final decision on the target levels. Second, two subsidiaries (CarSupCo Poland, ChemCo South EMEA) use **past performance-based** targets. In fact, the management accountants of these subsidiaries set the target levels by referring to the performance of the previous year. They carry forward the last year's performance without requiring an increase in the performance by a certain percentage or absolute value. Third, one subsidiary (TechCo Oman) aligns the target level for the Omanizaiton rate with the requirements of the Omani government. This is to avoid sanctions that may result from employing too few local people.

Concerning the **aggregation level** of the local targets, the subsidiaries use two contrasting approaches. On the one hand, one subsidiary (ChemCo South EMEA) uses the **same aggregation level** as defined in the parent-PMS. Thus, the target levels of the local-PMS are also only set on subsidiary level but not on product or team level. On the other hand, the three remaining subsidiaries (CarSupCo Poland, AgriCo France, AgriCo India) use target levels that are **more detailed** than those in the parent-PMSs. Thus, these subsidiaries do not only define targets on subsidiary level, but also define sub-targets on the level of production teams (AgriCo France, AgriCo India) and on product and production line level (CarSupCo Poland).

The **target evaluation** in the local-PMSs differs from that in the parent-PMS with respect to the type and frequency. Concerning the **type** of target evaluation, the management accountants prepare local, written performance reports and carry out local review meetings. The **local performance reports** exist in addition to the performance reports from the parent-PMSs. They contain either all performance measures of the local-PMSs (AgriCo France, AgriCo India, ChemCo South EMEA) or only those performance measures that are added by the subsidiaries' management accountants (CarSupCo Poland). The subsidiaries also hold **local review meetings**. In these local meetings, the subsidiaries' management accountants and managers discuss the results. For example, the managers have to explain negative deviations from targets and make suggestions on improving the performance of their area.

Concerning the **frequency** of target evaluation, two contrasting approaches prevail at the case companies' subsidiaries. On the one hand, one subsidiary (CarSupCo Poland) evaluates the targets at the **same frequency** as in the parent-PMSs, namely on a monthly basis. On the other hand, the three other subsidiaries (AgriCo France, AgriCo India, ChemCo South EMEA) **deviate from the frequency** of the parent-PMSs. At AgriCo' subsidiaries, the local review meetings are held more frequently (each month) than the review of AgriCo's parent-PMS (each quarter). At ChemCo South EMEA, the review meetings are held regularly (each month) rather than on an ad-hoc basis.

IT infrastructure

At all six subsidiaries having a local-PMS (CarSupCo Poland, MANuCo Germany, AgriCo France, AgriCo India, ChemCo South EMEA, TechCo Oman), the local-PMSs builds on an IT infrastructure. This IT-Infrastructure builds on the IT systems of the parent-PMSs (see Figure 6–53). In fact, the subsidiaries' management accountants use the IT systems of the parent-PMSs (ERP systems, BI systems, and spreadsheets) to obtain performance data on the performance measures that are also included in the parent-PMS.

For the performance measures that are only included in the local-PMS or that are changed in definition, the subsidiaries' management accountants create **spreadsheet software.** The choice of spreadsheet software has two reasons. First, spreadsheets are quick and inexpensive to implement by the subsidiaries' management accountants, because spreadsheet software is already implemented at the subsidiaries (*Horváth/Seiter* (2009), p. 402; *Allen et al.* (2017), p. 4). Second, self-developed spreadsheets are more flexible than ERP systems and BI systems implemented by the head offices (*Bange et al.* (2004), pp. 11-13; *Allen et al.* (2017), p. 4). In fact, the ERP systems and BI systems implemented at the case companies are standardized and do allow the subsidiaries' management accountants to add their own performance measures or to change the definition of performance measures.

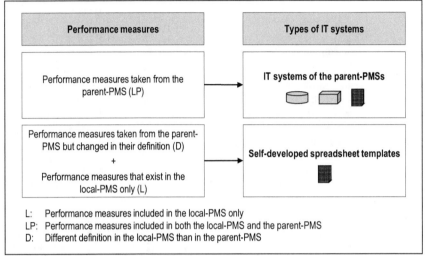

Figure 6–53: IT infrastructure of the local-PMSs

Overall, this section shows that local-PMSs differ from parent-PMSs regarding their performance measures, targets, and IT infrastructure. Concerning the performance measures, two different approaches prevail. On the one hand, almost all subsidiaries use the parent-PMS as a blueprint for designing the local-PMS. Thus, they take the performance measures of the parent-PMS and only add a few local performance measures. On the other hand, at one subsidiary the local-PMS contains only few performance measures that are also included in the parent-PMS. Concerning the targets, the subsidiaries' management accountants set local targets, which are often more detailed than the targets of the parent-PMS. The targets are evaluated based on local performance reports and local review meetings. Concerning the IT infrastructure, the subsidiaries' management accountants use the IT systems from the parent-PMS. They complement these IT systems with self-developed spreadsheet templates, which are fast and cheap to implement and provide them with a high degree of flexibility. These results add to the literature, which has almost exclusively dealt with the existence of local-PMSs but which has failed to provide descriptive evidence on the design of these systems (e.g., *Siti-Nabiha/Scapens* (2005); *Dossi/Patelli* (2008); *Mahlendorf et al.* (2012)).

6.2.3.3 Influencing factors of adoption

This section analyzes the factors that influence how the case companies' subsidiaries adopt the parent-PMSs. The factors are derived from the empirical data and are related to the theoretical framework based on NIS (see chapter 4). Consistent with this theoretical framework, the influencing factors are grouped into parent-PMS characteristics and host country and subsidiary characteristics.

6.2.3.3.1 Parent-PMS characteristics

According to NIS, the characteristics of a system determine how it is adopted at subsidiary level (*Oliver* (1991), pp. 156-157; *Kostova/Roth* (2002), p. 217). This is because these characteristics affect the subsidiaries' internalization of the system (*Oliver* (1991), pp. 156-157; *Modell* (2001), p. 461). Consequently, this study analyzes the impact of **parent-PMS characteristics** on the adoption of these systems at subsidiary level.

However, it is important to note that head offices and subsidiaries might differ in how they perceive the characteristics of the parent-PMS (*Tessier/Otley* (2012), pp. 175-176). For example, a MNC's head office might hold the opinion that it has selected performance measures that are relevant at subsidiary level, while the subsidiaries do not consider these performance measures as useful (*Lebas* (1995), p. 24). This could be the case if the head office does not know what is important at subsidiary level (*Ciabuschi et al.* (2011), pp. 961-962; *Schäffer/Mahlendorf* (2014), pp. 21-22; *Egelhoff/Wolf* (2017), p. 87). For the subsidiaries' internalization of the parent-PMS – and hence their adoption of the parent-PMS – it is relevant how the **subsidiaries** evaluate the parent-PMS characteristics (*Tessier/Otley* (2012), pp. 175-176; *Patelli* (2018), p. 37).

The management accounting literature (e.g., *Dossi/Patelli* (2008); *Schäffer et al.* (2010)) provides little evidence on the characteristics of parent-PMSs that influence their adoption. Based on prior evidence and the empirical data, **four** characteristics of parent-PMSs have been identified that affect the adoption at subsidiary level (see Figure 6–54).

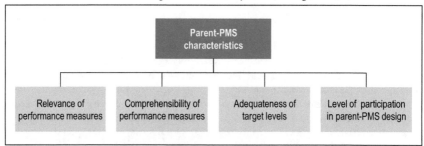

Figure 6–54: Overview of parent-PMS characteristics

Relevance of performance measures

The management accounting literature argues that head offices should select performance measures that are **relevant** at both head office and subsidiary level (*Lebas* (1995), p. 24; *Patelli* (2018), pp. 35-37).[144] However, subsidiaries might have a different opinion on the relevance of the performance measures included in parent-PMSs (*Lebas* (1995), p. 24). In particular, the subsidiaries might perceive (some of) the performance measures of the parent-PMS as irrelevant or might miss certain performance measures (*Schäffer et al.* (2010), p. 313; *Islam et al.* (2018), pp. 84-85; *Patelli* (2018), pp. 35-37). Despite these arguments,

---

[144] Cf. also *Atkinson et al.* (1997), p. 34; *Gleich* (2011), p. 298. Cf. also section 2.3.2.1.

the literature has not yet provided empirical evidence whether and how the subsidiaries' perceived relevance affects the adoption of the parent-PMSs.[145]

At the case companies, **six subsidiaries** (CarSupCo Poland, MaNuCo Germany, Agrico France, AgriCo India, ChemCo South EMEA, TechCo Oman) criticize the head offices' choice of performance measures. First, one subsidiary (AgriCo India) argues that the parent-PMS contains a performance measure that is **irrelevant** for the subsidiary, namely the absenteeism rate. According to the Indian management accountants, this is due to economic peculiarities in India, which result in the fact that this performance measure has no impact on the performance of the subsidiary.[146] Second, all six subsidiaries point out that the parent-PMSs **neglect** relevant performance measures:

> *"We need another performance measure that is not contained in the normal, standardized set. We need this performance measure because we have to meet the requirements of our government concerning the proportion of local employees."*

> *TechCo – Local CFO (Oman)*

> *"We have some performance measures in our local reports that are missing from the manufacturing report. These performance measures are very important for us – that is why we include them in our daily report."*

> *MaNuCo – Head of management accounting (Germany)*

Four of the six subsidiaries (CarSupCo Poland, MaNuCo Germany, ChemCo South EMEA, TechCo Oman) miss only one or two performance measures in the parent-PMS. For example, CarSupCo's Polish subsidiary criticizes that a performance measure dealing with the productivity of the production workers is missing in the parent-PMS. The two subsidiaries of AgriCo do not only miss single performance measures, but also criticize the lack of a whole measurement perspective. In fact, AgriCo's French and Indian subsidiaries point out that financial performance measures are missing in the parent-PMS, which makes it difficult to assess how the non-financial performance measures affect the financial performance of the subsidiaries. Furthermore, they are dissatisfied with the fact that the existing non-financial performance measures only relate to production processes but that they do not cover other processes (e.g., R&D processes).[147]

---

[145] Only *Dossi/Patelli* (2008) provide some evidence on this topic by showing that a higher number of measurement perspectives in parent-PMSs does not affect the extent to which subsidiaries use parent-PMSs (*Dossi/Patelli* (2008), pp. 137-140). However, the authors only examine the number of measurement perspectives but do not examine the subsidiaries' perception on the relevance of these measurement dimensions. In fact, a high number of measurement perspectives does not necessarily mean that these perspectives and the underlying performance measures are considered as relevant by the subsidiaries.

[146] The impact of economic differences between MNCs' home and host countries is discussed in section 6.2.3.4.2.

[147] This narrow focus on production processes is not only criticized by AgriCo's subsidiaries, but is also acknowledged by the case company's head office: *"One weakness is definitely that we do not evaluate all functional areas with our PMS [...]. For the future, we want to see if we also include other areas, such as administrative processes. Or research and development, which is something we have completely ignored so far."* *(AgriCo – Head of corporate management accounting)*

The subsidiaries' criticism of the relevance of the selected performance measures seems to affect the adoption of the parent-PMSs in **two ways**. First, AgriCo's Indian subsidiary indicates that the perceived relevance of the performance measures might influence the **use** of the parent-PMSs. Since the subsidiary does not see any relevance of the absenteeism rate, this performance measure is only used ceremonially and is therefore not discussed in local meetings, for example. Second, all six subsidiaries that perceive the parent-PMS as incomplete have **local-PMSs**. These local-PMSs are intended to support the functioning of the parent-PMSs by including the performance measures that the subsidiaries are missing. For example, the local-PMS of TechCo's Omani subsidiary includes a performance measure relating to the number of domestic employees.

Overall, these results indicate that the subsidiaries' perception on the relevance of the performance measures affects how they adopt the parent-PMSs. In fact, the subsidiary that perceives a performance measure as irrelevant uses this performance measure only ceremonially. The subsidiaries that miss certain performance measures include these performance measures in their local-PMSs.

Comprehensibility of performance measures

In addition to selecting relevant performance measures, head offices should ensure that the selected performance measures are **comprehensible** for their subsidiaries (*Atkinson et al.* (1997), p. 34; *Tangen* (2004), p. 728). The management accounting literature argues that head offices can achieve this by selecting performance measures that are clearly defined and easy to understand (*Maskell* (1991), p. 40; *Langfield-Smith et al.* (2006), p. 674).[148] If the head offices fail to do so, the subsidiaries may understand the performance measures in a different way than intended by the head office, which could affect the adoption of the parent-PMSs.

In line with this argumentation, the comprehensibility of the performance measures seems to affect the adoption at **AgriCo**. At this case company, the two subsidiaries complain about the low comprehensibility of some performance measures included in the parent-PMS:

> *"There is a guideline from the head office. In this guideline, there is a page for each performance measure showing how the performance values have to be calculated. The performance measures often measure the right thing, I would say, but they are often just too complex for our purposes."*

AgriCo – Head of management accounting (India)

> *"We always try to be in line with the central management accounting department in measuring the performance measures. However, the standards from the central management accounting department are not always clear."*

AgriCo – Management accountant (France)

In fact, AgriCo's subsidiaries argue that some performance measures and the underlying definitions are defined in an **ambiguous and too complex way** – even though the head

---

[148] Cf. also section 2.3.2.1.

office has issued a guideline that describes the objective and definition of each performance measure. This particularly holds for the performance measures of AgriCo's parent-PMS that are not automatically calculated and reported by the BI system, but that need to be measured and reported manually by the subsidiaries. One example is the employee productivity, which indicates how many productive hours the subsidiaries need to produce a machine. For this performance measure, AgriCo's subsidiaries find it difficult to distinguish between productive and non-productive hours.

The high complexity of some definitions is not only criticized by the subsidiaries, but is also acknowledged by AgriCo's head office:

> *"The measurement of certain performance measures is difficult. This is something we try to improve continuously. However, there are still some differences in calculating performance values between the different locations."*
>
> *AgriCo – Head of corporate management accounting*

AgriCo's subsidiaries respond to the low comprehensibility of some performance measures by **changing the definitions** of these performance measures. In fact, they create their own definitions of these performance measures in the local-PMS. For example, in its local-PMS, AgriCo's Indian subsidiary does not distinguish between productive and non-productive hours when defining the employee productivity, but only measures the total number of hours that is needed to produce a good. Therefore, two different definitions of the employee productivity exist at AgriCo's Indian subsidiary – one for the parent-PMS and one for the local-PMS.

At the other five case companies, in contrast, there is no evidence that the subsidiaries have problems with the comprehensibility of performance measures and underlying definitions. At these case companies, the subsidiaries **do not** create their own definitions of performance measures included in the parent-PMS. This might be due to two reasons. First, AgriCo's parent-PMS includes several non-financial performance measures that are company-specific and therefore do not have a commonly agreed definition (e.g., early hour failures, suppliers' delivery punctuality). At the other case companies, in contrast, the head offices rely more on common financial and non-financial performance measures. This might facilitate the subsidiaries' understanding of the performance measures and underlying definitions (*Dossi/Patelli* (2010), p. 503). Second, at two case companies (ChemCo, TechCo), all performance measures are automatically calculated by BI systems. This might reduce problems with the performance measures as the subsidiaries' management accountants do not have to collect and calculate data manually (*Bititci et al.* (2002), p. 1280; *Bange et al.* (2004), pp. 11-13).

Overall, these results indicate that the comprehensibility of performance measures might affect the adoption of parent-PMSs. In particular, subsidiaries might create their own definitions of performance measures when they consider the definitions in the parent-PMSs as ambiguous or too complex.

Adequateness of target levels

Another aspect of parent-PMSs which might affect its adoption is the adequateness of target levels. In fact, the management accounting literature argues that targets in parent-PMSs should be demanding but also achievable for the subsidiaries (*Malina/Selto* (2001), p. 53). Target levels that are perceived as too low or too high can have negative motivational effects on the evaluated employees (*Locke/Latham* (2002), pp. 705-706; *Ferreira/Otley* (2009), p. 271). Therefore, the subsidiaries' perceived adequateness of target levels might influence how they adopt the parent-PMS.

An influence of target levels on the adoption of parent-PMSs can be seen at **MaNuCo Poland**. Even though the target levels are determined by counter-flow planning between Ma-NuCo's head offices and the subsidiaries, the Polish management accountants perceive the negotiated targets as inadequate:

> *"We propose realistic targets [to the head office; added by the author]. But then they are telling us that the budget should look differently. Can we reach that? No! For instance, we shall increase the sales dramatically. How shall we do that? This is only in reach if the plan of our biggest competitor would burn. Otherwise it is not possible."*
>
> *MaNuCo – Head of management accounting (Poland)*

As illustrated by the quote above, the Polish subsidiary argues that the head office makes top-down adjustments that are **unachievable** for the subsidiary. Because the Polish management accountants consider the target levels as too high, they use the targets of the parent-PMSs only in a **ceremonial** way. In fact, they pretend to accept the head office's target adjustments but do not use the targets in a functional way. For example, they do not use them as a benchmark for the subsidiary's actual performance but rather compare the actual performance with the performance of the previous year.[149]

At the other four case companies, the subsidiaries do not complain about too high target levels. Accordingly, these subsidiaries use the targets included in the parent-PMSs in a **functional way**, for example by using them as benchmarks for their actual performance. These differences between MaNuCo and the other case companies could be explained by the fact that MaNuCo is owned by a private equity investor. This investor has high return expectations, which he communicates to MaNuCo's management board and which are then incorporated into the budgeting process:

> *"The investor bought all of our shares and he basically gives us the budget that we have to achieve each year [...]. The investor obviously wants to get the maximum and we always need to explain whether we are not able to achieve more."*
>
> *MaNuCo – Finance manager (EMEA)*

---

[149] At MaNuCo's German subsidiary, the target levels are not perceived as too high. This might be due to cultural differences between Poland and Germany and is discussed in the following section.

Overall, this result indicates that the subsidiaries' perceived adequateness of target levels might influence how they adopt the parent-PMS. In particular, subsidiaries might use targets only ceremonially and replace them by local targets if they consider the target levels as too high.

Level of participation in parent-PMS design

Finally, prior research suggests that the subsidiaries' level of participation in the parent-PMS design increases the extent to which subsidiaries use these systems (*Dossi/Patelli* (2008), pp. 138-139; *Schäffer et al.* (2010), p. 313). A participation in the parent-PMS design might influence the adoption in **two ways** (see Figure 6–55). First, a high level of participation might increase the likelihood that the parent-PMS design meets the subsidiaries' expectations (*Dossi/Patelli* (2008), pp. 131-132). For example, involving the subsidiaries in the selection of performance measures might lead to a set of performance measures that is perceived as relevant at subsidiary level.

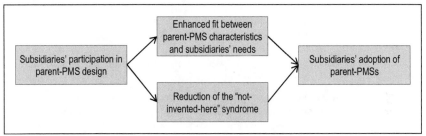

Figure 6–55: Impact of participation in parent-PMS design and adoption of parent-PMSs

Second, a participation in the parent-PMS design might increase the commitment of the subsidiaries towards the parent-PMS by reducing the so-called "*not-invented-here syndrome*" (*Kostova* (1999), p. 318, also cf. *Rautiainen/Järvenpää* (2012), p. 182). This term is used to describe a situation in which employees reject a system because it is not developed by themselves or their department but by other parts of the company (*Kostova* (1999), p. 318; *Antons/Piller* (2015), p. 206).

For analyzing the level of participation, this study distinguishes between the initial development of a parent-PMS design and later revisions of that design. At the **initial stage**, the subsidiaries of four case companies (CarSupCo, MaNuCo, ChemCo, TechCo) did not participate in designing the parent-PMSs. Instead, the head offices of these case companies implemented a parent-PMS that was solely developed at head office level. Thus, the head offices decided on their own on, for example, the performance measures and IT systems included in the parent-PMS. Only at one case company (AgriCo), the subsidiaries participated in the initial development of the parent-PMS design:

> *"When we started developing the system, the subsidiaries were actively involved. We asked them which performance measures they would like to see in the system and then developed the system together in workshops. However, this is over ten years ago. So*

many of the today's subsidiaries did not even exist and hence did not participate in these workshops."

AgriCo – Head of corporate management accounting

However, as expressed by the quote above, only a few subsidiaries participated in the design of the parent-PMS. This is because several subsidiaries were purchased or established after the initial development of the parent-PMS. This applies, for example, to the French and Indian subsidiaries, which were later acquired respectively established.

In addition to participating in the initial development, subsidiaries can also participate in **later revisions** of the parent-PMS. This applies to three case companies (CarSupCo, Ma-NuCo, ChemCo). At CarSupCo, the head office reviews the design of the parent-PMS on a regular basis. In fact, the head office asks their subsidiaries every year whether and which design elements of the parent-PMS they would like to alter or add. At MaNuCo and ChemCo, the subsidiaries are only asked occasionally, for example in review meetings, whether they have suggestions for improving the parent-PMS design. However, the head offices of the three case companies do not use the subsidiaries' proposals to create subsidiary-specific parent-PMSs. Instead, they retain the standardized approach and therefore apply changes in the parent-PMS design to all subsidiaries. Therefore, the head offices have to consider whether the proposed changes are appropriate for all subsidiaries, resulting in a low level of implemented proposals:

"The implementation rate of our proposals is rather low. This is because every proposal means that changes have to be made for all locations. Our head office therefore always asks us whether the change is advantageous for all locations. It quickly turns out that they say: 'We first have to talk to the other locations.'"

MaNuCo – Head of management accounting (Germany)

Overall, the subsidiaries seem to participate only to a small extent in the design of the parent-PMSs, especially in the initial development of the system. In later revisions, three head offices ask their subsidiaries for comments and suggestions for improving the parent-PMS design.

The low level of participation seems to affect the adoption of parent-PMSs at two case companies (MaNuCo and AgriCo). At AgriCo, both subsidiaries **criticize** the level of participation, while at MaNuCo only the German management accountants do so:

"A disadvantage of the system is that it is not customized to local needs. It would be better if they [management accountants from the head office; added by the author] would discuss the content with us and then customize it for us."

AgriCo – Head of management accounting (India)

"Interview partner: We were not involved in the selection of performance measures and the content and form of the reports. This has been decided on a global level.

Interviewer: Would you have preferred to be more involved?

*Interview partner: Yes. Absolutely. We know how we have to control our local oper-
ations, which performance measures we need, and how we find solutions. From my
point of view, it always makes sense to consult with the different locations."*

MaNuCo – Head of management accounting (Germany)

As expressed by the quotes above, the subsidiaries are **dissatisfied** with the fact that they
are not able to influence the selection of performance measures. In line with the argument
that the subsidiaries' participation might increase the fit between parent-PMS design and
subsidiaries' needs, the low level of participation at AgriCo and MaNuCo might lead to a
selection of performance measures that are not relevant at subsidiary level or to parent-
PMSs that are considered as incomplete by the subsidiaries (*Dossi/Patelli* (2008), pp. 131-
132). The former might lead to a ceremonial use of performance measures and the latter
might result in the development of a local-PMS.

Further evidence that the level of participation affects the adoption of parent-PMSs stems
from **CarSupCo**. At this case company, the subsidiaries comment **positively** on the level
of participation. The subsidiaries appreciate that they can make suggestions for improving
the design of CarSupCo's parent-PMS:

*"They [management accountants from the head office; added by the author] always
ask us if we have an idea or a suggestion. We do this on a yearly basis. But sometimes
there are points that should be done immediately – and then this is also possible.
They are very open for feedback."*

CarSupCo – Head of management accounting (Brazil)

*"We are able to make suggestions and to change things – at least to a certain extent.
For example, we eliminated a too detailed reporting of certain cost figures based on
our suggestions. It turned out that nobody was interested in these figures in the
group."*

CarSupCo – Head of management accounting (Poland)

At the Brazilian subsidiary, the participation might explain why the Brazilian subsidiary
perceives the performance measures included in the parent-PMS as relevant and hence does
not have a local-PMS. The Polish subsidiary explicitly provides an example that its participation has contributed to a change in the parent-PMS design, leading to an enhanced fit
between parent-PMS design and the subsidiary's needs. Nevertheless, the Polish subsidiary
has a local-PMS that includes additional performance measures. However, this might be
due to operational peculiarities of the Polish subsidiary that do not apply to CarSupCo's
other subsidiaries.[150] Since these operational peculiarities only apply to the Polish subsidiary, the head office cannot incorporate them in the design of the parent-PMS without de-
viating from the standardized approach.

Overall, the results support prior empirical evidence that the level of participation affects
the adoption of parent-PMSs. In particular, the results suggest that a low (high) level of

---

[150] See the analysis of operational differences in section 6.2.3.4.2.

participation negatively (positively) affects the subsidiaries' perceived relevance of the performance measures included in parent-PMSs (*Dossi/Patelli* (2008), p. 139).

Theoretical discussion

In the light of **NIS**, the results indicate that four parent-PMS characteristics affect the subsidiaries' internalization of the parent-PMS (*Oliver* (1991), pp. 156-157; *Modell* (2001), p. 461). Thus, these factors seem to determine the extent to which the subsidiaries "*see the value*" (*Kostova/Roth* (2002), p. 311) of adopting the parent-PMS. Thus, when having a high internalization of the parent-PMSs, the subsidiaries adopt them with high commitment (*Oliver* (1991), pp. 156-157; *Modell* (2001), p. 461). However, the subsidiaries' internalization can be constrained if the head offices and subsidiaries have different perceptions of the parent-PMS characteristics (*Tessier/Otley* (2012), pp. 175-176; *Patelli* (2018), p. 37). In case of a low internalization, the subsidiaries cannot simply reject the implementation of the parent-PMSs because they are dependent on the legitimacy of their head offices (*Oliver* (1991), pp. 156-157; *Modell* (2001), p. 461). The subsidiaries rather might evade the head offices' coercive pressures by using the parent-PMSs in a ceremonial way or by developing local-PMSs (*Siti-Nabiha/Scapens* (2005), pp. 46-49; *Dossi/Patelli* (2008), p. 140).

The subsidiaries' perception of the **relevance of performance measures** seem to affect the adoption of the parent-PMS at all case companies. In fact, at all case companies, at least one of two subsidiaries raise concerns about the relevance of the head offices' choice of performance measures. These concerns arise as existing performance measures are considered irrelevant and as the subsidiaries are missing relevant performance measures in the parent-PMS. Concerning the former, the results indicate that subsidiaries might tend to ignore performance measures that they consider as irrelevant by using them in a ceremonial way only. The subsidiaries that perceive the parent-PMS as incomplete tend to have a local-PMS that contains the missing performance measures. Thus, the results indicate that the choice of performance measures is an important lever for head offices to influence how valuable the subsidiaries perceive the parent-PMS and hence how they adopt these systems (*Kostova/Roth* (2002), p. 311).

Concerns about the **comprehensibility** of performance measures are only raised by AgriCo's subsidiaries, which react by creating local definitions. The subsidiaries' complaints about the comprehensibility of performance measures might be due to the fact that AgriCo's parent-PMS contains several non-financial performance measures for that no commonly agreed definition exists (*Dossi/Patelli* (2010), p. 503). The **adequateness of target levels** affects the adoption at CarSupCo's Polish subsidiary. This subsidiary perceives the target levels as too high and hence uses the targets of the parent-PMS only in a ceremonial way. The impact of target levels on the subsidiaries' internalization might be particularly strong at MaNuCo as this case company is owned by a private equity investor, who is involved in the budgeting process.

Finally, the **level of participation in parent-PMS design** seems to positively affect the internalization of CarSupCo's subsidiaries. At this case company, the head office reviews the design of the parent-PMS with the subsidiaries on a regular basis. This allows Car-SupCo's subsidiaries to suggest which performance measures to omit from the parent-PMS and which to add (*Dossi/Patelli* (2008), p. 139). This seems to have a positive effect on the relevance of the selected performance measures and hence increases the subsidiaries' internalization of the parent-PMSs.

6.2.3.3.2 Host country and subsidiary characteristics

In addition to characteristics of parent-PMSs, host country and subsidiary characteristics might influence how subsidiaries adopt these systems (*Cheng/Yu* (2012), p. 82; *Berry et al.* (2010), p. 1464). This is due to the fact that subsidiaries in MNCs are subject to **institutional duality**: The subsidiaries are not only dependent on the legitimacy of their head offices, but must also secure the legitimacy of their host countries (*Kostova/Roth* (2002), p. 216; *Roth/Kostova* (2003), p. 893).

Standardized parent-PMSs that are implemented by MNCs' head offices at the subsidiaries might not fit with the characteristics of the respective subsidiaries and host countries (*Westney* (1993), p. 61; *Vance* (2006), pp. 42-44). However, so far little empirical evidence exists whether and how host country and subsidiary characteristics affect the adoption of parent-PMSs. Based on the empirical data, **five** characteristics have been identified that are discussed in the following (see Figure 6–56).

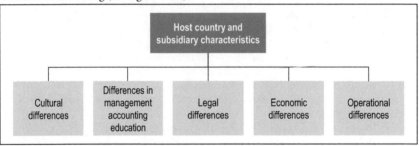

Figure 6–56: Overview of host country and subsidiary characteristics

Cultural differences

The subsidiaries of MNCs are embedded in the national cultures of their host countries (*Kostova/Roth* (2002), p. 215; *Drogendijk/Holm* (2012), pp. 384-385; *Fellner/Mitter* (2019), p. 471). This is the case, for example, because the subsidiaries hire local employees (*Roth/Nigh* (1992), p. 282; *Wu* (2015), p. 9). Given that each nation has its own distinctive culture, there are "*large cultural differences inside the MNC*" (*Drogendijk/Holm* (2012), p. 385). In general, culture can be defined as

> "*[...] the collective programming of the mind which distinguishes the members of one group or category of people from another.*"

(*Hofstede* (1994), p. 1)

Following this definition, a national culture refers to the collective mindset of the members of a nation (*Hofstede* (1994), p. 1; *Fellner/Mitter* (2019), p. 473). To analyze the effects of national culture on the adoption of parent-PMSs, the concept of national culture **needs to be operationalized** (*Chow et al.* (1999), p. 442; *Reisloh* (2011), p. 105). Management accounting research usually refers to *Hofstede* (*Chow et al.* (1999), p. 442; *Berry et al.* (2010), p. 1462), who uses six dimensions to describe and compare different national cultures (*Hofstede* (1991), pp. 13-15; *Hofstede* (2011), p. 8). For each of these dimensions, *Hofstede* assigns values between 0 and 100 to each nation, which are derived empirically (*Hofstede* (1991), pp. 13-15; *Harrison* (1993), p. 320).[151] Based on an analysis of the empirical data, the following four dimensions of national culture seem to be particularly relevant for explaining the adoption of the parent-PMSs at the case companies' subsidiaries:

- **Power distance (PD)** describes the extent to which nations accept power inequalities (*Hofstede* (1980), pp. 45-46; *Shore/Venkatachalam* (1996), p. 22). Nations with a higher (smaller) power distance tend (not) to accept power structures in which some members are more powerful than others (*Hofstede* (1980), pp. 45-46; *Chow et al.* (1999), p. 443).
- **Individualism (ID)** refers to the relationship between individuals and the groups that they are part of (*Hofstede* (1980), pp. 45-46; *Harrison* (1993), p. 323). This dimension orders nations on a continuum based on the extent to which the nations' members tend to take care of themselves (high individualism) or their group (low individualism) (*Hofstede* (1980), pp. 45-46; *Shore/Venkatachalam* (1996), p. 22).[152]
- **Uncertainty avoidance (UA)** refers to the extent to which a nation experiences discomfort with ambiguous situations and events (*Hofstede* (1980), p. 45; *Chow et al.* (1999), p. 443). Nations with a high (low) uncertainty avoidance are more (less) threatened by ambiguity and therefore tend (not) to avoid uncertain situations (*Hofstede* (1980), p. 45; *Shore/Venkatachalam* (1996), p. 22).
- **Masculinity (MA)** describes the extent to which a nation favors values such as *"assertiveness, the acquisition of money and things, and not caring for others, the quality of life, or people"* (*Hofstede* (1980), p. 46). Nations with a high (low) masculinity therefore (do not) tend to strive for material success and prestige (*Hofstede* (1980), p. 46; *Chow et al.* (1999), p. 443).

These cultural dimensions might affect **two aspects** of the adoption of parent-PMSs. First, literature shows that power distance and individualism can affect the **acceptance** of implemented practices and systems (*Chow et al.* (1999), p. 447; *van der Stede* (2003), p. 279; *Drogendijk/Holm* (2012), pp. 385-386). **Power distance** is relevant as it might explain how subsidiaries adopt systems that are implemented by more powerful actors such as head offices (*Hofstede* (1980), p. 46; *Merchant et al.* (1995), p. 622; *Drogendijk/Holm* (2012), p.

---

[151] Although management accounting research frequently used *Hofstede's* concept, there are also several points of critique on this concept (*Berry et al.* (2010), p. 1462). For a discussion of these concerns, cf. e.g. *Berry et al.* (2010), p. 1462, and *Reisloh* (2011), pp. 121-123.

[152] *Hofstede* uses the terms collectivism for a low level of individualism and femininity for a low level of masculinity (*Hofstede* (1980), pp. 45-49).

686). Subsidiaries in countries with a high (low) power distance tend to accept and comply with (oppose) systems that are implemented by head offices (*Chow et al.* (1999), p. 447; *van der Stede* (2003), p. 279; *Jiang et al.* (2015), p. 337). **Individualism** is relevant for the acceptance of implemented practices and systems as it affects the extent to which employees prefer to take decisions on their own rather than being guided by group decisions (*Shore/Venkatachalam* (1996), p. 22; *Chow et al.* (1999), p. 447). By implementing parent-PMSs, head offices restrict the subsidiaries' decision-making autonomy. For example, head offices specify the performance measures that the subsidiaries have to use for performance measurement (*Gleich* (2011), p. 215). Therefore, subsidiaries in host countries characterized by a high level of individualism might not accept the implementation of parent-PMSs (*Chow et al.* (1999), p. 447). Taking both cultural dimensions into consideration, it is expected that a high (low) power distance and a low (high) individualism increases (decreases) the subsidiaries' acceptance of parent-PMSs (*Chow et al.* (1999), p. 447; *Shore/Venkatachalam* (1996), p. 22; *van der Stede* (2003), p. 279).

At the case companies, the effect of national culture on the acceptance of the parent-PMS is particularly evident at **AgriCo**. At this case company, the subsidiaries differ greatly in how they adopt the parent-PMS:

> *"Cultural differences always play a role in the implementation. That is very colorful in this respect. The Chinese or Indian need a performance measure and want to be guided by it. The people in France, in contrast, see a performance measure more as orientation."*
>
> *AgriCo – Head of corporate management accounting*

> *"The acceptance of our system is very high in India I would say. This is because it is a very hierarchical country where things tend not to be questioned. If it is said from above that something must be done or reported in a certain way, then it will be accepted and done accordingly. In India, things are simply less questioned. What the boss says is done."*
>
> *AgriCo – Corporate Management accountant*

The Indian subsidiary accepts the parent-PMS to a high degree. This can be seen from the fact that the Indian management accountants use the parent-PMS in a functional way (with the exception of one performance measure), although they perceive weaknesses in the design of the parent-PMS such as a lack of financial performance measures. Furthermore, they develop a local-PMS with the intention to support the functioning of the parent-PMS. The French management accountants, in contrast, use the parent-PMS only ceremonially and have a local-PMS that replaces the parent-PMS.

These differences in the adoption of the parent-PMS might be explained by different levels of power distance and individualism between India and France. In fact, India is a country that is characterized by a high power distance and a moderate individualism (PD: 74, ID: 48).[153] The high power distance might be decisive for the subsidiary's desire to comply with

---

[153] All values for the national cultures are obtained from https://www.hofstede-insights.com/country-comparison/.

the head offices' intentions rather than to question the implementation of the parent-PMS (*van der Stede* (2003), p. 279). While the level of power distance in France is slightly lower compared to India, France has a much higher level of individualism (PD: 68; ID: 71). This high individualism might explain why the French subsidiary replaces AgriCo's parent-PMS by a local-PMS. In fact, due to the high level of individualism, the French management accountants might have the desire to decide on their own on, for example, the performance measures used to evaluate the subsidiary's performance (*Chow et al.* (1999), p. 447).

As a second aspect, national culture can affect the **subsidiaries' perceived adequateness of target levels** (*Chow et al.* (1999), p. 448; *Merchant et al.* (1995), p. 624; *Schuler/Rogovsky* (1998), pp. 165-166; *van der Stede* (2003), p. 268). Following the literature, this relationship can be explained by uncertainty avoidance and masculinity, which work in opposite directions (*Chow et al.* (1999), p. 448). In case of **high uncertainty avoidance**, subsidiaries prefer lower target levels, as this reduces the ambiguity whether they achieve the targets (*Chow et al.* (1999), p. 448; *Schuler/Rogovsky* (1998), pp. 165-166; *van der Stede* (2003), p. 268; *Paik et al.* (2011), p. 651). Subsidiaries operating in host countries with a **high masculinity**, is contrast, prefer higher target levels (*Chow et al.* (1999), p. 448; *van der Stede* (2003), p. 268). This is because subsidiaries that are subject to high masculinity opt for competition and aim to demonstrate their ability to achieve high targets (*Chow et al.* (1999), p. 448). Thus, uncertainty avoidance and masculinity might affect the subsidiaries' perceived adequateness of target levels, which in turn affects how they adopt parent-PMSs (see Figure 6–57).

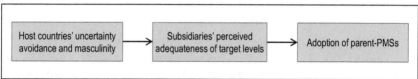

Figure 6–57: Impact of national culture on the adoption of parent-PMSs

In line with this argumentation, a relationship between national culture and subsidiaries' perceived adequateness of target levels can been seen at **ManuCo**. At this case company, the two subsidiaries differ in how they perceive the target levels of the parent-PMS. The German subsidiary considers the target levels to be appropriate and therefore uses them in a functional way. In contrast, the management accountants of the Polish subsidiary argue that the target levels are far too high and hence not achievable. Consequently, the Polish subsidiary only uses them ceremonially and defines local targets as benchmarks for the subsidiary's actual performance.[154]

National culture might explain the different perception of the target levels by ManuCo's German and Polish subsidiary. While both countries are very similar in terms of masculinity (MA Poland: 64; MA Germany: 66), there are major differences in the uncertainty avoidance. In fact, uncertainty avoidance is much higher in Poland (UA: 93) than in Germany

---

[154] Cf. section 6.2.3.4.1.

(UA: 65).[155] In line with the argumentation above, the high uncertainty avoidance in Poland therefore might explain why the Polish subsidiary perceives the target levels in the parent-PMS as too high (*Chow et al.* (1999), p. 448; *Schuler/Rogovsky* (1998), pp. 165-166; *van der Stede* (2003), p. 268). In fact, the Polish subsidiary might prefer lower target levels as this makes it more likely to achieve the targets – which in turn reduces uncertainty (*Chow et al.* (1999), p. 448). This effect might be particularly evident at ManuCo, because the target levels of ManuCo's parent-PMS are linked to the remuneration of the subsidiaries' employees (*Schuler/Rogovsky* (1998), pp. 165-166). For example, the bonus payment of the management and executive employees of ManuCo's subsidiaries depends on the EBITDA of the respective subsidiary. Therefore, target levels might be even more important for the employees of ManuCo's subsidiaries compared with the subsidiaries' employees of the other case companies (*Schuler/Rogovsky* (1998), pp. 165-166).

Overall, these results indicate that national culture might affect the adoption of parent-PMSs in two ways. First, in line with prior research (e.g., *Chow et al.* (1999), p. 447; *van der Stede* (2003), p. 279), a high power distance (high individualism) seems to positively (negatively) affect the subsidiaries' acceptance of the parent-PMS. This might explain the differences in the adoption of AgriCo's Indian and French subsidiaries. Second, the results indicate that uncertainty avoidance might affect the subsidiaries' perceived adequateness of target levels, which is in line with the results in prior literature (e.g., *Chow et al.* (1999), p. 448; *Merchant et al.* (1995), p. 624; *van der Stede* (2003), p. 268). Hence, differences in uncertainty avoidance might explain the different adoption of targets at ManuCo's German and Polish subsidiaries.

Differences in management accounting education

In addition to differences in national culture, MNCs' home and host countries can differ with respect to the **management accounting education** (*Endenich et al.* (2011), p. 365). In fact, extant literature shows that differences in management accounting education exist both within Europe (e.g., *Bhimani* (1996); *Ahrens/Chapman* (1999); *Endenich* (2012)) and between European countries and others parts of the world (e.g., *Hoffjan* (2008); *Brandau et al.* (2013)).[156] Given these differences in management accounting education, subsidiaries might understand the design of the parent-PMS in a different way than the head office. Therefore, differences in management accounting education may result in the subsidiaries adopting the parent PMSs differently than intended by the head office.

In line with this argumentation, differences in management accounting education seem to affect the adoption at **AgriCo**. The head office of this case company notes that it is difficult in some countries to hire management accountants that have a comparable education to that in Germany. This holds particularly for emerging countries such as India:

> *"In some countries, management accountants do not exist at all. In Russia and China, for example, this position is always done by financial accountants. Because*

---

[155] Poland has the highest uncertainty avoidance in the sample of this study.
[156] For a review of comparative management accounting studies, cf. *Endenich et al.* (2011).

they do not have a background in controlling, knowledge and methods are always an issue at our foreign locations."

AgriCo – Corporate management accountant

According to AgriCo's head office, problems with the adoption of the parent-PMS arise from recruiting financial accountants instead of management accountants. In particular, this causes problems in the subsidiaries' understanding of the performance measures and underlying definitions:

"In India, there is a strong focus on financial accounting and bookkeeping. Management accounting is not taught at any university [...] If performance measures then deviate too much from financial accounting, many employees are overwhelmed."

AgriCo – Head of corporate management accounting

Following the head office, the main problem of financial accountants is that they do not understand the definitions of the non-financial performance measures. This is in line with the finding that the Indian management accountants perceive these definitions as too complex.[157] This indicates that the lack of qualified management accountants in India might affect the **perceived comprehensibility** of performance measures.

The head offices of the other case companies **do not see problems** for the adoption of parent-PMSs resulting from differences in management accounting education. This might be due to several reasons. First, the sample of this study predominantly consists of subsidiaries from **European countries**. The literature indicates that differences in management accounting education are particularly large between Germany and emerging countries (*Brandau et al.* (2013), p. 467).[158] Second, it may be due to the fact that AgriCo's parent-PMS includes several **non-financial performance measures** for which no standardized definitions exist. The other case companies, in contrast, rely more on financial performance measures that are better understandable for financial accountants. Finally, the two largest case companies, ChemCo and TechCo, strongly make use of **expatriates**, who work in the local management accounting departments. This might reduce the negative effects of differences in management accounting education on the adoption of parent-PMSs.

Overall, these results indicate that differences in management accounting education might affect the subsidiaries' comprehensibility of performance measures (see Figure 6–58).

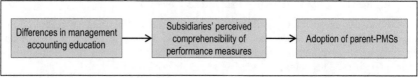

Figure 6–58: Impact of differences in management accounting education on adoption of parent-PMSs

---

[157] See the discussion on the subsidiaries' perceived comprehensibility of performance measures in the previous section.

[158] An exception is Brazil, which is strongly influenced by German management accounting concepts (*Brandau et al.* (2013), pp. 474-475). This might explain why there are no problems resulting from management accounting education at CarSupCo Brazil.

In particular, a lack of trained management accountants might reduce the comprehensibility of non-financial performance measures for that no commonly agreed definitions exist.

Economic differences

MNCs' home and host countries can differ with respect to their economic situation (*Vance* (2006), p. 42). Differences may exist, for example, in the national gross domestic products and in labor costs (*Berry et al.* (2010), pp. 1464-1465). The international business literature provides evidence that these economic differences affect a number of decisions in MNCs, for example MNCs' expansion strategies (*Berry et al.* (2010), pp. 1464-1465). However, there is no empirical evidence whether and how economic differences affect the adoption of parent-PMSs.

At **AgriCo**, economic differences seem to affect the adoption of the parent-PMS. At this case company, the two subsidiaries have different opinions on the relevance of a performance measure from the parent-PMS, namely the absenteeism rate. AgriCo's **Indian** subsidiary argues that this performance measure is not relevant due to low labor costs in India. In fact, given the low level of labor costs, the absenteeism rate only has a negligible impact on the subsidiary's performance. Therefore, it is used ceremonially by the Indian management accountants:

> *"The absenteeism rate makes no sense for India. In Germany, if a lot of people are ill, I know something is wrong. But in India, people don't stay at home unless they really can't come to work because they broke a leg or something. There is no such thing as paid holidays in India. Thus, the absenteeism rate makes no sense here. We only report it to Germany, because we have to."*

> *AgriCo – Head of management accounting (India)*

AgriCo's **French** subsidiary also notes the existence of economic differences between France and Germany:

> *"When we review our results with Germany, we also give economic explanations. For example, we look how the local market in France develops, how this can influence our performance, and what actions we should put in place to achieve our targets."*

> *AgriCo – Management accountant (France)*

However, in contrast to the Indian subsidiary, the French management accountants only see an impact of economic differences on their performance results, but not on the relevance of the performance measures. This could be due to the fact that the economic differences between Germany and France are smaller than the differences between Germany and India. This might be particularly true for labor costs, which are especially low in emerging countries such as India (*Das* (2012), p. 58; *Devajit* (2012), p. 30).

Overall, these results indicate that large economic differences between MNCs' home and host countries (e.g., emerging and developed countries) might affect the subsidiaries' perceived relevance of performance measures (see Figure 6–59).

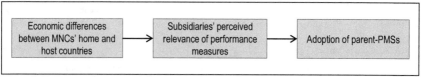

Figure 6–59: Impact of economic differences on adoption of parent-PMSs

This might explain why AgriCo's French and Indian subsidiaries differ in how they evaluate the relevance of the absenteeism rate.

Legal differences

Differences between MNCs' home and host countries can also exist in the legal systems (*Kostova/Roth* (2002), p. 215; *Berry et al.* (2010), p. 1464). Laws and standards of the local legal system might conflict with the standardized systems and practices that are implemented by MNCs' head offices (*Berry et al.* (2010), p. 1464). In this vein, the management literature provides evidence that legal differences affect the subsidiaries' adoption of management practices such as total quality management and HR systems (*Kostova/Roth* (2002), pp. 228-230; *Paik et al.* (2011), pp. 652-653). However, there is no empirical evidence whether and how legal differences influence the subsidiaries' adoption of parent PMSs.

An effect of legal differences on the adoption of parent-PMSs seems to be evident at **TechCo**. At this case company, the Omani subsidiary stresses the importance of a local law for the adoption of the parent-PMS:

> *"In Oman, the government attaches great importance that companies hire local employees. The government really requires a percentage of local employees that we have to meet. Otherwise, we are threatened with sanctions. So we need to take that into accounting when measuring performance."*

> *TechCo – Local CFO (Oman)*

The law prescribes that companies operating in Oman (including subsidiaries of foreign MNCs) must meet a minimum quota of domestic employees. Since non-compliance with the Omanization rate is associated with high sanctions, this rate is of particular importance for the subsidiary. For this reason, the subsidiary has decided to review the Omanization rate on a regular basis by including it as a performance measure in the local-PMS. This indicates that the local law has an impact on the adoption of parent PMS, even though it does not explicitly prescribe the design of parent-PMS. Instead, the local law seems to influence what the subsidiary considers important in controlling and managing the subsidiary. In fact, the local law puts the topic of Omanization on the agenda and thus affects the **subsidiaries' perceived relevance of performance measures**. Since a performance measure on the Omanization rate is not contained in TechCo's parent-PMS, the subsidiary includes it in the local-PMS.

TechCo UAE and the subsidiaries of the other case companies **do not** mention any local laws that are relevant for the adoption of the parent-PMSs. This could be due to the fact that management accounting and control systems such as parent-PMSs are not subject to legislation in most countries, especially in Europe (*Fischer et al.* (2015), p. 14; *Schulz* (2018), p. 15).

Overall, these results indicate that legal differences might affect the subsidiaries' perceived relevance of performance measures (see Figure 6–60). In particular, subsidiaries' might perceive the parent-PMSs as incomplete if local laws exist that put topics on the subsidiaries' agenda.

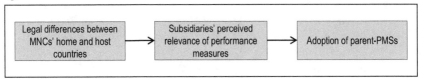

Figure 6–60: Impact of legal differences on adoption of parent-PMSs

Operational differences

Subsidiaries of MNCs can have different roles and tasks (*Jarillo/Martínez* (1990), p. 501; *Andersson/Forsgren* (2000), p. 330). For example, a subsidiary might be responsible for the production of a certain good (*Mahlendorf et al.* (2012), p. 689). Operational differences between subsidiaries might reduce the suitability of standardized parent-PMSs and hence might affect the adoption of these systems.

Operational differences seem to affect the adoption of **CarSupCo's** parent-PMS, which is adopted differently at the Brazilian and Polish subsidiaries. The **Brazilian** subsidiary perceives the performance measures of the parent-PMS as relevant. In fact, they do not miss any performance measure and do not consider performance measures from the parent-PMS as irrelevant. This is reflected in the fact, that the Brazilian subsidiary uses the parent-PMS in a functional way and does not develop a local-PMS.

In contrast, the **Polish** subsidiary perceives CarSupCo's parent-PMS as incomplete. In fact, the Polish management accountants miss performance measures dealing with the productivity of the production workers, the scrap level, and the fulfillment of production plans. These performance measures are therefore included in a local-PMS, as the following exemplary quote shows:

> *"What is really important for us is the measurement of the fulfillment of our production plan. It means we measure the percentage of the production orders that we complete in time."*
>
> *CarSupCo – Head of management accounting (Poland)*

Although both subsidiaries are responsible for the production and distribution of products, there are **operational differences** that might explain the different adoption at these subsidiaries. These differences mainly relate to the extent to which produced goods are sold on the local market. While the Brazilian subsidiary produces and sells exclusively for the local market, the Polish subsidiary mainly produces intermediate products that are shipped to CarSupCo's German production plants. This is because large quantities of these intermediate products can be manufactured at lower costs in Poland than in Germany. The Polish subsidiary receives the production schedules from CarSupCo's head office, which specify the kind, timing, and number of intermediate products that have to be shipped to Germany. Since the preliminary products still have to be finished in Germany, the punctual delivery of the preliminary products is an important aspect for the head office. However, according to the Polish subsidiary, a timely delivery of the intermediate products is sometimes difficult because the production schedules can change at short notice:

> *"So we are measuring whether we are in time with the shipment to Germany. This changes quite often, because the fluctuation of orders is quite unlimited. This is because we receive orders in a form of schedules [...] that can fluctuate significantly from one week to another."*

> *CarSupCo – Head of management accounting (Poland)*

The importance of a timely delivery might explain why the Polish subsidiary **perceives this as a relevant performance measure** and hence includes it as a performance measure in the local-PMS. This might also apply to employee productivity, as a higher productivity of production workers might positively affect the fulfillment of the production schedules. The scrap rate might also be perceived as relevant by the Polish subsidiary as the short-term changes of the production schedules could lead to a waste of materials, which negatively affect the production costs.

Overall, these results indicate that operational differences might affect what performance measures the subsidiaries perceive as relevant (see Figure 6–61). As CarSupCo's Polish subsidiary shows, subsidiaries might perceive the parent-PMS as incomplete if operational differences to other subsidiaries exist.

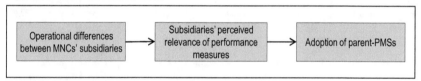

Figure 6–61: Impact of operational differences on adoption of parent-PMSs

Theoretical discussion

Based on **NIS**, it is discussed how the subsidiaries' institutional duality affects the adoption of parent-PMSs (*Kostova/Roth* (2002), p. 216; *Roth/Kostova* (2003), p. 893). These effects might result from the fact that the subsidiaries depend not only on the legitimacy of the head office, but also on that of the host country (*Oliver* (1991), pp. 154-456; *Siti-Nabiha/Scapens* (2005), pp. 46-49). At the case companies, **two opposing effects** of host country and subsidiary characteristics on the adoption of the parent-PMSs are evident.

On the one hand, cultural differences can **support** the adoption of the parent-PMS at subsidiary level. This is particularly evident at AgriCo India, where a high power distance of the host country seems to positively affect the subsidiary's acceptance of the parent-PMS. According to the NIS, this can be explained by the fact that the institutional pressures from AgriCo's head office and the host country work in the same direction (*Meyer/Rowan* (1977), pp. 352-353; *Kostova/Zaheer* (1999), pp. 67-68). In fact, both the head office's coercive pressure and the host country's cultural profile require the subsidiary to accept the parent-PMS. Since the head office's and host country's pressures are not in conflict, the subsidiary can secure the legitimacy of the head office and the host country by using the parent-PMS in a functional way (*Kostova/Roth* (2002), pp. 217-218).

On the other hand, host country and subsidiary characteristics can make it **more difficult** for the subsidiaries to adopt the parent-PMS. The results indicate that **cultural differences** complicate the adoption at AgriCo's French and ManuCo's Polish subsidiaries. At these subsidiaries, the host countries' high individualism (France) and high uncertainty avoidance (Poland) seem to negatively affect the acceptance of the parent-PMS and the adequateness of target levels (*Chow et al.* (1999), p. 447; *van der Stede* (2003), p. 279). According to NIS, the national cultures of these two subsidiaries are in conflict with the head offices' coercive pressures (*Kostova/Roth* (2002), p. 220). The subsidiaries, which require legitimacy from both sides, therefore are in a dilemma and react by pretending to use the parent-PMS and the targets, respectively. Through this ceremonial use, they secure the legitimacy of the head office, even if they do not actually use the parent-PMS and try to achieve the targets (*Oliver* (1991), pp. 154-156; *Walgenbach/Meyer* (2008), pp. 81-83).

Differences in **management accounting education** affect the adoption of the parent-PMS at AgriCo's Indian subsidiary. In fact, a lack of management accounting education in India lessens the subsidiary's perceived comprehensibility of performance measures. As a result, the subsidiary crates own definitions in the local-PMS. Since the subsidiary also continues to use the head office's definition when reporting the performance measures of the parent-PMS, the creation of local definitions does not endanger the legitimacy of the head office (*Ferner et al.* (2011), p. 178). Moreover, the results indicate that **economic differences** complicate the adoption at AgriCo's Indian subsidiary. In fact, the Indian subsidiary perceives the absenteeism rate as irrelevant due to differences in labor costs between Germany and India. By ceremonially using this performance measure, the subsidiary secures the head office's legitimacy without having to actually use it at subsidiary level (*Oliver* (1991), pp. 154-156; *Walgenbach/Meyer* (2008), pp. 81-83).

Legal differences seem to complicate the adoption of the parent-PMS at TechCo's Omani subsidiary. Because of a local law requiring the subsidiary to hire a certain amount of domestic employees, the subsidiary perceives the parent-PMS as incomplete. Therefore, it develops a local-PMS, which includes a performance relating to the number of local employees (Omanization rate). According to NIS, coercive pressures of the host country to follow the local law seem to affect the subsidiary's perceived relevance of performance measures (*Kostova/Roth* (2002), p. 216; *Walgenbach/Meyer* (2008), p. 35). By developing a local-PMS, which includes the Omanization rate, the subsidiary is able to track the percentage of domestic employees. This allows the subsidiary to comply with the host country's coercive pressures without losing the legitimacy of the head office (*Oliver* (1991), pp. 154-156; *Walgenbach/Meyer* (2008), pp. 81-83).

Finally, the results indicate that **operational differences** complicate the adoption at CarSupCo Poland. The subsidiary receives short-term changing production schedules from the head office, which leads to the fact that the subsidiary perceives the parent-PMS to be incomplete. The subsidiary includes the missing performance measures in the local-PMS, which allows the subsidiary to use the performance measures while at the same time maintaining the head office's legitimacy (*Oliver* (1991), pp. 154-156; *Walgenbach/Meyer* (2008), pp. 81-83).

Overall, host country and subsidiary characteristics predominantly complicate the adoption of the parent-PMS. As a result, the subsidiaries use the parent-PMS in a ceremonial way and develop a local-PMS. Only the host countries' national culture might also support the adoption of the parent-PMS. In fact, a high power distance might positively affect the subsidiaries' acceptance of parent-PMSs.

6.2.3.3.3 Summary

In summary, the results indicate that both parent-PMS characteristics and host country and subsidiary characteristics influence how the subsidiaries adopt parent-PMSs. However, both aspects do not seem to affect the adoption of parent-PMSs in isolation, but are connected to each other (see Figure 6–62).

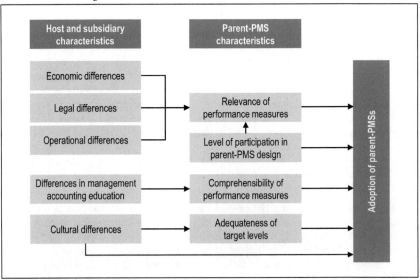

Figure 6–62: Summary of influencing factors

Economic, legal, and operational differences seem to affect the **subsidiaries' perceived relevance** of performance measures. In fact, subsidiaries seem consider performance measures of the parent-PMS as irrelevant or miss certain performance measures due to these differences. The results indicate that a **participation** of the subsidiaries in the design of the parent-PMS might positively affect their perceived relevance. This might be because a participation in the parent-PMS design allows the subsidiaries to address their individual needs resulting from economic, legal, and operational differences. In this vein, a participation of the subsidiaries seems to increase the fit between the performance measures included in the parent-PMS and the subsidiaries' needs.

The **comprehensibility** of performance measures seems to be affected by differences in management accounting education between MNCs' home and host countries. For instance, subsidiaries in host countries that lack qualified management accountants might perceive performance measures as incomprehensible and hence create their own definitions of these performance measures in the local-PMS. The subsidiaries' **perceived adequateness of target levels** might be influenced by the subsidiaries' national cultures. For instance, subsidiaries might prefer lower target levels to a high uncertainty avoidance.

6.2.3.4 Typology of adoption

This section carves out a **typology** of the adoption of parent-PMSs. The rationale for this is that identifying adoption types contributes to the theoretical generalization of a study (*Wrona* (2006), p. 207). Furthermore, typologies provide illustrative descriptions that can be used by both researchers and practitioners (*Doty/Glick* (1994), p. 230; *Kuckartz* (2018), p. 117).

As outlined in the chapter on the empirical research approach (chapter 5), the different adoption types are elaborated based on the empirical results and the theoretical framework of this study. In particular, the adoption types are based on the following three aspects:

1) Empirical results on the use of parent-PMSs,
2) Empirical results on the existence and design of local-PMSs,
3) Theoretical framework based on NIS.

Thus, the typology development combines the previous analyzes on the use of parent-PMSs and the development of local-PMSs. The results on the use of parent-PMSs contribute to the typology development by distinguishing between a **functional** and **dysfunctional** use of parent-PMSs. Concerning the results on the development of local-PMSs, the **existence** and **objectives of local-PMSs** are used to carve out different adoption types. Furthermore, the **extent of differences** in the design of parent-PMSs and local-PMSs contribute to the typology development.

The theoretical framework based on NIS serves as a lens to interpret the empirical results on the use of parent-PMSs and the development of local-PMSs (*Lukka/Vinnari* (2014), p. 1309; *Lukka/Modell* (2017), p. 40). In fact, the **four response types** to institutional pressures (acquiescence, modification, decoupling, and defiance) inform the typology development (*Oliver* (1991), p. 152; *Modell* (2001), p. 440). As proposed by the NIS, the concept of **internalization** is used to differentiate between these response types (*Oliver* (1991), p. 146; *Kostova/Roth* (2002), p. 217).

Based on these aspects, **three adoption types** are carved out (acquiescence, modification, and decoupling).

Acquiescence

First, three subsidiaries (CarSupCo Brazil, ChemCo North EMEA, TechCo UAE) adopt the parent-PMS in a way that can be related to the response type of **acquiesce** in NIS. According to NIS, acquiescence means that subsidiaries adopt parent-PMSs according to the head offices' intentions (*Kostova/Roth* (2002), p. 220). Subsidiaries do so in case of a **high internalization** of the parent-PMSs, which result from the fact that the parent-PMSs are in accordance with their expectations (*Oliver* (1991), p. 161; *Walgenbach/Meyer* (2008), p. 123).

In line with these theoretical underpinnings, the three subsidiaries have a **positive attitude** towards the parent-PMS. For example, they stress that the parent-PMS contains relevant performance measures and appropriate target levels:

> *"Interviewer: From your perspective, are there any performance measures that are missing in the reporting package of the head office?*
>
> *Interview partner: No, I would say no. The reporting package includes the important measures that we need here in Brazil. For example, the reporting package shows us how we manage our working capital or we can follow up our investments by looking at the capital expenditures. [...] The performance measures are well defined and transparent within the group in my point of view."*
>
> *CarSupCo – Head of management accounting (Brazil)*

In line with NIS, this can be interpreted as a **high internalization** of the parent-PMS at these subsidiaries (*Oliver* (1991), p. 146; *Kostova/Roth* (2002), p. 217).

The positive stance towards the parent-PMS is reflected in a **functional use** of these systems. Thus, the three subsidiaries do not pretend to use the parent-PMS but actually use them for several purposes. For example, the management accountants of these subsidiaries use the parent-PMS for monitoring their performance:

> *"To understand how our performance measures have developed, we look at the reports in the BI system. There we can filter a lot, for example by brand, customer, or product. If I see that our sales have dramatically improved or declined, I can check whether this is, for example, due to grinding paper or ink pots."*
>
> *ChemCo – Management accountant (EMEA North)*

With respect to the existence of local-PMSs, the subsidiaries within the first group have in common that they **do not have a self-developed local-PMS**. The parent-PMS implemented by the head office is therefore the only PMS that exists at these subsidiaries.

Supportive modification

Second, six subsidiaries (AgriCo India, CarSupCo Poland, MaNuCo Germany, MaNuCo Poland, ChemCo South EMEA, TechCo Oman) adopt the parent-PMS by **supportive modification**. Following NIS, supportive modification means that subsidiaries modify the parent-PMS in order to adapt them to their needs (*Cruz et al.* (2011), p. 414; *Ferner et al.* (2011), p. 178; *Cooper/Ezzamel* (2013), p. 292). This is the case if the subsidiaries **generally**

see the value of the parent-PMS, but are dissatisfied with individual aspects (*Cooper/Ezzamel* (2013), p. 292).

In accordance with the theoretical argumentation, the subsidiaries of the second group have a **positive attitude** towards the parent-PMS. However, different from the first group, they point out that the parent-PMSs also have some **weaknesses:**

> *"One strength of the system is that it makes the different locations comparable. In addition, it is very professionally developed and accepted within the group. I would even say that the system has its own corporate identity – everyone in the group knows it. The fact that the performance measures are displayed on movable walls makes it visible to everyone. The disadvantage is that you cannot adapt the system to local needs. As an example, I would like to mention this absenteeism rate, which is included in the system but which has practically no relevance for us here in India."*

> *AgriCo – Head of management accounting (India)*

> *"The performance measures from our head office reflect what is important for us – from the topline to the bottom line. We can easily check where we are. So yes, we are fine with the system [...]. But of course, we have some internal performance measures that are really important for us, such as the fulfillment of the production plan or the scrap-level of each production line."*

> *CarSupCo – Finance Director CarSupCo (Poland)*

> *"Continuity in the performance measures is always important. So that you do not come up with new performance measures every year. I think we make a good job here in the group concerning this continuity. But performance measurement also has to take conditions into account. For example, here in Oman we need another performance measure that is not contained in the normal, standardized set. We need this performance measure because we have to meet the requirements of our government concerning the proportion of local employees."*

> *TechCo – Head of management accounting (Oman)*

In particular, the subsidiaries criticize that the standardized parent-PMSs are not adapted to local conditions. They criticize, for example, that certain performance measures are missing in the parent-PMSs and that some performance measures from these systems are not relevant at subsidiary level. However, this criticism does not refer to the entire parent-PMS but only to single aspects. Therefore, the internalization within the second group can also be classified as **rather high** – albeit slightly lower than in the first group.

At the subsidiaries of the second group, the **use of the parent-PMS** is similar to the first group. In fact, the subsidiaries use the parent-PMS for several purposes such as monitoring performance and analyzing the outcomes of past decisions to develop best practices. Thus, the subsidiaries' management accountants use the parent-PMS in a **functional** way.[159]

The subsidiaries of the second group have in common that they have **local-PMSs**. With these self-developed PMSs, the subsidiaries' management accountants serve to **support the functioning** of the parent-PMSs. In fact, the local-PMSs shall compensate for the perceived weaknesses of the parent-PMSs. For example, the management accountants of TechCo's Omani subsidiary develop a local-PMS because the parent-PMS lacks a performance measure on the number of local employees. Another example is CarSupCo's Polish subsidiary, at which the management accountants develop a local-PMS because they miss a performance measure on the fulfillment of production plans, the scrap level, and employee productivity.

The objective of supporting the functioning of the parent-PMSs is also reflected in the **design** of the local-PMSs. The design of the local-PMSs **differs only slightly** from the design of the parent-PMSs. This is because the subsidiaries' management accountants build strongly on the parent-PMS in designing the local-PMSs. For example, the performance measures of the parent-PMSs are (fully) reflected in the local-PMSs. The local-PMSs differ from the parent-PMSs only in that they contain **additional elements** such as local performance measures, local performance reports, and local IT systems. These *"extra-local"* (*Cruz et al.* (2011), p. 421) elements allow the subsidiaries to mitigate the weaknesses of the parent-PMSs and hence support the functioning of these systems.

Decoupling

Finally, **decoupling** prevails at one subsidiary (AgriCo France). According to NIS, decoupling means that subsidiaries only pretend to adopt parent-PMSs without actually using them (*Meyer/Rowan* (1977), pp. 356-359; *Oliver* (1999), pp. 154-156; *Kostova/Roth* (2002), p. 220). This is the case if subsidiaries do not perceive the parent-PMS to be useful at subsidiary level (*Kostova/Roth* (2002), p. 220). In line with this argumentation, AgriCo's French subsidiary argues that the parent-PMS is a useful benchmarking tool for the head office, but which has **little relevance** at subsidiary level:

> *"The performance measures defined by our head office are more a way to make comparisons between different subsidiaries – but they are not a way to make some progress. That is why we have our own initiative [Manufacturing Balanced Scorecard; added by the author]."*

> *AgriCo – Management accountant (France)*

Thus, management accountants at this subsidiary spur a **low internalization** of the parent-PMS.

Concerning the **use of the parent-PMS**, the subsidiary does not use the system in a functional way. Thus, they do not use it, for instance, for guiding the behavior of the subsidiary's

---

[159] At two subsidiaries (AgriCo India, MaNuCo Poland) single elements of the parent-PMSs (absenteeism rate at AgriCo India and target levels at MaNuCo Poland) are used in a ceremonial way because these elements are not considered as useful. However, since these two subsidiaries use the main parts of the parent-PMSs in a functional way, they are grouped into the adoption type of supportive modification.

managers or for projecting the subsidiary's future performance. The management accountants at this subsidiary rather fulfill only the *"minimum requirements"* (*Rautiainen/Järvenpää* (2012), p. 169) of the parent-PMS, i.e. those requirements that are easily verifiable by the head office. For example, the management accountants report the performance measures and explain the performance in review meetings with the head offices. Therefore, the subsidiary's management accountants use the parent-PMS in a **ceremonial way** (*Siti-Nabiha/Scapens* (2005), p. 65).

As the subsidiaries of the second group, AgriCo's French subsidiary develops a **local-PMS**. However, this local-PMS **differs considerably** from the design of the parent-PMS. In fact, the subsidiary's management accountants select their own performance measures that are not included in the system implemented by the head office. This is because they do not consider the performance measures of the parent-PMS as useful at subsidiary level. The aim of the local-PMS is not to support the implementation or functioning of the parent-PMS, but to serve as an **alternative** that can be used for controlling the subsidiary.

Comparison of the adoption types

The three adoption types that are evident at the case companies' subsidiaries differ according to several aspects (see Table 6–25). First, the three types differ in the extent to which the subsidiaries' management accountants **internalize** the parent-PMS. Consistent with the argumentation in NIS, the internalization is highest at the subsidiaries acquiescing the parent-PMS and lowest at the adoption type of decoupling (*Oliver* (1991), p. 152; *Modell* (2001), p. 440). At the subsidiaries adopting the parent-PMS by supportive modification, the management accountants only disagree with single aspects of the parent-PMS.

Second, the three groups differ according to the **use** of the parent-PMS. At the first two adoption types (acquiescence and supportive modification), the subsidiaries' management accountants use the parent-PMSs in a functional way. The adoption type of decoupling differs from the first two adoption types by the fact that the parent-PMS is used in a ceremonial way only. With respect to the **existence and design of local-PMSs**, the subsidiaries of the first group do not develop any local systems. The subsidiaries of the other two groups, in contrast, develop local-PMSs. At the second group, the local-PMSs are intended to support the implementation of the parent-PMSs. They are similar in their design to the design of the parent-PMSs but contain additional performance measures. At the third group, the design of the local-PMS differs considerably from the design of the parent-PMS because the local-PMS contains other performance measures than the parent-PMS. The local-PMS serves as an alternative to the parent-PMS.

Characteristics	Adoption types		
	Acquiescence	Supportive Modification	Decoupling
Internalization of parent-PMSs	High (the subsidiaries are favorable of the entire parent-PMS)	Medium to high (the subsidiaries are favorable of the parent-PMS as a whole, but criticize single aspects)	Low (the subsidiary does not perceive the parent-PMS as useful at subsidiary level)
Use of parent-PMSs	Functional use (e.g., monitoring use, decision-making use)	Functional use (e.g., monitoring use, decision-making use)	Dysfunctional use (ceremonial use)
Existence and objectives of local-PMSs	Local-PMSs do not exist	The subsidiaries develop a local-PMS that is intended to support the functioning of the parent-PMS.	The subsidiary develops a local-PMS that is intended serve as an alternative to the parent-PMS.
Design of local-PMSs	Local-PMSs do not exist	The design of the local-PMS is similar to the design of the parent-PMS. The local-PMS contains additional performance measures.	The design of the local-PMS differs greatly from the design of the parent-PMS. The local-PMS mainly contains other performance measures than the parent-PMS.
Classification of the case companies' subsidiaries	CarSupCo Brazil ChemCo North EMEA TechCo UAE	CarSupCo Poland ManuCo Germany ManuCo Poland ChemCo South EMEA TechCo OMAN AgriCo India	AgriCo France

Table 6–25: Typology of the adoption of parent-PMSs

The three adoption types differ in how they fulfill the **head offices' objectives** of implementing parent-PMSs. The head offices' objective of **decision facilitation** is achieved for all three groups. In fact, none of the case companies' subsidiaries rejects to provide performance information to its head office. Instead, all subsidiaries provide this information, for example by reporting the performance measures of the parent-PMS to the head office.

For the head offices' objective of **influencing the subsidiaries' decisions,** the situation is different. The subsidiaries of the first and second group meet this objective. This is because these subsidiaries use the parent-PMS in a functional way. At the second group, the subsidiaries develop a local-PMS to support the functioning of the parent-PMS. The subsidiaries include additional performance measures in their local-PMS that they miss in the parent-PMS. This indicates that the subsidiaries are able to compensate for perceived weaknesses in the parent-PMS (e.g., missing performance measures). In this vein, the subsidiaries support the head offices in the implementation of the parent-PMS (*Cruz et al.* (2011), p. 413; *Cooper/Ezzamel* (2013), pp. 291-293).

In contrast, the subsidiary that decouples the parent-PMS does not meet the head office's objective of influencing decisions. In fact, this subsidiary only pretends to use the parent-PMS without actually using it. For example, the subsidiary's management accountants report the performance measures to the head office but do not discuss them in local meetings (*Siti-Nabiha/Scapens* (2005), p. 54). Thus, the head office is not able influence the decisions of this subsidiary. The subsidiary is rather influenced by a local-PMS that serves as an alternative to the parent-PMS (*Dossi/Patelli* (2008), pp. 143-144). This adoption type could have negative consequences for MNCs, as head offices are no longer able to influence the subsidiaries' decisions. Thus, subsidiaries might pursue their own goals, which could jeopardize the achievement of the MNCs' overall goals (*Dossi/Patelli* (2008), p. 140; *Rehring* (2012), p. 96; *Mahlendorf et al.* (2012), p. 705; *Wu* (2015), p. 10).

7 Conclusions

7.1 Main results and implications

Despite the high importance practitioners and scholars attach to parent-PMSs, two research gaps on these systems are prevailing in the literature and are hence addressed in this study. First, the literature lacks a **detailed description of the design of parent-PMSs.** In fact, many older studies on the design of parent-PMSs deal with financial performance measures only (*Schmid/Kretschmer* (2010), p. 225). These studies therefore do not provide evidence on how head offices measure the subsidiaries' non-financial performance. Furthermore, most of the newer studies that address non-financial performance measures have an explanatory focus and therefore provide little descriptive evidence. The few descriptive studies often confine to a single design element only. Thus, prior research provides an incomplete picture of the design of parent-PMSs. To address this research gap, this study describes the design of parent-PMSs based on **multiple design elements.**

Second, the management accounting literature has **failed to examine the adoption of parent-PMSs** for a long time (*Dossi/Patelli* (2008), p. 144; *Cruz et al.* (2011), p. 414). In fact, most studies have simply assumed that subsidiaries adopt parent-PMSs in accordance with the head offices' intentions (*Cruz et al.* (2011), p. 414). However, recent evidence suggests that subsidiaries might adopt parent-PMSs differently than expected by their head offices (e.g., *Siti-Nabiha/Scapens* (2005), p. 58; *Dossi/Patelli* (2008), p. 140). Since such an unintended adoption jeopardizes the objectives that head offices pursue with parent-PMSs, the adoption of parent-PMSs at subsidiary level deserves further attention (*Siti-Nabiha/Scapens* (2005), p. 58; *Dossi/Patelli* (2008), p. 140; *Rehring* (2012), p. 96). To address this research gap, this study examines how subsidiaries use parent-PMSs. Furthermore, this study investigates whether and how subsidiaries develop unofficial local-PMSs. In addition, factors that influence the adoption of parent-PMSs are explored. Finally, this study carves out different adoption types.

This study uses a **qualitative research approach** to address the research questions. In particular, this study conducts case studies of five German MNCs. This research approach was chosen because of the exploratory stage of the literature, especially on the adoption of parent-PMSs. At the case companies, interviews were conducted at both head office and subsidiary level. For the interviews at subsidiary level, two subsidiaries were selected at each case company, which stem from nine countries and three continents. In total, 33 experts from the case companies' head offices and subsidiaries were interviewed.

The remaining part of this section presents the main results concerning the design and adoption of parent-PMSs and their contributions and implications for management accounting research and practice.

Main results

RQ 1:   How are parent-PMSs designed?

For addressing the first research question, this study examines the design of parent-PMSs based on **four design elements**: performance measures, targets, link to rewards, and IT infrastructure.

With respect to the **performance measures**, the case companies evaluate the performance of their subsidiaries not only from a single perspective, but from multiple perspectives. However, only one case company (CarSupCo) addresses all four measurement perspectives outlined in the conceptual basis (financial, customer, internal process, and employee perspective). Looking at the types of measurement perspectives reveals that at one case company (AgriCo), the parent-PMS does not address the subsidiaries' financial perspective. This is contrary to the findings in the literature, which show that non-financial performance measures complement, but do not replace their financial counterparts (*Dossi/Patelli* (2010), pp. 507-511; *Abdallah/Alnamri* (2015), pp. 601-603). This can be explained by the fact that AgriCo's parent PMS was implemented as one part of a production system, which has a focus on the subsidiaries' production processes. The other case companies select financial performance measures for their parent-PMSs and perceive them as more important than the non-financial performance measures.

For describing the **targets** included in parent-PMSs, this study distinguishes between target setting and target evaluation. Concerning **target setting**, the results show that the case companies' head offices mainly use budget-based targets and past performance-based targets. The budget-based targets are used for determining target levels of financial and customer performance measures. Thus, for these performance measures the target levels are derived from the case companies' annual budgeting processes, in which the target levels are negotiated by counter-flow planning. For the performance measures relating to the subsidiaries' employees and internal processes, the head offices set targets based on the results of previous periods. For **evaluating** the target achievement, all case companies use performance reports and review meetings. Except ChemCo, all case companies evaluate the targets regularly (monthly or quarterly). Thus, the head offices use the parent-PMSs for regularly discussing the performance with the subsidiaries' management accountants. At ChemCo, the head office only intervenes in case the actual results are below expectations.

As regards the **link of parent-PMSs to rewards**, this study describes the types of rewards that the case companies' head offices use for the subsidiaries' management and staff. Furthermore, this study examines which performance measures are used to determine the bonus payments. The results show that all case companies except CarSupCo do not only use bonus payments for the subsidiaries' management, but also for the subsidiaries' staff. Three case companies (AgriCo, ChemCo, TechCo) do not use performance measures from their parent-PMS for rewarding the subsidiaries' management, which is in line with the results of prior studies (*Dossi/Patelli* (2008), p. 137; *Mahlendorf et al.* (2012), p. 708). Only the two smallest case companies (CarSupCo, MaNuCo) include a performance measure of the parent-PMS in their reward system. However, at CarSupCo the bonus payments depend on the performance of the entire MNC, which can be influenced only very indirectly by the individual manager. Four case companies (ManuCo, AgriCo, ChemCo, TechCo) use performance measures of their parent-PMS for rewarding the subsidiaries' sales staff and production workers. For example, the bonus of production workers depends on performance measures from the internal process perspectives of the parent-PMSs. These results complement prior literature (e.g., *Coates et al.* (1995); *Dossi/Patelli* (2008); *Mahlendorf et al.* (2012)), which exclusively deals with the rewards of the subsidiaries' management.

To examine the parent-PMSs' **IT infrastructure**, this study investigates which IT systems the case companies' head offices use. All head offices implement ERP systems, especially for collecting and storing performance data. However, these ERP systems are integrated to different degrees. On the one hand, ChemCo and ManuCo use the same ERP system throughout the whole MNC. On the other hand, the ERP system landscapes of CarSupCo, AgriCo, and TechCo are rather heterogeneous. In fact, the head offices of these case companies implement several ERP systems from different vendors at the subsidiaries. Regarding the combination of IT systems, two approaches are prevalent. The larger case companies (AgriCo, ChemCo, TechCo) combine the ERP systems with BI systems, which are used to calculate the performance values and to report them throughout the MNC. This approach is characterized by a high degree of automation and data quality. However, drawbacks of this approach are the time-consuming and expensive implementation. Due to these drawbacks, the smaller case companies (CarSupCo, ManuCo) combine the ERP systems with spreadsheet templates that the subsidiaries' management accountants have to report regularly. Since in this case the performance values are not calculated automatically, this approach causes a high manual workload for the subsidiaries' management accountants and is more prone to errors than the use of BI systems.

Adoption of parent-PMSs

RQ 2a:	How are parent-PMSs used?

Concerning the **use** of the parent-PMSs, the case companies' subsidiaries show both a functional and dysfunctional use (*Ferreira* (2002), p. 43; *Horváth/Seiter* (2009), p. 396). The functional use can be further classified into a decision-making use, monitoring use, attention-focusing use, and learning use. In addition to this functional use, a dysfunctional use is also evident at three subsidiaries. This supports initial findings in the literature (*Siti-Nabiha/Scapens* (2005), p. 65) that subsidiaries might use parent-PMSs differently than intended by their head offices. In fact, the management accountants of the three subsidiaries use the parent-PMS in a ceremonial way, meaning that they pretend to use the parent-PMS without actually doing so (*Ansari/Euske* (1987), pp. 561-564; *Siti-Nabiha/Scapens* (2005), p. 47). However, the extent of the ceremonial use differs at the three subsidiaries. Only at one subsidiary (AgriCo France), the management accountants use the entire parent-PMS ceremonially. The French management accountants do so because they perceive the parent-PMS as unsuitable for their subsidiary. At the other two subsidiaries, the management accountants only use individual elements of the parent-PMS, such as certain performance measures (AgriCo India) or targets (ManuCo Poland), in a ceremonial way. Thus, these results indicate that the ceremonial use should be understood as a degree rather than as an either-or issue.

RQ 2b: Do local-PMSs exist and, if yes, how are they designed?

As a second aspect regarding the adoption of parent-PMSs, this study analyzes the **existence** and the **design of local-PMSs** at the case companies' subsidiaries. At all case companies, at least one of the two subsidiaries develops a local-PMS. At one case company (AgriCo), both subsidiaries have a local-PMS. Responsible for developing the local-PMSs are the subsidiaries' management accountants, who are sometimes supported by employees from other departments (e.g., production and HR). Concerning head offices' awareness of the local-PMSs, the results are mixed. At the smaller case companies (CarSupCo, AgriCo, ManuCo), the head offices' management accountants stated that they are aware of the fact that some of their subsidiaries develop a local-PMS. For the two largest case companies (ChemCo, TechCo), the situation is different. In fact, the head offices of these case companies do not know whether their subsidiaries have a local-PMS, which might be explained by the high number of subsidiaries that these case companies have. With respect to the objectives that the subsidiaries pursue with the local-PMS, two contrasting objectives are evident (*Siti-Nabiha/Scapens* (2005), p. 65; *Cruz et al.* (2011), p. 413; *Cooper/Ezzamel* (2013), pp. 291-293). On the one hand, most subsidiaries develop the local-PMS to compensate the weaknesses of the parent-PMS. In this vein, the local-PMSs are supposed to support the functioning of the parent-PMSs at subsidiary level. On the other hand, one subsidiary (AgriCo France) developed the local-PMS as an alternative to the parent-PMS.

The **design of the local-PMSs** is described based on the four design elements mentioned above (performance measures, targets, link to rewards, and IT infrastructure). Concerning performance measures, the design of the local-PMSs depends on the objectives that the subsidiaries pursue with these systems. At the subsidiaries that develop the local-PMS for supporting the functioning of the parent-PMS, the local-PMS contains the same performance measures as the parent-PMS and a few additional performance measures. In contrast, the local-PMS that serves as an alternative to the parent-PMS (AgriCo France) includes several other performance measures than the parent-PMS. All subsidiaries having a local-PMS set and evaluate targets for the performance measures of the local-PMS. For the performance measures that are included in both the local-PMS and the parent-PMS, the target levels of the parent-PMS are used. For the performance measures that are included in the local-PMS only, the subsidiaries set local targets mainly based on past performance. The evaluation of targets is done based on local performance reports and local review meetings. None of the subsidiaries link their local-PMS to the rewards of the subsidiary's management and staff. As an IT infrastructure, the local-PMSs build on the IT systems of the parent-PMSs. In addition, the subsidiaries' management accountants prepare spreadsheet templates that are only used at subsidiary level.

RQ 2c: What influences the adoption of parent-PMSs?

Concerning the **factors that influence** the adoption of parent-PMSs, this study examined parent-PMS and host country and subsidiary characteristics. Parent-PMS characteristics that influence the adoption at subsidiary level are the relevance and comprehensibility of performance measures, the adequateness of target levels, and the level of participation in the parent-PMS design. For instance, subsidiaries tend to use performance measures ceremonially that they consider as irrelevant and add performance measures to their local-PMS that they miss in the parent-PMS. These parent-PMS characteristics are influenced by host country and subsidiary characteristics. In particular, legal, economic, and operational differences seem to affect the subsidiaries' perceived relevance of performance measures. The perceived comprehensibility of performance measures seems to be affected by differences in management accounting education between MNCs' home and host countries. Finally, cultural differences seem to affect the subsidiaries' acceptance of the parent-PMS and their perceived adequateness of target levels.

Based on the use of the parent-PMSs and the existence and design of local-PMSs, this study identified different **adoption types** that were derived from the New Institutional Sociology. At the case companies' subsidiaries, three adoption types are evident: Acquiescence, supportive modification, and decoupling. The subsidiaries of the first group use the parent-PMS in a functional way and do not develop a local-PMS. The subsidiaries of the second group differ from the first group by developing a local-PMS. These local-PMSs aim at supporting the functioning of the parent-PMSs and therefore contain some additional performance measures that the subsidiaries' management accountants are missing in the parent-PMSs. Finally, decoupling means that the parent-PMS is used ceremonially at subsidiary level and that the local-PMS serves as an alternative to the parent-PMS. The first two adoption types fulfill the objectives of the head offices, namely facilitating decision-making and influencing the decisions of the subsidiaries. The adoption type of decoupling, however, only fulfills the objective of decision facilitation as the parent-PMS does no longer influence the decisions of the subsidiaries.

Contributions and implications

These results provide several contributions for management accounting research and implications for practice. For management accounting researchers, this study contributes by describing the design of parent-PMSs based on **multiple design elements**. In fact, many prior studies only examine single design elements (e.g., performance measures or targets) or are focused on explaining the design of parent-PMSs.

Furthermore, by analyzing the adoption of parent-PMSs at subsidiary level, this study addresses a topic that has been **ignored** in the literature for a long time (*Cruz et al.* (2011), p. 414; *Cheng/Yu* (2012), p. 82). This helps management accounting researchers to understand what happens to the parent-PMSs once they have been implemented at the subsidiaries. In particular, this study sheds light on the use of parent-PMSs, the existence and design of local-PMSs, and the factors that influence the adoption. Thus, this study addresses several calls for research (*Dossi/Patelli* (2008), p. 144; *Cruz et al.* (2011), p. 414; *Cheng/Yu*

(2012), p. 82). Moreover, the results of this study can serve as a basis for other researchers who examine the adoption of parent-PMSs.

From a **methodological** perspective, the contributions of this study are twofold. First, by conducting interviews with experts from MNCs' head offices and subsidiaries, this study analyzes parent-PMSs at **both head office and subsidiary level.** Prior studies often examine only one of these two perspectives. For example, many studies only deal with the design of parent-PMSs from a head office point of view. By examining parent-PMSs at head office and subsidiary level, this study is able to capture different opinions and views on the parent-PMSs. Therefore, this study can assess how the subsidiaries' employees think about the parent-PMS. Based on these perceptions, this study explores which characteristics of the parent-PMSs influence the adoption of these systems. Second, this study contributes to management accounting research by using a **multiple case study approach.** Previous studies examine the adoption of parent-PMSs mainly by quantitative large-scale studies, which are not able to provide deep descriptions of the adoption (e.g., *Dossi/Patelli* (2008); *Schäffer et al.* (2010); *Mahlendorf et al.* (2012)). For example, these studies analyze the extent to which subsidiaries use parent-PMSs or capture the existence of local-PMSs by binary variables. The few qualitative studies are mainly single case studies that have a focus on joint ventures and domestic subsidiaries (e.g., *Siti-Nabiha/Scapens* (2005); *Cruz et al.* (2009); *Cruz et al.* (2011).[160] By using a multiple case study design, this study analyzes the adoption of parent-PMSs at foreign subsidiaries from different host countries. This allows, for example, to explore which host country characteristics affect the adoption of parent-PMSs.

In addition, this study makes a **theoretical contribution** by identifying three different adoption types based on New Institutional Sociology. Identifying these adoption types supports the theoretical generalizability of a study, which is an important objective of qualitative case studies (*Parker/Northcott* (2016), p. 1101; *Lukka/Modell* (2017), p. 43). Other researchers can use these adoption types for their studies, for example by examining the prevalence of these adoption types.

This study also provides implications for practitioners. For management accountants in MNCs' head offices, who are usually the designers of parent-PMSs, this study provides a detailed description of parent-PMSs. This allows the head offices' management accountants to **compare the design** of their parent-PMSs with the design of the case companies' parent-PMSs.

Furthermore, this study informs management accountants in MNCs' head offices on the adoption of parent-PMSs at subsidiary level. For the designers of parent-PMSs, it is important to **know how the subsidiaries' employees can deviate from their intentions,** for example by using the parent-PMS in a dysfunctional way or by developing a local-PMS as alternative to the parent-PMS. However, the results of this study also indicate that the existence of a local-PMS does not necessarily mean that the subsidiaries use the parent-PMS in a dysfunctional way. Instead, the subsidiaries can also develop a local-PMS for supporting the functioning of the parent-PMS. Therefore, it is important for management accountants in MNCs' head offices to be aware of the objectives that the subsidiaries pursue with the

---

[160] An exception is *Cooper/Ezzamel* (2013).

local-PMS. In this vein, the typology of the adoption of parent-PMSs might provide practitioners with a vivid description of the different adoption types.

In addition, this study has implications for the designers of parent-PMSs by analyzing the factors that influence how the subsidiaries adopt parent-PMSs. In fact, the results indicate that characteristics of the parent-PMSs affect how these systems are adopted. Therefore, the results of this study might help management accountants in MNCs' head offices to **design parent-PMSs that are adopted according to their intentions** (*Rehring* (2012), p. 118). For example, the results indicate that head offices should consider cultural and economic differences when designing parent-PMSs, as they might lead to a ceremonial use of the parent-PMSs at subsidiary level.

Finally, this study informs management accountants in MNCs' subsidiaries, who are supposed to use the parent-PMS and who are usually the designers of the local-PMS. The results of this study might help them in understanding the objectives that head offices pursue with parent-PMSs. Furthermore, the results might help them in designing local-PMSs that **support the functioning** of the parent-PMSs.

7.2   Limitations and future research

The following paragraphs present the limitations of this study and provide avenues for future research. Limitations arise from the qualitative case study approach in general and the particular research design of this study.

Even though **qualitative case studies** are particularly suitable for the research questions of this study (see chapter 5), they also have two main limitations. First, qualitative case studies do not allow inferring **statistically generalizable** results (*Eisenhardt* (1989), p. 537; *Scapens* (1990), p. 277). Thus, this study cannot provide evidence on the design and adoption of parent-PMSs on a large-scale. For example, this study cannot provide evidence on the prevalence of a dysfunctional use or of local-PMSs. However, it is explicitly not the aim of this study to provide large-scale evidence on parent-PMSs. This study rather aims at enhancing researchers' and practitioners' understanding of the design and adoption of parent-PMSs. Furthermore, this study intends to produce results that are generalizable from a theoretical point of view, which is the case if the results can be used by other researchers (*Scapens* (1992), pp. 378-380). For example, this study aims to make a theoretical contribution by carving out different adoption types of parent-PMSs.

The second limitation relates to the **subjectivity** that is inherent in qualitative research. This subjectivity comes from the researcher, for example when interpreting empirical data, and the research partners, for example when giving wrong answers purposefully or due to a lack of knowledge (*Tomkins/Groves* (1983), p. 369; *Scapens* (1990), p. 277). This study mitigates subjectivity in two ways. First, this study transparently discloses the research process and therefore makes clear how the data is collected and analyzed. Furthermore, this study reviews the research process based on disclosed quality criteria (*Flick* (2018), p. 73). These remedies allow other researchers to understand and assess how the results were produced and hence increases the traceability of this study (*Wrona* (2006), p. 207; *Messner et al.* (2017), p. 440). Second, this study reduces subjectivity of research partners by relying on three data sources, namely interviews, internal documents, and publicly available information (*Bebbington et al.* (2007), p. 369). Furthermore, this study uses multiple experts within each case, which allows to capture different perspectives (e.g., between employees from head offices and subsidiaries) within one case (*Patton* (2015), pp. 316-317).

In addition to the limitations that are inherent in each qualitative case study, further limitations arise from the particular research design of this study. The first limitation refers to the **selection of interview partners**. In fact, interviews were conducted exclusively with management accountants. This is because management accountants of MNCs' head offices are the designers of parent-PMSs and therefore can provide information on the design of these systems. At subsidiary level, management accountants were interviewed because they are expected to use the parent-PMSs and because they are the designers of the local-PMSs (*Euske et al.* (1993), pp, 288-289; *Dossi/Patelli* (2008), p. 127). However, at both head office and subsidiary level, employees from other departments are also involved in designing and adopting parent-PMSs. For example, employees from corporate production departments support the head offices' management accountants in selecting performance measures. By exclusively interviewing management accountants, this study does not capture the perspectives of the employees from other departments. However, this issue is partly mitigated by the fact that all of the interviewed management accountants are involved in the development of the parent-PMSs and therefore have profound knowledge of the design of these systems.

The second limitation arises from the **access to the case companies**. When studying MNCs, researchers can get access to the case companies through gatekeepers from head office and subsidiary level (*Kornacker* (2014), pp. 147-148; *Edwards et al.* (2011), pp. 411-412). However, both approaches have limitations. Gatekeepers from head offices might only establish contact to subsidiaries' employees who are favorable of the parent-PMSs, which would bias the results of this study. Gatekeepers from subsidiary level might not be willing to establish a contact to the head office, especially if they are not favorable of the parent-PMS (*Devers/Frankel* (2000), p. 265; *Lervik* (2011), pp. 237-238).

Furthermore, by using New Institutional Sociology as a theoretical basis, this study only explores influencing factors that arise from parent-PMSs characteristics and subsidiary and host country characteristics. Thus, this study ignores the **motives of individual employees** on the adoption of parent-PMSs (*Cooper/Ezzamel* (2013), p. 309). For example, it is not examined whether and how factors of individual employees, such as age or career status, affect the adoption of parent-PMSs.

Finally, this study examines the design and adoption of parent-PMSs **not over a longer period of time** as it is done in longitudinal case studies (*Scapens* (2004), p. 261). In fact, this study examines parent-PMSs only at a certain point in time. Therefore, this study is not able to examine and describe whether and how the design and adoption of parent-PMSs evolve over time.

Based on the results and limitations of this study, several avenues for future studies exist. First, a **longitudinal case study** could examine the adoption processes over a longer time span. For example, by conducting interviews and field observations, researchers could observe the implementation of parent-PMSs at subsidiary level. This would enrich the management accounting literature with a detailed description of the adoption processes that take place shortly before and after the implementation of the parent-PMSs by head offices. For example, prior to the implementation, the subsidiaries' employees might try to negotiate with the head office to abolish the implementation of the parent-PMS or might try to adapt the design of the parent-PMS to the local needs. It is interesting for both management accounting researchers and practitioners to know how the processes during the implementation of parent-PMSs affect the later outcome of the adoption.

Second, researchers could conduct further **multiple case studies** for examining different contexts. For example, this study does not examine subsidiaries from China or the USA, which are important economies. Especially China could be interesting to examine since it differs considerably in terms of culture from European countries (*Mahlendorf et al.* (2012), pp. 697-698). Extending the selection of subsidiaries would allow investigating additional factors that influence how subsidiaries adopt parent-PMSs.

Finally, **survey studies** could build on the results of this study by examining the prevalence of the three adoption types. Furthermore, researchers could examine the effects that the different adoption types have for the MNCs. For example, survey studies could test whether there is an association between the adoption types and the performance of the subsidiaries (*Dossi/Patelli* (2008), p. 142). Overall, there are several opportunities for researchers that want to contribute to the understanding of the adoption of parent-PMSs. In fact, the adoption of parent-PMSs at subsidiary level still deserves further attention by management accounting researchers.

Appendix A

Questions at head office level

I   Organization of performance measurement

- Which departments and persons are involved in measuring the subsidiaries' performance?
- Could you please describe how the subsidiaries are embedded in the organizational structure of your company?

II   Objectives and implementation of the performance measurement system

- Which goals does your company pursue with developing a performance measurement system?
- To what extent is the performance measurement system standardized/differentiated for the subsidiaries?
- Do you have guidelines, presentations, or trainings on the performance measurement system?
- What kind of changes have been made to the performance measurement system during the last five years?

III   Design of the performance measurement system

- Which performance measures do you use to measure the performance of the subsidiaries?
- How do you set performance targets for the subsidiaries?
- How do you evaluate the achievement of these targets?
- How do you use the performance measurement system for rewarding the subsidiaries' employees?
- Which IT systems do you use for performance measurement of the subsidiaries?
- From your point of view, what are the strengths of the performance measurement system of your company?
- Which aspects of your company's performance measurement system would you like to improve?

IV   Adoption of the performance measurement systems

- How do the subsidiaries adopt your performance measurement system?
- How do you make sure that the subsidiaries' employees use the performance measurement system according to your instructions?
- Do your subsidiaries have their own performance measurement systems that exist in addition to your performance measurement system?

Questions at subsidiary level

I Organization of performance measurement

- Could you please briefly describe the organizational structure of your subsidiary?
- Which departments and persons are responsible for reporting the subsidiary's performance to the head office?

II Design of the performance measurement system

- Which performance measures do you have to report to the head office?
- Which local performance measures do you have for measuring the performance of your subsidiary?
- How does the head office set performance targets for your subsidiary?
- How do you set local performance targets for your subsidiary?
- How does the head office use the performance measurement system for rewarding the employees of your subsidiary?
- How do you use the local performance measures for rewarding the employees of your subsidiary?
- Which IT systems does the head office implement for performance measurement?
- Which IT systems do you use for measuring and reporting your local performance measures?
- From your point of view, what are the strengths of the head office's performance measurement system?
- Which aspects of the head office's performance measurement system could be improved?
- What are the reasons for developing local performance measures, targets, rewards, and/or IT systems?

III Use of the performance measurement systems

- How do you use the head office's performance measurement system?
- Which role do your local performance measures, targets, rewards, and/or IT systems play for controlling the subsidiary?

Appendix B

Case company	Title	Organizational level
CarSupCo	Head of corporate management accounting	Head office
	Corporate management accountant	Head office
	Head of management accounting	Subsidiary Brazil
	Head of management accounting	Subsidiary Poland
MaNuCo	Corporate management accountant	Corporate head office
	Corporate management accountant	Corporate head office
	Management accountant for production & logistics	Corporate head office
	Management accountant for production & logistics	Corporate head office
	Finance manager	Regional head office of EMEA
	Head of management accounting	Subsidiary Germany
	Head of management accounting	Subsidiary Poland
AgriCo	Head of corporate management accounting	Head office
	Corporate management accountant	Head office
	Corporate management accountant	Head office
	Local management accountant	French subsidiary
	Local management accountant	French subsidiary
	Head of local management accounting	Indian subsidiary
ChemCo	Management accountant	Business unit head office
	Head of management accounting	Regional head office EMEA
	Management accountant	Regional head office EMEA
	Head of management accounting	Subsidiary North EMEA
	Head of management accounting	Subsidiary South EMEA

Table is continued on the next page

	Corporate management accountant	Corporate head office
	Divisional management accountant	Divisional head office
	Divisional management accountant	Divisional head office
	Divisional management accountant	Divisional head office
TechCo	Head of regional management accounting	Regional head office Middle East
	Regional management accountant	Regional head office Middle East
	Regional management accountant	Regional head office Middle East
	Management accountant	Subsidiary UAE
	Local CFO	Subsidiary Oman
	Commercial manager	Subsidiary Oman

List of references

A

Abdallah, W./Alnamri, M. (2015): Non-financial performance measures and the BSC of multinational companies with multi-cultural environment, in: Cross Cultural Management: An International Journal, Vol. 22, No. 4, 2015, pp. 594-607.

Abdel-Maksoud, A./Dugdale, D./Luther, R. (2005): Non-financial performance measurement in manufacturing companies, in: The British Accounting Review, Vol. 37, No. 3, 2005, pp. 261-297.

Aggarwal, R./Berrill, J./Hutson, E./Kearney, C. (2011): What is a multinational corporation? Classifying the degree of firm-level multinationality, in: International Business Review, Vol. 20, No. 5, 2011, pp. 557-577.

Agndal, H./Nilsson, U. (2010): Different open book accounting practices for different purchasing strategies, in: Management Accounting Research, Vol. 21, No. 3, 2010, pp. 147-166.

Aguinis, H./Joo, H./Gottfredson, R. (2013): What monetary rewards can and cannot do: How to show employees the money, in: Business Horizons, Vol. 56, No. 2, 2013, pp. 241-249.

Ahrens, T. (2008): Overcoming the subjective–objective divide in interpretive management accounting research, in: Accounting, Organizations and Society, Vol. 33, 2-3, 2008, pp. 292-297.

Ahrens, T./Becker, A./Burns, J./Chapman, C./Granlund, M./Habersam, M./Hansen, A./Khalifa, R./Malmi, T./Mennicken, A./Mikes, A./Panozzo, F./Piber, M./Quattrone, P./Scheytt, T. (2008): The future of interpretive accounting research – A polyphonic debate, in: Critical Perspectives on Accounting, Vol. 19, No. 6, 2008, pp. 840-866.

Ahrens, T./Chapman, C. (1999): The role of management accountants in Britain and Germany, in: Management Accounting: Magazine for Chartered Management Accountants, Vol. 77, No. 5, 1999, pp. 42-43.

Ahrens, T./Chapman, C. (2006): Doing qualitative field research in management accounting: Positioning data to contribute to theory, in: Accounting, Organizations and Society, Vol. 31, No. 8, 2006, pp. 819-841.

Alberti-Alhtaybat, L./Al-Htaybat, K. (2010): Qualitative accounting research: an account of Glaser's grounded theory, in: Qualitative Research in Accounting & Management, Vol. 7, No. 2, 2010, pp. 208-226.

AlHashim, D. (1980): Internal Performance Evaluation in American Multinational Enterprises, in: Management International Review, Vol. 20, No. 3, 1980, pp. 33-39.

Allen, D./Burton, F.G./Smith, S.D./Wood, D.A. (2017): Shadow IT Use, Outcome Effects, and Subjective Performance Evaluation, URL: https://papers.ssrn.com/sol3/papers.cfm?abstract_id=2993443 (16.08.2019).

Al-Sabri, H./Al-Mashari, M./Chikh, A. (2018): A comparative study and evaluation of ERP reference models in the context of ERP IT-driven implementation, in: Business Process Management Journal, Vol. 24, No. 4, 2018, pp. 943-964.

Anderson-Gough, F./Edgley, C./Sharma, N. (2017): Qualitative data management and analysis software, in: Hoque, Z./Parker, L. D./Covaleski, M. A./Haynes, K. (eds.), The Routledge Companion to Qualitative Accounting Research Methods, London 2017, pp. 405-431.

Andersson, U./Forsgren, M. (2000): In search of centre of excellence: Network embeddedness and subsidiary roles in multinational corporations: Management International Review, Vol. 40, No. 4, 2000, pp. 329-350.

Annavarjula, M./Beldona, S. (2000): Multinationality-performance relationship: A review and reconceptualization, in: The International Journal of Organizational Analysis, Vol. 8, No. 1, 2000, pp. 48-67.

Ansari, S./Euske, K. (1987): Rational, rationalizing, and reifying uses of accounting data in organizations, in: Accounting, Organizations and Society, Vol. 12, No. 6, 1987, pp. 549-570.

Antons, D./Piller, F. T. (2015): Opening the Black Box of "Not Invented Here": Attitudes, Decision Biases, and Behavioral Consequences, in: Academy of Management Perspectives, Vol. 29, No. 2, 2015, pp. 193-217.

Appleyard, A./Strong, N./Walton, P. (1991): Multi-currency budgeting by multinational companies, in: The British Accounting Review, Vol. 23, No. 2, 1991, pp. 105-121.

Artz, M. (2010): Controlling in Marketing und Vertrieb: Planung, Budgetierung und Performance Measurement, Wiesbaden 2010.

Artz, M./Homburg, C./Rajab, T. (2012): Performance-measurement system design and functional strategic decision Influence: The role of performance-measure properties, in: Accounting, Organizations and Society, Vol. 37, No. 7, pp. 445-460.

Atkinson, A. (1998): Strategic performance measurement and incentive compensation, in: European Management Journal, Vol. 16, No. 5, 1998, pp. 552-561.

Atkinson, A./Waterhouse, J./Wells, R. (1997): A Stakeholder Approach to Strategic Performance Measurement, in: MIT Sloan Management Review, Vol. 38, No. 3, 1997, pp. 25-37.

Austin, R. (1996): Measuring and managing performance in organizations, New York 1996.

Ayres, L./Kavanaugh, K./Knafl, K. (2003): Within-case and across-case approaches to qualitative data analysis, in: Qualitative Health Research, Vol. 13, No. 6, 2003, pp. 871-883.

B

Bange, C./Marr, B./Dahnken, O./Narr, J. (2004): Software im Vergleich: Balanced Scorecard - 20 Werkzeuge für das Performance Management – Eine Studie des Business Application Research Center BARC, München 2004.

Banker, R./Lee, S.-Y./Potter, G./Srinivasan, D. (1996): Contextual Analysis of Performance Impacts of Outcome-Based Incentive Compensation, in: Academy of Management Journal, Vol. 39, No. 4, 1996, pp. 920-948.

Bartol, K./Srivastava, A. (2002): Encouraging Knowledge Sharing: The Role of Organizational Reward Systems, in: Journal of Leadership & Organizational Studies, Vol. 9, No. 1, 2002, pp. 64-76.

Baxter, P./Jack, S. (2008): Qualitative Case Study Methodology: Study Design and Implementation for Novice Researchers, in: Qualitative Report, Vol. 13, 2008, pp. 544-559.

Bédard, J./Gendron, Y. (2004): Qualitative research on accounting: some thoughts on what occurs behind the scene, in: Lee, B./Humphrey, C. (eds.), The real life guide to accounting research, Amsterdam et al. 2004, pp. 191-206.

Behringer, S. (2018): Konzerncontrolling, Berlin et al. 2018.

Beitin, B. K. (2012): Interview and Sampling: How Many and Whom, in: Gubrium, J. F./Hostein, J.A./Marvasti, A. B./McKinney, K. D. (eds.), The SAGE Handbook of Interview Research: The Complexity of the Craft, 2nd edition, Thousand Oaks et al. 2012, pp. 243-253.

Berger, P./Luckmann, T. (1991): The Social Construction of Reality: A Treatise in the Sociology of Knowledge, New York 1991.

Berry, A./Otley, D. (2004): Case-based research in accounting, in: Lee, B./Humphrey, C. (eds.), The real life guide to accounting research, Amsterdam et al. 2004, pp. 231-255.

Berry, H./Guillén, M./Zhou, N. (2010): An institutional approach to cross-national distance, in: Journal of International Business Studies, Vol. 41, No. 9, 2010, pp. 1460-1480.

Bhimani, A. (1996): Management Accounting: European Perspectives, Oxford 1996.

Bititci, U./Nudurupati, S./Turner, T./Creighton, S. (2002): Web enabled performance measurement systems, in: International Journal of Operations & Production Management, Vol. 22, No. 11, 2002, pp. 1273-1287.

Borchers, S. (2000): Beteiligungscontrolling in der Management-Holding: Ein integratives Konzept, Wiesbaden 2000.

Borchers, S. (2006): Beteiligungscontrolling – Ein Überblick, in: Zeitschrift für Planung & Unternehmenssteuerung, Vol. 17, No. 3, 2006, pp. 233-250.

Bourguignon, A./Malleret, V./Nørreklit, H. (2004): The American Balanced Bcorecard versus the French Tableau de Bord: The Ideological Dimension, in: Management Accounting Research, Vol. 15, No. 2, 2004, pp. 107-134.

Bourne, M./Mills, J./Wilcox, M./Neely, A./Platts, K. (2000): Designing, implementing and updating performance measurement systems, in: International Journal of Operations & Production Management, Vol. 20, No. 7, 2000, pp. 754-771.

Bouwens, J./Speklé, R. (2007): Does EVA add value?, in: Hopper, T./Northcott, D./Scapens, R. W. (eds.), Issues in management accounting, 3rd edition, Harlow 2007, pp. 245-269.

Boxenbaum, E./Jonsson, S. (2017): Isomorphism, Diffusion and Decoupling, in: Greenwood, R./Oliver, C./Lawrence, T. B./Meyer, R. E. (eds.), The SAGE handbook of organizational institutionalism, 2nd edition, Los Angeles et al. 2017, pp. 79-104.

Brandau, M./Endenich, C./Trapp, R./Hoffjan, A. (2013): Institutional drivers of conformity – Evidence for management accounting from Brazil and Germany, in: International Business Review, Vol. 22, No. 2, 2013, pp. 466-479.

Breuer, F. (2010): Reflexive Grounded Theory, Wiesbaden 2010.

Breuer, F./Mey, G./Mruck, K. (2011): Subjektivität und Selbst-/Reflexivität in der Grounded-Theory-Methodologie, in: Mey, G./Mruck, K. (eds.), Grounded theory reader, 2nd edition, Wiesbaden 2011, pp. 427-448.

Brinkmann, S. (2014): Unstructured and Semi-Structured Interviewing, in: Leavy, P. (ed.), The Oxford handbook of qualitative research, Oxford/New York 2014, pp. 277-299.

Brühl, R. (2017): Wie Wissenschaft Wissen schafft: Theorie und Ethik, 2nd edition, Konstanz et al. 2017.

Brühl, R./Horch, N./Orth, M. (2008): Grounded Theory und ihre bisherige Anwendung in der empirischen Controlling- und Rechnungswesenforschung, in: Zeitschrift für Planung & Unternehmenssteuerung, Vol. 19, No. 3, 2008, pp. 299-323.

Bruns, W. (1968): Accounting Information and Decision-Making – Some Behavioral Hypotheses, in: The Accounting Review, Vol. 43, No. 3, 1968, pp. 469-480.

Buck, T. (2011): Case selection informed by theory, in: Marschan-Piekkari, R./Welch, C. (eds.), Rethinking the Case Study in International Business and Management Research, Cheltenham et al. 2011, pp. 192-209.

Burchell, S./Clubb, C./Hopwood, A./Hughes, J./Nahapiet, J. (1980): The roles of accounting in organizations and society, in: Accounting, Organizations and Society, Vol. 5, No. 1, 1980, pp. 5-27.

Burkert, M./Fischer, F./Schäffer, U. (2011): Application of the controllability principle and managerial performance – The role of role perceptions, in: Management Accounting Research, Vol. 22, No. 3, 2011, pp. 143-159.

Busco, C./Giovannoni, E./Scapens, R. (2008): Managing the tensions in integrating global organisations: The role of performance management systems, in: Management Accounting Research, Vol. 19, No. 2, 2008, pp. 103-125.

Busco, C./Quattrone, P. (2015): Exploring How the Balanced Scorecard Engages and Unfolds: Articulating the Visual Power of Accounting Inscriptions, in: Contemporary Accounting Research, Vol. 32, No. 3, 2015, pp. 1236-1262.

C

Cadestin, C./Backer, K. de/Desnoyers-James, I./Miroudot, S./Ye, M./Rigo/Davide (2018): Multinational enterprises and global value chains: New Insights on the trade-investment nexus, URL: https://www.oecd-ilibrary.org/docserver/194ddb63-en.pdf?expires=1566199596&id=id&accname=guest&checksum=AF4768EEE382EB4C8E505C732AFD6928 (16.08.2019).

Cadestin, C./Backer, K. de/Miroudot, S./Moussiegt, L./Rigo, D./Ye, M. (2019): Multinational enterprises in domestic value chains, URL: https://www.oecd-ilibrary.org/docserver/9abfa931-en.pdf?expires=1566199552&id=id&accname=guest&checksum=1CC3E035DE4F49C2EA9247326E944096 (16.08.2019).

Casas-Arce, P./Lourenço, S./Martínez-Jerez, F. (2017): The Performance Effect of Feedback Frequency and Detail: Evidence from a Field Experiment in Customer Satisfaction, in: Journal of Accounting Research, Vol. 55, No. 5, 2017, pp. 1051-1088.

Chang, E./Taylor, M. (1999): Control in Multinational Corporations (MNCS): The Case of Korean Manufacturing Subsidiaries, in: Journal of Management, Vol. 25, No. 4, 1999, pp. 541-565.

Charmaz, K. (2011): Grounded Theory Methods in Social justice Research, in: Denzin, N. K./Lincoln, Y. S. (eds.), The SAGE handbook of qualitative research, 4th edition, Los Angeles et al. 2011, pp. 359-380.

Cheek, J. (2011): The Politics and Practices of Funding Qualitative Inquiry, in: Denzin, N. K./Lincoln, Y. S. (eds.), The SAGE handbook of qualitative research, 4th edition, Los Angeles et al. 2011, pp. 251-268.

Cheng, H.-L./Yu, C.-M. (2012): Adoption of Practices by Subsidiaries and Institutional Interaction within Internationalised Small- and Medium-Sized Enterprises, in: Management International Review, Vol. 52, No. 1, 2012, pp. 81-105.

Chenhall, R. (2003): Management control systems design within its organizational context: findings from contingency-based research and directions for the future, in: Accounting, Organizations and Society, Vol. 28, 2-3, 2003, pp. 127-168.

Chenhall, R. (2005): Integrative strategic performance measurement systems, strategic alignment of manufacturing, learning and strategic outcomes: an exploratory study, in: Accounting, Organizations and Society, Vol. 30, No. 5, 2005, pp. 395-422.

Chenhall, R./Langfield-Smith, K. (2007): Multiple Perspectives of Performance Measures, in: European Management Journal, Vol. 25, No. 4, 2007, pp. 266-282.

Child, J. (1984): Organization: A guide to problems and practice, 2nd edition, London 1984.

Choi, F./Czechowicz, I. (1983): Assessing Foreign Subsidiary Performance: A Multinational Comparison, in: Management International Review, Vol. 23, No. 4, 1983, pp. 14-25.

Chong, V./Chong, K. (2002): Budget Goal Commitment and Informational Effects of Budget Participation on Performance: A Structural Equation Modeling Approach, in: Behavioral Research in Accounting, Vol. 14, No. 1, 2002, pp. 65-86.

Choong, K. (2013): Understanding the features of performance measurement system: a literature review, in: Measuring Business Excellence, Vol. 17, No. 4, 2013, pp. 102-121.

Choudhury, N. (1986): Responsibility Accounting and Controllability, in: Accounting and Business Research, Vol. 16, No. 63, 1986, pp. 189-198.

Chow, C. W./Shields, M. D./Wu, A. (1999): The importance of national culture in the design of and preference for management controls for multinational operations, in: Accounting, Organizations and Society, Vol. 24, No. 5-6, 2011, pp. 441-461.

Christmann, G. (2009): Telefonische Experteninterviews – Ein schwieriges Unterfangen, in: Bogner, A./Littig, B./Menz, W. (eds.), Experteninterviews, 3rd edition, Wiesbaden 2009, pp. 197-222.

Chua, W. (1986): Radical Developments in Accounting Thought, in: The Accounting Review, Vol. 61, No. 4, 1986, pp. 601-632.

Chung, L./Gibbons, P./Schoch, H. (2000): The influence of subsidiary context and head office strategic management style on control of MNCs: the experience in Australia, in: Accounting, Auditing & Accountability Journal, Vol. 13, No. 5, 2000, pp. 647-668.

Chung, L./Gibbons, P./Schoch, H. (2006): The Management of Information and Managers in Subsidiaries of Multinational Corporations, in: British Journal of Management, Vol. 17, No. 2, 2006, pp. 153-165.

Ciabuschi, F./Forsgren, M./Martin, O. M. (2011): Rationality vs ignorance: The role of MNC headquarters in subsidiaries' innovation processes, in: Journal of International Business Studies, Vol. 42, No. 7, 2011, pp. 958-970.

Clancy, D./Collins, F. (1979): Informal accounting information systems: Some tentative findings, in: Accounting, Organizations and Society, Vol. 4, 1-2, 1979, pp. 21-30.

Coates, J./Davis, E./Emmanuel, C./Longden, S./Stacey, R. (1992): Multinational companies performance measurement systems: international perspectives, in: Management Accounting Research, Vol. 3, No. 2, 1992, pp. 133-150.

Coates, J./Davis, T./Stacey, R. (1995): Performance measurement systems, incentive reward schemes and short-termism in multinational companies: a note, in: Management Accounting Research, Vol. 6, No. 2, 1995, pp. 125-135.

Collings, D./Dick, P. (2011): The relationship between ceremonial adoption of popular management practices and the motivation for practice adoption and diffusion in an American MNC, in: The International Journal of Human Resource Management, Vol. 22, No. 18, 2011, pp. 3849-3866.

Cooper, D./Ezzamel, M. (2013): Globalization discourses and performance measurement systems in a multinational firm, in: Accounting, Organizations and Society, Vol. 38, No. 4, 2013, pp. 288-313.

Cooper, D./Ezzamel, M./Robson, K. (2019): The Multiplicity of Performance Management Systems: Heterogeneity in Multinational Corporations and Management Sense-Making, in: Contemporary Accounting Research, Vol. 36, No. 1, 2019, pp. 451-485.

Cooper, D./Morgan, W. (2008): Case Study Research in Accounting, in: Accounting Horizons, Vol. 22, No. 2, 2008, pp. 159-178.

Corbin, J./Strauss, A. (1990): Grounded theory research: Procedures, canons, and evaluative criteria, in: Qualitative Sociology, Vol. 13, No. 1, 1990, pp. 3-21.

Coyne, I. (1997): Sampling in qualitative research. Purposeful and theoretical sampling; merging or clear boundaries?, in: Journal of Advanced Nursing, Vol. 26, No. 3, 1997, pp. 623-630.

Cray, D. (1984): Control and Coordination in Multinational Corporations, in: Journal of International Business Studies, Vol. 15, No. 2, 1984, pp. 85-98.

Cruz, I./Major, M./Scapens, R. (2009): Institutionalization and practice variation in the management control of a global/local setting, in: Accounting, Auditing & Accountability Journal, Vol. 22, No. 1, 2009, pp. 91-117.

Cruz, I./Scapens, R./Major, M. (2011): The localisation of a global management control system, in: Accounting, Organizations and Society, Vol. 36, No. 7, 2011, pp. 412-427.

D

Daniel, A. (2009): Perception Gaps between Headquarters and Subsidiary Managers: Differing Perspectives on Subsidiary Roles and their Implications, Wiesbaden 2009.

Das, P. (2012): Wage Inequality in India: Decomposition by Sector, Gender and Activity Status, in: Economic and Political Weekly, Vol. 47, No. 50, 2012, pp. 58-64.

Dechow, N./Granlund, M./Mouritsen, J. (2007): Management Control of the Complex Organization: Relationships between Management Accounting and Information Technology, in: Chapman, C. S./Hopwood, A. G./Shields, M. D. (eds.), Handbook of Management Accounting Research, 2nd edition, Amsterdam et al. 2007, pp. 625-640.

Dechow, N./Mouritsen, J. (2005): Enterprise resource planning systems, management control and the quest for integration, in: Accounting, Organizations and Society, Vol. 30, 7-8, 2005, pp. 691-733.

Demirag, I. S. (1988): Assessing foreign subsidiary performance – The currency choice of U.K. MNCs, in: Journal of International Business Studies, Vol. 19, No. 2, 1988, pp. 257-275.

Demski, J./Feltham, G. (1978): Economic Incentives in Budgetary Control Systems, in: The Accounting Review, Vol. 53, No. 2, 1978, pp. 336-359.

Denzin, N./Lincoln, Y. (2011): Introduction: The Discipline and Practice of Qualitative Research, in: Denzin, N. K./Lincoln, Y. S. (eds.), The SAGE handbook of qualitative research, 4th edition, Los Angeles et al. 2011, pp. 1-20.

Devajit, M. (2012): Impact of Foreign Direct Investment on Indian economy, in: Research Journal of Management Sciences, Vol. 1, No. 2, 2012, pp. 29-31.

Devers, K./Frankel, R. (2000): Study design in qualitative research: Sampling and data collection strategies, in: Education for health, Vol. 13, No. 2, 2000, pp. 263-271.

Dey, C. (2017): Ethnography, ethnomethodology and anthropology studies in accounting, in: Hoque, Z./Parker, L. D./Covaleski, M. A./Haynes, K. (eds.), The Routledge Companion to Qualitative Accounting Research Methods, London 2017, pp. 147-162.

Dey, I. (2005): Qualitative data analysis: A user-friendly guide for social scientists, London et al. 2005.

Dickson-Swift, V./James, E./Kippen, S./Liamputtong, P. (2007): Doing sensitive research: what challenges do qualitative researchers face?, in: Qualitative Research, Vol. 7, No. 3, 2007, pp. 327-353.

Dillard, J./Rigsby, J./Goodman, C. (2004): The making and remaking of organization context, in: Accounting, Auditing & Accountability Journal, Vol. 17, No. 4, 2004, pp. 506-542.

DiMaggio, P./Powell, W. (1983): The Iron Cage Revisited: Institutional Isomorphism and Collective Rationality in Organizational Fields, in: American Journal of Sociology Review, Vol. 48, No. 2, 1983, pp. 147-160.

DiMaggio, P./Powell, W. (1991): Introduction, in: Powell, W. W./DiMaggio, P. J. (eds.), The New Institutionalism in Organizational Analysis, Chicago/London 1991, pp. 1-38.

Döring, N./Bortz, J. (2016): Forschungsmethoden und Evaluation in den Sozial- und Humanwissenschaften, Berlin/Heidelberg 2016.

Dörrenbächer, C./Gammelgaard, J. (2016): Subsidiary Initiative Taking in Multinational Corporations: The Relationship between Power and Issue Selling, in: Organization Studies, Vol. 37, No. 9, 2016, pp. 1249-1270.

Dossi, A./Patelli, L. (2008): The decision-influencing use of performance measurement systems in relationships between headquarters and subsidiaries, in: Management Accounting Research, Vol. 19, No. 2, 2008, pp. 126-148.

Dossi, A./Patelli, L. (2010): You Learn From What You Measure: Financial and Nonfinancial Performance Measures in Multinational Companies, in: Long Range Planning, Vol. 43, No. 4, 2010, pp. 498-526.

Doty, D./Glick, W. (1994): Typologies As a Unique Form Of Theory Building: Toward Improved Understanding and Modeling, in: Academy of Management Review, Vol. 19, No. 2, 1994, pp. 230-251.

Doz, Y./Prahalad, C. (1984): Patterns of Strategic Control Within Multinational Corporations, in: Journal of International Business Studies, Vol. 15, No. 2, 1984, pp. 55-72.

Drew, A. (1997): From knowledge to action: the impact of benchmarking on organizational performance, in: Long Range Planning, Vol. 30, No. 3, 1997, pp. 427-441.

Drogendijk, R./Holm, U. (2012): Cultural distance or cultural positions? Analysing the effect of culture on the HQ–subsidiary relationship, in: International Business Review, Vol. 21, No. 3, 2012, pp. 383-396.

Drury, C./Tayles, M. (1995): Issues arising from surveys of management accounting practice, in: Management Accounting Research, Vol. 6, 1995, pp. 267-280.

Du, Y./Deloof, M./Jorissen, A. (2013): Headquarters–Subsidiary Interdependencies and the Design of Performance Evaluation and Reward Systems in Multinational Enterprises, in: European Accounting Review, Vol. 22, No. 2, 2013, pp. 391-424.

Dunning, J. (2003): Economic Analysis and the Multinational Enterprise, London 2003.

E

Edwards, T./Almond, P./Colling, T. (2011): Fleas on the backs of elephants: researching the multinational company, in: Marschan-Piekkari, R./Welch, C. (eds.), Rethinking the Case Study in International Business and Management Research, Cheltenham et al. 2011, pp. 411-430.

Egbe, I./Adegbite, E./Yekini, K. (2018): The influence of multinational enterprises on subsidiaries: context matters, in: Accounting, Auditing & Accountability Journal, Vol. 31, No. 2, 2018, pp. 703-724.

Egelhoff, W. (1988): Strategy and structure in multinational corporations: A revision of the stopford and wells model, in: Strategic Management Journal, Vol. 9, No. 1, 1988, pp. 1-14.

Egelhoff, W. (2010): How the Parent Headquarters Adds Value to an MNC, in: Management International Review, Vol. 50, No. 4, 2010, pp. 413-431.

Egelhoff, W./Wolf, J. (2017): The role of headquarters in the contemporary MNC: A contingency model, in: Dörrenbächer, C./Geppert, M. (eds.), Multinational Corporations and Organization Theory: Post Millennium Perspectives, Bingley 2017, pp. 71-98.

Eisenhardt, K. (1989): Building Theories from Case Study Research, in: The Academy of Management Review, Vol. 14, No. 4, 1989, p. 532.

Ellingson, L. (2011): Analysis and Representation Across the Continuum, in: Denzin, N. K./Lincoln, Y. S. (eds.), The SAGE handbook of qualitative research, 4th edition, Los Angeles et al. 2011, pp. 595-610.

Emmanuel, C./Otley, D./Merchant, K. (1990): Accounting for management control, London 1990.

Endenich, C (2012): Comparative Management Accounting – Ein Vergleich der Controllingforschung und –praxis in Deutschland und Spanien, Wiesbaden 2012.

Endenich, C./Brandau, M./Hoffjan, A. (2011): Two Decades of Research on Comparative Management Accounting – Achievements and Future Directions, in: Australian Accounting Review, Vol. 21, No. 4, 2011, pp. 365-382.

Euske, K./Lebas, M./McNair, C. (1993): Performance management in an international setting, in: Management Accounting Research, Vol. 4, No. 4, 1993, pp. 275-299.

F

Feichter, C./Grabner, I./Moers, F. (2018): Target Setting in Multi-Divisional Firms: State of the Art and Avenues for Future Research, in: Journal of Management Accounting Research, Vol. 30, No. 3, 2018, pp. 29-54.

Fellner, T./Mitter, C. (2019): Einfluss kultureller Unterschiede auf das Controlling – eine systematische Analyse des Forschungsstands, in: Feldbauer-Durstmüller, B./Mayr, S. (eds.), Controlling – Aktuelle Entwicklungen und Herausforderungen: Digitalisierung, Nachhaltigkeit und Spezialaspekte, Wiesbaden 2019, pp. 471-490.

Ferner, A./Almond, P. (2013): Performance and reward practices in foreign multinationals in the UK, in: Human Resource Management Journal, Vol. 23, No. 3, 2013, pp. 241-261.

Ferner, A./Edwards, T./Tempel, A. (2011): Power, institutions and the cross-national transfer of employment practices in multinationals, in: Human Relations, Vol. 65, No. 2, 2011, pp. 163-187.

Ferreira, A. (2002): Management Accounting and Control Systems Design and Use: An explanatory study in Portugal, University of Oporto 2002.

Ferreira, A./Otley, D. (2009): The design and use of performance management systems: An extended framework for analysis, in: Management Accounting Research, Vol. 20, No. 4, 2009, pp. 263-282.

Fischer, T. M./Möller, K./Schultze, W. (2015): Controlling – Grundlagen, Instrumente und Entwicklungsperspektiven, 2nd edition, Stuttgart 2015.

Fisher, J. (1992): Use of non-financial performance measures, in: Journal of cost management, Vol. 6, No. 1, 1992, pp. 31-38.

Fitzgerald, L. (2007): Performance measurement, in: Hopper, T./Northcott, D./Scapens, R. W. (eds.), Issues in management accounting, 3rd edition, Harlow 2007, pp. 223-241.

Flick, U. (2018): Designing Qualitative Research, London et al. 2018.

Flick, U. (2019): Qualitative Sozialforschung – Eine Einführung, 9th edition, Reinbek 2019.

Flyvbjerg, B. (2011): Case Study, in: Denzin, N. K./Lincoln, Y. S. (eds.), The SAGE handbook of qualitative research, 4th edition, Los Angeles et al. 2011, pp. 301-316.

Folan, P./Browne, J. (2005): Development of an extended enterprise performance measurement system, in: Production Planning & Control, Vol. 16, No. 6, 2005, pp. 531-544.

Franco-Santos, M./Kennerley, M./Micheli, P./.Martinez, V./Mason, S./Marr, B./Gray, D./Neely, A. (2007): Towards a definition of a business performance measurement system, in: International Journal of Operations & Production Management, Vol. 27, No. 8, 2007, pp. 784-801.

Franco-Santos, M./Lucianetti, L./Bourne, M. (2012): Contemporary performance measurement systems: A review of their consequences and a framework for research, in: Management Accounting Research, Vol. 23, No. 2, 2012, pp. 79-119.

Fülbier, R. (2004): Wissenschaftstheorie und Betriebswirtschaftslehre, in: WiSt – Wirtschaftswissenschaftliches Studium, Vol. 33, No. 5, 2004, pp. 266-271.

Furlong, P./Marsh, D. (2010): A Skin Not a Sweater: Ontology and Epistemology in Political Science, in: Marsh, D./Stoker, G. (eds.), Theory and Methods in Political Science, London 2010, pp. 184-211.

G

Giacobbe, F./Matolcsy, Z./Wakefield, J. (2016): An investigation of wholly-owned foreign subsidiary control through transaction cost economics theory, in: Accounting & Finance, Vol. 56, No. 4, 2016, pp. 1041-1070.

Gladen, W. (2014): Performance Measurement, Wiesbaden 2014.

Glaser, B./Strauss, A. (1967): The discovery of grounded theory: Strategies for qualitative research, New York, NY 1967.

Gläser, J./Laudel, G. (2010): Experteninterviews und qualitative Inhaltsanalyse als Instrumente rekonstruierender Untersuchungen, 4th edition, Wiesbaden 2010.

Gleich, R. (2011): Performance Measurement: Konzepte, Fallstudien und Grundschema für die Praxis, 2nd edition, München 2011.

Goddard, A. (2017): Grounded theory approach to accounting studies: Overview of principles, assumptions and methods, in: Hoque, Z./Parker, L. D./Covaleski, M. A./Haynes, K. (eds.), The Routledge Companion to Qualitative Accounting Research Methods, London 2017, pp. 91-111.

Goretzki, L./Strauss, E./Wiegmann, L. (2018): Exploring the Roles of Vernacular Accounting Systems in the Development of "Enabling" Global Accounting and Control Systems, in: Contemporary Accounting Research, Vol. 35, No. 4, 2018, pp. 1888-1916.

Grafton, J./Lillis, A./Mahama, H. (2011): Mixed methods research in accounting, in: Qualitative Research in Accounting & Management, Vol. 8, No. 1, 2011, pp. 5-21.

Granlund, M./Lukka, K. (1998): It's a Small World of Management Accounting Practices, in: Journal of Management Accounting Research, Vol. 10, 1998, pp. 153-179.

Granlund, M./Malmi, T. **(2002):** Moderate impact of ERPS on management accounting: a lag or permanent outcome?, in: Management Accounting Research, Vol. 13, No. 3, 2002, pp. 299-321.

Grochla, E. **(1978):** Einführung in die Organisationstheorie, Stuttgart 1978.

Groot, T./Lindahl, F. **(2010):** International Management Control Systems, in: Westerman, W./Van der Meer-Kooistra, J./Langfield-Smith, K. (eds.), International Management Accounting and Control, London 2010.

Guba, E./Lincoln, Y. **(1994):** Competing paradigms in qualitative research, in: Denzin, N. K./Lincoln, Y. S. (eds.), The SAGE handbook of qualitative research, Los Angeles et al. 1994, pp. 105-117.

Günther, T./Grüning, M. **(2002):** Performance Measurement-Systeme im praktischen Einsatz, in: Controlling, Vol. 14, No. 1, 2002, pp. 5-14.

H

Haas de, M. **(2000):** Strategic dialogue: In search of goal coherence, Eindhoven 2000.

Haas de, M./Kleingeld, A. **(1999):** Multilevel design of performance measurement systems: enhancing strategic dialogue throughout the organization, in: Management Accounting Research, Vol. 10, No. 3, 1999, pp. 233-261.

Hall, M. **(2010):** Accounting information and managerial work, in: Accounting, Organizations and Society, Vol. 35, No. 3, 2010, pp. 301-315.

Hammond, T. **(2017):** Oral history, in: Hoque, Z./Parker, L. D./Covaleski, M. A./Haynes, K. (eds.), The Routledge Companion to Qualitative Accounting Research Methods, London 2017, pp. 200-214.

Hannan, M./Freeman, J. **(1989):** Organizational Ecology, Cambridge et al. 1989.

Hansen, D. **(1997):** Worker Performance and Group Incentives: A Case Study, in: ILR Review, Vol. 51, No. 1, 1997, pp. 37-49.

Hansen, S./Otley, D./van der Stede, W. A. **(2003):** Practice Developments in Budgeting: An Overview and Research Perspective, in: Journal of Management Accounting Research, Vol. 15, 2003, pp. 95-116.

Harrison, G. L. **(1993):** Reliance on accounting performance measures in superior evaluation style – The influence of national culture and personality, in: Accounting, Organizations, and Society, Vol. 18, No. 4, 1993, pp. 319-339.

Harzing, A.-W./Sorge, A. (2003): The Relative Impact of Country of Origin and Universal Contingencies on Internationalization Strategies and Corporate Control in Multinational Enterprises: Worldwide and European Perspectives, in: Organization Studies, Vol. 24, No. 2, 2003, pp. 187-214.

Hayes, T./Mattimoe, R. (2004): To Tape or Not to Tape: Reflections on Methods of Data Collection, in: Lee, B./Humphrey, C. (eds.), The real life guide to accounting research, Amsterdam et al. 2004, pp. 359-372.

Haynes, K. (2017): Autoethnography in accounting research, in: Hoque, Z./Parker, L. D./Covaleski, M. A./Haynes, K. (eds.), The Routledge Companion to Qualitative Accounting Research Methods, London 2017, pp. 215-230.

Heenan, D. (1979): The Regional Headquarters Decision: A Comparative Analysis, in: Academy of Management Journal, Vol. 22, No. 2, 1979, pp. 410-415.

Heinicke, A. (2018): Performance measurement systems in small and medium-sized enterprises and family firms: a systematic literature review, in: Journal of Management Control, Vol. 28, No. 4, 2018, pp. 457-502.

Helfferich, C. (2011): Die Qualität qualitativer Daten, Wiesbaden 2011.

Henri, J.-F. (2006): Organizational culture and performance measurement systems, in: Accounting, Organizations and Society, Vol. 31, No. 1, 2006, pp. 77-103.

Hillman, A./Wan, W. (2005): The determinants of MNE subsidiaries' political strategies: evidence of institutional duality, in: Journal of International Business Studies, Vol. 36, No. 3, 2005, pp. 322-340.

Hoffjan, A. (2008): Comparative Management Accounting – Vergleich des anglo-amerikanischen Management Accounting und des deutschen Controllings, in: Controlling, Vol. 20, No. 12, 2008, pp. 655-662.

Hoffjan, A./Trapp, R./Endenich, C./Boucoiran, T. (2012): International budgeting— challenges for German-French companies, in: Journal of Management Control, Vol. 23, No. 1, 2012, pp. 5-25.

Hoffjan, A./Weide, G. (2006): Organisation des internationalen Controlling – Im Spannungsfeld zwischen Standardisierung und Differenzierung, in: Die Unternehmung, Vol. 60, No. 6, 2006, pp. 389-406.

Hofstede, G. (1980): Motivation, leadership, and organization: do American theories apply abroad?, in: Organizational dynamics, Vol. 9, No. 1, 1980, pp. 42-63.

Hofstede, G. (1991): Cultures and Organizations – Software of the mind, London et al. 1991.

Hofstede, G. (1994): The Business of International Business is Culture, in: International Business Review, Vol. 3, No. 1, 1994, pp. 1-14.

Hofstede, G. (2011): Dimensionalizing Cultures: The Hofstede Model in Context, in: Online Readings in Psychology and Culture, Unit 2, Subunit 1, Article 8, URL: https://scholarworks.gvsu.edu/cgi/viewcontent.cgi?article=1014&context=orpc (20.11.2019).

Hopper, T./Powell, A. (1985): Making sense of research into the organizational and social aspects of management accounting: A review of its underlying assumptions, in: Journal of Management Studies, Vol. 22, No. 5, 1985, pp. 429-465.

Hopwood, A. (1972): An Empirical Study of the Role of Accounting Data in Performance Evaluation, in: Journal of Accounting Research, Vol. 10, 1972, p. 156.

Hopwood, A. (1990): Accounting and Organisation Change, in: Accounting, Auditing & Accountability Journal, Vol. 3, No. 1, 1990, pp. 7-17.

Hopwood, A. (2009): The economic crisis and accounting: Implications for the research community, in: Accounting, Organizations and Society, Vol. 34, 6-7, 2009, pp. 797-802.

Hoque, Z. (2004): A contingency model of the association between strategy, environmental uncertainty and performance measurement: impact on organizational performance, in: International Business Review, Vol. 13, No. 4, 2004, pp. 485-502.

Horváth, P./Gleich, R./Seiter, M. (2015): Controlling, 13th edition, München 2015.

Horváth, P./Seiter, M. (2009): Performance Measurement, in: Die Betriebswirtschaft DBW, Vol. 69, No. 3, 2009, pp. 393-413.

Hronec, S. (1996): Vital Signs: Indikatoren für die Leistungsfähigkeit Ihres Unternehmens, Stuttgart 1996.

Hussain, M./Hoque, Z. (2002): Understanding non-financial performance measurement practices in Japanese banks, in: Accounting, Auditing & Accountability Journal, Vol. 15, No. 2, 2002, pp. 162-183.

Hyland, P./Beckett, R. (2002): Learning to compete: the value of internal benchmarking, in: Benchmarking: An International Journal, Vol. 9, No. 3, 2002, pp. 293-304.

Hyvönen, T./Järvinen, J./Pellinen, J. (2008): A virtual integration—The management control system in a multinational enterprise, in: Management Accounting Research, Vol. 19, No. 1, 2008, pp. 45-61.

I

Islam, S./Adler, R./Northcott, D. (2018): Managerial attitudes towards the incompleteness of performance measurement systems, in: Qualitative Research in Accounting & Management, Vol. 15, No. 1, 2018, pp. 84-103.

Ittner, C./Larcker, D. (1998): Innovations in performance measurment, in: Journal of Management Accounting Research, Vol. 10, 1998, pp. 205-238.

Ittner, C./Larcker, D. (2003): Coming up Short on nonfinancial Performance, in: Harvard Business Review, Vol. 81, No. 139, 2003, pp. 88-95.

J

Jaeger, A. (1983): The Transfer of Organizational Culture Overseas: An Approach to Control in the Multinational Corporation, in: Journal of International Business Studies, Vol. 14, No. 2, 1983, pp. 91-114.

Janghorban, R./Latifnejad Roudsari, R./Taghipour, A. (2014): Skype interviewing: the new generation of online synchronous interview in qualitative research, in: International journal of qualitative studies on health and well-being, Vol. 9, 2014, p. 24152.

Janvrin, D./Raschke, R./Dilla, W. (2014): Making sense of complex data using interactive data visualization, in: Journal of Accounting Education, Vol. 32, No. 4, 2014, pp. 31-48.

Jarillo, J. T./Martínez, J. I. (1990): Different Roles for Subsidiaries: The Case of Multinational Corporations in Spain, in: Strategic Management Journal, Vol. 11, No. 7, 1990, pp. 501-512.

Ji, S./Hoque, Z. (2017): A case study research project: personal reflections // The Routledge Companion to Qualitative Accounting Research Methods, in: Hoque, Z./Parker, L. D./Covaleski, M. A./Haynes, K. (eds.), The Routledge Companion to Qualitative Accounting Research Methods, London 2017, pp. 447-462.

Jiang, Y./Colakoglu, S./Lepak, D. P./Blasi, J. R./Kruse, D. L. (2015): Involvement work systems and operational effectiveness: Exploring the moderating effect of national power distance, in: Journal of International Business Studies, Vol. 46, No. 3, 2015, pp. 332-354.

Johansson, T./Siverbo, S. (2009): Why is research on management accounting change not explicitly evolutionary? Taking the next step in the conceptualisation of management accounting change, in: Management Accounting Research, Vol. 20, No. 2, 2009, pp. 146-162.

K

Kajüter, P./Schaumann, K./Schirmacher, H. (2019): Einfluss aktueller IT-Trends auf das interne Berichtswesen, in: Kümpel, T./Schlenkrich, K./Heupel, T. (eds.), Controlling & Innovation 2019: Digitalisierung, Wiesbaden 2019, pp. 135-153.

Kajüter, P./Schröder, M. (2017): Cross-National Differences in Cost Accounting of MNEs: Empirical Evidence from Anglophone Subsidiaries in Germany, in: Journal of International Accounting Research, Vol. 16, No. 2, 2017, pp. 71-100.

Kaplan, R. (1986): The role for empirical research in management accounting, in: Accounting, Organizations and Society, Vol. 11, 4-5, 1986, pp. 429-452.

Kaplan, R./Norton, D. (1992): The Balanced Scorecard: Measures that Drive Performance, in: Harvard Business Review, Vol. 1992, January-February, 1992, pp. 71-79.

Kaplan, R./Norton, D. (1996): Balanced Scorecard: Strategien erfolgreich umsetzen, Stuttgart 1996.

Kaplan, R./Norton, D. (2001): Transforming the Balanced Scorecard from Performance Measurement to Strategic Management: Part II, in: Accounting Horizons, Vol. 15, No. 2, 2001, pp. 147-160.

Kasanen, E./Lukka, K./Arto, S. (1993): The Constructive Approach in Management Accounting Research, in: Journal of Management Accounting Research, Vol. 5, No. 1, 1993, pp. 243-264.

Kaufmann, J. (2015): Das verstehende Interview: Theorie und Praxis, 2nd edition, Konstanz 2015.

Kelle, U./Kluge, S. (2010): Vom Einzelfall zum Typus: Fallvergleich und Fallkontrastierung in der qualitativen Sozialforschung, 2nd edition, Wiesbaden 2010.

Khalifa, R./Mahama, H. (2017): Discourse analysis in accounting research, in: Hoque, Z./Parker, L. D./Covaleski, M. A./Haynes, K. (eds.), The Routledge Companion to Qualitative Accounting Research Methods, London 2017, pp. 250-264.

Kihn, L. (2008): The determinants of multiple forms of controls in foreign subsidiary manager evaluations, in: International Journal of Accounting, Auditing and Performance Evaluation, Vol. 5, No. 2, 2008, p. 157.

Kilfoyle, E./Richardson, A./MacDonald, L. (2013): Vernacular accountings: Bridging the cognitive and the social in the analysis of employee-generated accounting systems, in: Accounting, Organizations and Society, Vol. 38, No. 5, 2013, pp. 382-396.

Kim, B./Prescott, J./Kim, S. (2005): Differentiated governance of foreign subsidiaries in transnational corporations: an agency theory perspective, in: Journal of International Management, Vol. 11, No. 1, 2005, pp. 43-66.

Kirsch-Brunkow, K. (2017): Vertriebscontrolling & Vertriebskennzahlen, Internatinaoler Contoller Verein, URL: https://www.icv-controlling.com/fileadmin/Assets/Content/AK/Berlin%20Brandenburg/Images/AK-Tagungen/60/Vertriebscontrolling.pdf (07.12.2019).

Klingebiel, N. (2001): Impulsgeber des Performance Measurement, in: Klingebiel, N. (ed.), Performance Measurement & Balanced Scorecard, München 2001, pp. 3-23.

Knauer, T./Silge, L./Sommer, F. (2018): The shareholder value effects of using value-based performance measures: Evidence from acquisitions and divestments, in: Management Accounting Research, Vol. 41, 2018, pp. 43-61.

Kornacker, J. (2014): Budgeting under the impact of contextual factors: Empirical evidence from German multinational enterprises in China, Hamburg 2014.

Kornacker, J./Trapp, R./Ander, K. (2018): Rejection, reproduction and reshaping – a field study on global budget control practices in multinational companies, in: Qualitative Research in Accounting & Management, Vol. 15, No. 1, 2018, pp. 24-52.

Körnert, J. (2006): Perspektiven der Balanced Scorecard: Eine theoretisch-konzeptionelle Analyse zur Auswahl geeigneter Balanced Scorecard-Perspektiven für Kreditinstitute, in: Zeitschrift für Planung & Unternehmenssteuerung, Vol. 17, No. 2, 2006, pp. 155-176.

Kornmeier, M. (2007): Wissenschaftstheorie und wissenschaftliches Arbeiten: Eine Einführung für Wirtschaftswissenschaftler, Heidelberg 2007.

Kostova, T. (1999): Transnational Transfer of Strategic Organizational Practices: A Contextual Perspective, in: The Academy of Management Review, Vol. 24, No. 2, 1999, pp. 308-324.

Kostova, T./Marano, V. (2019): Institutional Theory Perspectives on Emerging Markets, in: Grosse, R./Meyer, K. E./Kostova, T./Marano, V. (eds.), The Oxford Handbook of Management in Emerging Markets 2019, pp. 98-126.

Kostova, T./Roth, K. (2002): Adoption of an Organizational Practice by Subsidiaries of Multinational Corporations: Institutional and Relational Effects, in: Academy of Management Journal, Vol. 45, No. 1, 2002, pp. 215-233.

Kostova, T./Roth, K./Dacin, M. (2008): Institutional Theory in the Study of Multinational Corporations - A Critique and New Directions, in: Academy of Management Review, Vol. 33, No. 4, 2008, pp. 994-1006.

Kostova, T./Roth, K./Dacin, M. (2009): Theorizing on MNCs: A Promise for Institutional Theory, in: Academy of Management Review, Vol. 34, No. 1, 2009, pp. 171-173.

Kostova, T./Zaheer, S. (1999): Organizational Legitimacy Under Conditions of Complexity: The Case of the Multinational Enterprise, in: Academy of Management Review, Vol. 24, No. 1, 1999, pp. 64-81.

Kraus, K./Lind, J. (2010): The impact of the corporate balanced scorecard on corporate control—A research note, in: Management Accounting Research, Vol. 21, No. 4, 2010, pp. 265-277.

Kretschmer, K. (2008): Performance Evaluation of Foreign Subsidiaries, Wiesbaden 2008.

Krücken, G. (2017): Paul J. DiMaggio und Walter W. Powell: The Iron Cage Revisited: Institutional Isomorphism and Collective Rationality in Organizational Fields, in: Kraemer, K./Brugger, F. (eds.), Schlüsselwerke der Wirtschaftssoziologie, Wiesbaden 2017, pp. 195-200.

Kuckartz, U. (2010): Typenbildung, in: Mey, G./Mruck, K. (eds.), Handbuch Qualitative Forschung in der Psychologie, Wiesbaden 2010, pp. 553-568.

Kuckartz, U. (2018): Qualitative Inhaltsanalyse: Methoden, Praxis, Computerunterstützung, 3rd edition, Weinheim 2018.

Kuhn, T. (1970): The Structure of Scientific Revolutions, 2nd edition, University of Chicago 1970.

Küpper, H.-U./Friedl, G./Hofmann, C./Hofmann, Y./Pedell, B. (2013): Controlling: Konzeption, Aufgaben, Instrumente, 6th edition, Stuttgart 2013.

Kutschker, M./Schmid, S. (2011): Internationales Management, 7th edition, München 2011.

L

Ladley, D./Wilkinson, I./Young, L. (2015): The impact of individual versus group rewards on work group performance and cooperation: A computational social science approach, in: Journal of Business Research, Vol. 68, No. 11, 2015, pp. 2412-2425.

Lamnek, S./Krell, C. (2016): Qualitative Sozialforschung: Mit Online-Material, 6th edition, Weinheim/Basel 2016.

Langfield-Smith, K./Thorne, H./Hilton, R. (2006): Management Accounting: Information for Managing and Creating Value, 4th edition, New York et al. 2006.

Langfield-Smith, K. (1997): Management control systems and strategy: A critical review, in: Accounting, Organizations and Society, Vol. 22, No. 2, 1997, pp. 207-232.

Lasserre, P. (1996): Regional headquarters: The spearhead for Asia Pacific markets, in: Long Range Planning, Vol. 29, No. 1, 1996, pp. 30-37.

Lebas, M. (1995): Performance measurement and performance management, in: International Journal of Production Economics, Vol. 41, 1-3, 1995, pp. 23-35.

Lebas, M. (1996): Management Accounting Practice in France, Oxford 1996.

Lee, T. (1999): Using qualitative methods in organizational research, Thousand Oaks, Calif. 1999.

Lervik, J. (2011): The single MNC as a research site, in: Marschan-Piekkari, R./Welch, C. (eds.), Rethinking the Case Study in International Business and Management Research, Cheltenham et al. 2011, pp. 229-250.

Lewis, J./Ritchie, J. (2003): Qualitative research practice, London 2003.

Lilienthal, D. (1960): The Multinational Corporation, in: Anshen, M./Bach, G. L. (eds.), Management and Corporations, New York 1960, pp. 119-158.

Lillis, A./Mundy, J. (2005): Cross-Sectional Field Studies in Management Accounting Research—Closing the Gaps between Surveys and Case Studies, in: Journal of Management Accounting Research, Vol. 17, No. 1, 2005, pp. 119-141.

Lincoln, Y. (1995): Emerging Criteria for Quality in Qualitative and Interpretive Research, in: Qualitative Inquiry, Vol. 1, No. 3, 1995, pp. 275-289.

Lincoln, Y./Guba, E. (1985): Naturalistic inquiry, Beverly Hills 1985.

Lincoln, Y./Lynham, S./Guba, E. (2011): Paradigmatic Controversies, Contradictions, and Emerging Confluences, Revisited, in: Denzin, N. K./Lincoln, Y. S. (eds.), The SAGE handbook of qualitative research, 4th edition, Los Angeles et al. 2011, pp. 97-128.

Lingnau, V. (1995): Kritischer Rationalismus und Betriebswirtschaftslehre, in: WiSt: Zeitschrift für Studium und Forschung, Vol. 24, No. 3, 1995, pp. 124-129.

Llewellyn, S. (1992): The role of case study methods in management accounting research: A comment, in: The British Accounting Review, Vol. 24, No. 1, 1992, pp. 17-31.

Lounsbury, M. (2008): Institutional rationality and practice variation: New directions in the institutional analysis of practice, in: Accounting, Organizations and Society, Vol. 33, 4-5, 2008, pp. 349-361.

Luft, J./Shields, M. (2014): Subjectivity in developing and validating causal explanations in positivist accounting research, in: Accounting, Organizations and Society, Vol. 39, No. 7, 2014, pp. 550-558.

Lukka, K./Kasanen, E. (1995): The problem of generalizability: anecdotes and evidence in accounting research, in: Accounting, Auditing & Accountability Journal, Vol. 8, No. 5, 1995, pp. 71-90.

Lukka, K./Modell, S. (2010): Validation in interpretive management accounting research, in: Accounting, Organizations and Society, Vol. 35, No. 4, 2010, pp. 462-477.

Lukka, K. (2010): The roles and effects of paradigms in accounting research, in: Management Accounting Research, Vol. 21, No. 2, 2010, pp. 110-115.

Lukka, K./Mouritsen, J. (2002): Homogeneity or heterogeneity of research in management accounting?, in: European Accounting Review, Vol. 11, No. 4, 2002, pp. 805-811.

Lynch, R./Cross, K. (1995): Measure up!: Yardsticks for continuous improvement, 2nd edition, Cambridge 1995.

M

Macharzina, K./Wolf, J. (2012): Unternehmensführung: Das internationale Managementwissen: Konzepte - Methoden - Praxis, 8th edition, Wiesbaden 2012.

Macintosh, N./Quattrone, P. (2010): Macintosh, Norman B., and Paolo Quattrone. Management accounting and control systems: An organizational and sociological approach, Chichester 2010.

Mahlendorf, M./Rehring, J./Schäffer, U./Wyszomirski, E. (2012): Influencing foreign subsidiary decisions through headquarter performance measurement systems, in: Management Decision, Vol. 50, No. 4, 2012, pp. 688-717.

Maisonrouge, J. (1974): The mythology of multinationalism, in: Columbia Journal of World Business, Vol. 9, No. 1, 1974, pp. 7-12.

Malina, M./Selto, F. (2001): Communicating and Controlling Strategy: An Empirical Study of the Effectiveness of the Balanced Scorecard, in: Journal of Management Accounting Research, Vol. 13, No. 1, 2001, pp. 47-90.

Malmi, T./Brown, D. (2008): Management control systems as a package—Opportunities, challenges and research directions, in: Management Accounting Research, Vol. 19, No. 4, 2008, pp. 287-300.

Marr, B. (2005): Corporate Performance Measurement, in: Controlling – Zeitschrift für erfolgsorientierte Unternehmenssteuerung, Vol. 17, No. 11, 2005, pp. 645-652.

Marsh, D./Stoker, G. (2010): Theory and Methods in Political Science, London 2010.

Maskell, B. (1991): Performance measurement for world class manufacturing: A model for American companies, Cambridge 1991.

Matějka, M. (2018): Target Setting in Multi-Divisional Organizations, in: Journal of Management Accounting Research, Vol. 30, No. 3, 2018, pp. 13-27.

Maxwell, J. (2013): Qualitative research design: An interactive approach, 3rd edition, Los Angeles et al. 2013.

Mayring, P. (2016): Einführung in die qualitative Sozialforschung: Eine Anleitung zu qualitativem Denken, 6th edition, Weinheim 2016.

McInnes, J. (1971): Financial Control Systems for Multinational Operations: An Empirical Investigation, in: Journal of International Business Studies, Vol. 2, No. 2, 1971, pp. 11-28.

Menon, A./Varadarajan, P. (1992): A Model of Marketing Knowledge Use within Firms, in: Journal of Marketing, Vol. 56, No. 4, 1992, p. 53.

Merchant, K. (1987): How and why firms disregard the controllability principle, in: Kaplan, W.J.B./Bruns, W. J./Kaplan, R. S. (eds.), Accounting & Management: Field Study Perspectives, Cambridge 1987, pp. 316-338.

Merchant, K. A./Chow, C. W./Wu, A. (1995): Measurement, evaluation and reward of profit center managers: A cross-cultural field study, in: Accounting, Organizations, and Society, Vol. 20, No. 7-8, 1995, pp. 619-638.

Merchant, K./van der Stede, W. A. (2012): Management control systems: Performance measurement, evaluation and incentives, 3rd edition, Harlow 2012.

Messner, M./Becker, C./Schäffer, U./Binder, C. (2008): Legitimacy and Identity in Germanic Management Accounting Research, in: European Accounting Review, Vol. 17, No. 1, 2008, pp. 129-159.

Messner, M./Moll, J./Strömsten, T. (2017): Credibility and authenticity in qualitative accounting research, in: Hoque, Z./Parker, L. D./Covaleski, M. A./Haynes, K. (eds.), The Routledge Companion to Qualitative Accounting Research Methods, London 2017, pp. 432-443.

Meyer, J./Rowan, B. (1977): Institutionalized Organizations: Formal Structure as Myth and Ceremony, in: American Journal of Sociology, Vol. 83, No. 2, 1977, pp. 340-363.

Michel, A./Shaked, I. (1986): Multinational Corporations vs. Domestic Corporations: Financial Performance and Characteristics, in: Journal of International Business Studies, Vol. 17, No. 3, 1986, pp. 89-100.

Micheli, P./Mura, M./Agliati, M. (2011): Exploring the roles of performance measurement systems in strategy implementation, in: International Journal of Operations & Production Management, Vol. 31, No. 10, 2011, pp. 1115-1139.

Miles, M./Huberman, A./Saldaña, J. (2014): Qualitative Data Analysis: A Methods Sourcebook, 3rd edition London et al. 2014.

Modell, S. (2001): Performance measurement and institutional processes: a study of managerial responses to public sector reform, in: Management Accounting Research, Vol. 12, No. 4, 2001, pp. 437-464.

Modell, S. (2009): In defence of triangulation: A critical realist approach to mixed methods research in management accounting, in: Management Accounting Research, Vol. 20, No. 3, 2009, pp. 208-221.

Modell, S. (2010): Bridging the paradigm divide in management accounting research: The role of mixed methods approaches, in: Management Accounting Research, Vol. 21, No. 2, 2010, pp. 124-129.

Modell, S. (2017): Critical realist accounting research: In search of its emancipatory potential, in: Critical Perspectives on Accounting, Vol. 42, 2017, pp. 20-35.

Molinari, L./Abratt, R./Dion, P. (2008): Satisfaction, quality and value and effects on repurchase and positive word-of-mouth behavioral intentions in a B2B services context, in: Journal of Services Marketing, Vol. 22, No. 5, 2008, pp. 363-373.

Moll, J./Burns, J./Major, M. (2006): Institutional Theory, in: Hoque, Z. (ed.), Methodological Issues in Accounting Research: Theories, Methods and Issues, London 2006, pp. 183-206.

Möller, H.-P. (2000): IV-Controlling in der Softwarewartung, in: Dobschütz, L. von/Barth, M./Jäger-Goy, H./Kütz, M./Möller, H.-P. (eds.), IV-Controlling: Konzepte — Umsetzungen — Erfahrungen, Wiesbaden 2000, pp. 319-336.

Morse, J./Barrett, M./Mayan, M./Olson, K./Spiers, J. (2002): Verification Strategies for Establishing Reliability and Validity in Qualitative Research, in: International Journal of Qualitative Methods, Vol. 1, No. 2, 2002, pp. 13-22.

Muchiri, P./Pintelon, L. (2008): Performance measurement using overall equipment effectiveness (OEE): literature review and practical application discussion, in: International Journal of Production Research, Vol. 46, No. 13, 2008, pp. 3517-3535.

Myers, M./Newman, M. (2007): The qualitative interview in IS research: Examining the craft, in: Information and Organization, Vol. 17, No. 1, 2007, pp. 2-26.

N

Neely, A./Gregory, M./Platts, K. (1995): Performance measurement system design, in: International Journal of Operations & Production Management, Vol. 15, No. 4, 1995, pp. 80-116.

Neely, A./Yaghi, B./Youell, N. (2008): Enterprise Performance Management: The Global State of the Art, London 2008.

Nevries, P./Strauß, E./Goretzki, L. (2009): Zentrale Gestaltungsgrößen der operativen Planung, in: Controlling & Management, Vol. 53, No. 4, 2009, pp. 237-241.

Nienaber, M. (**2020**): Preparation Processes of Nonfinancial KPIs for Management Reports: Empirical Evidence on Process Design and Determinants, Frankfurt am Main 2020.

Nitzl, C./Sicilia, M./Steccolini, I. (**2018**): Exploring the links between different performance information uses, NPM cultural orientation, and organizational performance in the public sector, in: Public Management Review, Vol. 12, No. 1, 2018, pp. 1-25.

Norreklit, H. (**2000**): The balance on the balanced scorecard a critical analysis of some of its assumptions, in: Management Accounting Research, Vol. 11, No. 1, 2000, pp. 65-88.

O

Oliver, C. (**1991**): Strategic Respones To Institutional Processes, in: Academy of Management Review, Vol. 16, No. 1, 1991, pp. 145-179.

Otley, D. (**1999**): Performance management: a framework for management control systems research, in: Management Accounting Research, Vol. 10, No. 4, 1999, pp. 363-382.

Otley, D. (**2002**): Measuring performance: The accounting perspective, in: Neely, A. (ed.), Business performance measurement, Cambridge et al. 2002, pp. 3-21.

P

Pache, A.-C./Santos, F. (**2010**): When Worlds Collide: The Internal Dynamics of Organizational Responses to Conflicting Institutional Demands, in: Academy of Management Review, Vol. 35, No. 3, 2010, pp. 455-476.

Paik, Y./Chow, I./Vance, C. M. (**2011**): Interaction effects of globalization and institutional forces on international HRM practice: Illuminating the convergence-divergence debate, in: Thunderbird International Business Review, Vol. 53, No. 5, 2011, pp. 647-659.

Palinkas, L./Horwitz, S./Green, C./Wisdom, J./Duan, N./Hoagwood, K. (**2015**): Purposeful Sampling for Qualitative Data Collection and Analysis in Mixed Method Implementation Research, in: Administration and policy in mental health, Vol. 42, No. 5, 2015, pp. 533-544.

Parker, L. (**2012**): Qualitative Management Accounting Research: Assessing Deliverables and Relevance, in: Critical Perspectives on Accounting, Vol. 23, No. 1, 2012, pp. 54-70.

Parker, L./Northcott, D. (**2016**): Qualitative generalising in accounting research: concepts and strategies, in: Accounting, Auditing & Accountability Journal, Vol. 29, No. 6, 2016, pp. 1100-1131.

Parker, L./Roffey, B. (1997): Methodological themes, in: Accounting, Auditing & Accountability Journal, Vol. 10, No. 2, 1997, pp. 212-247.

Patelli, L. (2018): Properties of performance measurement and management systems used dialogically between parent companies and foreign subsidiaries, in: Advances in Management Accounting, Vol. 30, 2018, pp. 27-59.

Patton, M. (2015): Qualitative research & evaluation methods: Integrating theory and practice, Los Angeles, London, New Delhi, Singapore, Washington DC 2015.

Pausenberger, E. (1996): Controlling internationaler Unternehmungen, in: Engelhard, J. (ed.), Strategische Führung internationaler Unternehmen, Wiesbaden 1996, pp. 179-198.

Pfeffer, J./Salancik, G. (1978): The external control of organizations: A resource dependence perspective, New York et al. 1978.

Phillips, N./Tracey, P. (2009): Dialogue, in: Academy of Management Review, Vol. 34, No. 1, 2009, pp. 169-171.

Piekkari, R./Welch, C./Paavilainen, E. (2009): The Case Study as Disciplinary Convention, in: Organizational Research Methods, Vol. 12, No. 3, 2009, pp. 567-589.

Pla-Barber, J./Villar, C./Madhok, A. (2018): Co-parenting through subsidiaries: A model of value creation in the multinational firm, in: Global Strategy Journal, Vol. 8, No. 4, 2018, pp. 536-562.

Poland, B. (1995): Transcription Quality as an Aspect of Rigor in Qualitative Research, in: Qualitative Inquiry, Vol. 1, No. 3, 1995, pp. 290-310.

Poplat, T. (2013): Foreign Investments in BRIC Countries: Empirical Evidence from Multinational Corporations, Frankfurt am Main 2013.

Popper, K. (2005): Logik der Forschung, 11th edition, Tübingen 2005.

Pratt, M. (2008): Fitting Oval Pegs Into Round Holes, in: Organizational Research Methods, Vol. 11, No. 3, 2008, pp. 481-509.

Q

Qu, S./Dumay, J. (2011): The qualitative research interview, in: Qualitative Research in Accounting & Management, Vol. 8, No. 3, 2011, pp. 238-264.

Quattrone, P./Hopper, T. (2005): A 'time–space odyssey': management control systems in two multinational organisations, in: Accounting, Organizations and Society, Vol. 30, 7-8, 2005, pp. 735-764.

R

Ranjan, J. (2008): Business justification with business intelligence, in: VINE, Vol. 38, No. 4, 2008, pp. 461-475.

Raupach, A. (1998): Wechselwirkungen zwischen der Organisationsstruktur und der Besteuerung multinationaler Konzernunternehmungen, in: Theisen, M. R. (ed.), Der Konzern im Umbruch, Stuttgart 1998, pp. 58-167.

Rautiainen, A./Järvenpää, M. (2012): Institutional Logics and Responses to Performance Measurement Systems, in: Financial Accountability & Management, Vol. 28, No. 2, 2012, pp. 164-188.

Rehring, J. (2012): The Role of Performance Measurement Systems in Multinational Companies: Evidence from China, Vallendar 2012.

Reisloh, C. (2011): Influence of National Culture on IFRS Practice. An Empirical Study in France, Germany and the United Kingdom, Frankfurt am Main 2011.

Richards, G./Yeoh, W./Chong, A./Popovič, A. (2019): Business Intelligence Effectiveness and Corporate Performance Management: An Empirical Analysis, in: Journal of Computer Information Systems, Vol. 59, No. 2, 2019, pp. 188-196.

Richardson, A. (2012): Paradigms, theory and management accounting practice: A comment on Parker (forthcoming) "Qualitative management accounting research: Assessing deliverables and relevance", in: Critical Perspectives on Accounting, Vol. 23, No. 1, 2012, pp. 83-88.

Ridgway, V. (1956): Dysfunctional Consequences of Performance Measurements, in: Administrative Science Quarterly, Vol. 1, No. 2, 1956, p. 240.

Rikhardsson, P./Yigitbasioglu, O. (2018): Business intelligence & analytics in management accounting research: Status and future focus, in: International Journal of Accounting Information Systems, Vol. 29, 2018, pp. 37-58.

Ritchie, J./Lewis, J. (2014): Qualitative research practice, 2nd edition, London 2014.

Roberts, J. (2010): Designing incentives in organizations, in: Journal of Institutional Economics, Vol. 6, No. 1, 2010, pp. 125-132.

Roberts, J./Scapens, R. (1985): Accounting systems and systems of accountability — understanding accounting practices in their organisational contexts, in: Accounting, Organizations and Society, Vol. 10, No. 4, 1985, pp. 443-456.

Rolfe, S. (1970): The international corporation, in: The International Executive, Vol. 12, No. 1, 1970, pp. 1-3.

Roth, K./Kostova, T. (2003): The Use of the Multinational Corporation as a Research Context, in: Journal of Management, Vol. 29, No. 6, 2003, pp. 883-902.

Roth, K./O'Donnell, S. **(1996):** Foreign Subsidiary Compensation Strategy: An Agency Theory Perspective, in: Academy of Management Journal, Vol. 39, No. 3, 1996, pp. 678-703.

Roth, K./Nigh, D. **(1992):** The effectiveness of headquarters-subsidiary relationships: The role of coordination, control, and conflict, in: Journal of Business Research, Vol. 25, No. 4, 1992, pp. 277-301.

Rubin, H./Rubin, I. **(2012):** Qualitative Interviewing: The Art of Hearing Data, Los Angeles at al. 2012.

Ruggie, J. **(2018):** Multinationals as global institution: Power, authority and relative autonomy, in: Regulation & Governance, Vol. 12, No. 3, 2018, pp. 317-333.

S

Sageder, M./Feldbauer-Durstmüller, B. **(2018):** Management control in multinational companies: a systematic literature review, in: Review of Managerial Science, Vol. 22, 2018, p. 594.

Sandt, J. **(2004):** Management mit Kennzahlen und Kennzahlensystemen, Wiesbaden 2004.

Scapens, R. **(1990):** Researching management accounting practice: The role of case study methods, in: The British Accounting Review, Vol. 22, No. 3, 1990, pp. 259-281.

Scapens, R. **(1992):** The role of case study methods in management accounting research: A personal reflection and reply, in: British Accounting Review, Vol. 24, 1992, pp. 369-383.

Scapens, R. **(2004):** Doing Case Study Research, in: Lee, B./Humphrey, C. (eds.), The real life guide to accounting research, Amsterdam et al. 2004, pp. 257-279.

Schäffer, U./Heidmann, M. **(2007):** Der Beitrag von Controllingsystemen zur strategischen Früherkennung, in: Controlling & Management, Vol. 51, No. 2, 2007, pp. 66-73.

Schäffer, U./Mahlendorf, M./Rehring, J. **(2014):** Does the Interactive Use of Headquarter Performance Measurement Systems in Foreign Subsidiaries Endanger the Potential to Profit from Local Relationships?, in: Australian Accounting Review, Vol. 24, No. 68, 2014, pp. 21-38.

Schäffer, U./Rehring, J./Wyszomirski, E. **(2010):** Performance Measurement in chinesischen Tochtergesellschaften, in: Controlling & Management, Vol. 54, No. 5, 2010, pp. 309-313.

Schäffer, U./Steiners, D. **(2004):** Zur Nutzung von Controllinginformationen, in: Zeitschrift für Planung & Unternehmenssteuerung, Vol. 15, No. 4, 2004, pp. 377-404.

Schäffer, U./Weber, J. (2015): Mit den richtigen Kennzahlen steuern (Teil 1), in: Controlling & Management Review, Vol. 59, No. 3, 2015, pp. 34-40.

Schedler, S. (2005): Leistungsmessung in multinationalen Unternehmen, St. Gallen 2005.

Schmid, S./Kretschmer, K. (2010): Performance evaluation of foreign subsidiaries: A review of the literature and a contingency framework, in: International Journal of Management Reviews, Vol. 67, No. 10, 2010, p. 26.

Schnell, R./Hill, P./Esser, E. (2018): Methoden der empirischen Sozialforschung, 11th edition, Berlin/Boston 2018.

Scholz, C. (1984): Planning procedures in German companies—Findings and consequences, in: Long Range Planning, Vol. 17, No. 6, 1984, pp. 94-103.

Schröder, M. (2014): Cost Accounting in Anglophone Subsidiaries: Empirical Evidence from Germany, Frankfurt am Main 2014.

Schuler, R. S./Rogovsky, N. (1998): Understanding compensation practice variations across firms: The impact of national culture, in: Journal of International business studies, Vol. 29, No. 1, 1998, pp. 159-177.

Schuler, R./Fulkerson, J./Dowling, P. (1991): Strategic performance measurement and management in multinational corporations, in: Human Resource Management, Vol. 30, No. 3, 1991, pp. 365-392.

Schulz, A. (2018): Cost Accounting in German Multinational Companies: An Empirical Analysis, Frankfurt am Main 2018.

Schweitzer, M. (1978): Wissenschaftsziele und Auffassungen in der Betriebswirtschaftslehre – Eine Einführung, in: Schweitzer, M. (ed.), Auffassungen und Wissenschaftsziele der Betriebswirtschaftslehre, Darmstadt 1978, pp. 1-14.

Scott, W. (1995): Institutions and Organizations, London et al. 1995.

Scott, W. (2001): Institutions and organizations, 2nd edition, Thousand Oaks 2001.

Seal, W. (2001): Management accounting and the challenge of strategic focus, in: Management Accounting Research, Vol. 12, No. 4, 2001, pp. 487-506.

Sedgwick, M./Spiers, J. (2009): The Use of Videoconferencing as a Medium for the Qualitative Interview, in: International Journal of Qualitative Methods, Vol. 8, No. 1, 2009, pp. 1-11.

Sheu, C./Chae, B./Yang, C.-L. (2004): National differences and ERP implementation: issues and challenges, in: Omega, Vol. 32, No. 5, 2004, pp. 361-371.

Shore, B./Venkatachalam, A. R. (1996): Role of national culture in the transfer of information technology, in: Journal of Strategic Information Systems, Vol. 5, No. 1, 1996, pp. 19-35.

Simons, R. (1995): Levers of Control: How Managers Use Innovative Control Systems to Drive Strategic Renewal, Boston 1995.

Simons, R. (2000): Performance measurement & control systems for implementing strategy: Text and cases, Upper Saddle River 2000.

Siti-Nabiha, A.-K. (2009): Sensemaking in Interpretive Management Accounting Research: Constructing a Credible Account, in: International Journal of Qualitative Methods, Vol. 8, No. 1, 2009, pp. 41-53.

Siti-Nabiha, A./Scapens, R. (2005): Stability and change: an institutionalist study of management accounting change, in: Accounting, Auditing & Accountability Journal, Vol. 18, No. 1, 2005, pp. 44-73.

Speckbacher, G./Bischof, J./Pfeiffer, T. (2003): A descriptive analysis on the implementation of Balanced Scorecards in German-speaking countries, in: Management Accounting Research, Vol. 14, No. 4, 2003, pp. 361-388.

Speklé, R./Verbeeten, F. (2014): The use of performance measurement systems in the public sector: Effects on performance, in: Management Accounting Research, Vol. 25, No. 2, 2014, pp. 131-146.

Sprinkle, G. (2003): Perspectives on experimental research in managerial accounting, in: Accounting, Organizations and Society, Vol. 28, 2-3, 2003, pp. 287-318.

Stake, R. (2013): Multiple case study analysis, New York/London 2013.

Steiners, D. (2005): Lernen mit Controllinginformationen: empirische Untersuchung in deutschen Industrieunternehmen, Wiesbaden 2005.

Sturges, J./Hanrahan, K. (2004): Comparing Telephone and Face-to-Face Qualitative Interviewing: a Research Note, in: Qualitative Research, Vol. 4, No. 1, 2004, pp. 107-118.

Suchman, M. (1995): Managing Legitimacy: Strategic and Institutional Approaches, in: The Academy of Management Review, Vol. 20, No. 3, 1995, p. 571.

Sundaram, A./Black, J. (1992): The Environment and Internal Organization of Multinational Enterprises, in: Academy of Management Review, Vol. 17, No. 4, 1992, pp. 729-757.

T

Tangen, S. (2004): Performance measurement: from philosophy to practice, in: International Journal of Productivity and Performance Management, Vol. 53, No. 8, 2004, pp. 726-737.

Tarn, J./Yen, D./Beaumont, M. (2002): Exploring the rationales for ERP and SCM integration, in: Industrial Management & Data Systems, Vol. 102, No. 1, 2002, pp. 26-34.

Tessier, S./Otley, D. (2012): A conceptual development of Simons' Levers of Control framework, in: Management Accounting Research, Vol. 23, No. 3, 2012, pp. 171-185.

Tomkins, C./Groves, R. (1983): The everyday accountant and researching his reality, in: Accounting, Organizations and Society, Vol. 8, No. 4, 1983, pp. 361-374.

Tucker, B.P./Parker, L.D. (2014): Comparing Interview Interaction Modes in Management Accounting Research: A Case to Answer?, AAA 2015 Management Accounting Section (MAS) Meeting, URL: http://ssrn.com/abstract=2480247 (16.08.2019).

Tuomela, T.-S. (2005): The interplay of different levers of control: A case study of introducing a new performance measurement system, in: Management Accounting Research, Vol. 16, No. 3, 2005, pp. 293-320.

Turley, S. (2004): Research and public practice accounting, in: Humphrey, C./Lee, B.H.K. (eds.), The Real Life Guide to Accounting Research, Amsterdam et al. 2004, pp. 449-464.

U

UNCTAD (2019): World Investment Report 2019: Special Economic Zones,

V

Vaivio, J. (2008): Qualitative management accounting research: rationale, pitfalls and potential, in: Qualitative Research in Accounting & Management, Vol. 5, No. 1, 2008, pp. 64-86.

Vaivio, J./Sirén, A. (2010): Insights into method triangulation and "paradigms" in interpretive management accounting research, in: Management Accounting Research, Vol. 21, No. 2, 2010, pp. 130-141.

Vallurupalli, V./Bose, I. (2018): Business intelligence for performance measurement: A case based analysis, in: Decision Support Systems, Vol. 111, 2018, pp. 72-85.

van der Stede, W. (2001): The effect of corporate diversification and business unit strategy on the presence of slack in business unit budgets, in: Accounting, Auditing & Accountability Journal, Vol. 14, No. 1, 2001, pp. 30-52.

van der Stede, W. A. (2003): The effect of national culture on management control and incentive system design in multi-business firms: evidence of intracorporate isomorphism, in: European Accounting Review, Vol. 12, No. 2, 2003, pp. 263-285.

Vance, C. (**2006**): Strategic Upstream and Downstream Considerations for Effective Global Performance Management, in: International Journal of Cross Cultural Management, Vol. 6, No. 1, 2006, pp. 37-56.

Voss, C./Tsikriktsis, N./Frohlich, N. (**2002**): Case research in operations management, in: International Journal of Operations & Production Management, Vol. 22, No. 2, 2002, pp. 196-219.

W

Wagenhofer, A. (**2006**): Management Accounting Research in German-Speaking Countries, in: Journal of Management Accounting Research, Vol. 18, No. 1, 2006, pp. 1-19.

Walgenbach, P./Drori, G./Höllerer, M. (**2017**): Between Local Mooring and Global Orientation: A Neo-Institutional Theory Perspective on the Contemporary Multinational Corporation, in: Dörrenbächer, C./Geppert, M. (eds.), Multinational Corporations and Organization Theory: Post Millennium Perspectives, Bingley 2017, pp. 99-125.

Walgenbach, P./Meyer, R. (**2008**): Neoinstitutionalistische Organisationstheorie, Stuttgart 2008.

Walker, D./Myrick, F. (**2006**): Grounded theory: an exploration of process and procedure, in: Qualitative health research, Vol. 16, No. 4, 2006, pp. 547-559.

Weber, J./Schäffer, U. (**2013**): Balanced Scorecard und Controlling: Implementierung, Nutzen für Manager und Controller, Erfahrungen in deutschen Unternehmen, Wiesbaden 2013.

Weber, J./Schäffer, U. (**2016**): Einführung in das Controlling, 15th edition, Stuttgart 2016.

Weber, M. (**1949**): Max Weber on the methodology of the social sciences, Glencoe (Illinois) 1949.

Weinmann, T./Thomas, S./Brilmayer, S./Heinrich, S./Radon, K. (**2012**): Testing Skype as an interview method in epidemiologic research: response and feasibility, in: International journal of public health, Vol. 57, No. 6, 2012, pp. 959-961.

Welge, M./Holtbrügge, D. (**1999**): Individualisierung der Erfolgsbeurteilung in Multinationalen Unternehmungen, in: Controlling, Vol. 11, No. 12, 1999, pp. 569-573.

Westney, D. (**1993**): Institutionalization Theory and the Multinational Corporation, in: Ghoshal, S./Westney, D. E. (eds.), Organization Theory and the Multinational Corporation, Basingstoke 1993, pp. 53-76.

Whiting, L. (2008): Semi-structured interviews: guidance for novice researchers, in: Nursing standard, Vol. 22, No. 23, 2008, pp. 35-40.

Wrona, T. (2005): Die Fallstudienanalyse als wissenschaftliche Methode, Berlin 2005.

Wrona, T. (2006): Fortschritts- und Gütekriterien im Rahmen qualitativer Sozialforschung, in: Zelewski, S. v./Akca, N. (eds.), Fortschritt in den Wirtschaftswissenschaften, Wiesbaden 2006, pp. 189-216.

Wrona, T./Gunnesch, M. (2016): The one who sees more is more right: how theory enhances the 'repertoire to interpret' in qualitative case study research, in: Journal of Business Economics, Vol. 86, No. 7, 2016, pp. 723-749.

Wu, Y. (2015): The Decision-making Use of Performance Measurement Systems in the Headquarters-subsidiary Relationship: Evidence from China, Vallendar 2015.

Wu, Y./Schäffer, U. (2015): Organisational identification and decision-making use of decoupled performance measurement systems, in: China Journal of Accounting Studies, Vol. 3, No. 2, 2015, pp. 109-135.

Y

Yazdifar, H./Zaman, M./Tsamenyi, M./Askarany, D. (2008): Management accounting change in a subsidiary organisation, in: Critical Perspectives on Accounting, Vol. 19, No. 3, 2008, pp. 404-430.

Yin, R. (1981): The Case Study Crisis: Some Answers, in: Administrative Science Quarterly, Vol. 26, No. 1, 1981, p. 58.

Yin, R. (2018): Case Study Research and Applications: Design and Methods, 6th edition, London et al. 2018.

Z

Zucker, L. (1987): Institutional Theories of Organization, in: Annual Review of Sociology, Vol. 13, No. 1, 1987, pp. 443-464.

Münsteraner Schriften zur Internationalen Unternehmensrechnung

Herausgegeben von Peter Kajüter

www.peterlang.com